Doctor Who and Race

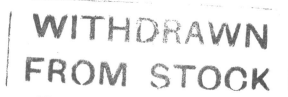

Doctor Who and Race

Edited by Lindy Orthia

intellect Bristol, UK / Chicago, USA

First published in the UK in 2013 by
Intellect, The Mill, Parnall Road, Fishponds, Bristol, BS16 3JG, UK

First published in the USA in 2013 by
Intellect, The University of Chicago Press, 1427 E. 60th Street,
Chicago, IL 60637, USA

A catalogue record for this book is available from the
British Library.

Cover designer: Holly Rose
Copy-editor: Emma Rhys
Production manager: Jelena Stanovnik
Typesetting: Contentra Technologies

ISBN: 978-1-78320-036-8
ePDF ISBN: 978-1-78320-124-2
ePub ISBN: 978-1-78320-123-5

Printed and bound by Hobbs, UK

Table of Contents

Acknowledgements

I thank Iona Yeager for e-mail discussions about race and *Doctor Who* that were the primary inspiration for this book; John Preston and Robert Monkman, whose correspondence provided further motivation; and Rachel Morgain and Vanessa de Kauwe, for invaluable discussions about the book at every stage.

I extend sincere thanks to the Australian National University Publication Subsidies Committee, which provided generous funding towards publication of the book.

Many thanks to the staff at Intellect Books who were supportive, helpful and honest throughout the publication process. In particular I thank Jelena Stanovnik for being an absolutely legendary production manager. Thanks to Holly Rose for her design work and patience, Emma Rhys for stellar copy-editing, and Melanie Marshall and James Campbell for their assistance and support.

Thanks to all the contributors for giving insightful feedback and suggestions on each others' essays, improving the book in numerous respects. Thanks also for writing such interesting essays to begin with – they were such a pleasure to work with.

Last but not least, thanks to those who expressed interest in contributing but were unsuccessful or unable to prepare a proposal in time, and to the hundreds of people from 43 countries who contributed to the 3355 visits to the 'call for papers' blog in 2011. Your interest in the project was very encouraging. Please consider sharing your ideas at http://doctorwhoandrace.wordpress.com, or if you publish elsewhere, posting a link there.

Introduction

In 2008 the actor David Tennant, then cast as *Doctor Who*'s central character, the Doctor, announced that he would vacate the role at the end of 2009. Tennant was the tenth actor to play the Doctor in the television series since its inception in 1963, and it was noted at the time – as it had been many times before – that all ten actors had been white men. Many viewers felt it was time for a change. *Doctor Who* is the longest running science fiction television series in the world, is watched in over fifty countries and routinely garners millions of viewers for each episode. *Doctor Who* – including its representations of race – matters to a lot of people.

Speculation abounded in the media that the British Broadcasting Corporation (BBC), which produces *Doctor Who*, would cast a black or female actor as the Eleventh Doctor.[1] For months before the final decision was made, bookmakers were tipping black actor Paterson Joseph as the front-runner for the job, and the BBC itself reported this when interviewing Joseph about the role.[2] Ultimately the BBC announced that the role went to Matt Smith, continuing the tradition of casting white men.

The decision was a surprise and a disappointment to many, not because Smith is a bad Doctor, but because he is white.[3] The disappointment is partly attributable to the fact that *Doctor Who*'s twenty-first century incarnation is so strikingly diverse in its casting of other characters, particularly compared to the programme's past. *Doctor Who*'s original series was produced between 1963 and 1989, and it was only in the last few years of its production that black and Asian actors were given prominent roles in the program on anything like a routine basis. The programme was cancelled for 16 years just as that trend was building, with only a telemovie made in 1996, and was not revived until 2005. During the 16-year hiatus, numerous *Doctor Who* spin-off media were published including novels, short stories and audio books, which picked up where the television series left off. These broadened and deepened the outlook of the *Doctor Who* universe, making it more adult in the absence of a requirement to appeal to child audiences,[4] and in effect setting a new standard for *Doctor Who*. The hiatus seemed to make an immense difference to many aspects of the programme when it was revived in 2005, including the new series' assertive engagement with a cosmopolitan Britain – a Britain not only diverse with respect to race, but also sexuality, gender, regionality, class and sub-culture.[5] Casting a black actor as the Doctor seemed to fit this new picture.

Yet the Doctor's 'race' is more complicated than a simple decision of 'colour-blind casting'. Race is a sociopolitical category contextualized by history and geography, related to imperialism, colonialism, slavery, nationalism, and more. Thus the whiteness, blackness or brownness of a fictional character as complex and long-lived and well-loved as the Doctor carries tremendous significance. The Doctor is ostensibly an alien who travels through time and space, but *Doctor Who* is not just a silly children's show about silvery wetsuitoids and CGI spacecraft. Beneath the special effects and technobabble, it reflects and examines the cultural politics of the society that made it. The programme emerged from and continues to dwell in the post-empire period of British history, a potent time when formerly colonized people were migrating to Britain in larger numbers than before as well as reclaiming their cultural heritage and political independence elsewhere in the world, transforming conceptions of Britishness, the meaning of 'race' on the global stage, and the ways in which the western media understand and deal with racism. *Doctor Who* has captured and repackaged many of the race-oriented ideas and ideologies from this environment, sometimes deliberately and sometimes inadvertently. It has often explored sociopolitical themes in great depth – including imperialism, colonialism, slavery and nationalism – and has proselytized on the nature of good and bad, right and wrong, in almost every episode. In other words, *Doctor Who* takes a stand. More than that, the Doctor takes a stand. And while, as the essays in this book attest, the particular stand taken at any given moment varies considerably, in general *Doctor Who*'s ideological frame is historically and geographically specific: it is liberal humanist.[6] In this, and in the Doctor's godlike mastery of science as universal problem solver, his Victorian clothing throughout the original series, and his propensity for tea and the European aristocracy, *Doctor Who* is a child of the British Enlightenment.[7] Perhaps it was some of these elements that led the BBC Wales Head of Drama, Piers Wenger, to describe Matt Smith as having "that 'Doctor-ness' about him" when he was given the role.[8] While the Doctor may aspire to a world in which race does not matter, the programme itself is not culturally neutral. Which makes it less surprising – though no less disappointing – that Paterson Joseph is not the Eleventh Doctor.

On the other hand, *Doctor Who* is the product of literally thousands of cast and crew members over its fifty year history. Its negotiation of race-related themes has been diverse and complex across the decades – if this was not the case, this would be a very short book. As we will demonstrate in the pages to follow, its representations of race have been, by turns, insightful and ignorant, utopian and pessimistic, oppressive and liberatory. It has offered great hope for people opposed to racism in its many forms, and has perpetuated discourses of race that are deeply problematic. Going by its track record it is infinitely possible that Paterson Joseph – or indeed anyone else – could play the Doctor one day.

The essays in this book traverse 128 of the 231 *Doctor Who* stories televised between 1963 and 2012, plus some spin-off media, including the recent television series *Torchwood* (2006–11). They examine the many facets of race as they are represented in *Doctor Who*. This includes not only the racial identity of the Doctor, but also the casting and characterization of his companions and more minor characters, allegorical or historical representations of European imperialism and slavery, engagement with multiculturalism and xenophobia, and links between race and biology, race and history, race and ethics. *Doctor Who*'s longevity, complexity and sheer popularity make it a rich resource for us to think about, analyse, enjoy, critique, praise, condemn, and through that, better understand the place of race in the society we live in.

Previous writings about race and *Doctor Who*

Given its richness, it is surprising is that relatively little attention has been paid to race in previous books and academic publications about *Doctor Who*. Even the godfathers of *Doctor Who* scholarship, John Tulloch and Manuel Alvarado, did not discuss race except in passing in their highly esteemed 1983 analysis of *Doctor Who*, *The Unfolding Text*.[9] The earliest paper in an academic journal to focus on race politics in *Doctor Who* is a 1999 one page opinion piece by Nick Caldwell in which he reflected on *Doctor Who*'s colonialist or anti-colonialist tendencies.[10] Brian Boyd touched on colonialism in *Doctor Who* in a 2002 popular style essay for a book about archaeology,[11] but his emphasis was elsewhere. Many other *Doctor Who* commentators across the years have discussed imperialist tendencies in the program, for example in Peter B. Gregg's 2004 analysis of the 1975 serial *The Ark in Space*,[12] and discussions of Britishness and national identity have appeared in innumerable books about *Who*, but race was never the primary interest of these texts. To find explicit and in-depth focus on race and *Doctor Who* in the academic literature, we had to wait until the 2007 publication of the wonderful *Doctor Who* essay anthology *Time and Relative Dissertations in Space*, in which Alec Charles argued that much of *Doctor Who* is imperialistic, including the way the programme characterizes and colonizes time itself.[13] In 2010, in the award-winning anthology, *Chicks Dig Time Lords*, K. Tempest Bradford wrote about aspects of race as they pertained to the Doctor's companion Martha Jones.[14] I published an essay that year which examined representations of colonialist pasts and cosmopolitan futures in *Doctor Who* across its history, and argued that the programme depicted very little of the racist and oppressive postcolonial present that we face in reality today.[15] More recently, J.P.C. Brown has written about the Doctor as "a very British alien" reflecting British imperialist history.[16] These works signal a growing interest among writers and publishers in talking about *Doctor Who* and race, though compared to the sheer weight of writing on *Doctor Who* that has proliferated in recent years, it is still fairly marginal.

This relative dearth of academic discussion about *Doctor Who* and race may not surprise some. Isiah Lavender III has noted that scholarly attention to race in science fiction in general has been sparse, and indeed that some publishers, fiction writers and commentators in the field have been openly hostile to engaging with race.[17] Lavender has asserted that more concerted study of race and science fiction is needed,[18] because science fiction is a significant venue for working through issues, questions and problems that we face in the real world, including racism, colonialism and nationalism. That is one reason this book is timely, if not long overdue.

It is noteworthy that academic publications lag behind the rest of the world on this. Since the advent of the new series of *Doctor Who* in 2005, the blogosphere has erupted with opinions and debate and extensive discussion of the programme's representations of race, including about the casting of the Eleventh Doctor as discussed above, and more recently speculation about the casting of future Doctors to follow Matt Smith.[19] Blogger The Angry Black Woman initiated a thread of this conversation with a post that celebrated the depiction of Martha Jones, because she felt the programme recognized the brown colour of Martha's skin when it mattered, but ignored it the rest of the time.[20] Other online commentators, including blogger karnythia,[21] were much more critical of the way Martha was treated by both the Doctor and *Doctor Who*'s writers. Blog-based discussions about race have not been limited to the new series; Philip Sandifer, for example, has delved into representations of race and colonialism in many of his reviews of original series *Doctor Who* stories.[22]

All of this is another reason why this volume is timely: while blogs enable many of us to express our opinions freely and cheaply, blogs and other websites are inherently ephemeral, anarchically organized, and notorious in the academic world for being unreliable sources. Bringing some of this debate to the formal publishing arena seems important for posterity's sake, and to cement the credibility of *Doctor Who* bloggers who have valuable perspectives to add to academic discussion but may not be taken seriously if they only publish on blogs. Some people who contributed to these online discussions – Fire Fly, Iona Yeager, Linnea Dodson and Kate Orman – have further developed their ideas for this volume. In addition, ten of the essays in this book are 1000–2000 word commentaries (similar to blog posts), a style of essay invited in order to break down ivory tower walls policed by word counts, and to expand publishing opportunities for people who do not think in 6000–8000 word academic chunks (the form the other 12 essays take). As it happens, some of the authors who contributed short reflections are academics by profession, and some of those who contributed longer, academic-style essays are not, so the ivory tower walls are crumbling.

About *Doctor Who*

Before proceeding to the essays, it is important to give some background information about *Doctor Who* for the uninitiated. *Doctor Who*'s central character, the Doctor, is a Time Lord from the planet Gallifrey, and he travels through time and space in his ship, the TARDIS. The Doctor's body is able to completely regenerate if he is ever killed, and it is this device that has allowed the programme to continue for half a century with different actors playing the part. The Doctor almost always travels with one or more companions, who are frequently humans from contemporary Earth. The names of companions discussed in this book are Rose, Mickey, Jack, Sarah, Martha, Donna, Amy, Rory and River Song from the new series; Barbara, Ian, Vicki, Steven, Dodo, Jamie, Zoe, the Brigadier, Jo, Sarah, Harry, Leela, Romana, Adric, Tegan and Ace from the original series; and also Benny from spin-off media. Much of the blog discussion about race and *Doctor Who* has concerned Martha and Mickey, who were each hailed at different times as *Doctor Who*'s 'first black companion'.[23] Although Mickey (played by Noel Clarke) was a regular character from the first episode of the new series in 2005, the BBC did not include him among its lists of companions until well after Freema Agyeman was cast as Martha in late 2006, causing numerous fans to question why.[24] For some viewers, this exemplified the poor treatment in *Doctor Who* of 'characters of colour',[25] casting a pall over what should have been a wholly positive transition in *Doctor Who* from the overwhelmingly white cast in the original series to the visibly diverse cast of the new series.

Doctor Who is serialized, which means that any production season comprises a number of stand-alone stories (serials), each made up of one to several episodes. In most of the original series the serials were named and episodes numbered, for example, *Genesis of the Daleks*, Episode 3. When discussing these serials in this book, we italicize their names, and also give the year they were first broadcast in the United Kingdom. In the new series, it is mostly episodes that are named, and one, two or three episodes can comprise one serial: when discussed in this book, we indicate narratively-linked episodes by a slash if the whole serial is important to the discussion, for example, *Daleks in Manhattan/Evolution of the Daleks*, and subsequently by the name of the first episode, for example, *Daleks in Manhattan*, as well as giving the year of first broadcast. Space forbids us from listing all cast and crew details for every serial here, so readers are encouraged to look them up on the Internet Movie Database and/or BBC website, or better yet to find a comfy chair to sit on or hide behind and watch the programme itself.

The essays

The essays in this book represent diverse points of view about *Doctor Who* and race, and take different theoretical or personal approaches to the topic. They do not conform to any editorial line, aside from opposition to racism. Some of the essays find fault with the way that *Doctor Who* has engaged with race. Others discuss elements of *Doctor Who* that actively oppose and confront racism. Still others find more neutral reflections of real-world racial discourses within *Doctor Who*. We hope that the collection will inspire debate and conversation on this topic.

The essays are organized into five parts, each unified thematically, and arranged with shorter essays up front and longer essays following. Parts 1 and 2 each comprise four or five shorter essays followed by one longer essay, and the final shorter essay is the first of Part III.

Part I focuses the analytical frame on the Doctor, his companions and race. Fire Fly's essay draws from the discipline of whiteness studies, identifying some of the ignorantly racist attitudes and behaviours displayed by the New Series Doctor that are too often exhibited by white people in the real world. Iona Yeager then examines Martha Jones's historical journeys to England in 1599 and 1913, problematizing *Doctor Who*'s simplistic depiction of these 'olden days' as racist, and mourning the lost opportunities for Martha and viewers to explore historical resistance to racism as well as the complexities of racism itself. Linnea Dodson reviews the companions of colour in New Series *Who*, concluding that the BBC's aspirations towards colour-blind casting fell short of the mark with those characters, including Martha and Mickey. Amit Gupta takes the discussion back to the original series, discussing the racial significance of the Victorian cricketing attire worn by the Fifth Doctor (played by Peter Davison, 1982–84), given the racist history of international cricket and its place in English identity. Quiana Howard and Robert Smith? take a different tack on the programme's main character, arguing that the Doctor is a race-traitor, being a racially 'other' alien who sides not with other aliens, but instead with (white) humanity against them. Mike Hernandez completes this section with a longer essay that frames the Doctor as a diasporic traveller separated from his culture, and examines the great potential that reading holds for casting a black actor in the role of the Doctor.

Part II concerns questions about racialized representation and diversity in *Doctor Who*'s casting and characterization decisions beyond the Doctor and companions. The first two essays both compare how characters of colour were represented in the new series' early seasons under show runner (head writer and producer) Russell T Davies (2005–09) with those appearing more recently under show runner Steven Moffat (2010–). Emily Asher-Perrin focuses on representations of interracial relationships, and Rosanne Welch on the class affiliations of characters of colour, and both conclude that Davies's characters were more diverse and well-rounded than Moffat's. Stephanie Guerdan discusses the dearth of East Asian characters in new *Who*, detailing the missed opportunities for including characters from Japan and China or British Asian characters, and how the programme might improve in this respect. George Ivanoff notes how his perceptions of race in *Doctor Who* have changed since his childhood, by discussing the representations of race in 1972's *The Mutants* and 1977's *The Talons of Weng-Chiang*, two racially loaded serials he first saw as a child. In the final, longer, essay in this section, Kate Orman undertakes a detailed study of *The Talons of Weng-Chiang*, in which a Caucasian actor was cast as the main Chinese character, in light of the legacy of the Fu Manchu novels and films and the history of anti-Chinese racism in England.

Part III features four essays about European colonialism, imperialism, race-related slavery and the postcolonial diaspora, as depicted literally or allegorically in *Doctor Who*. In the final short essay of the book, Leslie McMurtry examines the 1964 serial *The Aztecs*, finding racist mythologies within it that can be traced back to the words of Columbus and Cortés, the European conquerors of Central America. Erica Foss then discusses parallels between the racist historical idea of 'natural born slaves', which was used to justify the European slave trade, and the discourses surrounding *Doctor Who*'s New Series slave species, the Ood. John Vohlidka compares four 1970s *Doctor Who* serials that featured allegorical imperialism scenarios, and shows how each represented a different perspective on imperialism and changing British attitudes to the British Empire. Vanessa de Kauwe rounds out the section with her analysis of the 1966 serial *The Ark*, in which she argues that what appears on first critical glance to be racist stereotyping can alternatively be interpreted as a depiction of postcolonial trauma, and that it takes the 'coloured eyes' of one who has experienced postcolonial transition to identify this.

Part 4 consists of four essays that address the nexus of xenophobia, nationalism and national identities in *Doctor Who* television serials and spin-off media. Alec Charles discusses allegorical representations of race in the 2011 serial *The Almost People/The Rebel Flesh* and 2011 spin-off series *Torchwood: Miracle Day*, in the context of racist media commentary about the 2011 UK urban riots, and argues that all of these reveal that 'race' itself is a fiction. Richard Scully revisits a popular topic for *Doctor Who* commentators – *Doctor Who*'s critique of Nazi Germany, particularly through its most famous villains, the Daleks – from the original perspective of asking why *Doctor Who* has dealt with Nazism metaphorically countless times, but has rarely depicted Nazi characters and settings in a literal sense. Marcus K. Harmes disputes the common view that *Doctor Who* is quintessentially English by analysing the depiction of the Church of England in *The Dæmons* (1971), *Ghost Light* (1989) and *The Curse of Fenric* (1989), discussing historical links between the Church and Englishness as a racial identity, and the Church's changing role in an increasingly multicultural Britain. Finally, Catriona Mills describes and discusses three *Doctor Who* short stories from the early 2000s in which Australian fan authors used *Doctor Who*'s characters and formula to reflect upon Australian national identity and the racial dynamics that problematize it.

Part 5 examines connections between race and science in *Doctor Who*. Kristine Larsen explores the parallels between real life human eugenics movements and the Daleks' many attempts over the decades to achieve and police racial purity through genetic engineering activities. Rachel Morgain examines intersections of race and science in the 2010 serial *The Hungry Earth/Cold Blood*, finding racially problematic discourses in the story from the fields of anthropology, geography and biological taxonomy. My own essay, the last for the book, discusses *Doctor Who*'s ideological supposition that societies evolve in stages from savagery through barbarism to civilization, its assumption that western society is naturally at the top stage, and its use of western-style science as the measuring stick for judging real and fictional societies' place on that ladder.

We believe these essays make an important contribution to discussions of race and *Doctor Who*. Yet we have examined the topic with frames of reference particular to our experiences and interests. For example most of the contributors, though identifying with diverse ethnic backgrounds, live in or hail from Australia or the United States, so many of the essays approach 'race' from perspectives relevant to events in those nations' histories, such as colonialism, the dispossession of indigenous lands and Europeans' enslavement of Africans. Given the size and diversity of the Earth's population, and *Doctor Who*'s popularity across the world, this book is not the end of the conversation. No doubt there will be – and should be – many more books, blogs and other discussions on this topic in the years to come that broaden our collective outlook still further. We hereby invite readers to continue the conversation with us on the blog associated with the book, doctorwhoandrace.wordpress.com. We know you have opinions, so please come and share them with us.

Lindy Orthia

Notes

1   e.g., Anon., "Favourites for next Doctor Who emerge", *The Telegraph*, 30 October 2008; Anita Singh, "Catherine Zeta Jones to be the next Doctor Who?", *The Telegraph*, 18 December 2008. Notably no actors who were both black and female were touted prominently as contenders.

2   Tim Masters, "Who favourite talks Time Lords" (20 November 2008), *BBC News*. Retrieved 19 August 2012 at http://news.bbc.co.uk/2/hi/7739408.stm. See also Simon Cable, "Casualty star Paterson Joseph could become first black Dr Who as BBC set to announce David Tennant's replacement" (2 January 2009), *Daily Mail*.

3   e.g., Caroline Davies and David Smith, "Dr Who? Big names lose out to Matt Smith", *The Guardian*, 3 January 2009; Graeme McMillan, "Why This Doctor Disappoints" (4 January 2009), *io9*. Retrieved 19 August 2012 at http://io9.com/5122806/why-this-doctor-disappoints; see also comments by dish and Dervag, "Introducing The Eleventh Doctor ... Matt Smith!" (4 January 2009), *Giant in the Playground Forums*. Retrieved 19 August at http://www.giantitp.com/forums/archive/index.php?t-101247.html.

4   Dale Smith, "Broader and deeper: The lineage and impact of the Timewyrm series", in David Butler, ed., *Time and Relative Dissertations in Space: Critical Perspectives on Doctor Who*, Manchester: Manchester University Press, 2007, 263–79.

5   For more on this see Lindy A. Orthia, "'Sociopathetic abscess' or 'yawning chasm'? The absent postcolonial transition in *Doctor Who*", *The Journal of Commonwealth Literature*, 45, 2 (2010), 207–25.

6   See e.g., James Chapman, *Inside the TARDIS: The Worlds of Doctor Who*, London: I.B. Tauris, 2006; John Fiske, "Popularity and Ideology: A Structuralist Reading of *Doctor Who*", in Willard D. Rowland, Jr. and Bruce Watkins, eds., *Interpreting Television: Current Research Perspectives*, Beverly Hills: Sage Publications, 1984, 165–98.

7   For more on this see Lindy A. Orthia, *Enlightenment was the Choice: Doctor Who and the Democratisation of Science*, Ph.D. thesis, Canberra: Australian National University, 2010.

8   Anon., "New Doctor actor is youngest ever" (4 January 2009), *BBC News*. Retrieved 19 August 2012 at http://news.bbc.co.uk/2/hi/7808697.stm.

9   John Tulloch and Manuel Alvarado, *Doctor Who: The Unfolding Text*, London: Macmillan Press, 1983.

10 Nick Caldwell, "A decolonising Doctor? British SF invasion narratives", *M/C: A Journal of Media and Culture*, 2, 2 (1999), online.

11 Brian Boyd, "The Myth Makers: Archaeology in *Doctor Who*", in Miles Russell, ed., *Digging Holes in Popular Culture: Archaeology and Science Fiction*, Oxon: Oxbow Books, 2002, 30–37.

12 Peter B. Gregg, "England Looks to the Future: The Cultural Forum Model and Doctor Who", *The Journal of Popular Culture*, 37, 4 (2004), 648–61.

13 Alec Charles, "The ideology of anachronism: Television, history and the nature of time", in David Butler, ed., *Time and Relative Dissertations in Space: Critical Perspectives on Doctor Who*, Manchester: Manchester University Press, 2007, 108–22.

14 K. Tempest Bradford, "Martha Jones: Fangirl Blues", in Lynne M. Thomas and Tara O'Shea, eds., *Chicks Dig Time Lords: A Celebration of Doctor Who by the Women Who Love It*, Des Moines: Mad Norwegian Press, 2010, 168–74.

15 Orthia, "'Sociopathetic abscess' or 'yawning chasm'?"

16 J. P. C. Brown, "Doctor Who: A Very British Alien", in R. C. Neighbors and Sandy Rankin, eds., *The Galaxy is Rated G: Essays on Children's Science Fiction Film and Television*, Jefferson: McFarland & Co., 2011, 161–82.

17 Isiah Lavender III, *Race in American Science Fiction*, Bloomington: Indiana University Press, 2011, 10, 25, 31 and 36.

18 Lavender, *Race in American Science Fiction*, 25.

19 e.g., Emmanuel Akitobi, "As Matt Smith hints at jump to Hollywood, could Paterson Joseph's name re-emerge for 'Doctor Who'?" (27 October 2011), *Shadow and Act/Indiewire*. Retrieved 19 August 2012 at http://blogs.indiewire.com/shadowandact/as_matt_smith_ hints_at_jump_to_hollywood_could_paterson_josephs_name_re-eme; Alasdair Shaw, "A Question of Colour" (24 June 2012), *Kasterborous*. Retrieved 19 August 2012 at http:// www.kasterborous.com/2012/06/a-question-of-colour/.

20 The Angry Black Woman, "ABW's TV Corner – Doctor Who" (9 May 2007), *The Angry Black Woman*. Retrieved 19 August 2012 at http://theangryblackwoman.wordpress. com/2007/05/09/abws-tv-corner-doctor-who/.

21 karnythia, "Martha as Mammy and yet more 'ism's in the Whoverse" (2 July 2007), *Life on Martha*. Retrieved 19 August 2012 at http://lifeonmartha.livejournal.com/268192.html.

22 Philip Sandifer, *TARDIS Eruditorium: A Psychochronography in Blue*. Retrieved 19 August 2012 at http://tardiseruditorum.blogspot.com.

23 Ciar Byrne, "*Doctor Who* gets his first black assistant", *The Independent*, 5 July 2006; Richard Simpson, "Exit Billie as Doctor Who Gets First Black Side-Kick", *Daily Mail*, 5 July 2006; Anon., "Mickey Smith" (n.d.), *TARDIS Index File*. Retrieved 19 August 2012 at http://tardis. wikia.com/wiki/Mickey_Smith.

24 See essay by Linnea Dodson, this volume. The essay is based on a blog post she published in 2007: neadods, "Mickey, Martha, and the Message that Doesn't Belong on Who" (1 July 2007), *Life on Martha*. Retrieved 19 August 2012 at http://community.livejournal.com/ lifeonmartha/259659.html?thread=2812491.

25 'Characters of colour' is a contested term for a number of reasons, so I use it reservedly. For an insightful discussion and links to sites of debate, see Fire Fly, "On the term 'people of colour'" (23 June 2010), *The Long Way Home*. Retrieved 19 August 2012 at http://ardhra. wordpress.com/2010/06/23/on-the-term-people-of-colour/.

PART I

The Doctor, his companions and race

Chapter 1

The white Doctor

Fire Fly[1]

Since the screening of Series 3 of the new series of *Doctor Who* in 2007, there has been considerable critical analysis and discussion among *Doctor Who* fans, particularly amongst fans of colour, of Martha Jones as a Black female character; especially of how her characterization reflects on the social position of Black women.[2] However, there has been less discussion of the racial characteristics of the Doctor. Although the Doctor is, within the series, an alien, the character is informed by whiteness[3] and the racial anxieties of the show's white British creators, such that the Doctor embodies a number of characteristics of whiteness.

Race is a recurrent theme in Series 3. It's used as a cipher to develop the Doctor's character and to reveal new information about the Time War and the genocide of the Time Lords. At the same time, however, race is treated in a supremely naïve manner in the season, with outright historical inaccuracy portrayed in order to reassert a normative white moral centre for the show.

The Doctor's whiteness, and the white perspective of the series, is manifest in a number of ways, but particularly in the characters for whom compassion is cultivated, the Doctor's lack of accountability in his transient adventures, and the context in which the series was created and has developed.

Race is set up as an implicit theme in Series 3 before the beginning of the season proper, in the denouement of the 2006 Christmas special episode *The Runaway Bride*. When the Doctor reveals to the Racnoss Empress that he is from Gallifrey, the Racnoss Empress protests that Gallifreyans wiped out the Racnoss, leading to their present predicament in having no home planet. When the Empress rejects the solution the Doctor proposes – to take all the remaining Racnoss to another planet – the Doctor chooses to commit genocide instead, completing the task his ancestors began.

This is a rather grim conclusion for a character who is typified by his willingness to give second chances, and his belief that all forms of life deserve the opportunity to survive. He has even given the Daleks such opportunities, and many others, specifically *in contrast to* his human companions.

However, in making the Doctor's unresolved grief, guilt and self-blame over the genocide of his people the central dramatic theme in the series, the series makes the grief, guilt and suffering of real human beings due to racial violence a vehicle for the personal angst of the Doctor. His acts of genocide are treated as important because of what they reveal about the Doctor's pain; the Racnoss' pain is not given such treatment, nor is any enemy species the Doctor chooses not to believe in, setting up clear categories of characters worthy of compassion versus those who are not. The Doctor's inconsolable grief over the death of the Master in *Last of the Time Lords* (2007) contrasts tellingly with his dismissiveness towards the Racnoss. It is clear that, for Russell T Davies, characters who do not resemble white men aren't important enough to grieve or feel guilt over.

In the past decade and a half in Australia this has been how issues around genocide have played out. White Australia has grappled with trying to displace guilt over committing and benefiting from the genocide of Aboriginal people, a programme that Britain shares culpability for. The national Apology to the Stolen Generations in February 2008 characterizes how white society would like to address its culpability for genocide against Aboriginal and Torres Strait Islander people in Australia: words without efforts behind them,[4] just as the Doctor moves on from committing genocide without remaining answerable to the societies he intervenes in.

In the second episode of the season, *The Shakespeare Code* (2007), the Doctor advises Martha to "just walk about like you own the place. It works for me" after she expresses concern that she might be abducted and sold as a slave because she's Black. The Doctor then retorts that he is an alien, implying that real racial inequality among humans is analogous to fictional differences between species.

This exchange betrays the ignorance of the writers about both historical racial violence and contemporary white privilege. The episode is set in 1599, while Portugal and Spain were transporting African slaves to the Americas, and Britain was establishing its colonies. Black slaves were present in London since early in the sixteenth century,[5] making it entirely reasonable for Martha to feel anxious about her security. Furthermore, by implying that anyone could "walk about like [they] own the place" the role of whiteness is normalized – nobody else *could* "own the place."

It is telling that one of the greatest injustices on Earth of the last 500 years hardly merits notice from the Doctor, who'll jump at a chance to depose tyrannical regimes in alien societies; injustice in human society is natural and normal to the *Doctor Who* writers, as is a white man's capacity to move about anywhere unmolested.

This is particularly apparent since *Doctor Who* was originally conceived as a family television series that would educate school-age children about history.[6] As it began in 1963, there were considerable cultural and intellectual upheavals around race and Britain's involvement in colonialism, accompanied by migration programmes to attract Black and South Asian migrants to Britain. Most British colonies became independent by the end of the 1960s. Postcolonial theory, multicultural education, and anti-racist social movements challenged white-centred ways of looking at the world. Yet, at the same time, nativism, Merchant-Ivory films, and the National Front gained popularity. While colonialism was being challenged politically, economically and culturally, there was an equally strong white supremacist backlash, and *Doctor Who* needs to be situated in terms of that conflict.

The Doctor himself as a character represents a very nineteenth-century ideal of technical mastery and intellectual detachment.[7] He travels alone, never becoming too attached to a place or its people, and is unburdened by caregiving responsibilities. He can inhabit an imperialist Enlightenment ideal of objectivity, with no emotional attachment to the people he meets in his travels. Yet the audience is still supposed to judge that he has a sound moral compass, despite the fact that he's a mass murderer, often lies, steals and leaves people to suffer or die, usually without seeming to really care.

Series 3 re-establishes this characterization of the Doctor, but this time he works through his guilt around genocide by subjugating Black characters. *Human Nature/The Family of Blood* (2007) and *Last of the Time Lords* feature all the Jones family women as maids to Time Lords. This is deeply significant, as a major field that Black women were employed in, as slaves, indentured servants and underpaid workers, was domestic service – a site of physical, sexual, economic and cultural violence for many Black women through history. In these roles, not only were Black women economically dependent and exploited by white people, but they played a secondary role in wealthy whites' domestic life as providers of home comfort and stabilizers of family relationships, forever deferring their emotional needs and those of their families. Continual invocation of this past in contemporary media tends to reinscribe this role for Black women: the Mammy stereotype.[8]

The Doctor's silent acceptance of Martha, her mother and sister in subservient roles, echoes the position wider white society prefers for people of colour: even in the process of liberation, even anti-racist liberation, they are secondary to white, male heroes. Like Martha walking the Earth for a year to liberate humans from the Master's tyranny in *Last of the Time Lords*, people of colour are expected to laud the power of white male heroes to liberate – to be maids, not masters, of liberation.

After Series 4 screened there was considerable speculation that Black British actor Paterson Joseph would be cast as the Doctor.[9] It turned out to be unfounded after Matt Smith was announced as the next lead for the series. The dominance of the white perspective in *Doctor Who* indicates why the Doctor continues to be played by a white, male actor. While a Black actor would be able to portray the same tropes and narratives, the writers might not be able to dismiss genocide and slavery so casually as they have done. The Doctor might not be able to blithely 'walk about like he owns the place', which would make for a very different story. But perhaps it's a story that needs to be told.

Notes

1   This pseudonym is used by the author across several social media and online publishing platforms. This essay is a revised version of one written in 2007, reproduced at *The Long Way Home* (5 April 2009). Retrieved 19 August 2012 at http://ardhra.wordpress.com/2009/04/05/white-doctor/.

2   e.g., Savannah J. Frierson (writing as bana05), "Martha Jones and Love: a Rant/Meta" (9 October 2007), *A literary and elegant woman*. Retrieved 19 August 2012 at http://bana05.livejournal.com/178351.html.

3   Whiteness and blackness as concepts have been extensively addressed in critical race theory and critical whiteness studies. Prominent whiteness studies texts include Richard Dyer, *White*, London: Routledge, 1997; Ruth Frankenberg, *White Women, Race Matters: The social construction of whiteness*, London: Routledge, 1993; Ruth Frankenberg, ed., *Displacing Whiteness: Essays in social and cultural criticism*, Durham: Duke University Press, 1997; Aileen Moreton-Robinson, ed., *Whitening Race: Essays in social and cultural criticism*, Canberra: Aboriginal Studies Press, 2004; Toni Morrison, ed., *Playing the Dark: Whiteness and the literary imagination*, Cambridge: Harvard University Press, 1992. For a more comprehensive bibliography see Infinity Foundation (n.d.) *Bibliography of Whiteness Studies*. Retrieved 19 August 2012 at http://www.infinityfoundation.com/mandala/BibliographyOfWhiteStudies/Biliography.pdf.

4   Alexander Reilly, "How Sorry Are We?: The limits of the Apology to the Stolen Generation", *Alternative Law Journal*, 34, 2 (2009), 97–101.

5   Anya Langmead and National Archives, "Adventurers and Slavers" (n.d.), *Black Presence: Asian and Black History in Britain, 1500–1850*. Retrieved 19 August 2012 at http://www.nationalarchives.gov.uk/pathways/blackhistory/early_times/adventurers.htm.

6   J. P. C. Brown, "Doctor Who: a Very British Alien", in R. C. Neighbors and Sandy Rankin, eds., *The Galaxy is Rated G: Essays on Children's Science Fiction Film and Television*, Jefferson: McFarland & Co., 2011, 161–82.

7   Lindy A. Orthia, *Enlightenment was the Choice: Doctor Who and the Democratisation of Science*, Ph.D. thesis, Canberra: Australian National University, 2010, 131–75.

8   Patricia Hill Collins, *Black Feminist Thought: Knowledge, Consciousness and the Politics of Empowerment*, New York: Routledge, 1991.

9   e.g., Ian M. Cullen, "Patterson Joseph is the Next Doctor?" (November 2008), *SciFiPulse*. Retrieved 19 August 2012 at http://scifipulse.net/2008/11/patterson-joseph-is-the-next-doctor/.

Chapter 2

Too brown for a fair praise: The depiction of racial prejudice as cultural heritage in *Doctor Who*

Iona Yeager

1988, *Remembrance of the Daleks*: the Seventh Doctor ponders how the craving for sugar has influenced Humankind's destiny. The black British waiter tells the Doctor the history of his African ancestor's capture and enslavement. The Doctor expresses his sympathy and respect without judgement.

Twenty-first century: the Tenth Doctor's fair-complexioned companions, Rose Tyler and Donna Noble, protest humanity's abuse and exploitation of the fictional enslaved species, the Ood.[1]

2007, *The Shakespeare Code*: Martha Jones, the Doctor's companion most likely to be directly affected by the British slave trade, voices her concern about visiting Elizabethan London: "I'm not exactly white," Martha notes. "I'm not even human," the Doctor retorts, then adds: "Elizabethan England is not so different from your time." On cue, two black actresses dressed in modest period costume walk onto the set. As we don't see these women or any other character of colour in this episode again, the characters' narrative purpose is mere reassurance to Martha and her audience, that Martha's fears of being captured as a slave are groundless.

It is unclear if the writers intended to deny the existence of the British Slave Trade or suggest that it is ongoing in 2007. Historically, in 1596, Queen Elizabeth I issued this statement: "there are of late divers Blackmoores brought into the Realme, of which kinde of people there are all ready here to manie",[2] and then proceeded to award Dutch merchant Caspar Van Senden licence to detain "Blackamoores here in this Realme and to transport them into Spaine and Portugall."[3]

Considering that Martha's concerns were supported by history, the Doctor's attitude appears insensitive and recklessly naïve. Whatever the Doctor's reasoning, the script silences Martha's opportunity to voice her opinion regarding the institution of slavery, and denies the character agency to view her black British ancestors' experience in context.

The Doctor's dismissal of Martha's concerns becomes censorship when Shakespeare, floundering for a suitable complement for Martha's beauty, uses a spate of archaic terms. The Doctor describes Martha's reaction as "political correctness gone mad" and suggests the only offence is Martha's hypersensitive reaction.

The Doctor's response confirms his ignorance of dark-complexioned Britons' exclusive journey. In spite of period portraits depicting Africans as servants in King James IV and Elizabeth I's court, or historical records of existing African Kingdoms, the Doctor informs Shakespeare that Martha Jones comes from the fictional country of Freedonia.

Freedonia is the name of the fictional, despotic nation in the 1933 Marx Brothers' film, *Duck Soup* (Director: Leo McCarey). This would not be the only instance in which writers use questionable terms and references in relation to Martha Jones. In a now deleted scene[4] from *The Lazarus Experiment* (2007), Martha asks if she looks alright in her evening dress. The Doctor ignores the question and pulls out a draft of the Declaration of Independence, and speaks of inspiring Jefferson. Jefferson's disparaging remarks on the appearance of Africans are often quoted by white supremacists in the United States and United Kingdom.[5] It is unclear as to whether these potential slights were intentionally inserted into the scripts, however the writers do not shrink away from the possibility that Doctor may share human bias. In *Utopia* (2007) Jack Harkness informs Martha that the Doctor is less likely to abandon a blonde companion, and later he accuses the Doctor of prejudice when he refers to Jack's difference as "wrong."

Evidence of cultural or familial heritage rather than 'racial incident' connects an audience to historical drama, yet a few minutes into *The Shakespeare Code*, the Doctor deprives Martha of any tangible connection to any earthbound nation; nor is she allowed to explore the journey of her African British ancestors. When Donna and Rose travel to the past, they meet persons of all social classes who resemble them. At one point the Doctor and Rose acknowledge that they met the ancestor of *Torchwood* cross-over character Gwen Cooper. As neither Rose nor Donna is Irish, Welsh or Scottish, there is no need to stress that they are meeting the persons who helped shape their cultural and political history. However, fair-complexioned companion Amelia Pond, as both a child and young adult, speaks often of her Scottish heritage and her dislike of English culture.

The journey of African Britons encompasses Britain's involvement in slavery, and the violent oppression of African nations during Britain's colonial period. Critics and fans may argue that portraying these elements of British history would either be too disturbing for family viewing, or serve as instigators of ethnically divisive dialogue. Why, however, is it not possible for the Doctor and his companion to confront racial prejudice and oppression as they would any other form of adversity?

In *The Shakespeare Code* the Doctor employs a nonsense diagnosis to describe suspicious death because he explains "this lot has still got one foot in the dark ages." Would not the same explanation serve to explain – not justify – Elizabethans' xenophobia and seeming acceptance of slavery?

Denial of the existence of the British slave trade subverts the knowledge of Queen Elizabeth I's outrage upon hearing reports of John Hawkins' brutal slave raids. "[I]t would be detestable," she declared, "and call down the vengeance of heaven upon the undertakers."[6]

The Queen would later – slavery was profitable – become a silent partner with slavers. And although she would forbid slavery in England, she did try to deport Africans from England on the basis of faith. Queen Elizabeth's edict to deport her African subjects failed. Van Senden suffered bankruptcy when fair-complexioned Britons rushed to defend their 'Blackamoor' neighbours and servants. When Van Senden appealed to the Crown for help,

Sir Robert Cecil's concerns about the welfare of his servant, Fortunatus, found more favour with the ageing Queen.[7]

Martha Jones inspired Shakespeare's Dark Lady Sonnets, yet she never encountered an historical Briton who shared her blended heritage.

The rich ancestry of Freema Agyeman[8] (who portrayed Martha Jones) presented the *Doctor Who* creative team with new avenues of exploration. However in the episodes that did address Ms Agyeman's African ancestry, instances of subjugation, prejudice and oppression are portrayed as a natural element of white British mentality. In *Human Nature/The Family of Blood* (2007) we learn that racial prejudice is so endemic in the nature of twentieth-century Britons that the Doctor, once he becomes a white, human male of 1913, adopts racial and class prejudices as part of his identity. The script hints that had John Smith been more evolved, it would have signalled to the predatory aliens that he was the Doctor, although they were hunting a Time Lord, not a member of the 1913 British Liberal Party.

The *Doctor Who* creative team visualized Paul Cornell's *Human Nature* as representing a more innocent era in British history before the First World War.[9] It is fascinating that the writers consider colour and class prejudice an element of 'innocence'.

In all fairness, *Human Nature* celebrates the love story between the suddenly human Doctor and Joan Redfern. The TARDIS chooses a time and place where the Doctor can take refuge and enjoy the privilege of a white, male Briton. Martha Jones, in spite of her erudition, supposedly could only assume a subservient position. Although he charges Martha with his care, the Doctor informs Martha she must improvise, oblivious to what is apparent: in 1913 rural England, Martha is The Alien.

The entitled, white middle-class lovers John Smith and Joan Redfern constantly remind Martha of 'her place' as prescribed in their minds by her complexion and class. Although John Smith believes Martha is his inherited family servant, he voices doubts about her intellectual discernment because of her 'cultural differences'.

Martha is as English as Smith believes he is, therefore it is clear that Smith – whom the Doctor invented – not only considers Martha's complexion a 'cultural difference', but the source of her perceived intellectual deficiency.

Nurse Redfern's scepticism that Martha can train as a physician – "but hardly a skivvy and hardly one of your colour" – defies British history which records that American abolitionist Sarah Remond matriculated at London's Bedford College for Ladies before studying medicine in Italy in the late nineteenth century.[10] Indian British Dr Rukhmabai graduated from the London School of Medicine for Women in 1895.[11] African/Briton Agnes Savage, who studied at Edinburgh,[12] is recalled as one of the two "black lady doctors" who attended the Pan African Congress in London in 1900, only 13 years before Joan confronts Martha.[13]

Chambermaid Martha delivers a newspaper dated the 10th of November 1913 to John Smith. In November 1913, London papers carried the story that white, male district leaders had elected African/Irish/British John Archer as Mayor of Battersea.[14]

Accepting the post, John Archer praised the people of Battersea saying: "You have shown that you have no racial prejudice, but recognize a man for what you think he has done."[15] Considering Archer's words, should not the *Doctor Who* audience question whether John Smith's attitude towards class and skin colour reflects the inescapable mentality of the time period or the Doctor's personal beliefs?

Joan's scorn of Martha's abilities and prospects appears due to the matron's isolation and ignorance of 1913's current events. Knowledge that greater opportunities exist in her present fuels Martha's defiant reply.

The election of John Archer was an exceptional event. However, encountering Shakespeare was also an exceptional event. Yes, Martha would have faced adversity in 1913, but we must ask if she would have also found hope and inspiration in the lives and accomplishments of Britons of Colour in that time.

Unfortunately, because the script focuses on the existence of racial and class oppression, rather than the struggle against it, Martha and her audience remain unaware of the efforts of their ancestors to make the opportunities of their present possible.

Notes

1   *The Impossible Planet/The Satan Pit* (2006) and *Planet of the Ood* (2008).

2   Queen Elizabeth I, "An Open Letter about 'Negroes' Brought Home" (1596), *The National Archives: Exhibitions and Learning Online: Black Presence: Early Times*. Retrieved 19 August 2012 at http://www.nationalarchives.gov.uk/pathways/blackhistory/early_times/elizabeth. htm. Elizabeth issued similar statements in 1599 and 1601.

3   Miranda Kaufmann, "Caspar Van Senden, Sir Thomas Sherley and the 'Blackamoor' project", *Historical Research*, 81, 212 (2008), 367.

4   BBC, *Doctor Who: The Complete Third Series*, DVD release, 2007.

5   Cathy Boekmann, *A Question of Character: Scientific racism and the genres of American Fiction, 1892–1912*, Tuscaloosa: University of Alabama Press, 2000, 26–29.

6   John Wesley, *Thoughts Upon Slavery*, Philadelphia: Joseph Crukshank, 1774.

7   Kaufmann, "Caspar Van Senden", 369.

8   IMDb, "Freema Agyeman: Biography" (2012), *The Internet Movie Database (IMDb)*. Retrieved 19 August 2012 at http://www.imdb.com/name/nm1303956/bio.

9   Ailsa Jenkins (director), "Bad Blood" (2007), *Doctor Who Confidential*, UK: BBC.

10 National Women's History Museum, "Sarah Remond (1826–1894)" (n.d.), *Education & Resources: National Women's History Museum: NWHM*. Retrieved 19 August 2012 at http:// www.nwhm.org/education-resources/biography/biographies/sarah-remond/.

11 Antoinette Burton, "From child bride to 'Hindoo Lady': Rukhmabai and the debate on sexual respectability in imperial Britain", *The American Historical Review*, 103, 4 (1998), 1119–46.

12 Charles Tetty, "Medical practitioners of African descent in colonial Ghana", *The International Journal of African Historical Studies*, 18, 1 (1985), 139–44.

13 David Killingray, "Doctors", in David Dabydeen and John Gilmore, eds., *The Oxford Companion to Black British History*, Oxford: Oxford University Press, 2007, 131.

14 Mike Phillips and the British Library, "John Archer (1863–1932)" (2005), *Black Europeans*. Retrieved 19 August 2012 at http://www.bl.uk/onlinegallery/features/blackeuro/pdf/archer.pdf.

15 Phillips and the British Library, "John Archer."

Chapter 3

Conscious colour-blindness, unconscious racism in *Doctor Who* companions

Linnea Dodson

Once upon a time, there was a science fiction show that I adored. It was a product of its time, displaying unspoken prejudices and stereotypes, but the overall message – that there was an all-powerful alien who adored all the various peoples of Earth – was an uplifting one.

That show was cancelled. Time – and attitudes – moved on. Then *Doctor Who* came back, updated for a whole new century. I was thrilled. I watched breathlessly. And I became more and more disappointed in the disconnect between the uplifting message and the depressing reality until, three seasons in, I was horrified at the end of *Last of the Time Lords* (2007). The BBC kept insisting that it had overcome old prejudices, that it was colour-blind when the actors were cast. What the BBC was really blind to was how characters of colour were consistently cast as unloved and/or servants. How could the Doctor, who supposedly loves humanity as a whole, continually treat companions of colour as second class?

Mickey: Neither idiot nor tin dog

Viewed objectively, Mickey was the type of character usually called the salt of the Earth. He had a steady job, was devoted to his girlfriend Rose, and even had the compassion to forgive and befriend Rose's mother despite her accusing him of murder. These are excellent personal qualities to have even before Mickey starts helping defeat a host of Whovian monsters.

The Doctor usually praises loyalty, dependability and empathy, but in this case the Doctor can't even be bothered to remember his name, calling him "Ricky the idiot." The Doctor considers this an endearment, although Mickey makes it clear several times that he's insulted. Rose, who is white, doesn't treat him much better. She doesn't notice that Mickey's been replaced by an auton in *Rose* (2005), treats him like a delivery service in *Boom Town* (2005), and ignores him completely in *The Age of Steel* (2006) as she and the Doctor laugh together about adventures he never shared.

In *Rise of the Cybermen* (2006), Mickey finally voices what has been clear all along: the woman he loves doesn't care. "It's just you and him, isn't it? We had something a long time ago, but not anymore." He's so desperate for respect that he's willing to leave not just them but his home universe behind, taking nothing but the clothes he's wearing. Rose asks him not to leave, but doesn't deny that she stopped loving him. The Doctor, left with a last chance to show his appreciation for all that Mickey has done, chooses instead to shake his hand, give him a set of orders – and call him "idiot."

Even the British press overlooked him. Although Mickey has known the Doctor from the first reboot episode, fought beside him, and travelled with him, the *Daily Mail* called Martha Jones the first black companion.[1]

Martha Jones: Not the rebound companion

Martha, we were told, was the rebound companion; that's why the Doctor never returned her love the way he did Rose's. There's only one problem with this point of view: Martha wasn't the Doctor's next companion. Shouldn't the "rebound companion" be the one who was introduced literally seconds after the Doctor said goodbye to Rose? But that character, Donna, never hears things like: "You're not replacing [Rose]." "Rose would know what to do." "Just one trip and back home." At the end of *The Runaway Bride* (2006), Donna's invitation to travel with the Doctor is unconditional.

Martha, the companion *after* the companion after Rose, the woman who literally gave her last breath to save the Doctor in her first adventure, is the one constantly hit with limits and comparisons by the Doctor. The "just one trip" warnings come so often that Martha eventually has to put her foot down and demand to either be treated as a fully accepted companion or be left to the life she'd planned for herself.

It's not as though the Doctor doesn't trust Martha. He relies on her – as support staff. In *Blink* (2007), she financially supports them both while marooned. In *Human Nature/ The Family of Blood* (2007), she is literally a servant, protecting the hidden TARDIS and the amnesiac "John Smith" (who is adding to the racism, sexism and hard manual labour she must endure). The hardship was doubtless good training for Martha's global trek through a post-apocalyptic world (*Last of the Time Lords*), where her contribution to saving the planet wasn't to fight, like Rose and Jack did in *The Parting of the Ways* (2005), or to help build defences like Rose did in *Doomsday* (2006), but to talk incessantly about how wonderful the Doctor is – despite the less than wonderful way he's treated her. To underline the racial imagery, Martha's entire family of successful professionals are reduced to literal slaves of an abusive master.

How does the Doctor acknowledge this incredible effort and devotion? Just "thank you" and factual statement: "Martha Jones, you saved the world." No wonder she says, "I spent a lot of time with you thinking I was second best." If ever there was a time for the Doctor to tell her – as he told Rose – "I only take the best" (*The Long Game*, 2005), it's now. But he never says anything to praise her. There are four Martha goodbye scenes: when she first leaves, when she comes immediately back to make it clear to him how badly he's hurt her feelings, when she leaves after *The Doctor's Daughter* (2008), and when she returns to help save the entire universe in *Journey's End* (2008). Four chances, and the Doctor never gives her a word of praise.

Nor will the Doctor be as generous to her as he is to his white companions. In *Journey's End*, Rose has a reunited family and a Doctor substitute. In *The End of Time* (2009–10) Donna has a winning lottery ticket. Even Sarah Jane will get a new K-9, sonic lipstick and scanner watch after *School Reunion* (2006). Martha does get a job recommendation, but nothing else; no help for her traumatized family, no riches, and no alien toys. (Mickey doesn't even get the job recommendation. In *The End of Time*, the Doctor watches Mickey leave for the second time with nothing but the clothes he's wearing.)

Rosita: The problem summed up in a single scene

In *The Next Doctor* (2008), Rosita fought Cybermen side-by-side with the Tenth Doctor, and she saves him and her Doctor from a potentially fatal fall. Yet her ultimate fate is a condensed replay of all the problems with the way companions of colour are treated in New Who: her future, and the only compliment she will receive, is discussed between two white men just out of her earshot. What she wants, what she hopes, doesn't matter; she's going to be the nanny.

The Moffat era: Meet the new boss, same as the old boss

Steven Moffat tried to take steps in the right direction with Liz 10 (*The Beast Below*, 2010) and Mels (*Let's Kill Hitler*, 2011). Unfortunately, although they are strong characters, both of them remain deeply problematic as positive depictions of women of colour.

Liz hides her face behind a white mask, not one that reflects her skin tone. Furthermore, although she claims to love and want to protect her subjects, she was complicit in creating a totalitarian society where children disappear and the adults (including herself) continually choose to erase their memories of the things they should change.

Mels is erased in an even more drastic manner. Moffat writes storylines that span multiple seasons and have long, subtle build ups … but he somehow overlooks having Amy and Rory mention their best friend, not even once in passing. If that isn't dismissive enough, Mels lasts just long enough to be introduced, killed off – and literally whitewashed. Right before our eyes an overlooked woman of colour becomes the white woman who's been driving the plot.

The solution

Some people have told me that complaining how companions of colour are treated is to actually say that no companion of colour should be cast, or that certain storylines should never be done. Far from it! The solution isn't to avoid storylines or actors; it's for the BBC to give a more diverse cast a wider set of roles to play. When the Doctor has a companion of colour that he treats with exactly the same affection and respect that he's given others, that's when there will be true colour-blindness – and how the show could truly display equal love for all of humanity in its diversity.

Note

1 Richard Simpson, "Exit Billie as Doctor Who Gets First Black Side-Kick", *Daily Mail*, 5 July 2006.

Chapter 4

Doctor Who, cricket and race: The Peter Davison years

Amit Gupta[1]

It was perhaps inevitable that when Peter Davison assumed the role of the Doctor in 1982 his persona would include a cricketing reference – in this case he assumed the garb of a Victorian cricket player. As Davison himself put it, "I'll be wearing a kind of Victorian cricketing outfit to accentuate my youth. I'd like my Doctor to be heroic and resourceful."[2] In Margaret Thatcher's Britain, however, the reference to cricket was more than being youthful, heroic and resourceful. To the British elite the game represented the epitome of Englishness as well as a vehicle through which British imperialism gained acceptance in the colonies. Cricket, therefore, formed the perfect bridge between the politics of the times, Britain's lost self-image, and the role of the new Doctor.

Davison's Doctor portrayed the amateur English cricketer of the late nineteenth century during which period the game was characterized by both racial and class distinctions. Cricket was a semi-amateurish game whose decision making process was dominated by the white nations of the British Empire. The game was semi-amateurish for several reasons. Until 1962, it maintained an amateur-professional divide in England, the birthplace of the game. Cricket also had a role in maintaining the status of British imperialism through the exercise of soft power as it was successfully inculcated by the colonial elites.[3] The game was restrictive in its decision making process, for unlike other international sports, cricket, at the highest levels, sought to exclude nations from the most prestigious form of competition in the game – Test match cricket.[4] Thus the division in cricket was characterized as that between the white nations – England, Australia, South Africa and New Zealand – and the black nations – the West Indies and the South Asian countries – and the goal of the former was to prevent a takeover of the game's administration and ultimately its future by the latter.[5]

Race was also central to the British dominated game as witnessed by the determined efforts of the English, Australian and New Zealand cricket boards to keep apartheid South Africa in the international sporting community despite domestic protests and the international efforts of the 'black' nations. Thus through the 1960s and early 1970s the Caucasian nations were to try and keep an increasingly isolated South Africa within cricketing circles.[6]

For Thatcherite Britain, which sought national revival after years of self-doubt and the post-Second World War decline of imperial power, images and institutions that preserved this self-image that had been lost due to economic and political realities were welcomed. As Tulloch and Alvarado write, the BBC for much of its history has been "deeply implicated in the transmission of British ruling culture."[7]

In the Peter Davison years *Doctor Who* established a cricketing persona with the Doctor wearing the garb of a Victorian cricketer and in one serial (*Black Orchid*, 1982) actually playing in a cricket match. Davison himself decided to go with the cricketing persona both for its Englishness and to make a complete break from Tom Baker's bohemian Doctor.[8] The use of cricket in the Davison years symbolized not just Englishness but also the England of a bygone era where the International Cricket Council was dominated by the white nations who set the rules of the game. By the 1980s, the West Indies dominated world cricket and terms like "Blackwash" were being used to describe the ritual drubbing that the cricketers from the Caribbean had begun to inflict on their sporting opponents from the Caucasian nations. In fact, a team of rebel West Indians went to South Africa and defeated the apartheid team of the 1980s, thereby dispelling beliefs of South African racial and cricketing superiority.[9]

The Doctor, therefore, in his Victorian cricketer's garb, represented a class and race identity that had begun to vanish in both British and international society. The Doctor, always being an upper-class English gentleman – even in his most Bohemian incarnations – naturally had to play the most English of games, especially one so identified with British cultural superiority. Yet, while cricket symbolized Englishness and an upper-class, white identity, John Major, former Prime Minister and someone who served in a variety of government positions during the Davison years, put it best when he wrote:

> Although cricket is the very essence of England, the skills of Bradman and Sobers, of Hadlee and Tendulkar, are evidence that the game has far outstripped the land of its birth. England no longer owns cricket. Like radar, penicillin, electricity, the steam engine, railways, the jet engine, computers and the worldwide web, cricket is an English invention; an export as potent as the English language itself. At one level it is a game and no more; at another it helped cement an Empire and bind a Commonwealth. Its legacy is a fellowship of cricket-lovers across continents and through generations.[10]

Davison's cricketing Doctor therefore represented far more than youth and physical fitness. It once again saw the BBC using *Who* to promote a racial and class nostalgia that had already outlived its validity in British society.

It took the advent of the Matt Smith era for the Doctor to get a different sporting persona – that of a football player. Smith's Doctor plays a game of football in Lionel Messi-like form, taking the ball from his part of the field to the other goal and repeatedly scoring (*The Lodger*, 2010). Britain had changed by the 2000s, as football had replaced cricket as the true national game of England, and the heroes of the game came from both the working class – rather than the elite that dominated cricket – as well as from multiracial backgrounds. Moreover, cricket itself had become a game whose financial roots and viewership had shifted to India and South Asia.[11]

Davison's portrayal of the Doctor as a Victorian cricketer, therefore, remains locked in nostalgia for a Britain that was once the hegemonic international power and for a game where race and class shaped the character of the sport.

Notes

1　Amit Gupta is an associate professor in the Department of International Security Studies at the USAF Air War College. The views in this essay are his own and do not necessarily represent those of the United States Air Force or the Department of Defense. E-mail: amit.gupta1856@gmail.com.

2　Anon., "New Who", *Radio Times*, 2 January 1982.

3　Brian Stoddart, "Sport, Cultural Imperialism, and Colonial Response in the British Empire", *Comparative Studies in Society and History*, 30, 4 (1988), 651.

4　Football, in fact, only became a truly global phenomenon when the Federation of International Football Associations (FIFA) expanded the World Cup from 16 to 32 contesting nations under the visionary leadership of the Brazilian Joao Havelange – who increased the number of African and Asian teams that could compete in the tournament.

5　Mike Cronin and Richard Holt, "The imperial game in crisis: English Cricket and decolonization", in Stuart Ward, ed., *British Culture and the End of Empire*, Manchester: Manchester University Press, 2001, 115–18.

6　Peter May, *The Rebel Tours: Cricket's Crisis of Conscience*, Cheltenham: SportsBooks, 2009, 11–15 and 32.

7　John Tulloch and Manuel Alvarado, *Doctor Who: The Unfolding Text*, New York: St. Martin's Press, 1983, 35.

8　Anon., "New Who."

9　May, *The Rebel Tours*, 262–66.

10　John Major, "Why Cricket is more important than being Prime Minister", *Daily Mail*, 28 April 2007.

11　Amit Gupta, "The IPL and the Indian Domination of Global Cricket", *Sport in Society*, 14, 10 (2011), 1316–25.

Chapter 5

Humanity as a white metaphor

Quiana Howard and Robert Smith?

*D*octor Who is a show about a man called the Doctor, who travels through time and space. On these adventures, he fights against invaders, brings unseen threats into the light and often saves the day through unconventional thinking. With a few notable exceptions, humanity is mostly presented as an ideal that must be protected and preserved at all costs. Humanity's defender is the Doctor, who is himself an alien. Not only does the Doctor defend us from aliens bent on invasion, he often pulls us up on our own morality, showing us how to be the best humans we can possibly be.

Let's just stop and think about that for a moment. A large but weak hegemony (humans) who live in fear of the 'other' (aliens) nevertheless adopt one of those others (the Doctor) not only into their society, but they make him their saviour and moral compass. Now recast this into our westernized society: replace 'humans' with 'white' and 'aliens' with all things not white, and what you have is a very mixed message from the show. And the obvious question is: who is the Doctor in this metaphor? We'll come to that in a moment.

Part of the Doctor's safe nature is due to his alienness often being played for laughs. Examples include a post-regeneration Fourth Doctor in the serial *Robot* (1974–75) in his first interactions with the Brigadier and Harry Sullivan, who are bemused by the Doctor's wacky behaviour – dressing as a Viking, skipping, mocking the Brigadier's assumptions about foreigners – yet quickly find him acceptable. His alienness here is reduced to human-level eccentricity; you can imagine someone who's never seen *Doctor Who* never realizing that he isn't human.

A similar situation happens when the Eleventh Doctor meets a young Amy Pond for the first time in *The Eleventh Hour* (2010). This strange man comes falling to Earth, and his differences are boiled down to laughs – he comically climbs out of the TARDIS, he doesn't like human food, he gets undressed in public – making him 'safe' enough for humanity to interact with. It's almost as if the Doctor becomes like Uncle Remus, a stereotypical black narrator from the 1800s, who simultaneously presented as comic relief and wise mentor. The Doctor usually forsakes his differences in favour of humanity, which makes him seem more human and therefore 'safe'. This draws direct parallels with the Uncle Tom stereotype of lore: forming a bond with those who would otherwise seek to destroy him and his kind.

To be sure, the Doctor is not always a comedy character. Indeed, when facing down monsters or standing up to villains, including human villains, he's often deadly serious. But it's worth examining his general attitude to species. When aliens try to do evil, he stops them and invariably destroys their entire species. When humanity does, he's ... disappointed. He may make a token speech about our failings, but he's soon back to appreciating the good in us and admiring our many virtues.

In the real world, especially the cultural milieu of the Global North from which *Doctor Who* hails, the dominant white power structure exists to oppress the racialized other, largely out of fear and a desire to protect one's own 'kind'. By co-opting members of the oppressed group into their cause, as conservative groups sometimes do with racialized or gay members, the veneer of civility is maintained, while allowing the overall oppression to continue.

In *Doctor Who*, we see the Doctor play this role. Defender of humanity, yet not human, he thus releases us from fears that we may be 'species-ist'. The Doctor becomes our moral compass, choosing whether aliens have the right to live, based on a code of ethics that ostensibly comes from him, but that nevertheless serves humanity's interests time and time again.

An example of this would be with the Saturnynians from *The Vampires of Venice* (2010). They were driven from their homes by the cracks in time and space. All they wanted was a single water-logged town in order to rebuild their society, but were aggressive in their pursuits against humans. Rather than negotiating a compromise where both sides could share the planet, the Doctor becomes the arbiter on their right to survive, thus protecting humanity. Interestingly, Rosanna even proposes to him, as a fellow outsider.

A more subtle example plays out in 2011's *Closing Time*. In the pre-credits teaser, the Doctor detects a strange anomaly in Craig's house (in actuality, his baby). He then bursts into the baby's room, sonic screwdriver held out like a weapon, with the instant demand, "Whatever you are, get off this planet!" Although played for laughs, the joke hinges upon the idea of the Doctor as an unquestioning defender of humanity against the alien. His first response isn't to question the creature or investigate it, but simply to demand its removal from Earth.

There's a startling parallel today in the United States with its leader, Barack Obama. Just like the Doctor, the president is a member of the racialized 'other' and also in the position where he must protect the white authority. His role as leader and protector is in direct opposition to his being a member of the 'alien' group. He then must forgo his fellow 'others' to protect the white humanity, while still being 'safe' enough for whites to interact with. The president walks the fine line of where his loyalties lie. For one, he was born and raised as a member of an 'alien' group. He knows first hand what being a member of that group means and the lifelong 'label' that carries. But those ties to the 'alien' group are forsaken because of his role as leader of the United States. As leader, he must adopt a 'neutral' role, regardless of the colour of his skin. He must readapt and become a person that the majority of people will feel comfortable looking up to and taking direction from, often acting as their moral compass.

Doctor Who has almost always reflected the times in which it was made. However, in positing the Doctor as a safe outsider who defends the weak but dominant hegemony, we see that *Doctor Who* was, in an unusual way, decades ahead of its time. Whether or not that is a good thing, we leave to the reader to decide.

Chapter 6

"You can't just change what I look like without consulting me!": The shifting racial identity of the Doctor

Mike Hernandez

The Doctor and race

Race in *Doctor Who* always gives viewers something to think about, from the casting and characterization of companions to the treatment of alien races. Yet it is the Doctor himself whose racial identity has yet to be fully understood and whose full potential is still to be realized. In terms of character development, the Doctor's relationship with the Time Lords has grown to greater and greater importance, from the starkly antagonistic and satirical characterization in the classic series to one tinged with guilt and regret in the revived series. Since the show's return in 2005, the Doctor's struggle to understand his new identity as the last of his species has brought a new perspective to the character; more emotional, more mature in its consideration of grave consequences. Another element of the Doctor's characterization, however, has yet to change in a significant way. In discussing the Doctor's identity crisis, this essay also discusses long-frustrated hopes for diversity in the casting of the Doctor. Every regeneration could bring an actor of a different gender or race, yet the Doctor is as much a white male in 2012 as he was in 1963. And, as this essay will show, the Doctor's racial and cultural significance have a meaning that is currently only partially realized and just faintly legible.

In order to understand what the Doctor could mean, it is important to understand what the show stops short of meaning. After all, unfulfilled potential can be as important a message as what the show says outright. So, after nearly fifty years in which the show has avoided diverse casting, viewers might infer this message: a quintessential British character can be an alien – as long as he remains a white male. *Doctor Who* is certainly reaching the point at which this implication becomes inescapable, almost deliberate. In 2007, *The Sound of Drums* featured the first black actor cast as a Time Lord. In 2011, *The Doctor's Wife* established that Time Lords can change gender. In the same year, River Song's regeneration in *Let's Kill Hitler* set a precedent for one Time Lord to be portrayed by a white actor and a black actor in different incarnations. The possibility even goes as far back as the 1969 serial *The War Games*, in which the Doctor refuses several new bodies offered to him by the Time Lords, including one resembling a black male. The Doctor refused the possibility then and show runners have avoided it in all the regenerations after. With the possibility established, it seems logical for viewers to see it happen. That is, unless this is a line show runners and producers are implicitly saying they will not cross. Even the revived series of *Doctor Who*, which often raises emotional and problematic situations more deliberately than the classic series, avoids new cultural significance by avoiding greater variation in the Doctor's casting, variation that could expose something which has gone unnoticed despite being in front of viewers' faces the entire time – hidden in plain sight.

Since *Doctor Who*'s revival in 2005, fans and commentators have wondered when there will be more diverse casting in the title role. In recent years, tabloids have reported actors such as Paterson Joseph and Colin Salmon as potential Doctors.[1] Yet for all the rumours, viewers have continued waiting for a more diverse Doctor. When one considers the Doctor's status in popular culture, disappointment does not seem unwarranted. Simply having a black actor in the title role of the BBC's flagship show, one with a legacy, a cult following and growing mainstream popularity abroad, would be a massive step toward more diverse representation in media. Instead, the exclusive casting of white male actors as a character who battles injustice, champions individuality and saves the universe on a seasonal basis seems to squander some of the character's potential. Considering the persistence of token characters in television, the Doctor offers the opposite with his depth and individuality. Even – no, especially – the Doctor's flaws create a complexity to counter an inequality that persists in television today. In an age when shows still rely on stereotypes, the Doctor could be one of the most positive roles a black actor could play. Furthermore, this kind of change is what has ensured the show's survival; *Doctor Who* only functions to its full potential when it has the ability to surprise.

It may be surprising to readers, then, just what we can see in the Doctor's character by looking to the thoughts and lives of postcolonial theorists. Like these intellectuals, the Doctor has a complicated relationship with both his home culture and his adopted culture, understanding both and identifying wholly with neither. The Classic Series *Doctor Who* depicts political, personal and ideological strife between the Doctor and his own people, but the revived series builds on that a more complex subject, saddled with the uncomfortable burden of representation. To draw out this reading of the Doctor, I will rely on the thoughts of Frantz Fanon, Stuart Hall, and scholars influenced by Hall. These ideas will help explain why continuing to cast the Doctor exclusively white is actually counterintuitive to the direction *Doctor Who* has taken for some years now. Consider, for example, the problem of West Indian immigrants to Britain in the late twentieth century, living there without any feeling of belonging. Although they are now a significant component of British society, they may find a less prominent role for themselves in the national identity. With this in mind, this essay will carry out a reading of the Doctor as a metaphor, a reflection and site of crisis for British national identity in the face of diaspora and an ever-increasing need for inclusivity. As the only one left to decide what it means to be a Time Lord, the Doctor takes the responsibility of representing his culture while also demonstrating how flexible that identity can be. And, as a cultural phenomenon, *Doctor Who* is emblematic of British culture both domestically and internationally. With this in mind, it seems that the character and casting of the Doctor could possibly embody and demonstrate the flexibility – the inclusive potential – of British national identity.

The Doctor and cultural identity

Before substantial analysis can be made, it is important to clarify some terms and define a few ideas. The essay is about race, yet the term can mean different things. Within the confines of the show, *Doctor Who* usually refers to the Time Lords as the Doctor's race, but they are more accurately described for our purposes as a species. Time Lords are usually described as being a race in the zoological sense, having a common physiology, DNA, and so on. However, the way we generally discuss race is in the sociological sense, as a cultural construction. Regardless of variations such as facial features and skin colour, what we call race is a human invention,[2] used to separate – and exploit – other groups. People use various traits, physical and cultural, to support racist claims, hate crimes, discrimination and stereotyping; these things are products of a basic idea, referred to as a 'guarantee' by Stuart Hall.[3]

Throughout history, different guarantees have been used to affix racial identities on groups of people. Take, for example, the claims by some colonists that the peoples they met were soulless beasts, viable candidates for slavery: the religious guarantee. Or, take the spurious science around brain size that supported further subjugation: the biological guarantee. And later came the genetic excuse for racism, which facilitated ludicrous claims about black intellectual inferiority.[4] Clearly, the Time Lords are not quite a race in the same way we might see humans described as races. These are the limitations that shape this essay. It relies on diaspora and postcolonial writing for ideas about personal identity, national identity and race, but it does not argue that the Doctor suffers outright racism. Racism, oppression, subjugation: these injustices prompt people to theorize about race, but cannot be found in the Doctor's story. The Doctor is generally cast in a position of privilege, travelling (usually) as he pleases, righting wrongs as he sees fit, the intellectual superior of all and the moral superior of most. And while it is true that the Doctor is an outcast among his people, their differences are still defined by his relative superiority. If the Doctor is oppressed, then it is only by his own people and at nowhere near the extremity of slavery or colonization; the Doctor's personal cultural conflict is that of someone who disagrees with the politics of his nation, not that of an enslaved or racially discriminated 'other'.

This is not to say there is nothing in the Classic Series Doctor to discuss; instead this analysis will show how the story's latent symbolic potential makes a more diverse Doctor a natural progression for the series. To do this, we must first establish historical and theoretical context. The shadow that race and racism cast over individual lives is relevant to our discussion of race in *Doctor Who*. The cultural constructions and racial stereotypes that linger and fester in the wake of colonialism have a deep psychological effect, as described by Fanon in the case of black people in former French colonies.[5] Furthermore, postcolonial politics also influence individual and national identities, as described by Hall in the case of the West Indian diaspora in England.[6]

By the time *Doctor Who* first aired in 1963, Jamaican immigrant and sociology professor Stuart Hall had already been studying culture, racial identity and media for several years. His thought on race and culture is influenced by both Marxist and semiotic structural theory, emphasizing race as something whose meaning shifts based on time and place, determined by history and politics.[7] At the same time, Hall's thought is shaped by his own complicated relationship with race, separated from those around him by education and class and then placed in a new context as a student at Oxford.[8] By the time Hall returned home, it no longer existed as he knew it, changed fundamentally by decolonization and the formation of a new national identity which he did not share.[9] This displacement has an effect on identity that is particularly relevant to a discussion of the Doctor; it offers the displaced an atypical perspective, understanding culture from multiple positions simultaneously.[10] Helen Davis explains it this way:

> Journeying from the largely agrarian, colonised and racially complex, ethnic and class oriented society of Kingston in Jamaica, to a predominantly industrialised homogenous society of England in the early 1950s, must have induced a series of profound reflections. We can see the importance of race, colour, class, and ethnicity to Jamaican society in Hall's analysis. The relative hothouse environment of Oxford followed by periods in poorer areas like Brixton and Birmingham certainly contributed enormously to Hall's sense of displacement. Paradoxically, these moves simultaneously afforded him greater awareness of and access to the different levels and institutions of British culture.[11]

Note that displacement and greater awareness of culture reach an extreme in the character of the Doctor. Neither he nor Hall could ever return to the intellectual position from which they started, but both can be said to construct new identities. Hall, instead of identifying personally with the immigrants of the West Indian diaspora who followed him, had to approach the issue from his intellectual, political standpoint and renegotiate his cultural identity, creating it anew instead of simply returning home.[12]

That psychological element, that personal element both Fanon and Hall describe, is reducible to this: the feeling of having lost part of yourself and having to remake that part of your identity. When the Doctor returned to television seeking refuge from a war in which all his people died, he began to address the same element. The Time Lords were taken for granted by the Doctor in the classic series, so they became difficult for him to identity with after their extinction. Beneath franchise-saving regenerations, plot twists, even the fall and genocide of the Time Lords at the Doctor's hands, the inspiration for this essay is a tale of shifting identity. Shifting identity is integral to Hall's thought on diaspora, in which he describes the need to reconstruct a heritage, to revise identity after a removal from the Caribbean preceded distantly by a removal from Africa. It is helpful here to turn to Hall's own words on the subject:

> [Cultural identity] is not a fixed origin to which we can make some final and absolute Return. Of course, it is not a mere phantasm either. It is something – not a mere trick of the imagination. It has its histories – and histories have their real, material and symbolic effects [...] [The past] is always constructed through memory, fantasy, narrative and myth.

Cultural identities are the points of identification, the unstable points of identification or suture, which are made, within the discourses of history and culture. Not an essence but a positioning. Hence, there is always a politics of identity, a politics of position, which has no absolute guarantee in an unproblematic, transcendental 'law of origin'.[13]

According to Hall, every origin and shared history is a partial invention because they are relative to historical moments. In a different context, one origin can actually grow from the site of a previous breach. As an immigrant in Britain, Hall saw his point of origin, the place that determined his identity, as Jamaica. Yet, he understood at the same time that this place was partially a place of his own construction, for his own needs. It is this idea of constructing an identity based on a partially invented past, the creation of a story to which one can relate, that resonates with the current portrayal of the Doctor and the foundation of the character as a result. The Doctor has to invent his past and identity through memory and fantasy precisely because the classic series showed him actively rejecting his Time Lord identity. So too, the next section of this essay will examine the relationship between the Doctor and the Time Lords in the classic series, reconstructing a past from stories initially devoid of racial significance and explaining how the Doctor could say more about culture, race and identity. If this essay argues for a repositioning of the Doctor, then it is necessary to understand what this new position is made against.

Unfulfilled potential: Time Lords in classic *Doctor Who*

Since its early days, *Doctor Who* has used the Time Lords in various ways to construct the Doctor's identity. As with other elements of the show, writers draw on different elements in its history, advancing the story while maintaining a sense of continuity, highlighting different aspects in order to tell a compelling story. The extinction of the Time Lords, for example, is arguably the most interesting innovation of Russell T Davies's revival of *Doctor Who* because it takes an element of the Doctor's identity and makes it new by adding emotional significance. Throughout the classic series, however, the Doctor's species, culture and civilization usually served as foils for the Doctor. Keeping in mind that this Classic Series dynamic is not marked by racial strife, let us consider the Doctor's relationship with this group of people, this species and culture with which he is supposed to identify. In their mysterious initial appearance, the Time Lords are a great and powerful people who loom over the Doctor's life. Yet, by the time viewers see the Doctor return home to Gallifrey, the Time Lords are (like most other characters in the show) foils to emphasize the Doctor's superiority. Take, for example, the notorious overreaction of the President of the Doctor Who Appreciation Society to the first Gallifrey story, *The Deadly Assassin* (1976):

I've spoken to many people [...] and they all said how this story shattered their illusions of the Time Lords and lowered them to ordinary people. Once, Time Lords were all-powerful, awe-inspiring beings, capable of imprisoning planets forever in force fields, defenders of truth and good (when called in). Now, they are petty, squabbling, feeble-minded, doddering old fools. WHAT HAS HAPPENED TO THE MAGIC OF DOCTOR WHO?[14]

Overreaction aside, it seems that the real magic of *Doctor Who* was to use the Time Lords, cast as oppressors, fools and villains, to emphasize the Doctor's anti-authoritarianism and superior intellect. This narrative strategy, flattening other characters to bring out the positive traits of a round character, goes back at least as far as the nineteenth-century British novel.[15] The strategy, while not only used on Time Lords in *Doctor Who*, sends a message about the individual in relation to the group. Flattening the Time Lords in comparison with the Doctor implies that the Doctor is an exception, an intelligent, heroic character in spite of being of a Time Lord. Just consider the number of villainous Time Lords the Doctor has to fight in the classic series: the Meddling Monk, the War Lord, Morbius, the Rani and, of course, the Master. And what about the evil Time Lord historical figure Omega, who tried to trap the Doctor in an anti-matter universe in his stead and later returned to steal the Doctor's body? In *The Three Doctors* (1973) and *Arc of Infinity* (1983), the Doctor has to literally fight his cultural heritage in the form of one of his society's founders.

Even the Doctor's Time Lord companion, Romana, had to turn away from the Time Lords to be her own person. Upon her introduction in *The Ribos Operation* (1978), Romana is arrogant and antagonistic towards the Doctor, but becomes more like him after they travel together. Although she is initially as small-minded as any Time Lord of the era, Romana eventually declines returning to the Time Lords after seeing the excitement of wandering the universe. Just as the Doctor is set to take her home in *Full Circle* (1980), Romana becomes upset and runs from the console room. When he follows her, Romana says: "Doctor, I don't want to spend the rest of my life on Gallifrey – after all this." When the Doctor says she cannot fight the Time Lords, Romana replies, "you did", making him something of a role model in his rejection of their people. The argument is only settled when the Doctor says that he lost to the Time Lords. In one short exchange, individuals cast their people as boring, adversarial and oppressive.

In Classic Series examples like this, the message the Doctor sends is that one's own culture can be a hindrance to individualism, an oppression to be escaped. Whether we recognize a racial conflict in a fictional scenario or find fictional species too abstract to be metaphors for race, the same problem underlies both: the uneven balance between sameness and individuality in representation. In a story with a more racial context, the implication would be that a character's race is a handicap to be overcome.

A significant missed opportunity for cultural and racial allegory is the 1986 season-long story *The Trial of a Time Lord*, in which the Doctor finds himself charged by his peers with "conduct unbecoming a Time Lord." The charge of "conduct unbecoming" adds racial policing to the alternative history of the Doctor. This form of racism is all the more troubling for originating within one's own racial group. Today, black public figures must champion individuality against those who would have members of a racial group conform to the stereotypical, even against people who do this within their own racial group.[16] From a positive point of view, the Doctor might be someone who frustrates stereotypes and expands the definition of Time Lord by his actions. The positive racial message to be found in *The Trial of a Time Lord* would contribute to the positive aspects of a black actor playing the Doctor. From a negative point of view, the Doctor might be seen as a sort of traitor. The viewer is stuck taking a side in this conflict when the Time Lords prosecute the Doctor and he attacks them back. Of course, this is no problem as it stands because there are no racial differences between the Doctor and the Time Lords. The differences remain political at this stage, yet they could easily have offered complex and problematic racial conflict.

The burden of representation

It is no wonder the Doctor suffers a crisis of identity once the Time Lords are gone; he has defined himself against them all of his life. Despite the avoidance of racial connotations in *Doctor Who*, the story of group membership in conflict with personal identity meshes well with a racial reading. In both cases, we see this conflict's jarring effect. Fanon describes the loss of racial identity as existentially and psychologically disorienting, writing this about realizing his own loss:

> In all truth I tell you, my shoulders slipped out of the framework of the world, my feet could no longer feel the touch of the ground. Without a Negro past, without a Negro future, it was impossible for me to live my Negrohood. Not yet white, no longer wholly black, I was damned [...] the Negro suffers in his body quite differently from the white man. Between the white man and me the connection was irrevocably one of transcendence.[17]

The Doctor certainly suffers from displacement and disorientation, even an identity crisis, after losing the Time Lords. However, it seems he takes Fanon's journey backwards. As the burgeoning racial message of the series demonstrates, the Doctor is not yet black, but no longer wholly white. Perhaps it is fitting that the Classic Series Doctor, who ran from home and rejected his identity, was played by white men; his body reflected the freedom, the transcendence, which he enjoyed. The revived series, however, wrestles with and engages his responsibility. If his body reflected racial transcendence in the classic series, the overdetermined body of a black actor seems appropriate for the Doctor who can no longer shirk the weight of his heritage.

Fanon explains this as well, contrasting anti-Semitic behaviour with anti-black behaviour:

> [T]he Jew can be unknown to his Jewishness. He is not wholly what he is. One hopes, one waits. His actions, his behavior are the final determinant. He is a white man, and, apart from some rather debatable characteristics, he can sometimes go unnoticed.[18]

In the past, the Doctor's rejection of his culture in favour of his own individuality reflected that same freedom from external determination. Yet today, the 'last of the Time Lords' mentality of the Doctor acknowledges an inescapability of cultural identity that seems closer to Fanon's description of experience as a black man:

> The Jew is disliked from the moment he is tracked down. But in my case everything takes on a new guise. I am given no chance. I am overdetermined from without. I am the slave not of the 'idea' that others have of me, but of my own appearance.[19]

Although the Doctor's external appearance does not mark him off immediately as a Time Lord, Fanon's description resonates with the idea that certain parts of his identity are inescapable. The Doctor now accepts his heritage in a mature way, not going back to some past Time Lord identity, but coming to terms with his past and creating a new identity.

In the revived series, the Doctor demonstrates a need to represent that which he has always had difficulty relating with. He regularly refers to himself as "last of the Time Lords" and multiple stories focus on his struggle to form a new identity or come to terms with his heritage, sometimes placing a nostalgic gloss over their memory. Despite the often unmitigated conflict between the Doctor and his people, he must revise history in order to regain a piece of his heritage. One of the most interesting examples of his attempt to fulfil that need, to tell a story that fits with his identity, comes upon the brief return of the Time Lords in *The End of Time* (2009–10). As their return approaches, his friend Wilfred Mott is excited, but the Doctor describes them as having become evil, simultaneously remembering/constructing some golden past for them:

WILFRED: But I've heard you talk about your people – how they're wonderful.

THE DOCTOR: That's how I choose to remember them. The Time Lords of old. But then they went to war. An endless war. And it changed them. Right to the core. You've seen my enemies, Wilf. The Time Lords are more dangerous than any of them.

While the contrasts in *Doctor Who* are more exaggerated than those in our critical source material, we must put aside the obvious differences between postcolonial immigration and cosmic genocide for a moment; this space opera story device is a means to a deeper analysis (as well as simply a way to inject emotional gravitas into the series). Yes, the Doctor eventually admits that the Time Lords died at his hands, to end a war in which they had lost their way and become evil. But what is this, if not an extreme metaphor for the Doctor's rejection of the Time Lords and the permanent consequences of his actions? What the Doctor's remembrance of the Time Lords really represents here is the same mythmaking about one's origins that Hall described. What connects the bombastic fiction of the Doctor to the real world postcolonial experience is the emotional process of renegotiating a cultural identity.

Unlike the Doctor of the classic series, today's Doctor (usually) has no living Time Lords against which to rail. He continually revises both his idea of the Time Lords and his concept of himself as one. He goes from renegade to exile to outcast to "last of the Time Lords" to "lonely god" to "Time Lord victorious." His remembrances range from idealistic to regretful to even-handed. While *The End of Time* still shows a general opposition between the Doctor and the Time Lords, the Doctor's preferred memory of his people reflects a sense of what was good about them. At the core, beneath the megalomania of the Time Lords and their status as villains, the central idea is that he has to fashion a Time Lord identity with which he can live. And now that the basis has been laid for a potential racial message in *Doctor Who*, it is time to flesh it out by placing relevant elements of the Doctor in the context of diaspora and postcolonialism.

Claiming and reclaiming identity

In 1950, the West Indian community in Britain was near 30,000; by the 1970s, it had risen past one million.[20] In 1981, Hall delivered a lecture in which he argued that the complicated dual identity of the Caribbean diasporic subject was a gift rather than a burden; rather than losing one culture, he argued, immigrants gained another. Arguing for immigrants' rightful place in British society, Hall said: "The first thing I want you to get out of your mind is that you are not visitors here … you belong here. You are living here, part of English society."[21] In effect, this is the same thing that this essay argues for, a more inclusive and accurate conception of British culture. Television, particularly iconic British legacy television, is an important area for inclusion, especially in a story with such unique diasporic potential. Just as Hall encouraged a proactive addition of the English identity to the Caribbean identity, the identity of the original home, so *Doctor Who* can promote an active model of cultural and racial identity formation.

An interesting, if problematic, example of this is *The Waters of Mars* (2009), in which the Doctor violates the Time Lord rule of making major changes to history. The Doctor takes control over time as his inherited right, speaking like a megalomaniac when he says: "For a long time now, I thought I was just a survivor, but I'm not. I'm the winner! That's who I am: the Time Lord Victorious!" Even if the Doctor's attempt to assert his Time Lord identity is somewhat troubling, it still signifies an attempt by the Doctor to integrate his dead heritage into his normal identity; that this attempt is unsuccessful stresses the difficulty of re-engaging with heritage, the struggle to represent a culture and oneself at the same time. It is very interesting that there is actually a wrong way for the Doctor to be a Time Lord. Against his better judgment, the Doctor saves the Mars station crew; while he is shown coming to this decision, sound bites from previous episodes play, describing the extinction of the Time Lords and repeating that he is the last of them. The connection is clear between the decision and the Doctor's idea of what it means to be the last Time Lord. If we keep in mind the metaphor of the Doctor as the paragon of Britishness within popular culture, embodied by an alien, we can see the growing pains of a mind reconciling his individual identity with a community identity and not always meeting success.

The conflict within the Doctor's mind reflects the crisis the show is in, attempting to integrate an identity in flux. The stories have taken on a new kind of significance while the casting lags behind ideologically. The show can continue to present this hero while also bringing out the latent message of inclusivity not only in British television, but in British national identity; to show that the Doctor's face is not fixed in one colour is also to say that British identity is not a single default colour. The diasporic connotations of the character becoming more noticeable would inherently acknowledge that the immigrant, postcolonial experience is essential to British culture, something to be reflected in national cultural institutions, which *Doctor Who* certainly is. What's more, the Doctor's casting promises a role that is not bound to represent what anyone thinks of as a 'black role'. The Doctor stands as a British cultural phenomenon, but within the show he is an alien; the character is fleshed out in such detail now that an actor like Paterson Joseph should not be at risk of playing racial stereotypes in the role.

This is key. A common barrier to innovative black art is its frequent relegation to the niche of multicultural art, saddled with the burden of representation. Writing in response to Hall, Kobena Mercer describes the process by which ethnicity becomes a determinant, dictating what black artists can and can't do or seem to be doing:

> To the extent that multiculturalism implicitly prescribes black artists to be ethnically representative, and thus visibly different, arts policy is reduced to a simplistic equation whereby retroactive inclusion supplements and compensates an institutional fetish in a regime of visuality more or less continuous with the ethnocentric ideology it sought to modify.[22]

Another way to think about this is through Hall's idea of the positive guarantee, the notion that black art, thought or politics should be valued simply for being black. Hall explains that this assumption hinders the success of black artists, making it an undeniable concern; he finds that "it leads to a kind of mechanistic anti-racist politics, not a thoughtful one, not a self critical one, not a reflexive one."[23] However, it is precisely because *Doctor Who* offers a diasporic theme that the casting of a black actor would not simply be a concession to multiculturalism. When a film version of *Wuthering Heights* (Director: Andrea Arnold, 2011) featuring a black actor as Heathcliff was dismissed by some as "multicultural nonsense",[24] it was actually Joseph who took to the editorial section of *The Guardian*, presenting historical research and explaining why black actors have a rightful place in British period drama. His conclusions are strikingly similar to those of Hall and Mercer, in that they locate the real problem in reductive portrayal:

> Drama must give us a view not just of what was but of what could be, and when we say that all that black people were or ever could be to us are 'problems' or 'issues', or buzz

words like 'knife/gun crime', we take our broad and beautiful richness and diminish it to stunted cliché and narrow world view. As an actor, I want to be in works that reflect black presence in the UK throughout the nation's history.[25]

Joseph's once rumoured role as the Doctor, however, promises a significance to match the richness he refers to. While the diasporic potential of the Doctor offers a certain relevance to the black component of British identity, it is not a blunt metaphor. The Doctor as diasporic subject that I argue for is something that has developed gradually, an evocative characterization too haphazard to be simplistic or cliché. It would be exciting, to say the least, to see Joseph play the Doctor in the future. Having played characters like the Marquis de Carabas in Neil Gaiman's *Neverwhere* (1996), he possesses the charisma that is so central to the role. And what's more, he seems to realize the potential of roles for black actors in Britain that this essay is concerned with.

The Doctor as diasporic intellectual

On the face of it, the Doctor is simply a privileged white traveller. Beneath this reading, however, are the makings of a diasporic intellectual. Eschewing the typical expectations of someone in his own cultural group, he comes to situations from his own unique position, doing something far more interesting as a result. He resists reduction to stereotypes and frustrates expectations, at least within the species-level dynamic of the series; we are constantly reminded in both incarnations of the show that the Doctor is not the typical Time Lord. It is a pity then that this champion of individuality is not played by an actor from a community which is so often reduced to stereotypes, defined primarily by race. The Doctor's individuality is not limited by his cultural identity; in fact, his uniqueness comes from his complex cultural position. For a white actor in the role, the lack of limits on individuality is often a matter of course. This is important because the role relies on the ability to frustrate expectations, the ability to give mystery to the series and keep it sustainable over the long term. *Doctor Who* scholar Matt Hills calls this *endlessly deferred narrative*.[26] Part of the classic series' stagnation in the 1980s resulted from too much being known about the Doctor (and the Time Lords). Before production stopped in 1989, script editor Andrew Cartmel had started a story arc teasing viewers with lines about how the Doctor wasn't "just another Time Lord" (1988's *Silver Nemesis*). Endless deferral in *Doctor Who*, as Piers Britton explains, refers to the ultimate unknowability of the Doctor, "focused on a central theme or character which is inherently mysterious."[27] Just when you think you know him, his body explodes into flames and a stranger takes his place. Viewers experienced this recently at the conclusion of Series 6, *The Wedding of River Song* (2011). The final unanswered question "Doctor who?" reiterates the titular, fundamental conceit of the show: we've known the Doctor for years and still don't even know his real name. He is a familiar stranger to us, on television long enough to become a part of British cultural language, yet still surprising enough to keep viewers interested.

There are also risks to be acknowledged, obstacles to the diversification of a legacy character like the Doctor. There is no way of knowing exactly what the effect will be until the day comes that the Doctor is played a black actor. It may be that the Doctor's diversification will then make more viewers pause and reassess what they watch. One can foresee an effect that is both positive and problematic. The worst that could really happen is the reduction of the character to the 'black Doctor', the avoidance of the kind of message I have outlined above. What 'black Doctor' means is a phenomenon any consumer of culture can imagine. By using blackness to establish difference, we reduce an actor or performance to a single characteristic, one that restricts agency and individuality. But then, reductive characterization is frequently imposed upon black characters and actors alike. To approach the Doctor as if his skin colour was his most interesting feature would be a waste; this is why this essay focuses on both the underlying message and the casting. Consider the actor Idris Elba's response to the rumour that he would be the next James Bond. As a successful black actor under consideration for another British legacy role, Elba expresses a similar concern:

> I just don't want to be the black James Bond. Sean Connery wasn't the Scottish James Bond, and Daniel Craig wasn't the blue-eyed James Bond, so if I played him, I don't want to be called the black James Bond.[28]

Just as Elba seeks to be appreciated in his own right and not simply as 'the black James Bond', our fictional alien would need to be considered in his own right, regardless of skin colour. Accomplishing this is a responsibility for both the actor and the audience. It also helps to remember the controversy surrounding the new Spider-Man in 2011. When Marvel's "Ultimate" universe saw the death of Peter Parker, it was announced that the new Spider-Man would be of black and Hispanic descent.[29] At the ugliest end of public reaction were the people who commented on USA Today's coverage of the event, dismissing the character as a worthless attempt to gain political correctness points.[30] While comment boards invite the outliers of offensive remarks, we should not forget that people still say things like, "Why not make him a dyslexic homosexual too, and cover all the politically correct bases, then we will really be 'enlightened.'"[31] Before Miles Morales's first issue of Ultimate Comics: Spider-Man (2011) debuted, there was significant controversy and backlash. While some people saw the new Spider-Man as a positive change coming from a large corporation, others saw gratuitous stunt casting to bring in new readers and generate news headlines.[32]

Yet as Joseph's comments show, black British actors are often excluded from their own national identity in film and television. White actors can play individualistic, dynamic characters who frustrate the expectations on them because there are fewer expectations to reject. The preconceptions a black actor faces are more overwhelming, making it all the more impressive, all the more appropriate for a role like the Doctor. This is not simply for the benefit of black actors, black audiences or sympathetic viewers either. This is an important message on British national identity. When Hall told Caribbean immigrants that they had a place in English society, it wasn't only for their benefit. Reading Hall another way, Bill Schwarz finds that "the theme underlying [Hall's] lecture suggests that it is only the black presence that allows the formerly imperial nation to fully see itself and thereby (in his terms) to realize its own modernity."[33]

Consider in closing the background and historical place that produced Stuart Hall's unique thought, described by Grant Farred: "Hall is a thinker who learned, however belatedly, how to negotiate between the unspeakabilities of his Caribbean past from a disjunctive locale: an intellectual formed in the cauldron of the 1950s (and beyond) white British politics."[34] So it is with the Doctor, formed in the context of twentieth-century British politics, a product of England by way of a mysterious and far off place. For black actors to be denied such a role is not only exclusive, it is also counter to the surprising diasporic undercurrent within the series.

Notes

1   Anon., "Colin Salmon to be first black Doctor Who?" (11 July 2008), *What's On TV?*. Retrieved 19 August 2012 at http://www.whatsontv.co.uk/drama/doctor-who/news/colin-salmon-to-be-first-black-doctor-who/4345; Simon Cable, "Casualty star Paterson Joseph could become first black Dr Who as BBC set to announce David Tennant's replacement", *Daily Mail*, 2 January 2009.
2   Ivan Hannaford, *Race: The History of an Idea in the West*, Washington, D.C.: The Woodrow Wilson Center Press, 1996.
3   Stuart Hall, *Race, the Floating Signifier*, Northampton: Media Education Foundation, 1997, 1–17.
4   Hall, *Race*, 6.
5   Frantz Fanon, "The Negro and Psychopathology", *The Fanon Reader*, London: Pluto, 2006, 59–99.
6   Stuart Hall, "Cultural Identity and Diaspora", in Jonathan Rutherford, ed., *Identity: Community, Culture, Difference*, London: Lawrence and Wishart, 1990, 222–37.
7   Claire Alexander, "Introduction: Stuart Hall and 'race'", *Cultural Studies*, 23, 4 (2009), 457–82.
8   Caryl Phillips and Stuart Hall, "Stuart Hall", *BOMB*, 58, 1 (1997), 38–42.
9   Phillips and Hall, "Stuart Hall", 39.
10 Alexander, "Introduction", 461.
11 Helen Davis, *Understanding Stuart Hall*, London: Sage, 2004.
12 Grant Farred, *What's My Name?: Black Vernacular Intellectuals*, London: University of Minnesota Press, 2003.
13 Hall, "Cultural Identity", 226.
14 BBC, "The Deadly Assassin" (n.d.), *Doctor Who Classic Episode Guide*. Retrieved 19 August 2012 at http://www.bbc.co.uk/doctorwho/classic/episodeguide/deadlyassassin/detail.shtml.

15 Alex Woloch, *The One vs. the Many: Minor Characters and the Space of the Protagonist in the Novel*, Princeton: Princeton University Press, 2004.

16 Touré, *Who's Afraid of Post-Blackness: What It Means to Be Black Now*, New York: Free Press, 2011, 75–114.

17 Frantz Fanon, "The Fact of Blackness", *The Fanon Reader*, London: Pluto, 2006, 127–48.

18 Fanon, "Fact", 131.

19 Fanon, "Fact", 131.

20 Farred, *What's My Name?*, 161.

21 Bill Schwarz, "Becoming Postcolonial", in Paul Gilroy, Lawrence Grossberg and Angela McRobbie, eds., *Without Guarantees: In Honour of Stuart Hall*, London: Verso, 2000, 268–81.

22 Kobena Mercer, "A Sociography of Diaspora", in Paul Gilroy, Lawrence Grossberg and Angela McRobbie, eds., *Without Guarantees: In Honour of Stuart Hall*, London: Verso, 2000, 239.

23 Hall, *Race*, 4.

24 Paterson Joseph, "Why Wuthering Heights gives me hope", *The Guardian*, 11 November 2011.

25 Joseph, "Wuthering Heights."

26 Matt Hills, *Fan Cultures*, London: Routledge, 2002.

27 Piers D. Britton, *TARDISBound: Navigating the Universes of Doctor Who*, London: I.B. Tauris, 2011.

28 Linda Holmes, "Idris Elba: The Man Who Is Luther, Was Stringer, And Could Be James Bond" (28 September 2011), *NPR*. Retrieved 19 August 2012 at http://www.npr.org/blogs/monkeysee/2011/09/28/140870300/idris-elba-the-man-who-is-luther-was-stringer-and-could-be-james-bond.

29 Brian Truitt, "Half-black, half-Hispanic Spider-Man revealed", *USA Today*, 2 August 2011.

30 Rich Johnston, "Fear of a Black Spider-Man" (2 August 2011), *Bleeding Cool*. Retrieved 19 August 2012 at http://www.bleedingcool.com/2011/08/02/fear-of-a-black-spider-man/.

31 Johnston, "Fear of a Black Spider-Man."

32 Alexandra Petry, "Sorry, Peter Parker: The response to the black Spiderman shows why we need one", *Washington Post,* 3 August 2011.

33 Schwarz, "Becoming Postcolonial", 281.

34 Farred, *What's My Name?*, 153.

PART II

Diversity and representation in casting and characterization

Chapter 7

No room for old-fashioned cats: Davies era *Who* and interracial romance

Emily Asher-Perrin

Television perplexes us enough with its insistence on sticking to the 'token ethnic character' model, but what's more disheartening is how uncommon it is to find couples of different racial backgrounds. Is it the result of a patent disbelief in their existence? Or are we being subtly assured that these relationships have no place in mainstream entertainment? In either case, there was a point in time when one television show regularly featured couples, married or otherwise, who did not share the same ethnic heritage …

It was 2005, and *Doctor Who* was back on television. The new companion, Rose Tyler, was in many respects still a kid. She was 19 years old, working a crappy job at a large retail outlet, living at home with her mother, and waiting for nothing special to happen to her. She had a boyfriend named Mickey Smith who fixed cars and met her on her lunch breaks to goof around and eat bad fast food.

Mickey and Rose were the first interracial couple audiences met on the new *Doctor Who*, and they were far from the last. Show runner Russell T Davies had a penchant for diversifying his casts in everything from colour to sexual orientation, but it is perhaps even more noteworthy how many mixed race couples we saw during his tenure. The Tenth Doctor's other companions, Martha (a black woman) and Donna (Caucasian), also upheld Rose's initial trend; Martha was engaged to the very pale Tom Milligan, and both Donna's first fiancé and her husband, Lance and Shaun, were black. There was Foon and Morvin from *Voyage of the Damned* (2007), Milo and Cheen in *Gridlock* (2007), even Sally Sparrow's flirtation with DI Billy Shipton – who proceeds to marry a white woman after he is stranded in the 1960s by the Weeping Angels – in *Blink* (2007). An Indian woman and a Caucasian man without names, credited as 'Female Programmer' and 'Male Programmer', in *The Parting of the Ways* (2005) shared a mutual crush, and Martha's cousin Adeola had a romantic rendezvous with white Gareth in *Army of Ghosts* (2006).

Other social boundaries were addressed and crossed in these relationships. In *The Next Doctor* (2008), a tale set in 1851, the Doctor seemed somewhat perturbed that white Jackson Lake was only appointing his black 'companion' Rosita to the position of nanny after they found his son. Though Jackson dismissed the Doctor's comments in confusion, a mark of the era he lived in, the Doctor advocated their potential together. A deleted scene from *The Age of Steel* (2006) showed Mickey finding out that his alternate universe counterpart, Ricky, was white Jake's boyfriend, creating *Doctor Who*'s first gay interracial couple.[1] If you decide to count human/alien relationships as another form of interracial expression, the series gets even more muddied. There's cat-man Brannigan and his human wife Valerie in *Gridlock*. There's also Tallulah's choice to stay with Laszlo after he has been turned into a pig-person in *Daleks in Manhattan/Evolution of the Daleks* (2007), and Lady Eddison's affair with a Vespiform in *The Unicorn and the Wasp* (2008). Love jumped hurdles at every turn during these years on *Who*, and no one was excluded from those trials.

And what has changed since Davies's departure? In juxtaposition, subsequent show runner Steven Moffat seems entirely unconcerned with picking up where Davies left off. The only interracial flirting we've observed in his run at the time of writing (post-Series 6) is Tony and Nasreen from *The Hungry Earth/Cold Blood* (2010). White Canton Delware III made mention of his black partner in *The Impossible Astronaut* (2011), but we never *see* the man – he's relegated to the punchline of a joke, a way of unnerving the conservative President Nixon. If we count aliens again then we have the Silurian, Madame Vastra, and her companion, Jenny, from *A Good Man Goes to War* (2011). In wake of the Davies years, the romantic diversity that was once comfortably settled at the core of *Doctor Who* has all but vanished.

But what was the purpose of constantly showcasing these people and their relationships? Russell T Davies excelled at bringing all backgrounds, ages and lifestyles together on *Doctor Who*. His era seemed to be marked by a pervasive insistence, embedded in the characters he created and all they accomplished together, that these things should no longer be shocking to us. That there is no need to make a fuss over the colour of two people who love each other, because that love is worthy of recounting all on its own.

Some might choose to point out that not all of these pairs stayed put; Rose was left with the Doctor's clone, and Martha broke it off with Tom and married Mickey. But those final choices were ultimately character driven, as we all knew that Rose wanted to be with the Doctor after experiencing that adventurous life with him, and Martha and Mickey were liable to fall in love after they discovered how much they had in common – starting with the fact that they had both been on the wrong side of the same love triangle. With a few exceptions, all of these mixed relationships – whether or not they lasted – were supportive, undoubtedly loving, and *real*. No one on the show asked these couples what they saw in each other, or if it was strange to be attracted to someone of a different heritage. They were all simply people, which is, more importantly, the way that *the Doctor* sees us. Just human beings … ordinary, brilliant, ridiculous human beings.

Whether or not the show is poorer for the lack of this diversity should not be in question. The template that the show followed with Russell T Davies' guidance showed the world an ideal that we've yet to reach on our own steam, and good fiction – especially fiction with the optimistic bent that *Doctor Who* has always possessed – should do just that. The only way we can move forward is to allow everyone to help create the future, no matter the colour of their skin or who they fall in love with. The Doctor certainly believes it, and the show that bears his name should continue to as well.

Note

1   BBC, *Doctor Who: The Complete Second Series*, DVD release, 2006.

Chapter 8

When white boys write black: Race and class in
the Davies and Moffat eras

Rosanne Welch

A funny thing happened on my way to writing this essay comparing the way the first two show runners of new *Who* have handled race representation on *Doctor Who* … I found the opposite of what I had assumed to be true. Since many fans heralded the arrival of Steven Moffat as the superior writer thanks to his work on *The Empty Child/The Doctor Dances* (2005) and *Blink* (2007) among other scripts written under the executive producing of Russell T Davies, I had imagined Moffat would also be the one to have handled race more creatively. Instead, after studying the three major characters of colour created by each writer, I found that it was Davies who brought the most fully realized, three-dimensional characters of colour into the Whoniverse.

First Davies began his rebooting of *Who* by giving the Doctor a lower-class companion of colour in Mickey Smith. Mickey arrived as part of an interracial relationship as Rose Tyler's boyfriend and the Doctor's reluctant companion. When Mickey discovered he was their 'tin dog' in *School Reunion* (2006) he began to grow and challenge himself until he became a rogue alien hunter in his own right, mighty enough to earn the love of the Doctor's first full-time companion of colour, Martha Jones, in *The End of Time* (2009–10). While the BBC essentially required all the diversity that appeared in his productions through their policy of colour-blind casting,[1] it's also something Davies championed. In a personal interview conducted for *Written By Magazine*, Davies told me, "For a white writer to go see a night's television with a minority family, frankly it's embarrassing to see how they're presented or how little they are represented at all." Davies has had such nights with black family friends and gay family friends and almost always feels the need to apologize for the content they are seeing. As an apology he created Martha Jones, also a three-dimensional sexual being complete with an attraction to the Doctor and the strength of character to understand that being the rebound woman wasn't enough for her. It is interesting to note that when the Doctor said goodbye by saving Martha and Mickey from the bulls-eye of the Sontaran gun, Martha appeared with her hair in long cornrows – possibly reflecting comfort with her African heritage – rather than with the straight hair she had worn as the assimilating-into-white-society intern in *Smith and Jones* (2007).

Finally Davies created Rosita Farisi in *The Next Doctor* (2008) who again was in love with her imagined Doctor, Jackson Lake. While some viewed Rosita as a copy of Rose, largely due to the name play, my take on her character is that she was meant to be an alternative universe copy of Martha. The fact that Rosita loves Jackson's Doctor and he's oblivious to her love makes her much more like Martha (above and beyond the fact that she is of African descent).

Her possibly winning Jackson's heart in the end satisfies the romantics who were sad that Martha would never win her Doctor. Clearly, the Jackson/Rosita romantic relationship had more potential than any involving the real Doctor. While some fans argued that Rosita is merely a cheap prostitute as evidenced by Miss Hartigan's line of dialogue, "I doubt he paid you to talk", in actuality she saves both the real Doctor and Jackson Lake from a Cybershade, making her a valuable companion to both. In the end of the episode the real Doctor says to Jackson Lake, "Take care of that one. She's marvellous", a line that reads as a suggestion for their future relationship and highlights the fact that Davies gave all his characters of colour a backstory and a future, a beginning, middle and end as it were, which is not always the case with characters of colour in Moffat's imagination.

While Davies began with a character or colour from the lower class, Moffat's first character of colour was of the highest class possible. Liz Ten, the future British Queen of undeclared African descent, was unattached, intelligent and independent. She first appeared in *The Beast Below* (2010), the second episode after Moffat had taken the Executive Producer role and created Doctor 11, played by Matt Smith and his yet again white companion, Amy Pond. She later appeared in *The Pandorica Opens* (2010) in order to allow River Song to steal a painting. While I expected great things from Moffat's beginning with a monarch of colour, Liz Ten stands as an example that all his characters of colour are Talented Tenth[2] types, coming from the upper classes and the world of higher education, but oddly two-dimensional in that they operate solely as stepping stones to the Doctor's stories. They are never shown to grow or change or have lives outside of their usefulness to the Doctor. For his second character of colour Moffat created a surprising Time Lord of colour when we learned Mels, short for Melody, was in fact an earlier regeneration of River Song taking the time to grow up as her mother and father's best school chum. While quick-witted and clever, Mels as a teenager served her purpose to the story – and to the writer – in that her being a person of colour kept the audience from guessing she was a young River, even though she carried Melody's name. It smacked of being a bit of a writer's trick and again left us with a character of colour with nowhere to grow. Moffat's latest character of colour at the time of writing was Rita in *The God Complex* (2011), and he went so far as to make her not just a person of colour not often seen in *Who*, but also a person of a faith never before seen in the new series. Though that was innovative in a post 9/11 world, the character was never even given a last name, and while she can be said to have experienced growth in her faith, she had no future.

Whoopi Goldberg has said she agreed to appear on *Star Trek: The Next Generation* (Creator: Gene Roddenberry, 1987–94) in order to show young black children that their people would survive into the future.[3] My brief study of race representation on *Doctor Who* shows that Moffat, originally assumed to be the more creative writer, has been messing with that desire, while Davies, the admitted (in his book *The Writer's Tale*)[4] deadline-chasing, impulsive writer, has supported the idea. Can it be because as an openly gay man Davies understands the need for three-dimensional minority representation more than the heterosexual, white Moffat? I'd hate for it to come down to that.

Notes

1   Rosanne Welch, "The Doctor is In America", *Written By Magazine* (Summer 2011) 30.

2   The 'Talented Tenth' is a term coined by W. E. B. Du Bois, who felt that the Negro race would only succeed if they focused on educating the 'best of the race'. He elaborated on that idea in "The Talented Tenth", *The Negro Problem: A Series of Articles by Representative American Negroes of To-day*, New York: James Pott and Company, 1903, 31–75.

3   See e.g., Lee Winfrey, "Whoopi Goldberg joins 'Star Trek' crew", *The Modesto Bee*, 28 November 1988, B-7; and Baobao Zhang, "Meet Whoopi Goldberg, born Caryn Elaine Johnson, Academy Award-winning actress, panelist on 'The View'", *Yale Daily News*, 16 April 2010.

4   Russell T Davies and Benjamin Cook, *Doctor Who – The Writer's Tale: The Final Chapter*, London: BBC Books, 2010.

Chapter 9

Baby steps: a modest solution to Asian under-representation in *Doctor Who*

Stephanie Guerdan

Ever since I watched *Rose* (2005) one bleak December night during my final exam week, I've had an insatiable love for the Doctor and his companions and their adventures. I raced through the episodes in an emotional whirlwind and was caught up in the 2005 series by the Series 5 Christmas special two and a half weeks later. (I still haven't gotten around to watching any of Doctors 1–8, despite my best intentions.) Amidst my unabashed fangirling and attempts to proselytize my family and friends to the way of the Doctor, however, I found a question starting to grow in my mind: Where were all the Asians?

Some background: as the most stereotypical sort of Japanese major, I spend most of my time watching Japanese or other Asian-inspired or -created media. Because of this, it was a bit of a shift to go from that to a show that doesn't have a single East Asian recurring character. Off the top of my head, I can name Naoko Mori, who played the scientist who studied the fake alien/pig in *Aliens of London* (2005) (and who went on to star in *Torchwood* as Toshiko Sato. Fun fact: she's billed in that episode as Dr Sato, but Tosh in *Torchwood* is a computer genius, not a biologist), the sinister fortune teller who tries to mess with Donna's past in *Turn Left* (2008) and Mia Bennett, Bowie Base One's geologist in *The Waters of Mars* (2009). (I hope there's more that I just can't recall, but I'm not holding my breath waiting to find out.)

So what do we see of East Asian countries in *Doctor Who*? Well, the Ninth Doctor, Rose and Jack show up on Satellite Five in *Bad Wolf* (2005) via Kyoto in the late Muromachi Period, but you don't actually *see* them in Japan at all. During the Tenth Doctor's tenure we hear how the Master systematically killed all the Japanese during the Year that Never Was (Martha was the only person to leave Japan alive). Japan was also polluted with poison gas by the Sontarans in *The Poison Sky* (2008) and invaded by Daleks in *The Stolen Earth* (2008). China's military is transformed into Master clones in *The End of Time* (2009–10), and Korea, Mongolia and Taiwan might as well not exist for all that they are mentioned in new *Who*. No East Asian settings or named characters of Asian descent show up at all in the Eleventh Doctor's two seasons to date (at the time of writing).

A year ago, I'd have said the fix was just to reverse that: add some plots based in Asian countries; add some Asian characters (they don't even have to be companions, although that would be great; but seriously, just an episode like *Vincent and the Doctor* (2010) about a figure in Korean history or at least a memorable recurring character like Jack Harkness or Craig from *The Lodger*, 2010/*Closing Time*, 2011, would be nice). *Doctor Who* goes to the distant future and far-off planets routinely. It shouldn't be that hard to accurately portray a select group of people from an already-existing country at some point in said country's past, present or future.

Unfortunately, since then I've watched the BBC's *Sherlock* (Creators: Steven Moffat and Mark Gatiss, 2010–), another project helmed by *Doctor Who*'s current show runner Steven Moffat. Its second episode, *The Blind Banker* (2010), deals with a Chinese smuggling gang, and although it was entertaining on a superficial level, I had a hard time looking past all the glaring inconsistencies and flat-out racism related to the Asian culture portrayed. And so I'm worried. I'm concerned that if the BBC ever deigned to put some Asians in our *Doctor Who* so that we could have diversity while we watched sci-fi, they would let these same sorts of unpleasant orientalist clichés slip past editors. The last thing the BBC needs is more of that.

So what can they do? It would be great to have an Asian companion. He or she (most likely she, given *Doctor Who*'s conventions) doesn't have to be deeply involved in his or her cultural heritage – just having a non-white main character would have some value for fans of the show who don't see themselves represented at all in an otherwise diverse cast. Just ask any fan of Martha Jones.

It would be great to have an Asia-related plotline or episode. We glorify western history so much, but Asia and the Middle East have millennia of exciting historical events that have remained untapped on the show. It would be awesome for the Doctor to visit some of the big historical events in distant (or recent) Asian history.

But what I think would be most awesome would be an Asian Doctor. The Doctor is something of a cultural hero. I think it would be inspiring for viewers of colour to see a non-white Doctor, and I think it would show considerable chutzpah and thoughtfulness on the part of the BBC for being brave enough to push past their prejudices and cast one. And this would skirt past all of the sketchy potential problems posed by *Sherlock*. Because although in a perfect world I'd trust the BBC's writers to portray Asian culture fairly and correctly, I think what's really called for now is baby steps. The Doctor is and always will be a Time Lord from Gallifrey. That's his race, ethnicity and cultural background. The Doctor's planet of origin is already well-defined; no matter what he looks like, he'll still be the Doctor. He'll probably always be played by a British actor, but Britishness is not limited to a single race of people. And perhaps with that first baby step on the part of the BBC, placing an Asian man (or woman!) in what has always been a white man's leading role, people will start to take their own baby steps, out of a mindset coloured by prejudice and into a world where people of all races are equally represented.

Who knows? If the Doctor has taught me anything, it's to have hope, and to trust in the inherent goodness of the human race. I can only hope, therefore, that the show that I've come to love so much can grow to represent the entirety of that great human race, without exception.

Chapter 10

That was then, this is now: How my perceptions have changed

George Ivanoff

The past, they say, is a different country. They did things differently back then … especially on television. Television programmes from the 1970s were very different from television programmes made today. Techniques and technology were different. Society's morals and expectations were different. As a long-running series, spanning the decades from the 1960s through to the present day, *Doctor Who* is a perfect example of this.

The differences are not only evident in the actual programme itself, but in the viewer expectations. My reactions to watching *Doctor Who* as an adult are different from when I was a child. Watching *Doctor Who* for the first time in the late 1970s, I did not notice the wobbly sets, the strings and the dodgy camera work. I did not see that some stories were progressive, while others reinforced stereotypes. All I saw was the marvellous adventures of a time-travelling alien in a police box.

No two stories illustrate this more clearly to me than *The Mutants* and *The Talons of Weng-Chiang*. Separated by five years – the former broadcast in 1972 and latter in 1977 – they are completely different in approach to the issue of race. Christopher Barry, perhaps picking up on the racial issues of the story he was directing, chose to perform a rare piece of 'colour-blind casting', having a black actor, Rick James, play the part of Cotton in *The Mutants*. In *The Talons of Weng-Chiang* director David Maloney cast Caucasian actor John Bennett as the Chinese magician Li H'sen Chang. Of course, the story itself depicts Chinese people in a rather stereotypically unflattering light, using them only as villains: it's all opium dens, gangs and the abduction of young women.

Viewing these two stories as a child of 11 years, I did not see these differences. To me at the time, they were both equally exciting and entertaining. All I saw was the adventure and the monsters and the Doctor fighting evil. I did not notice the parallels to South Africa's apartheid policies in *The Mutants*, and I did not see the racial stereotyping in *The Talons of Weng-Chiang*. And I didn't even notice that Li H'sen Chang was a Caucasian actor in make-up. But I did not live in a multicultural community. I lived in a very white, middle-class Australian suburb, I went to a very white, middle-class, Catholic primary school and I socialized with white, middle-class kids. Racial differences were not uppermost in my mind at the time, and so I did not notice them in the programmes I watched on television.

But, with experience, perceptions change over time. I went to an independent secondary school with a significant intake of overseas Asian students, particularly from China. And then I went to university and my horizons were broadened even further by the racial mix of the student body. Then I entered into the real world, the workplace again providing me with exposure to people of different ethnicities (particularly my first job as a sales assistant).

Re-watching those *Doctor Who* stories recently, as an adult with a very different view of the world, my reaction to them was quite different.

I started off with *The Mutants*. Despite a few minor hiccups, I thought it was a well-written, intriguing story. Colonialism and the treatment of native peoples were clearly the main thrust of the story, and the thinly veiled references to apartheid in South Africa were glaringly obvious. It was, in many ways, a story well ahead of its time, in terms of what a family-oriented television series was willing to tackle; and it probably got away with it because it was science fiction and therefore removed from reality in the minds of most people, particularly BBC executives. I was also struck by the ambitious nature of the production. Even though it did not always work, it aimed for an epic quality with its location shooting, its set design and costumes, and its more complex than usual special effects. Given these ambitious elements, perhaps the 'colour-blind casting' is not such a surprise, as the director seemed willing to take risks.

Then, watching *The Talons of Weng-Chiang*, I was struck by the contrast. Even though it was made five years later than *The Mutants*, the views it put forward were so far behind. People often dismiss the casting of a Caucasian actor as a Chinese character as being the done thing at the time.[1] And yet, the director would have had the power to cast as he saw fit – as Christopher Barry did, casting Rick James in *The Mutants*; and as Timothy Combe did in *The Mind of Evil* in 1971, when he cast Chinese actress Pik-Sen Lim as Captain Chin Lee. So David Maloney probably could have cast a Chinese actor if he really wanted to.

Knowing all this, watching it as an adult, I couldn't help but feel disappointed by the writer and director. Yes, they were making this story at a particular point in time, when racial stereotyping and racist casting were not only accepted, but were the norm in mainstream British culture. They weren't doing anything out of the ordinary. But that's the point: they made the choice to go with the flow. The writer could have chosen to avoid racial stereotypes, but he didn't. The director could have chosen to cast a Chinese actor. He certainly found it acceptable to cast Chinese extras – but a Chinese lead actor?

Beyond the disappointment and the awareness, I also found myself watching this story with a slight sense of guilt. Despite the casting, despite the stereotyping, I still found myself immersed in the story, being carried away with the adventure and enjoying it all a great deal. I even found myself appreciating John Bennett's performance, despite the 'yellowface'. The fact of the matter is that *The Talons of Weng-Chiang* is a well-written and well-produced *Doctor Who* story. And even though on an intellectual level I can abhor the decision to cast a Caucasian actor, I can recognize that individual actor's talent and the subtle and layered nature of his performance.

All this then begs the question: how should current audiences view past examples of the depiction of race? Should we condemn the poor examples, as we praise the forward thinking ones? Or should we accept the poor ones as products of their time?

I enjoyed watching *The Talons of Weng-Chiang*. As a *Doctor Who* fan I will, no doubt, watch it again. And despite that slight feeling of guilt I will, no doubt, enjoy it again. And I'm reasonably comfortable doing this because of context. But if the current series of *Doctor Who* were to present me with such blatant racism, I would like to think that I would switch it off.

Note

1   e.g., "A Caucasian actor, John Bennett, portrayed Li H'sen Chang, using make-up and an accent, a practice probably not acceptable today, but more widespread in 1976, when *The Talons of Weng-Chiang* was made and aired." Anon., "Li H'sen Chang" (n.d.), *TARDIS Index File*. Retrieved 19 August 2012 at http://tardis.wikia.com/wiki/Li_H'sen_Chang; and "[…] casting a Caucasian actor as the Chinese villain. But that's kind of a product of the times, I guess." Christopher Barry, comment to "Dr. Who: The Talons of Weng Chiang" (11 April 2004), *El Skin Project*. Retrieved 19 August 2012 at http://www.exisle.net/ESP/mb/index.php?showtopic=14852.

Chapter 11

"One of us is yellow": Doctor Fu Manchu and
The Talons of Weng-Chiang

Kate Orman

Maybe we wouldn't get away with it these days.

– Philip Hinchcliffe[1]

Introduction

As a Chinese doctor who fan, I just want to say Talons of Weng-Chiang was so horrible for me that I didn't manage to finish watching it ... Why did I even try to watch it, knowing there're evil Chinese stereotypes? I should have known better. I love my show and it's painful to watch.[2]

The Talons of Weng-Chiang (1977), a long-standing favourite, has only two real flaws in the eyes of *Doctor Who* fans: the casting of white actor John Bennett as Chinese villain Li H'sen Chang, and an unconvincing giant rat. While the rat can be smiled at, the story's use of 'yellowface' has to be explained away. Paradoxically, the intense moral opprobrium attached to calling something 'racist' helps to obscure the presence of racism. If racism is anathema, then when a story we cherish contains racially charged elements, we must show that it's not *really* racist – and neither are we for loving it.

The rat and the yellowface are both forgiven by fans on the same grounds: the exigencies of 1970s television production. Neither technology nor attitudes were as advanced then as they are now, and maybe Asian actors were rarer in those days.

I think the fan discussion around Bennett's casting misleads us. Even if, say, Burt Kwouk, Anthony Chinn, Robert Lee, Kristopher Kum or Cecil Cheng[3] had been cast as Chang, it still wouldn't have fixed *Talons*. The yellowface is only the most conspicuous component of a collection of contemptuous clichés in which *Talons* is involved – up to its epicanthic eyebrows!

The Devil Doctor

JAGO: You mean to say the Celestial Chang was involved in all these Machiavellian machinations?

THE DOCTOR: Yes, up to his epicanthic eyebrows.

Hostile racial caricatures don't just appear from thin air: they're created for a reason. Politicians and the press may be trying to justify a war or scapegoat immigrants. However, the early-twentieth-century English novelist Arthur Sarsfield Ward, better known as Sax Rohmer, had a different reason: to make money. As his biographers note, "Conditions for launching a Chinese villain on the market were ideal [...] The Boxer Rebellion had started off rumours of a Yellow Peril which had not yet died down. Recent events in Limehouse had again drawn public attention eastwards."[4]

Drawing on the anti-Chinese stereotypes which had long been promoted by British newspapers, boys' magazines[5] and politicians,[6] Ward conjured up not the first but by far the most influential[7] oriental criminal mastermind bent on world domination: Fu Manchu. The 'Devil Doctor' made his first appearance in 1912, reaching the pinnacle of his fame in the 1920s and 1930s.[8] Thanks to Fu, Ward became "one of the most widely read and highly successful authors of popular fiction in the world."[9]

Plenty of *Doctor Who* stories share the general pulpish conceits of the Fu Manchu milieu. Ward, who confessed "I know nothing about the Chinese",[10] drew heavily on western ideas, such as secret societies with esoteric knowledge[11] (as do, for example, *The Tomb of the Cybermen*, 1967; *Invasion of the Dinosaurs*, 1974; and *Torchwood*) and mesmerism (both Fu in *The Face of Fu Manchu* [Director: Don Sharp, 1965] and the Master in *Terror of the Autons*, 1971, leave a hypnotized substitute to die in their place).[12]

Unlike those stories, however, *The Talons of Weng-Chiang* is an intentional Fu Manchu pastiche, featuring multiple elements borrowed from Fu-land: superscience, hypnosis, fanatical cults, secret lairs, exotic drugs and poisons, and white women in peril. While many *Doctor Who* stories have some of these elements, only *Talons* has them all – and only *Talons* puts them into the context of colourful, deceiving, opium-smoking Chinese villainy.

Producer Philip Hinchcliffe remarked, "I'd never read any of the Sax Rohmer stories, but I sort of vaguely knew that it must be Chinese, Limehouse, and skulduggery, opium dens and things."[13] Most probably, then, he and scriptwriter Robert Holmes drew on the 1960s Fu Manchu movies starring Christopher Lee (the BBC had screened *Face* in March that year),[14] much as they had drawn on Hammer Film Productions versions of the Mummy, Frankenstein and Dracula for *Pyramids of Mars* (1975), *The Brain of Morbius* (1976) and the postponed vampire story that eventually became *State of Decay* (1980).[15] In *The Face of Fu Manchu*, Fu's henchmen infiltrate the 'Museum of Oriental Studies' via the sewer tunnels beneath London; in *Talons*, the Tong of the Black Scorpion use London's sewers to sneak around from one secret lair to another. The nefarious plan in *Face* involves a poison made from a rare Tibetan flower; in *The Blood of Fu Manchu* (1968), the poison comes from a rare snake. In *Talons*, the Tong of the Black Scorpion prefer to hatchet their victims, but carry around "concentrated scorpion venom" in case of capture. In *The Brides of Fu Manchu* (1966), Fu's elaborate, exotic lair is an Ancient Egyptian temple; in *Talons*, it's the House of the Dragon, "ornately furnished in the style of a Chinese temple"[16] and sporting a four-faced, eight-armed golden idol.

For *Talons*, the character of Fu Manchu has been split between Magnus Greel, aka Weng-Chiang,[17] and his acolyte Li H'sen Chang.[18] Greel is a time-travelling Dr Mengele from the fifty-first century. He provides the story's fantastical elements, including the cult of fanatical followers ready to kill or die at his command, and the 'Peking Homunculus', aka 'Mr Sin', a miniature killer robot. However, Greel's ethnicity is never made clear; it's Li H'sen Chang who provides the Fu Manchu look, with rubber eyelids, the eponymous moustache and, for his performances onstage at the Palace Theatre, ornate Chinese costume.

As Greel's servant, Chang's chief job is to procure young white women for his master. This being *Doctor Who*, Greel's intention is only to distil the women's "life essences"; the sexual implications are left to the viewer's imagination.[19] (Well, *mostly* left to their imagination. Perhaps *Brides* provided *Talons* with its imagery of helplessly hypnotized women in their underthings.) Lines perhaps not surprisingly cut from the script include Greel explaining that "Maidens at the point of puberty are ideal material" for distillation, and ordering his victims: "take those clothes off!"[20]

Throughout the West in the late nineteenth and early twentieth century, Chinese men greatly outnumbered Chinese women. A horror of the inevitable liaisons – which could "lower the white type" by creating "a mongrel race"[21] – became a major element of the 'Yellow Peril'. Unlike the United States and Canada, Britain did not pass laws to keep Chinese men and white women apart; but, as in those countries, the UK press ran baseless stories that Chinese men were kinky sexual predators on the lookout for white women to dope, seduce and/or sell into 'white slavery'. Surprisingly, however, this racial paranoia has seldom been a major part of the Fu Manchu oeuvre.[22] In both the novels[23] and the 1960s Lee movies, Fu seems sexless; despite their deshabille, the *Brides of Fu Manchu* are not 'brides' but hostages.[24] As in *Talons*, the sexual content is always available to the viewer, but is never addressed outright.

By contrast, exotic drugs are front and centre in Rohmer's stories; Fu himself is an opium addict. Stories of the corruption of white women in Chinese opium dens made sensational content for early-twentieth-century British newspapers.[25] This fitted into a journalistic and literary tradition of voyeuristic visits to London's multicultural, poverty-stricken East End – the site of "the vilest scenes of depravity and degradation", as pathologist Professor Litefoot warns the Doctor. Limehouse, with its tiny but conspicuous Chinese population, became a particular site of fascination – and fantasy: its depiction in fiction and newspapers "veered from glamour to the Gothic [...] as appealing as it [was] frightening."[26] Limehouse is the natural site for Fu Manchu's HQ – and for Magnus Greel's lair. Although the drug itself makes only a brief, medicinal appearance, Greel sneers that his followers are "opium-sodden scum"; he also uses ether or chloroform to incapacitate Leela, and two kidnapped women are knocked out by the unidentified "broth of oblivion."

"More Mickey Finn than shark's fin"

Introducing a 1997 reprint of *The Insidious Dr Fu-Manchu*, editor Douglas G. Greene remarks, "Rohmer's novels remain popular not because they say anything about what was going on in the world in his time or in ours, but because they are almost pure fantasy, appealing to the armchair adventurer."[27]

Derived from racial paranoia and propaganda, Rohmer's novels actually tell us a great deal about 'what was going on in the world'. *Talons*, too, may seem like mere escapism, but contains elements which refer to the everyday world of British viewers in 1977.

The print Fu Manchu prolongs his life with an "elixir vitae", which, like Greel's "secret of life", requires what the Doctor describes as "cannibalism." The Doctor quips of Greel's catalytic extraction chamber, "I'll have the Bird's Nest Soup … isn't this where you do the cooking?" He explains that the narcotic "broth of oblivion" is "a Chinese soup." Lines were dropped expanding on both of these gags, with the Doctor additionally ordering "Foo Yung with noodles" and describing the "broth of oblivion" as "more Mickey Finn than shark's fin."[28] These jokes about Chinese food connect the story to the British institution of the Chinese takeaway – and especially to the perennial western suspicion of its ingredients. (As recently as 2011, a Yorkshire restaurant's business was badly damaged by false rumours about dog meat in its dishes.)[29] The British Chinese experience more racial harassment and property damage than any other ethnic minority – and the "contact zone" of the isolated, conspicuous takeaway[30] is the most likely target.[31]

Set well before the takeaway boom of the 1960s and 1970s, *Talons* instead features its predecessor, the Chinese laundry, which serves as a front for an opium den and criminal hideout. (Rather than putting poison into Litefoot's food, the Tong put Mr Sin into his laundry.) This was another panic of 1970s Britain – the exaggerated dread of the Tongs and Triads, of Chinese immigrants seeming to meekly wash clothes or serve food while secretly importing drugs and crime.

Though fans might defend the Fu Manchu tales or *The Talons of Weng-Chiang* as fantasy, Ward's own defence was the opposite – he claimed that he was being realistic:

> Of course, not the whole Chinese population of Limehouse was criminal. But it contained a large number of persons who had left their own country for the most urgent of reasons. These people knew no way of making a living other than the criminal activities that had made China too hot for them. They brought their crimes with them.[32]

This description is another product of Ward's fertile and malicious imagination. In fact, the Chinese were described by their British neighbours as "perfectly well-conducted citizens" noted for their peacefulness and honesty.[33] Chinese migration at the time was driven not by crime but by the economic chaos resulting from war and natural disaster.[34] The bulk of the Chinese population of Limehouse, which never totalled more than a few hundred, were sailors in the employ of the East India Company.[35] Few had planned to settle; some were laid off, some were "dumped" by "unscrupulous ship-owners", and some chose to jump ship rather than continue to endure "extreme exploitation."[36] But the myth sold.

Writing in 1977, the year *Talons* was broadcast, sociologist James L. Watson described the Chinese as "the least understood of all Britain's immigrant minorities", overlooked by researchers and government bodies:

> The mass media have simply exacerbated the problem: after completely ignoring the Chinese for over a decade, British newspapers have begun a series of sensationalised reports focusing on gangland activities in Soho […] In the last two years, dozens of newspaper articles and at least two prime-time television programmes have focussed on these problems.[37]

Though the offenders in these cases were few, and were as likely to be non-Chinese as Chinese, the papers still reported the crimes as the work of "secret Chinese triad societies", creating "a new stereotype of the Chinese restaurant worker as an infiltrator and a dangerous purveyor of drugs" – or rather, resurrecting the old stereotype of the dangerous Chinese immigrant.[38]

These links would be less significant if there had not been so few images of Chinese people available on British screens around this time, and if those images had been more realistic and/or more varied. Viewers could titter at the halfwit immigrant caricatures of *Mind Your Language* (1977–86), including Pik-Sen Lim as Chung Su-Lee, always ranting about "capitarists"; or the *It Ain't Half Hot Mum* (Creators: Jimmy Perry and David Croft, 1974–81) episode *Pale Hands I Love* (1976), in which the usual Indian stereotypes are varied by dog meat gags and the poisonous threat of – no kidding! – the Tong of the Black Scorpion. Action lovers might tune in to see the *New Avengers* (Creators: Brian Clemens and Albert Fennell, 1976–77) episode *Trap* (1977) and the bizarre, laryngitic performance of Terry Wood as sweaty criminal mastermind Soo Choy. (As our heroes drag their defeated foes away, they can't resist joking: "Chinese takeaway!") Or, if viewers preferred real Chinese actors, *Gangsters* (Creator: Philip Martin, 1976–78) featured the exotic rituals of the drug-smuggling Triads.[39]

For British TV in the late 1970s, the Chinese were comical at best, dangerous at worst, but almost always peculiar outsiders. *Talons* did not break this pattern.

Men behaving inscrutably[40]

However, *Talons* does deviate in some ways from the Fu Manchu template. As destructive as the story's villains are, they are not "a menace to the civilized world" like Fu Manchu, whose plan for a "giant Yellow Empire" threatens the survival of "the entire white race."[41] The Doctor does say that the Tong of the Black Scorpion expect Weng-Chiang to "rule the world"; but all Greel seems to want to do is to restore his "protenoid balance" and depart to "some distant time and place." His use of the malfunctioning time-travel cabinet will cause a "huge implosion", but the Doctor says only that this will destroy Greel's lair; there's no mention of a threat to London or Earth. Though there isn't even a token Chinese goodie, this is not a race war.

Also notable about the Chinese characters in *Talons* is that none of them are 'inscrutable'.[42] John Bennett could easily have reproduced the blank cool assumed by Lee as Fu Manchu, or Joseph Wiseman as *Dr No* (Director: Terence Young, 1962). To his credit, he instead gives us a sympathetic performance which humanizes Chang, undermining his resemblance to the inhuman, demonic Fu, who "belongs to some significantly foreign category of being, toward which the reader need feel little or no responsibility."[43]

Of the two chief villains, "the crafty Chang" (as the novelization's blurb calls him) is by far the more interesting character. While Greel lurches around his lair, bellowing, Chang the illusionist negotiates the surrounding hostile alien culture – brilliantly, by turning its own assumptions against it. Chang, who speaks immaculate English, drops into his stage patter whenever he needs to convince someone he is a harmless and comical 'Chinee'. At the police station in Episode 1, he is debonair: "Not at all, Sergeant. I'm always happy to be of service to the police. What can I do for you this time? [...] You seem remarkably well-informed, Doctor. Alas, I know nothing of these matters." But onstage, Chang plays to his audience's assumptions and prejudices, speaking stilted English, exaggerating his accent ("First tlick velly simple!"), and when the Doctor strolls out of the "cabinet of death", quipping, "The bird has flown. One of us is yellow." There is sometimes an edge of satire to Chang's remarks: when the Doctor asks, "Don't I know you?" Chang smilingly answers, "I understand we all look the same."

Though once a "humble peasant", Chang is neither a credulous bumpkin nor a mindless zealot. Chang is no superstitious dupe; he simply believes his own eyes. The Doctor dismisses Weng-Chiang's legendary powers, such as the ability to kill "with a white light that shone from his eyes", as "superstitious rubbish." This attitude is a perennial trap in *Doctor Who* for those who consider themselves superior to the "superstitious savage."[44] The Doctor neglects Chang's warning to "beware the eye of the dragon", and is struck down by the white light from the statue's eyes – in this case, a laser weapon.

Chang argues with his god about the risks involved in going out to search for his lost time machine, and in kidnapping more and more women. Though devoted, Chang is also motivated by self-interest: with Greel's help, "Next month, the Great Chang would have performed before the Queen Empress at Buckingham Palace. I, the son of a peasant." When his benefactor turns against him, shaming him before his theatre audience, he in turn betrays the "false god."

The character of Li H'sen Chang presents us with layer after layer of illusions: a white actor dresses up to play the role of a Chinese man, who in turn dresses up to play the role of an entertaining 'Chinaman' (as did numerous white stage magicians of the time, such as William Robinson, aka 'Chung Ling Soo').[45] Chang's stage mesmerism is actually real mesmerism, "mental powers undreamt of in this century" bestowed on him by Greel. His ventriloquist's 'dummy' is actually alive.

This layered illusory nature crops up throughout *Talons*. The holographic ghost in the theatre cellar hides a genuine phantom (of the opera). The Doctor dresses up as Sherlock Holmes, but then actually does play the role of the detective assisting the police. Weng-Chiang, as a mock god, is the ultimate in fakery[46] – but his powers are no less real. No surprise, then, that the story's very first image is of the Palace Theatre stage, and its last image a poster of Li H'sen Chang advertising his "Amazing Artistry." Chang never resembles Fu Manchu more than when he is onstage in glittering mandarin costume, putting the 'fluence on the young ladies and smilingly deceiving his audience.

But unlike Christopher Lee's Fu Manchu, who was blown up at the end of every movie only to promise he would return (with increasing comic effect at each iteration), and unlike Greel's bathetic collapse in his own extraction machine, Chang's death is played as tragic. His career destroyed by Greel, he flees into the sewers, and we hear his cry as the giant rat attacks him. For many villains, this poetic justice would have been the last we saw or heard of them. However, a badly injured Chang returns for a melancholy final scene, our only visit to the opium den. The pipe he is smoking to relieve his pain gives him lyrical visions of his ancestors coming to greet him: "They are smiling and carry gifts of fruit and flowers." Chang's last act is to struggle to tell the Doctor the whereabouts of Greel's lair. As it turns out, this bit of information is irrelevant to the plot. The scene is there not to give our heroes a vital clue, but to give the character of Chang a proper exit.

Excursus: Chin Lee, Fu Peng and *The Mind Of Evil*

It's striking that six years earlier, *Doctor Who* portrayed the Chinese in such a completely different way. In *The Brides of Fu Manchu*, the evil genius plans to destroy an international arms conference with a death ray and take over the world; in *The Mind of Evil* (1971), the Master plans to destroy an international peace conference with a nerve gas missile and take over the world. The Chinese delegates to the conference are just as much the Master's victims as everyone else. Was scriptwriter Don Houghton's story a deliberate inversion of *Brides*, or a more general response to recent the-Chinese-take-over-the-world movies such as *Battle Beneath the Earth* (Director: Montgomery Tully, 1967) and the James Bond franchise?

As well as giving its Chinese characters a more sympathetic role, *The Mind of Evil* accomplishes something that *Talons* fails to: it satirizes British ignorance of Chinese culture by contrasting it with the Doctor's broader understanding:

BRIGADIER: We are going to see the new Chinese delegate, Mr Fu Peng.

THE DOCTOR: Fu Peng? He must be Hokkien.

BRIGADIER: No, no, no, Doctor, he's Chinese. Now, come along.

While the Brigadier naturally wants to get down to business at once, the Doctor does what any guide to Chinese business etiquette will advise you to do: he makes a bit of small talk first. Even better, he does it in Fu Peng's own language. (Later, he speaks to Chin Lee in Cantonese.) While there's the inevitable joke about weird Chinese food – Fu Peng promises the Doctor a dinner of "dried squid and stewed jellyfish" – the punchline here is that the Doctor is entirely comfortable with this menu.

Houghton had a considerable advantage: he was married to Pik-Sen Lim, who played Chin Lee. (She continues to appear on stage and TV and in movies to this day.) Lim assisted him with the Hokkien dialogue, and coached Jon Pertwee in his delivery.[47] She may have had other input into the script: the ill-fated delegate Cheng Taik was presumably named for her father, Lim Cheng Taik.

In *Talons*, the Fourth Doctor shows off his knowledge of Chinese, boasting that he knows "all the dialects", then – with no Pik-Sen Lim on set to coach Tom Baker in his lines – speaks gibberish.[48] More significantly, his little speech is no more effective than police Sergeant Kyle's pidgin: "Him jaw-jaw plenty by and by, eh, Johnny?" There's nothing that contrasts the Doctor's wisdom, manners or attitudes with those of the Englishmen around him.

And that brings us to the awkward problem of Professor Litefoot.

The awkward problem of Professor Litefoot

Unease about contamination or retaliation by the colonized – "reverse colonization"[49] – manifests itself as exotic threats such as 'voodoo', the mummy and aliens such as the Wirrn in *The Ark in Space* (1975), who, driven from their home by human colonists, in turn literally colonize human bodies. As historian Stephen Gong explains: "It's about the British people reflecting back the fears that the people they had subjugated would do their best to take them down."[50]

Although China was never fully colonized, the threat of conquest by the 'Yellow Peril' was a "complete inversion of the actual power relations between East Asia and the West."[51] China's attempts to stop the illegal importation of opium by British merchants, which had created millions of addicts, resulted in Britain's repeated, successful wars against China, forcing it to do business.

The loveable Professor Litefoot suggests Sherlock Holmes's offsider Doctor Watson, but is more likely drawn from the Lee movies' pathologist and sidekick, Doctor Petrie. Professor Litefoot tells us that his father was part of the "punitive expedition of 1860", part of the Second Opium War; Litefoot senior, then, was part of the joint British–French force which engaged in arson and looting. Was this the source of some of the Litefoot's collection of valuable Chinese *objet d'art*?

Litefoot's father "stayed on as a palace attaché" after the war, and young George was brought up in China. Yet despite this long exposure, he remarks, "they're a mysterious lot, the Chinese. Enigmatic. I never got anywhere near to understanding them." The young George Litefoot was akin to the son of a conqueror, growing up in a defeated, humiliated and economically damaged China. Perhaps it's not so surprising, then, that he looks down on the inexplicable Chinese – and that he casually refers to two corpses as "a couple of inscrutable Chinks."

Fans who can happily tolerate great amounts of implicit racism balk at its explicit statement, especially by a favourite character. Litefoot's use of what is still the standard anti-Chinese insult in Britain[52] is excused as either depicting or satirizing the attitudes of less enlightened times. And yet, there's nothing parodic about it. Had the line come from the theatrical Henry Gordon Jago, we might understand it as the blustering of a comic dimwit; but Litefoot is sensible and matter-of-fact, a sober, educated man.

More importantly, the Doctor, who would normally be our moral guide, doesn't bat an eyelid at Litefoot's comment, any more than he does at Sergeant Kyle's taunts. More than one opportunity is missed to suggest to the viewer that Litefoot's attitudes are questionable: later, when the Professor ruefully remarks, "Things are coming to a pretty pass when ruffians will attack a man in his own home," the Doctor replies, "Well, they were *Chinese* ruffians." This line could have been delivered as impatience with, or mockery of, Victorian prejudice; but it, too, is played straight. Nowhere in the story is racism portrayed as anything but normal. Only Chang's clever reflection of the assumptions surrounding him draws any attention to them at all.

The man with the yellow face

"In a perfect world, we should all be able to play anything we want," said [actress Kim] Miyori, "(but while) it's acceptable for Caucasian actors to play Asians, it is not acceptable for Asian actors to play Caucasians."[53]

Why didn't the *Doctor Who* show runners cast an Asian actor as Li H'sen Chang? Perhaps they were simply following a so far unbroken tradition: no Asian actor has ever taken the part of Fu Manchu. In fact, they may have been trying to specifically recreate the look of Christopher Lee's rubber-eye-lidded Fu: John Bennett's make-up as Li H'sen Chang included rubber prostheses which were attached to his face in a three-hour process, paralleling the rubber mask of many a *Doctor Who* monster. From an acting perspective, this had a definite disadvantage: Bennett had to be careful not to blink beneath his rubber forehead while on camera,[54] lest the prosthesis become obvious.

Like blackface, yellowface – the playing of Asian roles by white actors in make-up – began on stage long before the origin of cinema.[55] However, Hollywood made an institution of it: anxious about making their money back, they would cast established white stars in Asian roles. Early British films followed the same practice.[56] As insulting as this was to Asian moviegoers, from the point of view of Asian actors, the real damage was that they were denied the chance to break out and become stars – creating a vicious circle.[57]

Interviewed about the breakthrough series in which he starred, *The Chinese Detective* (Creator: Ian Kennedy Martin, 1981–82), David Yip remarked:

> But for me it really was a question of getting a chance as an actor, instead of just being offered walk on parts as a Chinese waiter. I suffered as a lot of ethnic minority actors do – that they can go for months, years in fact taking small parts and then something huge comes along because a writer has either written a part which suits them down to the ground or some enlightened director has given them a lead.[58]

In 1992, a decade after *The Chinese Detective*, David Yip ran a drama workshop; its "several dozen" Chinese participants were as frustrated as he was about "the stereotyped image that he, as an actor, was expected to perpetuate."[59] At the launch of a civil rights organization in 2002, Yip pointed out that in twenty years British television had not produced another Chinese "role model", remarking, "In no shape or form has there been seen on television a person of Chinese extraction doing anything of real importance."[60] At a 2004 theatre seminar, Asian British actors expressed their frustration that white actors continue to "yellow up" for Asian roles.[61]

These protests are not just the product of recent, more enlightened times. The stereotypes of the Fu franchise were criticized "from the very outset."[62] In the 1910s and 1920s, Chinese students in Britain vigorously protested numerous stage productions such as *Mr Wu* and *The Yellow Mask*;[63] these plays, which featured secret societies, poison, torture and imperilled white women, also drew official diplomatic protests in 1913 and 1928 for their "vicious" representation of Chinese people (as did *The Mask of Fu Manchu* [Director: Charles Brabin, 1932] in the United States).[64]

No one listened. Decades later, reviewing *The Face of Fu Manchu*, *Time* magazine remarked that the film-makers "are clearly aware that the nonsense of yesteryear taps a jumpy vein of contemporary anxiety – all those diabolical Chinese, seeking ways and means to make western civilization heel to the Yellow Peril."[65] And in 1982, Canadian educational network TV Ontario declined to broadcast *The Talons of Weng-Chiang* after privately showing it to members of the Chinese community for their comments.[66] This was only five years after the story's original UK broadcast.

Conclusion

Actress Elizabeth Chan points out that:

> although we are the fourth-largest minority ethnic group in the UK, we are virtually invisible in public life, principally the arts, media and politics […] Chinese characters rarely appear

on our television screens, but when they do, you can bet they'll be DVD sellers, illegal immigrants, spies or, in the case of last year's *Sherlock*, weird acrobatic ninja types.[67]

While yellowface would be hard to get away with on British TV today, the stereotypes that Fu Manchu embodies and *Talons* is based on – the weird, treacherous, cruel and criminal Chinese – are still alive and kicking. British Chinese people continue to be portrayed as importers of organized crime, "only deemed newsworthy if they conform to acknowledged negative stereotypes – whether as members of 'triads' or as mass victims of gangs or gangmasters."[68] A visit to criminal Chinatown has become a stock element of movies[69] and police TV shows.[70] As recently as 2010, *Sherlock* (Creators: Steven Moffat and Mark Gatiss, 2010–) featured an assassin who strangles his victims with lengths of cloth (perhaps borrowed from the deadly 'Tibetan prayer scarves' of the Christopher Lee movies) and a fiendish slow-torture device which would not have been out of place in *The Mask of Fu Manchu*.

Ultimately, the problem is not in front of the camera, but behind it. The British television industry is still overwhelmingly white, giving non-white Britons little chance to represent themselves.[71]

Perhaps the only way to rehabilitate *Talons* would be to have Chang step off the stage of the Palace Theatre, retire to his dressing room, and remove his eyelids and make-up – much as Chung Ling Soo (and John Bennett) would have done after each performance. There's no reason a white man could not have met Greel in China and become his servant. After all, Fu Manchu is not a Chinese character, but a western one. But what would be the point of a Fu Manchu pastiche without Fu?

I seriously doubt that Philip Hinchcliffe, Robert Holmes, David Maloney, John Bennett or any of the production team had any intention to denigrate or demonize the Chinese. Nonetheless, in making *The Talons of Weng-Chiang*, they reproduced stereotypes which were created with *exactly* that intention. Because realistic Chinese characters are even now scarce on British TV, such stereotypes still have the power to harm the Chinese British community, with non-Chinese Britons absorbing suspicion and distrust, and young Chinese Britons absorbing a "negative self-image."[72] Stereotypes "are particularly damaging for a small and dispersed population, with few counterexamples of their own in popular culture."[73] The high level of racial abuse and attacks experienced by British Chinese people – including street harassment, school bullying, vandalism, assault, arson and murder[74] – is on the increase.

Writing in 2008, researchers Gregor Benton and Terence Gomez noted: "Resentment at media transmission of offensive images of 'orientals' – as inscrutable, exotic, cruel, mysterious, and so forth – is a recurrent theme of British Chinese writing and creative output."[75] Nearly a century after Fu's creation, his shadow still hangs over the British Chinese.

When fans downplay or defend the racism in *The Talons of Weng-Chiang*, we, too, are helping to keep Arthur Sarsfield Ward's cruel creation alive. But because we *are* fans, we're capable of being sophisticated, thoughtful viewers, able to see both a story's successes and its failings. If we can still love and laud *Talons* while ruefully acknowledging the rubbish giant rat, I think we can acknowledge the racist elements of the story too.

Notes

1   Steve Broster (director), *The Last Hurrah* (supplementary documentary on *The Talons of Weng-Chiang* DVD release), BBC, 2010.

2   myfavouriteplum, comment to "Talons of Weng-Chiang: racist?" (9 July 2010), *Doctor Who Livejournal*. Retrieved 19 August 2012 at http://doctorwho.livejournal.com/6464482. html?thread=96569058#t96569058.

3   This is a sample of male Chinese actors, of comparable age and career length to Bennett, who were working in British TV at the time. In this essay, 'British Chinese' (or simply 'Chinese') is an umbrella term for people of Chinese ancestry living in Britain, including British-born Chinese people, people born in China and Taiwan, and ethnic Chinese people from former British colonies such as Hong Kong and Singapore, and from other countries such as Vietnam and Malaysia. As you can see, British Chinese identity is complex. Britons self-identifying as Mixed Race add further complexity to the picture.

4   Cay Van Ash and Elizabeth Sax Rohmer, *Master of Villainy: A Biography of Sax Rohmer*, Bowling Green: Bowling Green University Popular Press, 1972.

5   George Orwell's 1940 list of foreign stereotypes in boys' weekly papers includes "Chinese: Sinister, treacherous. Wears pigtail." George Orwell, *Essays*, London: Penguin, 2000, 78–100. Schools taught almost nothing about China, so the boys' and girls' magazines went uncontradicted by fact: "these images were to breed fear and righteous indignation in generations of British youth." Kathryn Castle, *Britannia's Children: Reading colonialism through children's books and magazines*, Manchester: Manchester University Press, 1996, 146.

6   This essay focuses on the United Kingdom, but there was similar hostility to Chinese immigrants in the United States, Canada, New Zealand, South Africa and my own country of Australia – including harassment, discrimination, race riots and anti-Chinese immigration laws, fuelled by an inimical press.

7   Jess Nevins, "On Yellow Peril Thrillers" (2001), *Aunt Violet's Book Museum*. Retrieved 19 August 2012 at http://www.violetbooks.com/yellowperil.html.

8   Karen Kingsbury, "Yellow Peril, Dark Hero: Fu Manchu and the 'Gothic Bedevilment' of Racist Intent", in Ruth Bienstock Anolik and Douglas L. Howard, eds., *The Gothic Other: Racial and Social Constructions in the Literary Imagination*, Jefferson: McFarland & Co, 2004, 104–19.

9   Thomas J. Cogan, "Western Images of Asia: Fu Manchu and the Yellow Peril", *Waseda Studies in Social Science*, 3, 2 (2002), 37–64.

10 Quoted in Douglas G. Greene, "Introduction", in Sax Rohmer, *The Insidious Dr. Fu-Manchu*, New York: Dover, 1997, i–vii.

11 Ward himself may have been a member of the Hermetic Order of the Golden Dawn and the Rosicrucians. Kingsbury, "Yellow Peril", 107.

12 Another source Ward used was himself: Fu's intense green eyes were one of several of Ward's "own characteristics, both real and imagined" with which he invested his villain. Kingsbury, "Yellow Peril", 114. (One might even remark that, as a flattering authorial self-insertion, the character was Ward's Mary Fu.) In *Talons*, Chang's eyes literally flash as he hypnotizes his

victims; Fu's eyes "sometimes burned like witch lamps." Sax Rohmer, *The Return of Doctor Fu Manchu*, New York: A.L. Burt Company, 1916, 284.

13 Stella Broster (producer), Victoriana and Chinoiserie – References in The Talons of Weng-Chiang (supplementary documentary on *The Talons of Weng-Chiang* DVD release), BBC, 2010.

14 Martin Wiggins, "Infotext" (commentary in subtitles), *Doctor Who: The Talons of Weng-Chiang* DVD release, BBC, 2010.

15 Fu flicks of an earlier generation may also have had some input: Mr Sin's inhuman face resembles Boris Karloff's in *The Mask of Fu Manchu*.

16 Terrance Dicks, *Doctor Who and the Talons of Weng-Chiang*, London: Target Books, 1977, 102.

17 There is no such "ancient Chinese god", though there is a river in Guangdong Province with this name (now more usually transliterated as 'Wengjiang'). We might speculate that Greel arrived here and was taken to be the god of the river.

18 The apostrophe in 'H'sen' seems to be an error – perhaps a cousin of the variably present hyphen in 'Fu-Manchu'. Kingsbury, "Yellow Peril", 117n2.

19 Is there a hint of sexual threat about Chang's remark to Leela on their first encounter? "I'm sure we shall meet again … Perhaps under more pleasant circumstances."

20 Wiggins, "Infotext."

21 "Australia objects to them [Asians, Africans and Pacific Islanders] because they introduce a lower civilisation. It objects because they intermarry with white women, and thereby lower the white type, and because they have already created the beginnings of a mongrel race, that has many of the vices of both its parents and few of the virtues of either." *The Bulletin*, 22 June 1901, 6. Quoted in Bill Hornadge, *The Yellow Peril: A squint at some Australian attitudes towards Orientals*, Dubbo: Review Publications, 1971, 33.

22 By contrast with, e.g., Ming the Merciless's lust for the white Dale Arden in the *Flash Gordon* serials (Director: Frederick Stephani, 1936).

23 Kingsbury, "Yellow Peril", 110.

24 There are notable exceptions, such as the pre-Hayes Code *The Mask of Fu Manchu* (1932), in which Fu rallies his troops thusly: "Then conquer and breed … kill the white man … and take his women!" In both that film and the Lee films of the 1960s, Fu Manchu's daughter is a disturbing sexual sadist with a taste for the whip. (This female equivalent of Fu, the alluring but treacherous 'Dragon Lady', is thankfully absent from *Talons*, but she did crop up in the New Series story *Turn Left*, 2008.) For an example closer to the time of *Talons*, see *Thoroughly Modern Millie* (Director: George Roy Hill, 1967) and its 'white slavery' storyline.

25 Julia Lovell, *The Opium War*, Sydney: Picador, 2011.

26 Stella Broster (producer), *Limehouse – A Victorian Chinatown* (supplementary documentary on *The Talons of Weng-Chiang* DVD release), BBC, 2010.

27 Greene, "Introduction."

28 Wiggins, "Infotext."

29 Anon., "Chinese restaurant bankruptcy fear after false dog meat rumour", *Daily Telegraph*, 13 October 2011.

30 David Parker, "Rethinking British Chinese Identities", in Tracey Skelton and Gill Valentine, eds., *Cool Places: Geographies of Youth Cultures*, London: Routledge, 1998.

31 Sue Adamson, Bankole Cole, Gary Craig, Basharat Hussain, Luana Smith, Ian Law, Carmen Lau, Chak-Kwan Chan and Tom Cheung, *Hidden from Public View? Racism against the Chinese Population*, London: The Monitoring Group, April 2009.

32 Van Ash and Rohmer, *Master of Villainy*.

33 Gregor Benton and Edmund Terence Gomez, *The Chinese in Britain, 1800–present: Economy, Transnationalism, Identity*, Basingstoke: Palgrave Macmillan, 2008, 292–93.

34 Kingsbury, "Yellow Peril."

35 Broster, *Limehouse*.

36 Benton and Gomez, *Chinese in Britain*, 24–26.

37 James L. Watson, "The Chinese: Hong Kong Villagers in the British Catering Trade", in James L. Watson, ed., *Between Two Cultures: Migrants and Minorities in Britain*, Blackwell: Oxford, 1977, 181–213.

38 *Doctor Who* would return to the same theme two decades later: Chang Lee, the decent but misguided kid in the 1996 television movie, is a member of a San Francisco gang.

39 Meanwhile at the cinema, there was *One of our Dinosaurs is Missing* (Director: Robert Stevenson, 1975), a sort of comic Disney Fu Manchu packed with British stars, including a yellowface Peter Ustinov gabbling gibberish at his criminal gang. Imported action movies from Hong Kong did offer an alternative view of Chinese culture for 1970s Britain, albeit creating their own stereotype in the process.

40 See Kate Solomon (director), *The Missing Chink*, Channel 4, 2004.

41 Rohmer, *Insidious*.

42 Anthony Then, who plays Chang's assistant Lee, is well worth keeping an eye on throughout the story: with no lines and no close-ups, he nonetheless gives a thoughtful performance. Then was an accomplished musician, teacher, dancer and choreographer who would go on to co-found the Singapore Ballet Company. Bill Henkin, *The Rocky Horror Picture Show Book*, New York City: Hawthorn/Dutton Books, 1979.

43 Kingsbury, "Yellow Peril", 112.

44 This is Professor Scarman's dismissive remark to his fleeing Egyptian assistant in *Pyramids of Mars* (1975). Scarman ignores Achmed's warning and is promptly killed.

45 Jim Steinmeyer, *The Glorious Deception: The Double Life of William Robinson, aka Chung Ling Soo, the "Marvellous Chinese Conjurer"*, New York: Carrol and Graf, 2005.

46 In a sense, Greel too is in yellowface, in that he's impersonating a Chinese deity, his real face hidden not by rubber or make-up but by a mask (Jonathan Blum, personal communication).

47 Andrew Pixley, "The Mind of Evil: Archive", *Doctor Who Magazine* 208, 19 January 1994.

48 A Chinese Australian friend of mine mentioned that this reduced his family to helpless laughter.

49 Broster, *Limehouse*.

50 Arthur Dong (director), *Hollywood Chinese*, United States: Deep Focus Productions, 2007.

51 Kingsbury, "Yellow Peril", 108.

52 The other usual epithet is 'yellow', also used matter-of-factly in *Talons*, in this case by Leela who refers to Chang as "the yellow one." Adamson et al., *Hidden From Public View?*.

53 Yayoi Lena Winfrey, "Yellowface: Asians on White Screens" (2011), *IMdiversity.com*. Retrieved 19 August 2012 at http://www.imdiversity.com/villages/asian/arts_culture_media/archives/winfrey_yellowface_asians_hollywood.asp.

54 John Bennett, commentary to Episode 1, *Doctor Who: The Talons of Weng-Chiang* DVD release, BBC, 2010.

55 Robert B. Ito, "A Certain Slant: A Brief History of Hollywood Yellowface", *Bright Lights Film Journal*, 18 (1997), online.

56 Mark Duguid and Ling-Wan Pak, "British-Chinese Cinema" (n.d.), *BFI screenonline*. Retrieved 19 August 2012 at http://www.screenonline.org.uk/film/id/475755/index.html.

57 Dong, *Hollywood Chinese*.

58 Alan Clarke, "Interview with David Yip, the Chinese Detective", *Marxism Today*, October 1983, 19–23.

59 Benton and Gomez, *Chinese in Britain*.

60 Ian Burrell, "Chinese actor blames racism for lack of role models", *The Independent*, 16 April 2002.

61 Benton and Gomez, *Chinese in Britain*.

62 Kingsbury, "Yellow Peril", 105.

63 Benton and Gomez, *Chinese in Britain*, 313.

64 Darrell Y. Hamamoto, *Monitored peril: Asian Americans and the politics of TV representation*, Minneapolis: University of Minnesota Press, 1994.

65 Anon., "Cinema: Chinaman's Chance", *Time Magazine*, 19 November 1965.

66 Anon., "Overseas Overview", *Doctor Who Monthly*, 71, December 1982.

67 Elizabeth Chan, "Chinese Britons have put up with racism for too long", *The Guardian*, 11 January 2012.

68 Adamson et al., *Hidden From Public View?*.

69 Maria Noëlle Ng, "Representing Chinatown: Dr. Fu-Manchu at the Disappearing Moon Cafe", *Canadian Literature*, 163 (Winter 1999), 157–75.

70 Parker, "Rethinking."

71 Owen Gibson, "Diversify or die: Equality chief's stark message to broadcasting industry", *The Guardian*, 17 July 2008.

72 Stuart Brown, Isobel Hawson, Tony Graves and Mukesh Barot, *Eclipse: Developing strategies to combat racism in theatre*, London: Arts Council England, 2002.

73 Parker, "Rethinking."

74 Adamson et al., *Hidden From Public View?*.

75 Benton and Gomez, *Chinese in Britain*, 349–50.

PART III

Colonialism, imperialism, slavery and the diaspora

Chapter 12

Inventing America: *The Aztecs* in context

Leslie McMurtry

The Aztecs (1964) is often viewed as a seminal piece of *Doctor Who*: it has the distinction of being the first time the Doctor has romantic inclinations, serves as a template for understanding the cumulative effects of time travel, and is held up as an example of the 'pure historicals'.[1] It has other distinctive features too: taking place in pre-conquest Aztec Mexico, it is very much companion Barbara's story. Barbara, when mistaken for the priest/god Yetaxa, attempts to remove the blood sacrifice element of the Aztecs' culture. Yet Barbara's understanding of the Aztecs comes from biased sources, and in wanting to change Aztec society the moment she arrives, she is unable to experience the untouched culture first-hand. Writer John Lucarotti contributed a historically sound script, but the story works within a framework of 'good' and 'bad' Indians.[2] This dichotomous concept was introduced in the journal of Christopher Columbus and developed by conqueror of the Aztecs, Hernán Cortés.[3]

Although the High Priest of Knowledge in *The Aztecs* is fictional character Autloc not real-life Aztec leader Moctezuma, like almost all subsequent writing about this period, the serial takes its lead from the Quetzalcóatl myth we first hear about in Cortés's *Second Letter*. We as astute readers and viewers should be suspicious of accepting this myth because there really is no evidence to suggest its validity other than Cortés's word, which judicious reading throws into some doubt. The main goal of Cortés's *Letters from Mexico*, written to King Charles of Spain between 1519 and 1526, was to establish the justice of his command. Cortés was in a tight spot as he composed these letters – he had committed treason, ignoring a last minute recall from his expeditionary mission. It is difficult but important to separate the historical Moctezuma from the character presented by Cortés for King Charles's benefit in the *Second Letter*. In it, Cortés repeatedly cited Divine intervention in his success at subduing the Aztec empire, emphasizing the role of the semi-Divine king in this statement. Cortés records Moctezuma as saying, "See that I am of flesh and blood like you and all other men, and I am mortal and substantial."[4] However, it is difficult to imagine such a Christianized discourse coming from the lips of the pagan Moctezuma; Anthony Pagden in his translator's notes goes so far as to say, "[Moctezuma] could never have held the views with which Cortés accredits him."[5]

In *The Aztecs,* Autloc's unfailing ability to accept everything that Barbara-as-Yetaxa says, despite supposedly being a representative of reason and intellect, chimes with the way Cortés represented Moctezuma. Cortés says that Moctezuma and his people accept and welcome Cortés and his men as a representative or reincarnation of the Aztec deity

Quetzalcóatl. It could be that Cortés is referring to an actual Aztec myth, the legend of the Aztecs' principal god, Huitzilopochtli, but even if Moctezuma offered Cortés the ceremonial regalia of Quetzalcóatl at the time of his landing it doesn't necessarily mean that he thought that the stranger was, or represented, the god.[6]

Tlotoxl in *The Aztecs* similarly does not accept Barbara-as-Yetaxa's 'divinity', and it is partly this that establishes the 'good Indian/bad Indian' dichotomy. To the western mind, John Ringham's performance as High Priest of Sacrifice Tlotoxl evokes nothing so much as Shakespeare's *Richard III* (1592). That eponymous anti-hero's evil nature is summed up in his limp, his hunchback and his leer, all of which Tlotoxl seems to share, with the added bonus of black face paint or tattooing. Tlotoxl is at the centre of the 'good/bad Indian' dichotomy; his physical ugliness makes him both antagonist to our heroes' intentions and the representative of that 'barbaric' practice of human sacrifice, which is, in fact, very similar to the treatment of the '*canibale*' Indians in Columbus's writings.

Peter Hulme supplies a strong theory for why it might have been to Columbus's advantage to make the distinction between tribes that 'seemed' timid and the tribe that actively resisted. After being privately assured that there are no "Oriental courts" to be found on the new continent, Columbus reverts to the "Herodotean discourse of savagery."[7] In general, he praises the beauty of the peoples he meets, but there is one person who is described disparagingly, ugly because of "extrinsic cultural features."[8] This individual just happens to be part of the tribe said to eat other people: "Columbus 'judges' that the native is a man-eating Caribe."[9] How convenient is it that the tribe that attacks Columbus's men is the one that Columbus paints as cannibals?[10] Tlotoxl is not lovely to look upon and thus makes an excellent scapegoat for all the sins of the Aztecs.

Despite her aspirations towards objectivity in being a history teacher, Barbara's crusade to rehabilitate the Aztecs shows her to be at least influenced by the motif of the noble savage. The concept of the noble savage – the native in a prelapsarian state of innocence and purity – in some form arrives with Columbus, but it was French Protestant Jean de Léry who in 1553 described his intention "simply to declare what I have myself experienced […] among the American savages."[11] Janet Whatley notes that "savage" stands in here for the French *sauvage*, "the word [that] most often means simply 'living in a state of nature'."[12] The linguistic distinction is an important one, especially in light of de Léry's Spanish predecessors, who referred to the natives as *los indios*. Yet by using the word *sauvage*, de Léry highlighted his Calvinist duty to convert a people "without religion."[13]

For many viewers of *The Aztecs*, the serial is their first glimpse into a historical pre-Columbian civilization and as such, it is an admirable introduction. Nevertheless, it is coloured by the calculated writings of Cortés and his contemporaries. "Oh, don't you see?" cries Barbara to the Doctor. "If I could start the destruction of everything that's evil here, then everything that's good will survive when Cortés lands." All that is good is in the eye of the beholder.

Notes

1 BBC, "The Aztecs" (n.d.), *Doctor Who Classic Episode Guide*. Retrieved 19 August 2012 at http://www.bbc.co.uk/doctorwho/classic/episodeguide/aztecs/detail.shtml; Shannon Sullivan, "The Aztecs" (3 April 2005), *A Brief History of Time (Travel)*. Retrieved 19 August 2012 at http://www.shannonsullivan.com/drwho/serials/f.html.

2 We see this dichotomy again in *Doctor Who*, in *Black Orchid* (1982), in which the 1920s British hero/villain has been mutilated and maddened by a 'bad' South American tribe, while nurtured by a 'good' tribe.

3 With Yetaxa's death around 1430 and Cortés's arrival in 1519, Lucarotti's novelization's date of 1507 is plausible. Tat Wood and Lawrence Miles, *About Time 1: The Unauthorized Guide to Doctor Who, 1963–1966, Seasons 1 to 3*, Des Moines: Mad Norwegian Press, 2006, 70.

4 Hernán Cortés, "The Second Letter", *Letters from Mexico* (trans. Anthony Pagden), New Haven: Yale University Press, 1986, 86.

5 Pagden, note to Cortés, *Letters from Mexico*, 467.

6 Ross Frank, "The Codex Cortés: Inscribing the Conquest of Mexico", *Dispositio*, 14, 36–38 (1989), 200.

7 Peter Hulme, *Colonial Encounters: Europe and the Native Caribbean, 1492–1797*, London: Metheun, 1986, 31–33.

8 Hulme, *Colonial Encounters*, 40.

9 Hulme, *Colonial Encounters*, 40.

10 Christopher Columbus, *The Four Voyages: Being His Own Log-Book, Letters and Dispatches with Connecting Narratives* (trans. J. M. Cohen), New York: Penguin Classics, 1992.

11 Jean De Léry, *History of a Voyage to the Land of Brazil* (trans. Janet Whatley), Berkley: University of California Press, 1993, 3.

12 Whatley, notes to De Léry, *History of a Voyage*, 232.

13 De Léry, *History of a Voyage*, xlix.

Chapter 13

The Ood as a slave race: Colonial continuity in the Second Great and Bountiful Human Empire

Erica Foss

In the world of *Doctor Who*, by the forty-second century, humanity seems to have worked out the little kinks that caused so much political and social turmoil on Earth. They've expanded across three galaxies and are well on their way to becoming the centre of all the activity in the universe. The Second Great and Bountiful Human Empire has become an economic powerhouse; and all the humans seem to be getting along just fine. As the Tenth Doctor explains this to Donna Noble in *Planet of the Ood* (2008) it's difficult not to feel a sense of pride at the resilience of humanity as we have overcome global warming, nuclear war and the million other things that were supposed to destroy the race over time. The Doctor's love of humanity is often attributed to this strength, and as he shows Donna Noble the map of the Empire's reach, the audience grins along with him.

When the Doctor and Donna encounter Ood Operations (OO), however, we quickly come to realize that this great and bountiful empire has a much darker side. Ood Operations sells members of an alien species, the Ood, as slaves to humanity. Although the public face of the Empire and of OO uses a framework of paternalism and benevolence, the reality of the ways in which the Ood are used as chattel slaves is easy for the Doctor and Donna to find. The Ood are seen by their owners as a docile servant race when they first appear in *The Impossible Planet/The Satan Pit* (2006). "They like it" is the justification that the slaveholders use, and they emphasize the cordiality of relations between the Ood and humanity. Despite this public face, however, it becomes clear that the rationalization for enslaving the Ood has everything to do with humanity's tendency to other. The term 'othering', reinvented by Edward Said in the late 1970s, suggests that people define themselves in relation to what they are not. Discursively, if *we* are not savage and *they* are not like us, then they must be savage. Conversely, if *we* are powerful and civilized and *they* are not, then they become the other.[1] Historically, humanity has found various ways of dealing with this other, from creating an exotic and wild image of them, to simply dominating them 'for their own good'. This latter model fits nicely with humanity in the Whoniverse. Human captains of industry found a race so unlike their own, docile and vulnerable, that it was easy for them to portray themselves to the consuming public as the saviours of Oodkind, giving them purpose in life.

To understand the dynamics of this new human Empire, and how the Ood were represented to potential buyers as another incarnation of 'a natural slave race', it is useful to look back to imperial practices in the fifteenth–nineteenth centuries. There are strong parallels between the historical Age of Exploration and Empire[2] and the fictitious Age of the Second Human Empire. In human history, nation states fought for supremacy over the globe. The Portuguese and Spanish, followed by the Dutch and the English, all fought to maintain the most powerful empires in the world. Rather than seeing this fight continue in the space age, the Whoniverse allows this battle to be played across galaxies. And just as the public records of early European explorers and conquerors emphasized the importance of the 'civilizing mission' and described native populations as natural-born slaves, the industrious owners of OO play up the naturalness of having Ood servants and claim that they "rescued" the Ood from a life of savagery. Both the expansion of the human race, and the naturalistic, scientific arguments they make about slavery, suggest that far from overcoming the problems of the past, the Second Great and Bountiful Human Empire has simply outsourced them. This society continues to other what it does not understand, primarily for the sake of power and profit. As such, the relationship between the Ood and the Empire, with all of its parallels to the past, serves as a morality tale not just for Donna, but for the audience as well. By forcing us to consider the moral cost of human expansion and resilience, the Ood remind us that in the forty-second century, and even in the twenty-first, humanity still has a long way to go.

Empire and expansion

With the boom of overseas exploration in the fifteenth century from Western Europe, powers sought new lands to serve as a generator of wealth and prestige. Portugal headed up this quest, followed quickly by Spain. Both nations, though their motivations were complex and varied, competed for empires that were the biggest and best. Once the Netherlands, England, France, Germany and Belgium joined the race in the eighteenth and nineteenth centuries, empire became an all out war for dominance. Although much of this exploration was motivated by economic concerns, the centuries-long bid to occupy the globe also rested on concerns about world power and superiority.[3] This desire for global dominance led to both small- and large-scale power struggles throughout the period of 1848–1914, which historian Eric Hobsbawm has termed both "the Age of Capital" and "the Age of Empire."[4]

Social scientist David Abernathy has argued that the European drive for empire was characterized by a strong "explore-control-utilize syndrome" that led to the eventual exploitation of peoples.[5] The model that he has created can be applied from the earliest European imperial endeavours to the height of expansion in the late nineteenth century. In this way, all of the political, social and economic complexities underlying expansion can be boiled down to dominant nations laying claim to the resources of weaker ones. While this model certainly has problems, it works well when analysing the relationship between the imperial metropole and the colonial periphery.[6] In exploiting the colonies for their raw materials and natural resources, European powers focused far less on settling their own populations and far more on utilizing the wealth of those places. Abernathy's model here characterizes well the goals of Europe in controlling and using colonies like wealth factories. Putting little in and using up the resources available, European powers would simply move on once they had gotten what they needed. There are myriad examples of this, but perhaps one of the most vivid here is the extraction of rubber from central Africa in the late nineteenth century.[7] King Leopold II's deputies in what became known as the Belgian Congo used the native populations to extract rubber from their land under threat of death and dismemberment for native men and their families. This excursion into what Joseph Conrad has termed "the Heart of Darkness" had nothing to do with settlement, or even of 'civilizing' Africans, with its discourse of salvation and good intentions (regardless of devastating consequences). It was unabashedly, and unapologetically, exploitative, and many Europeans who later found out about this were shocked that such actions were being taken so late in the imperial game.[8]

Under this model, the 'undiscovered countries' of the world were quickly found, and after the scramble for Africa at the turn of the twentieth century, the opportunities for new imperial expansion dwindled to nothing by the end of the twentieth century.[9] In the Whoniverse, the opportunity re-emerges with humanity's ever broadening knowledge of other worlds and star systems. As humanity moves forward into the Space Age, their playing field broadens exponentially. Indeed, by the forty-second century, humanity has expanded across three galaxies. Because of Earth's colonial past, it is unsurprising to see that humanity has expanded their reach into new galaxies and created a space empire. The Doctor is generally impressed by this feat of human indefatigability. The Time Lord assumes, most of the time, that humanity is inherently good, and that their natural inclination to explore the universe "because it [is] there" (*The Impossible Planet*) will lead to an ever-evolving and benevolent species. However, on more than one occasion, we see the Tenth Doctor question his assumptions about humanity's goodness. The first is immediately after his regeneration and Prime Minister Harriet Jones has just destroyed the Sycorax vessel. Enraged by her disproportionate reaction, the Doctor tells her "I sent the wrong message. I should have told them to run, run and hide, because the monsters are coming […] The human race" (*The Christmas Invasion*, 2005). While perhaps Jones is justified in her reaction to the invasion, the response is concerning for its implications about humanity's willingness and ability to be a threat to others in the universe. In 2005, the PM's reaction can be termed aggressive defence, but by the forty-second century, this defensive protectionism has morphed into an insatiable drive to expand, though the Doctor's concerns about humanity's violence remain. As he tells the crew on the impossible planet, not only could they fuel the empire with the energy they find, they could start a war.

When we see how expansive the empire has become in *Planet of the Ood*, Donna asks the Doctor "Is that good or bad though? I mean, are we like, explorers or more like a virus?" Both the Doctor and the audience remain unsure. We have already seen that humanity's history has been fraught with conflict, expansion and exploitation, so Donna's question makes perfect sense. But her word choice – virus – is also important. Viruses don't integrate – they destroy. Tellingly, at this point in human history the empire has remained largely homogenous. The buyers who visit Ood Operations are all human, as are the employees. Even 150,000 years later in the Fourth Great and Bountiful Human Empire, the workers on Satellite Five (*The Long Game*, 2005) were all human. In their eagerness to explore the galaxies of the universe, humanity has not let go of the imperialist dogma that speaks to Abernathy's model of conquest. They have expanded their borders without expanding their lived experience. This trend is not without a ray of hope, however. As we travel with the Doctor even further into the future, we see evidence that humanity will finally mix more fully with other species, to the point that no 'pure' humans will remain by the year five billion (*The End of the World*, 2005). But in the early days of the Human Empire, little has changed, and the exploitation of peoples and cultures seems par for the course.

The science of slavery

Within this exploitative colonial system of the Human Empire, we must still ask the question of how the owners of OO justify enslaving the Ood. The twenty-first century was characterized by concerns about human rights, although violence and crime was still widespread. If humanity has had two thousand years to evolve, why are they still conquering and enslaving other beings? The Ood have physiological weaknesses that make them susceptible to exploitation. With their hindbrain in their hands, Donna points out, "they'd have to trust anyone!" (*Planet of the Ood*). This leads to familiar justifications from OO that the Ood are natural born slaves. They never protested their enslavement; therefore they must be okay with it.

This line of reasoning is not new to the forty-second century. The Age of Exploration brought with it encounters between Europeans and 'new' types of people with unfamiliar language, culture and appearance. Although the beginnings of the Atlantic slave trade are filled with complexities, there is a clear trend of explorers justifying their actions through the idea that slaves were not protesting their own enslavement, and that slavery was nothing new to the indigenous peoples they encountered. When the Spanish and Portuguese began exploring the Americas, many accounts described the natives as "willing slaves" or "natural born servants."[10] This had little to do with those men and women offering their services, but rather with the fact that their technology was less advanced and they would be easy to subdue. Although some thinkers, usually clergymen, spoke out against the ill treatment of indigenous populations, none suggested that they be treated as equals to white Europeans.[11] The conception that Europeans were civilized while others had 'primitive' technology and less 'advanced' infrastructure was pervasive through the period of early exploration. The natural born slaves of the tropics were largely described, not in terms of race, but in their environmental suitability for hard labour. Europeans often saw themselves as too delicate, too prone to disease and too important to do the physically demanding work of mining raw materials. Controversially, historian John Thornton has argued that Europeans did not, in fact, transform New World societies through the development of slavery. Slavery existed within (particularly) African cultures long before European explorers arrived, and

Europeans simply tried to capitalize on an already thriving human market.[12] Even with this being true, however, many historians have argued that Europeans changed the way that slavery operated. Rather than something local and political, explorers used slavery to reinforce their own sense of superiority and came to see all indigenous people as potential slaves.[13]

This reasoning continued well into the nineteenth century with the development of scientific theories about race. Darwin's theories of evolution led to the creation of the ideologies of Social Darwinism, and phrenology and physiognomy. Championed by thinkers such as Francis Galton and Herbert Spencer, the new science of modern life led to the belief that certain races were biologically better than others.[14] Darwin's theory of natural selection played prominently here, as Europeans argued that their industry and modernity proved their superiority. The idea of 'survival of the fittest' became a hugely influential justification for colonialism and the oppression of non-white peoples.[15] Very quickly, people of differing races were placed on a hierarchy based on their level of 'civilization' and 'savagery'. As Dana Hale has suggested, this hierarchy was disseminated to the public along with visual images and material examples to reinforce white superiority in the minds of ordinary citizens.[16] In Europe by the late nineteenth century, official slavery was not a part of this, though the spectacle of racism and the socio-economic differences between white Europeans and 'savage' races amounted to much the same thing.

For the CEO of Ood operations, Klineman Halpern, this scientific racism is perfectly sound. He tells the Doctor that when humanity discovered Ood Planet, they found its inhabitants little better than wild beasts, running chaotically around the countryside. He says, "they welcomed it! It's not like they put up a fight" (*Planet of the Ood*). For him and his company, a lack of active resistance was tantamount to complicity. Like the arguments made in the infancy of the Atlantic slave trade, the myth of acceptance fuelled the enslavement of the Ood. In their first appearance in the Whoniverse, the Ood are described by their human masters as low-level telepaths that are "too stupid" to even let their owners know when they are ill (*The Impossible Planet*). They are always described in animalistic terms that belie the Ood's unusual intelligence. To their masters, including human scientists, the Ood are no more than cattle – livestock that must be kept alive because of the service that they provide to humanity. They have no value in themselves, but are defined entirely in relation to the human race. Even the Ood themselves echo this statement once they have been processed into slavery, saying, "humanity defines us" and "[to serve] is all we crave – we have nothing else in life." The Ood are so removed from their own natural instincts, that they do not even understand the concept of liberty. The Doctor, of course, turns this supposed scientific fact on its head by proclaiming that "a species born to serve could never evolve in the first place", and later finds that "processing" an Ood means to cut off their amygdala. It is the torture of lobotomy – torture, for one can assume they do not anaesthetize the Ood first – that makes them submissive and servile. Whatever pseudo-scientific justifications humanity had been using for exploiting their 'servant race' are immediately debunked, and Donna is left in shock and horror.

Also essential to the enslavement of the Ood is the cultural collaboration of the human population. Public relations representative Solana's sales pitch is a perfect example of the way that the rest of humanity is lulled into apathy with spun language:

> As you can see, the Ood are happy to serve and we keep them in facilities of the highest standard. We like to think of the Ood as our trusted friends. We keep the Ood healthy, safe and educated. We don't just breed the Ood, we make them *better*. After all, what is an Ood, but a reflection of us? If your Ood is happy, you'll be happy too. (*Planet of the Ood*)

When an outraged Donna asks what people would do if they knew that the Ood were treated as chattel slaves, Solana replies, "Don't be so stupid! Of course people know […] they don't ask. Same thing." At this statement, the audience realizes that the veil of imperialism is indeed quite thin, and the oppression of a people is tacitly accepted. This again has parallels to the empires on earth in the nineteenth century. The British Empire at its height had its own imperial culture, and Britons embraced their own imperial power quite actively.[17] Europe in this period was characterized by power struggles, class conflict and tense gender relations; the Empire gave Britons a sense of belonging.[18] Along with tacit acceptance is a wilful misunderstanding of the treatment of the Ood. The ethics officer on Century Base Six explained to Rose, "The Ood offer themselves. If you don't give them orders, they just wither away and die" (*The Impossible Planet*). Whether apathy or misinformation, however, humanity has spent hundreds of years in blissful ignorance, happily endorsing the torture and enslavement of another race or species, whether the slaves and 'savages' of the old empire, or the Ood in the future.

Of course, not all of humanity accepted the Ood as slaves unquestioningly; just like the abolitionist movements in the nineteenth century, Friends of the Ood commit themselves to raising awareness and ending the slavery. Much like in the nineteenth century, the people in these movements are ridiculed.[19] When Rose expresses outrage at the enslavement of the Ood in *The Impossible Planet*, the crew of the space station mock her for her concern. Moreover, the movement itself is not terribly influential. It takes Doctor Ryder ten years to infiltrate the company and try to free the Ood brain. Nevertheless, after 200 years of enslavement, this will allow the Ood to stage their 'revolution' and win their freedom. Through their connection to the hive brain, the Ood are able to channel their repressed rage and use their communication devices – the shackles of slavery – as weapons against their oppressors. We can see this revolt in many ways as parallel to the numerous slave uprisings in the nineteenth century, as abolitionists raised awareness while slaves participated in rebellions. This was most prevalent in the United States, where slavery was legal for much longer than in Europe.[20] The abolitionists offer a glimmer of hope in the greed of empire, where beings are bought and sold for profit. Small groups of people in both periods move against the accepted science and practices of the time; these are the types of people that the Doctor continually recruits as his companions – the best of humanity.

'Othering' the Ood

Deeply connected to the science of slavery is the cultural perception of the other. For many years, historians and social scientists have studied how various interpersonal and group interactions operate on an 'us/them' dichotomy. From gender relationships, to religious differences, to racial dichotomies, human history is rife with socially constructed group struggles. This 'politics of difference' is rarely peaceful and almost always results in the dominant group violently oppressing the weaker.[21] In the colonial context, this manifests itself in the most obvious model of physical dominance and enslavement. Edward Said specifically coined the term 'orientalism' to refer to the ways in which European societies have exoticized, eroticized and fetishized the cultures of the East. In labelling them 'oriental', he argued, the West has created a false idea of their colonial holdings and made it impossible to truly understand the peoples who lived in them.[22] For imperial explorers in the early modern world, the language of othering took the form of 'civilization' and 'savagery'. European nations self-consciously labelled themselves as paragons of virtue, Christian ethics and modernity; the indigenous peoples they encountered, with their unfamiliar ways of life, were classified as Godless, savage and dangerous.[23]

Misconceptions and a lack of communication fuel much of this discourse, and when the Doctor and Rose first sight the Ood, their experience is much the same. Upon landing on the Century Base Six station in *The Impossible Planet*, the first beings they encounter are a dozen Ood. Unlike anything either of them have ever seen, the Ood have reptilian skin, beard-like tentacles, enormous wide-set eyes and an orb device through which they speak. At first, both our travellers and the audience assume that the Ood are about to attack. They repeat, "we must feed … we must feed," as they advance toward the Doctor and Rose. Finally, one of the Ood shakes his speech device and repeats, "we must feed … you. If you are hungry." Immediately we realize that these beings are not threatening, but serving. Both of the travellers, though relieved, seem somewhat disconcerted by this. At the time, the Doctor accepts that the Ood are a benign, harmless race of servants, and it is not until he encounters them again in *Planet of the Ood* that he decides he owes them their freedom. Although Rose will ask pointed questions about the Ood's enslavement throughout this story arc, it is surprising that the Doctor so readily accepts the situation. The shock of his first contact with this species and the far more scientifically fascinating situation of a planet in orbit around a black hole, made the Doctor blind to the uglier reality of the human empire. Fulfilling his role as saviour, the Doctor was forced to ignore the 'minutiae' of injustice against the Ood in order to save the crew of the base. Later, on Ood Planet, he will tell Donna that he was "a bit busy" battling the devil during their last encounter and that he now owes the Ood his assistance. The Doctor shows the audience that even he isn't infallible. However, while othering and acceptance may be a natural reaction to a new culture or species, the Doctor shows the way to correct those mistakes.

As we have seen, the Second Human Empire operates publicly under a system of benevolence and paternalism that allows humans to enslave the Ood and to justify this with the idea that slavery is their natural place. Yet this enslavement is sugar-coated for the investors and potential buyers of Oodkind, as the Ood themselves are whipped and chained. As we have already noted above, Solana asks them to "think of the Ood as your friend." Obviously, she is not talking about a friend/confidante, but a friend/pet. These creatures, obviously not human, are treated as 'less than'. So far removed are they from the operations, thinking and lifestyle of humanity that it becomes easier for them to be thought of as akin to animals that can be treated as such. This treatment of the Ood reflects the discourse of othering as well. On Century Base Six, when the Ood are infected with the spirit of 'the devil', the crew attempt to use a strategy that will eject them all out of the airlock to their deaths. At Ood Operations, on their own planet, the Ood are shackled like chattel slaves and transported like non-organic cargo in huge containers packed as full as possible. Halpern suggests that when the "livestock" is contaminated, all they have to do is carry out "the old foot and mouth solution" and kill off the entire batch with poisonous gas. Because the Ood are literally dehumanized, it makes the task of enslavement and even genocide infinitely easier to justify. Because the Ood aren't human, it is easy to see them as 'less than'; because they communicate telepathically, it is even easier to manipulate them and adapt them for slavery. Othering and enslaving the Ood makes humanity with its great Empire a true player in the quest for universal power. At a time in which humanity itself seems to have unified and moved beyond its own petty differences, the urge to other remains strong. If they cannot other themselves, but are not strong enough to conquer truly threatening races, the discovery of Ood Planet presented the perfect opportunity for humanity to exert its power.

Conclusion

Humanity's treatment of the Ood, through scientific racism and the discourse of the other, backfires against the humans on more than one occasion. On Century Base Six, the computer is not programmed to recognize the Ood as proper life forms with sentient thought. When the Ood are infected with red-eye and become violent, the crew cannot track their movements. On Ood planet, the translator ball acts as a weapon that can channel Oodkind's rage at humanity. But ultimately, the natural, unprocessed Ood truly are benign and peaceful. After gaining their freedom and exacting revenge on Halpern, Ood Sigma claims that Ood must never kill, but will look after the newly transformed Halpern as one of their own. This contrast with the greed and ignorance of the human race is striking and it seems that even in the forty-second century we are still in our infancy when it comes to encountering other cultures.

Although the Ood ultimately win their liberty with the assistance of the Doctor and Donna, we are left wondering about the character of humanity. On the one hand, humanity's drive to exist is nothing if not impressive. Throughout the Doctor's travels, we see them survive to the year 100 trillion. That spirit to live and keep going is one of the reasons that the Time Lord is so enamoured with the human race. On the other hand, we are often left wondering at whose expense humanity has survived so long. Though Donna is outraged that in the forty-second century, the empire is built on slavery, the Doctor points out that it's not so different from her own time. And even that is not so different from the nineteenth century and before. There is a cycle of oppression, exploitation, and othering that the human race cannot seem to break, and we see evidence of this throughout the Doctor's travels. The Whoniverse suggests that this continuity may not bode well for the future of humanity. Although Earth's population has had moments of progress and integration, the fear of difference and the drive to excel remains a danger to humanity's potential to fulfil the Doctor's high aspirations for us. For those in Donna's time – the audience – the example of the Ood serves as a reminder that humans must never cease to strive for progress, tolerance and understanding.

Notes

1   Jean Paul Sartre was in fact, one of the first to use the term. However, his conceptions of otherness are based in interpersonal relationships and not group dynamics. He argues that the internal process of 'othering' is instinctual and natural. He does not, however, discuss collective difference such as race or gender. Simone de Beauvoir would also use the language of Other to describe women as man's Other. But it was Edward Said who first brought the term to postcolonial studies, and his use of the term is how I utilize it in this essay, though I accept Sartre's insistence on the inherency of othering. For more on these theories, see Jean-Paul Sartre, *Being and Nothingness,* New York: Citadel, 2001 [1956]; Simone de Beauvoir, *The Second Sex*, New York: Vintage, 2011 [1949]; Edward Said, *Orientalism*, New York: Vintage, 1978.

2   For the purposes of this essay, the Age of Exploration and Empire are periodized together as roughly from 1500–1900. Though broad, this allows us to encompass the key watershed moments of Empire and race relations. C. A. Bayly acknowledges that this period is wrought with imperial battles as Europe struggled for dominance over the globe. For more, see C. A. Bayly, *The Birth of the Modern World: 1780–1914*, London: Blackwell, 2003.

3   H. L. Wesseling, *The European Colonial Empires, 1815–1919*, Edinburgh: Pearson Longman, 2004; P. J. Cain and A. G. Hopkins, *British Imperialism, 1688–2000*, London: Longman, 2001.

4   These conflicts include the Indian Mutiny of 1857, the Boer War in 1901, the Franco-Prussian War, the Opium Wars, the Crimean War and the First World War. Eric Hobsbawm, *The Age of Capital: 1848–1875*, New York: Vintage, 1996; Eric Hobsbawm, *The Age of Empire: 1875–1914*, New York: Vintage, 1989.

5   David Abernathy, *The Dynamics of Global Dominance: European Overseas Empires, 1415–1980*, New Haven: Yale University Press, 2000, 34.

6   Catherine Hall uses these terms as loaded ways to describe the economic and cultural relationship of power that empires had over their subjects. For more on this, see Catherine

Hall, *Civilizing Subjects: Colony and Metropole in the English Imagination, 1830–1867*, Chicago: University of Chicago Press, 2002.

7   Of course, earlier examples from the Spanish conquistadors in the Mayan and Aztec empires are also poignant examples of squeezing the land and people dry in the quest for wealth.

8   This incident has some of the most interesting popular culture interpretations, including Joseph Conrad's *Heart of Darkness* (1902), the later film adaptation *Apocalypse Now* (Director: Francis Ford Coppola, 1979), and the popular history by Adam Hochschild, *King Leopold's Ghost*, Boston: Mariner Books, 1998. For further histories, see Kevin C. Dunn, *Imagining the Congo: The International Relations of Identity*, New York: Palgrave MacMillan, 2003; W. J. Samarin, *The Black Man's Burden: African Colonial Labor on the Congo and Ubangi Rivers, 1880–1900*, Westview: Boulder, 1989.

9   I say 'new' expansion very specifically; there are plenty of imperial struggles that continued through the twentieth century. However, those struggles were largely between autonomous political actors rather than powerful explorers exploiting raw materials and peoples.

10 Much of this is taken from Aristotle's defence of 'natural slavery', as well as biblical references to slaves and general Christian doctrine. There were many debates about the treatment of natives by Spanish conquistadors, and one of the main defenders of slavery was Juan Ginés de Sepúlveda. See Paolo G. Carozza, "From Conquest to Constitutions: Retrieving a Latin American Tradition of the Idea of Human Rights", *Human Rights Quarterly*, 25, 2 (2003), 281–313.

11 Among these dissenters were Bartolemé de las Casas, bishop of Chiapas in 1550, who participated in the Valladolid debate about the righteousness of slavery in the New World, and St Peter Claver (1580–1654), a Spanish Jesuit who actively denounced the enslavement of fellow Christians.

12 John Thornton, *Africa and the Africans in the Making of the Atlantic World, 1400–1680*, Cambridge: Cambridge University Press, 1992.

13 Paul E. Lovejoy, *Transformations in Slavery: A History of Slavery in Africa*, Cambridge: Cambridge University Press, 2000; David Brion Davis, *Inhuman Bondage: The Rise and Fall of Slavery in the New World*, New York: Oxford University Press, 2005.

14 Francis Galton coined the term 'nature versus nurture', and championed the idea that if people procreated more selectively, the species would keep improving. His ideas of eugenics remained popular through the Second World War. Herbert Spencer is considered the father of social Darwinism, and coined the phrase 'survival of the fittest'.

15 Cecil Rhodes's *Confession of Faith* is an excellent, if extreme, example of common racial ideology and its connections to imperialism in the late nineteenth century. He argues that the English are the finest race in the world, and that they have a responsibility to subdue, civilize and otherwise control the inferior and savage races across the globe. See Robert I. Rotberg, *The Founder Cecil Rhodes and the Pursuit of Power*, New York: Oxford University Press, 1988.

16 Hale has argued that, particularly in France in the late nineteenth century, black Africans were regarded as the most uncivilized, North Africans were 'mysterious' and Indochinese were industrious and gentle. These classifications were based overwhelmingly on second hand racial imagery and an ingrained culture already fascinated with orientalist 'primitivism'.

Dana Hale, *Races on Display: French Representations of Colonized Peoples 1886–1940*, Bloomington: Indiana University Press, 2008. See also Alice Conklin, *A Mission to Civilize: The Republican Idea of Empire in France and West Africa, 1895–1930*, Stanford: Stanford University Press, 1997.

17 Although Bernard Porter has contested this, most scholars acknowledge that there was, to varying degrees, an 'imperial culture' within Britain that was embraced by its citizens. For more on this debate, see Bernard Porter, *The Absentminded Imperialists: Empire, Society, and Culture in Britain*, Oxford: Oxford University Press, 2005; and John MacKenzie, *Propaganda and Empire: The Manipulation of British Public Opinion, 1880–1960*, Manchester: Manchester University Press, 1988.

18 See Linda Colley, *Britons: Forging the Nation 1707–1837*, New Haven: Yale University Press, 1994; Jennifer Pitts, *A Turn to Empire: The Rise of Imperial Liberalism in Britain and France*, Princeton: Princeton University Press, 2005.

19 See Julie Roy Jeffrey, *Abolitionists Remember: Antislavery Autobiographies and the Unfinished Work of Emancipation*, Chapel Hill: UNC Press, 2008; Jean Fagan Yellin, *Women and Sisters: The Antislavery Feminists in American Culture*, New Haven: Yale University Press, 1992.

20 Slavery was abolished in England in 1772 and in France in 1794 under Jacobin rule in the Revolution. Slavery in the United States was not abolished until 1865. Although many forms of slavery persist in the present day, legal chattel slavery in the West is the most analogous to the situation of the Ood in the Whoniverse.

21 For a theoretical, policy perspective on this issue, see Iris Marion Young, *Justice and the Politics of Difference*, Princeton: Princeton University Press, 1990.

22 Said, *Orientalism*.

23 Matthew Day, "Godless Savages and Superstitious Dogs: Charles Darwin, Imperial Ethnography, and the Problem of Human Uniqueness", *Journal of the History of Ideas*, 69, 1 (2008), 49–70.

Chapter 14

Doctor Who and the critique of western imperialism

John Vohlidka

B y the 1970s, the sun was setting on the British Empire. This required the British public to adopt a new world view defining its place in history. Britain's view of itself was left without a rudder and the public needed a new form of self-identification defining their wants, values and composition. *Doctor Who* helped fill this need. When the original series began airing, it was a reflection of a society that still had not made sense of its place in the world, particularly and specifically concerning its post-imperial phase. This reflection demonstrates that, as a society, the British remained uncertain as to their role with the loss of their empire bringing about conflicting opinions and emotions.[1] This decade saw the coming of age of the first generation less engaged in British imperialism and freer to confront it directly as a critique. The series created a dialogue with the audience to confront these issues.[2]

With the Empire in its last throes, the show was capable of addressing imperialism head on. This article will look at four stories from the 1970s: *Colony in Space* (1971); *The Mutants* (1972); *The Face of Evil* (1977); and *The Power of Kroll* (1978–79). These stories were meant not just to entertain, but also to create a dialogue with the British viewers over issues of racism, capitalism and technology in an imperialist context. While the stories were decidedly anti-imperialist and anti-racist in intent, the different perspectives of the writers meant that the programme's message on these issues varied. Often, these stories fell into a racist trap: arguing against imperialism but from a pro-western view.

The four stories deal directly with the themes of imperialism, colonialism and racism in what I call the 'Imperialist Model'. The 'Imperialist Model' is a storyline within a set situation containing a conflict between two groups: one that is portrayed in the story as 'civilized', a group or society whose attributes are defined by technology, city-style culture and rationalism, and the other as 'native', a group or society whose attributes are defined as being 'close' to nature (living off the land) or described in the story as 'primitive' or 'savage'. Natives are usually portrayed as misunderstood non-technological victims of an excessive western capitalistic system. They are not necessarily portrayed as non-white (often they are white actors, masked or in bright green make-up), but they function as non-white victims of imperialism for the purpose of the stories. This conflict is characterized by distrust, violence, racism and exploitation of one group by the other. Into this mix comes the Doctor, whose primary role is to end the conflict, usually aiding the 'native' society against the 'civilized' one. The Doctor, as the main character and the 'hero', serves as a model of correct behaviour and as a guide for the audience through these tensions.[3]

Background

While we may think of the series as being about whatever time or place the TARDIS lands, it is really a reflection of British society at the time the serials were produced. This is not a particularly new idea. John Tulloch and Manuel Alvarado argued that the show was capable of presenting ideological values of the liberal/consensual type.[4] John Fiske examined *Doctor Who* as a textual work, noting that the popularity of such a text stemmed from its reflection of the corresponding ideologies of the audience.[5] John Kenneth Muir argued that *Doctor Who* presented an ethical perspective that was anti-empire and pro-democracy.[6] While Alan McKee's 2004 study showed *Doctor Who* is not political to a small sampling surveyed, that does not mean the series did not reflect the current political and cultural climate in the time it was produced. Nor does it mean the show had no impact on shaping the opinions, values or emotions of any audience members.[7] John R. Cook and Peter Wright pointed out that television in a general sense constituted cultural criticism.[8] Finally, Alec Charles argued that a significant portion of the series is either pro-imperialist (or nostalgic) in nature or presented imperialists as good-natured bumblers.[9]

The Doctor represents science in these four serials. This is particularly true of the Third Doctor (Jon Pertwee) portrayed first and foremost as a scientist, and to a lesser extent, the Fourth Doctor (Tom Baker), whose representation as a scientist was lessened somewhat by his charismatic personality, but nevertheless tended to represent science in many of his stories. Pertwee's Doctor was even visually reminiscent (with his frills and cape), of the great scientific age, the Enlightenment.[10] Baker's Doctor was more eclectic, suggestive of those Bohemian intellectuals of the early nineteenth century.[11] As a true (or 'goodie') scientist, the Doctor is a champion of western ideals who sides with the natives/victims to liberate them. In a stereotypical bit of benevolent racism, the Doctor (the white scientist) uses his superior western scientific knowledge to liberate the inferior natives.

Historical context

Post-war Britain was typified by a period of economic hardship beginning in the late 1940s, followed by a period of limited economic prosperity that began in the 1960s.[12] The British Empire did not end overnight. Initial decolonization began under the Atlee government in 1945. After the disastrous attempt to retake the Suez Canal in 1956 under Anthony Eden, Britain was humiliated and made to appear an American satellite.[13] Margaret Thatcher referred to the political mindset that followed as "Suez Syndrome."[14] In 1960, Harold Macmillan referred to "the wind of change blowing through this continent" while speaking in Cape Town.[15] This marked the beginning of an acceleration of decolonization. This decolonization was mainly peaceful disengagement, although some colonies turned towards civil war.

By the 1970s, decolonization was not yet complete, although comparatively few colonies remained. This resulted in a British society that was left in a confused state. Their great empire was, for liberal internationalists, in its last throes.[16] Some British thinkers were wistful of the glory days of Great Britain.[17] Some people were glad of the new direction Britain was taking, while others directed hostility towards new immigrants entering the country.[18] In short, Britain was in a state of cultural and political flux with its population divided over imperialism.

Britain in the late 1960s and early 1970s was in a state of transition. It was becoming a multiracial society as subjects from the ex-colonies were migrating to Britain and assuming full British citizenship thanks to the British Nationality Act of 1947. Britain also had become socially fragmented. The affluence and apparent public contentment of the 1960s was starting to crack by the early 1970s; racial tensions resulting from these new migrations, runaway inflation, and terrorist bombings were heralding darker times ahead.[19] These tensions influenced *Doctor Who*.[20]

Colony in Space

Colony in Space, by Malcolm Hulke, was primarily an adventure story in which the Doctor and Jo try to foil arch-villain the Master's attempt to acquire a doomsday weapon, and get caught up in a dispute between some Earth colonists and the Interplanetary Mining Corporation (IMC). In this story, the importance of the once great indigenous peoples, now called Primitives, is downplayed: they communicate telepathically so do not speak; they attack the main characters and are generally portrayed as 'simple' or in a state of 'degeneration'. In fact, the overall attitude towards the natives of Uxarieus is that they are primitive. The colonists treat them with wary respect, but many are quick to believe IMC's chicanery that the natives are deceitful and hostile. Even the Doctor is somewhat contemptuous of their culture. Upon the Master's explanation of how the natives had degenerated, the Doctor remarks, "I see. So the super-race became *priests* of a lunatic religion worshipping machines instead of gods." This is not the Doctor respecting other peoples' belief systems. To worship a machine is 'lunacy' in his opinion.[21] In the end, the natives make the ultimate sacrifice asking the Doctor to destroy the weapon so it cannot be used for evil, showing they are truly more civilized than thought.

In Hulke's story, the Doctor seems less concerned about the Primitives (what would happen to them if the colonists were successful and multiplied is not even discussed) than he is about the colonists and IMC.[22] This main storyline can be seen to have a number of parallels with the American colonies and their War of Independence. Many Americans in favour of breaking away from England felt their homeland was unjustly exploiting them and the resources of the colonies. Crown and Parliament were more concerned with profit through taxes, gathering of raw materials/natural resources, and seeing the colonies as a market for British goods, than creating a better homeland for the settlers. For the purposes of *Colony in Space*, the colonists (Americans) are intruded upon by IMC (British Parliament) in the name of commercialism. The colonists settled on Uxarieus hoping to establish a new life based on the ideals of freedom, self-government and independence, similar to why many European settlers moved to America. Their goal is to create a new and hopefully better life away from a crowded Earth. IMC is only interested in pillaging the land for its valuable minerals and resources. Their interests are primarily economic, much as the British Parliament (which was closely allied with business interests) in the 1760s and 1770s saw the Thirteen Colonies primarily as a source of revenue and sought to dominate their economic systems.[23] "What's good for IMC is good for Earth," says the IMC's Captain Dent, reinforcing the economic-political connection. In contrast, the colonists in both this story and colonial America are willing to fight for their new home and their ideals. In this story, the colonist's leader gives his own life to outsmart IMC, allowing the other colonists to remain on the planet. As in the War of Independence, *Colony in Space* sees a ragtag group of colonists fight a well uniformed (with red as the primary colour), armed and skilled enemy to protect their liberty and way of life. In the end, ideals win out over greed.[24]

Neither side, however, seems particularly concerned with the Primitives. In this sense, the Primitives take on the role of Native Americans ('Indians') who figure incidentally in the storyline as they did in histories of the War of Independence.[25] In popular history, Native Americans were rarely considered a factor in the American War of Independence despite it being just as much a war for their land and sovereignty as for the colonists or British to retain control of the land from which they drove the 'Indians'. Colonists have shaky truces with the 'Indians'/Primitives, yet are not all that trusting of them. Dent uses the power of rumour to sow seeds of distrust by sending a fake colonist in to describe how his settlement was attacked by Primitives. It is really this imposter who murders a colonist and his native assistant, claiming he killed the Primitive after witnessing him murder the human and attempting sabotage. The other colonists are more willing to believe the story of the white stranger than their own past experience with the benevolent native.

Distrust, fear and propaganda overshadowed how Native Americans were viewed. The famous Boston Tea Party had colonists dress as 'Indians' to hide their identity. IMC uses the Primitives as pawns, pretending they are attacking, even killing, colonists. Propaganda in the American colonies played up 'Indian' attacks and put the British behind stirring them up. The US Declaration of Independence accused King George III of exciting "domestic insurrections amongst us and [endeavouring] to bring on the inhabitants of our frontiers, the merciless Indian Savages."[26]

While *Colony in Space* was clearly dealing with imperialism, it is primarily concerned with the colonists and their revolution (even the doomsday weapon, the whole reason for the Time Lords sending the Doctor to Uxarieus, is only dealt with at the very end of the story). The Primitives, whose appearance in the story is full of racist undertones (their skin colour, the colonist's easily awakened distrust of them), are not focused on in the story. They are present, but have little impact on the narrative, except to occasionally complicate matters, and are the guardians of the weapon. Some colonists get substantial character development, while the Primitives get none.

The Mutants

According to director Christopher Barry, *The Mutants*, written by Bob Baker and Dave Martin, was supposed to be a satire of the British Empire, but that aspect was later played down.[27] Nevertheless, it is clear that topics of imperialism, racism and science permeate the story. This critique of empire also critiques certain aspects of western civilization. Western civilization is an elusive concept, tricky to nail down.[28] Its definition is both complex and paradoxical, containing a number of different elements that sometimes contradict each other, and changes through time as well. For example, one aspect of western civilization is imperialism combined with racism particularly during the nineteenth and early twentieth centuries, but then so is the rejection of those concepts in the late twentieth century. This story is a western critique of the West's previous practices.

The racial tension in *The Mutants* is between the humans, called the Overlords (imperialists), and the Solonians (natives). Atmospheric changes made by the Overlords are interfering with the natural life-cycle of the Solonians, transforming them into insect-like Mutts. The Overlords in charge of Skybase use race (particularly illustrated by segregated teleportation tubes) as a marker to define the cultural differences between themselves and the Solonians.[29] The Solonians are seen by the Overlords as a conquered people who are racially inferior. The Marshal takes advantage of this by playing different groups against each other and fostering distrust and hatred towards the Mutts, demonizing them in moves designed to keep himself in control of the conquered people. He goes so far as to frame Solonian Ky for murder, in a move to cement his authority and distrust of the natives. It is really Varan, another Solonian and rival of Ky, who the Marshal employed to arrange the murder. This is historically a classic move of empires to keep subject peoples at odds with each other, dating back at least as far as the Romans dealing with the Germanic Cherusci in the first century.[30] The Marshal clearly represents all the evils of imperialism, and, by implication, western civilization. He is portrayed as greedy, fat and self-centred. He wants to make Solos hospitable to humans. Doing so would be to his benefit and keep him in charge, basically creating his own empire. Demonstrating the West's addiction to comfort, with aide from scientist Jaeger, he prepares to change Solos's atmosphere, committing genocide to keep his comfortable position and give humans a planet where they can breathe in comfort.[31]

Breathing in comfort might not seem an outlandish idea on the surface. Consider this: a society having the technology to build and maintain Skybase obviously has the skills for artificial atmosphere within dwellings. The humans in the story live in the enclosed environment on Skybase. Why not just build a domed city protected from the Mutts and toxic air outside? The long run of *Doctor Who* is peppered with examples of self-contained, enclosed living environments (*The Ark*, 1966; *Midnight*, 2008). Being able to go outdoors and breathe the air is a luxury in this respect. Jaeger and the Marshal are prepared to commit genocide for something which is not necessary for human survival, only desired.[32]

While the Marshal is the stereotypical 'bad' imperialist, the Doctor is another western stereotype. The Doctor represents the purity of science coupled with moral superiority.[33]

He and Jo are thrust into the middle of the dispute. Seeing injustice, the Doctor cannot resist getting involved. He attempts to stop the Marshal, fighting for what is right and against what he sees as an abuse of science. He is thus the white hero who saves the day for the poor natives.

While attempting to be a commentary on the British Empire, Baker and Martin's story falls into a racist trap. The Solonians are depicted as a primitive people being taken advantage of by the Marshal. Despite their apparent longing for independence as shown with the actions of the rebel leader Ky, they were incapable of changing their situation until the white scientist (the Doctor) shows them the way. It requires the superior scientific knowledge of the Doctor (and human Professor Sondergaard to a lesser degree) to free the Solonians, by showing them how to transform themselves into a higher state of being rather than Mutts, and therefore achieve independence. It is only once Ky is transformed (thanks to the Doctor and Sondergaard) into an ethereal being that he is able to destroy the Marshal and free his people. To use an old imperialist term, they need to be civilized to be independent. That the Solonians are backward natives is demonstrated by the point that they were unaware that the mutations were part of their own natural order of things, despite the fact it was apparently part of their natural life-cycle.[34] It requires the Doctor's interference to act as a catalyst.

In counterpoint to this, human Professor Jaeger is portrayed as someone who has sacrificed his scientific credentials in order to obey the Marshal's plans. When the Doctor tricks Jaeger to make his escape, it is seen as deserved since Jaeger has strayed from the path of science by lending his talents to an excessive capitalistic imperial endeavour. This compromises his scientific ability, which is demonstrated by his inferior scientific skills (his increasing reliance on the Doctor, his inability to follow much of what the Doctor does in the lab, how he is easily tricked by the Doctor) compared to the Doctor, who is scientifically and morally superior.[35] In contrast, Sondergaard actually conforms to the popular culture stereotype of the good scientist as 'maverick' by separating from his fellows and 'going native' to help them.[36] The Doctor's willingness to work with him reinforces this.

Both *Colony in Space* and *The Mutants* are criticisms of the British imperial system. Why critique what was essentially a past event? As Jeremy Black pointed out, "an organic appreciation [of historical movements] ensures that past events become present grievances and thus wrongs to be righted in the future."[37] In other words, these stories were not just critiques of Britain's past behaviour, but also a criticism of current behaviour. As the villains in both stories are either corporate stooges or connected to business in some way, the stories are a means to criticize globalization. *The Mutants* also critiques racism at home. Large numbers of immigrants had arrived in Britain in the last decade and a considerable number of Britons were not happy about it. Enoch Powell warned darkly of "rivers of blood" years earlier and had predicted an "explosion" early in 1971, the year the story was written.[38] Powell clearly had some grass roots support. His "rivers of blood" speech got him dismissed from the Shadow Cabinet, but he received over 100,000 letters of support.[39] The character of the Marshal was clearly designed to reflect this view, as typified by his intolerance/racism towards the Solonians, and the treating of the Mutts as diseased. The other Earthlings in the story easily believe his lies, despite rather sketchy evidence. Their willingness to believe seems largely based on their inherent distrust of indigenous peoples. The envoy sent to investigate matters at Skybase appears wary of the Marshal at first. Once he catches sight of a Mutt, he shifts his full support behind the Marshal.

The writers of each story have their own take on imperialism and how they portray it. *Colony in Space* is a straightforward, old-fashioned, underdog-triumphs story. Hulke, who was born in 1924, grew up with the British Empire still intact and meaningful to many of that generation. He reaches back to an old example (American colonists versus Britain) of imperialism. While his story is anti-imperialist with the British Empire as the bad guy, it hearkens back to history for the basis of its critique and typically ignores the inherent racism embedded in the empire during his youth. The focus of his critique is thus historical, avoiding the messiness of racism demonstrated in nineteenth-century imperialism. Baker and Martin, born in 1939 and 1935 respectively, were from a younger generation. Coming of age in the 1950s, they would have been more disconnected from the responsibilities of empire and freer to be more critical of it. This could account for their more cartoonish portrayal of the Marshal as a wannabe dictator with expansionist dreams who wants to eliminate an entire race standing in his way.

The imperialist critique in the Pertwee years was direct and straightforward. If anything, the characterization was a little over the top. The character of Captain Dent is a clearly uncaring capitalist focused only on profit over human lives. The Marshal is portrayed as a blatant racist, who hates the Solonians just because they are different and in his way. No deeper cause of his hatred is explored. Later stories during the Baker era, however, are more nuanced. Both *The Face of Evil* and *The Power of Kroll* had a slightly more complicated take on a similar set-up.

The Face of Evil

By 1977, Britain was becoming more insular and less involved in colonialism (most of the former colonies were now gone). This is reflected in Chris Boucher's *The Face of Evil* being a studio-bound story relying on sets and lighting to portray a dark and moody planet. While not a true imperialist tale, it demonstrates the evils of technology run amok in a colonial context.

This story is essentially tension between two peoples, the Sevateem and the Tesh. The twist is that both are being manipulated by the same source – the computer of a crash-landed spaceship, Xoanon – which the Doctor had repaired long ago and inadvertently driven mad. Xoanon split the crew into the survey team (Sevateem) and the technicians (Tesh) and had them war on each other. While the Sevateem initially appear to be the more 'native' and less intellectual of the two groups, relying on nature for everything from shelter to weapons, living in huts with dirt floors and using poisonous thorns to kill, it is the Tesh who eventually are shown to be set in their ways, unquestioningly worshipping a computer.

The uniformed Tesh appear more 'civilized' with their telepathic powers, white hallways, technology and calm, organized behaviour, but they actually turn out to be as brutal as the supposedly inferior, more 'savage' Sevateem.[40] The Tesh are the more rigid, finding it difficult to comprehend anything outside their belief system; conformity appears to be a central aspect of their lives, as demonstrated by their lack of emotion and that everyone wears the same uniform. The Sevateem are more individualistic; a number of characters are shown to have conflicting motivations and goals. Even Neeva, the high priest of the Sevateem, demonstrates an ability to grow mentally, turning against the mad computer/god. In this, Boucher condemns western civilization and its worship of the new and the technological, warning that contemporary viewers are in danger of replacing their own belief systems with the worship of science and technology, which would be a blow against individual liberties.[41]

In the Imperialist Model, the Tesh represent the imperialists. They can be seen as an example of 'white man's prestige'. To keep control over natives, the British thought they had to dress a certain way, have a well-maintained home, stick together and have a stiff upper lip. This is reflected in the Tesh's style of living and lack of emotion. British imperialists believed that emotion was destructive to their mystique.[42] Likewise, the Sevateem represent the natives. To further accentuate this, Louise Jameson was originally going to wear dark make-up as Leela, and several test shots of this were done before the idea was dropped.[43]

Boucher's story is also a condemnation of a particular aspect of British imperialism: the White Man's Burden. This was the argument that white Europeans had a duty to colonize other parts of the world to bring native peoples the benefits of western civilization. This form of benevolent racism was still racism and presupposed that the other non-white civilization was inferior. The story demonstrates that this sort of thinking led to meddling with other cultures (the Doctor fixing the computer and unintentionally leaving his imprint on it) that was not to their advantage, leading to strife and even civil war. The troubles in *The Face of Evil* were caused by the Doctor. "I thought I was helping them," he says, realizing his fault. His interference led to driving the computer mad, which led to the divisions of the Sevateem and the Tesh and their civil war. This also demonstrates a more mature understanding of the role of science in society. Science is not necessarily good or right, it depends on how it is used. The Doctor, the scientist, misuses his knowledge (albeit accidentally), leading to division and strife.

Most of the former British colonies did not turn to civil war after decolonization. Rhodesia had, however, and a civil war was raging there throughout the 1970s when this story was written and transmitted. Boucher's argument for the cure of the White Man's Burden is seen in the Doctor's actions that resolve the story. Unlike *The Mutants*, where the Doctor's pivotal role is to act, his role is the opposite in *The Face of Evil*. He wipes his personality from the computer core. In other words, he takes himself out of the equation. This is a full endorsement of decolonization. The only cure to the miseries created by British imperialism is to pull out of the colonies. Instead of fixing the problem, the white hero has to leave.[44]

The Power of Kroll

The Power of Kroll, by Robert Holmes, essentially follows the same pattern as *The Mutants*, but is more nuanced in its approach. Apart from being a tighter story (four episodes compared to six) it also shows greater complexity in its characterization and therefore has a different moral. *The Power of Kroll* comes in the middle of the 'parody' phase of *Doctor Who*.[45] There is clearly a satirical air to Holmes's story that particularly relates to European imperialism in Africa. Of note is the character of Rohm Dutt, who is dressed for the African bush (strange attire for someone visiting a swamp) à la Alan Quatermain from the H. Rider Haggard stories. Unlike the Primitives who were in costume or the Solonians who were all white males, *Kroll*'s native 'Swampies' are essentially humanoid with green skin and dyed knitted wool for hair. They are also referred to as having been relocated (like Native Americans or Australian Aboriginal peoples).[46]

Although visually more outlandish than the Solonians, the Swampies' characterization is more varied. While their leader appears mired in superstition, others of the tribe demonstrate a more sceptical attitude, particularly toward the Swampie god, Kroll, a giant squid. Also, as in *The Mutants*, those imperialists not in charge and younger seem more tolerant and understanding toward the natives. The same can be said of the younger Swampies, who question why there cannot be peace with the imperialist methane miners. The younger characters dare to ask why they do not get along. They were not instilled since birth with the imperialist rhetoric.

John Kenneth Muir compares the story with *King Kong* (1933): tribal natives worship a gigantic creature as their god and offer it a white woman (Romana) as a sacrifice. There is much more to the story than this. Muir notes that the story deals with race hatred, genocide and land exploitation and compares the Swampies with Native Americans.[47] The Swampies are already displaced onto a reservation and face being moved again or extinguished because they are at odds with Thrawn, the leader of the methane refinery. As in history, the Swampies' claim to the land is disregarded and the land is considered as *terra nullius*, or unowned land, because they did not develop it in a western fashion.[48] The miners' intention to exploit the land gives them, in their opinion, a superior claim to the land for the benefit of civilization. The story is calling into question the attributes and moral values of western civilization. As in *The Mutants*, the Doctor's position on civilization is ambiguous.

FENNER: Tell me. Would you let a small band of semi-savages stand in the way of Progress?

THE DOCTOR: Well 'progress' is a very flexible word. It can mean just about anything you want it to mean.

Miner Fenner is clearly attempting to equate civilization with progress. The Enlightenment saw progress as a concept closely linked with western science and referred to the creation of a better future through science. This definition lasted until the second half of the twentieth century when the term became more ambiguous.[49] The Doctor's comment about the term's flexibility exposes this sham for what it was: a term used to justify anything. The Doctor thus damns the desacralization of this word and consequently how progress as a scientific term had been hijacked by outside interests, particularly the trend towards a single global marketplace. He thus demonstrates that what Fenner means by progress is exploitation.

This is a stronger condemnation than anything Pertwee's Doctor says in *The Mutants*. When told that the Marshal's plan to change Solos's atmosphere would result in the extinction of the natives, he responds: "Genocide as a side effect! You ought to write a paper on that Professor." Pertwee's Doctor is making a distinct condemnation towards the bastardization of science being used for illicit or immoral purposes. It is also fairly academic in nature. While he is condemning Jaeger, he does so in 'academic' terms (writing of a scholarly paper), arguing that Jaeger is retreating from the reality of what he is doing into the safety of his position as an academic. Baker's Doctor however is making a comment towards all of society which fits in with the general dissatisfaction[50] of the later 1970s.

The Power of Kroll was a satire of imperialism and decolonization. The Swampies appear to be a group of 'savages' mired in superstition and their worship of Kroll. But a number of them demonstrate, in the terms of the story, a growing and healthy scepticism towards Kroll, demanding to know from their high priest why Kroll attacked them as well as their enemies. This is similar but distinct from *The Face of Evil* where the only members of the Sevateem to doubt Xoanon do so for personal reasons (either personal affection for Leela on the part of Tomas, or Calib who sought to wrest leadership of the tribe). In both stories, however, scepticism is seen as a virtue, in keeping with the scientific nature of the stories while at the same time making a rationalist judgement about native cultures. This, in effect, promotes modernity (rationalism, efficiency, scepticism) as superior to tradition (fatalism, indiscipline, adherence to custom) and modernity is an important aspect of western dominance.[51] So while this 'scepticism' is presented as a positive trait, it is only positive from a western view. Along with *The Mutants*, these two stories also fall into a racist trap.

The satire of decolonization is found in the resolution in *The Power of Kroll*. The solution to Kroll himself and the destruction he causes is for the Doctor to touch him with the Key to Time tracer, transferring Kroll's power into a Key to Time segment and reverting him back to an ordinary squid. In other words, the white hero must remove the outside contamination to put things right with what is essentially a magic wand.

The Power of Kroll and *The Face of Evil* can be seen to be on almost opposite sides of the spectrum: one is nature run amok (the giant squid); the other technology (the mad computer). Holmes, born in 1928, is from the same generation as Hulke, but, unlike Hulke, he brings a somewhat jaundiced bent to his stories. As in *The Sun Makers* (1977) from the season before, Holmes uses satire to mock not just imperialism and racism, but simplistic story conventions that purport to be solutions to such issues. This story is similar to the 'damsel in distress' action stories (such as those by Edgar Wallace), which were popular during his youth, with the modern twist of science thrown in, combined with both an homage to the giant monster films of the 1950s and 1960s and a tongue-in-cheek mocking of those conventions. Comparatively, Boucher, born in 1943, is the youngest of the authors dealt with in this essay. His story deals the most with technology. He grew up in a world fully aware of the true danger/power of science thanks to the atomic bomb. He was part of the first generation to experience the rapid rise of technology in the western lifestyle. Unlike Baker and Martin's story where science is the solution, it is the villain in Boucher's story. He suggests that it is the removal of the contamination of western science (and, in a sense, the white influence, since it is the Doctor's imprint driving the computer mad) that is the solution to heal the evils caused by imperialism.

Conclusion

The four stories are all allegories of British imperialism which was in its final phase. British society was uncertain as to its place in the world and as to how it felt about its now nearly defunct empire. These stories demonstrate a wide range of opinions on how to deal with the loss of prestige, racism and other issues confronting society.

Colony in Space represented an older view of colonialism from an eighteenth century Euro-American perspective. In Hulke's story, the colonists, not natives, fought for and demonstrated their right for self-rule. *The Mutants* was an outright and blatant critique of the British Empire from younger writers arguing against those who lamented the empire's fall. The story, in which the Marshal was described as 'mad', argues that anyone in favour of the empire was mad as well. In other words, imperialism itself, it is argued, is a form of madness. The solutions suggested by the story however, were a trap. The story argued even greater interference was necessary to end the evils of colonialism. By the mid-1970s, Boucher's *The Face of Evil* argued for the merits of decolonization, suggesting not everyone in society felt that way. This story argued that outside (read British) meddling in other cultures whether for the purposes of benevolence or the attributes of science, merely resulted in a chaotic native culture. The only cure was outsiders removing themselves from the equation. *Doctor Who* is a fantasy, and that is particularly true of the solution to this story. The Doctor, using science and technology (showing technology is a double-edged sword and its 'goodness' depends on how it is used) is able to remove all traces of his interference. This is an unrealistic solution in reality, where cultural cross-contamination is pervasive and varied and therefore impossible to remove. *The Power of Kroll* was a satirical look at decolonization. Again, as in *The Face of Evil* and unlike the first two stories, modernity is taken to task. Imperialism did not help the Swampies and 'progress' was prepared to sweep them aside. Only the fantasy solution of the Doctor, who stands outside such dilemmas, is able to provide a resolution.

The show's position on imperialism (and racism inside the Imperialist Model) was not consistent; nor could it be considering the variety of people involved in producing the show during that decade. It is interesting to note that the show's criticism of imperialism became more subtle as the decade wore on. This reflected British society's confusion in the early 1970s over the loss of empire and the emerging challenges of their newly integrated immigrant population. Britons wished for quick fixes to the problems, as demonstrated in the first two stories discussed. By the late 1970s, the British people, influenced by economic recession, IRA bombings and widespread strikes, knew quick and easy solutions were a fantasy. The later stories epitomized this feeling by shifting to the more absurd for their resolutions. This reflected how society had become less enamoured by easy fixes as well.

Doctor Who became an anchor of British popular culture. It created a dialogue for its viewers; presenting varied opinions on a subject that still would have been a talking point at the time. The show's messages were not always consistent, but it gave its viewers, young and old alike, something to think about.

Notes

1   Christine Cornea, "British Science Fiction Television in the Discursive Context of Second Wave Feminism", *Genders*, 54 (2011), 22.
2   James Chapman, *Inside The TARDIS: The Worlds Of Doctor Who*, New York: I.B. Tauris, 2006, 5.
3   Chapman firmly places the Doctor in the liberal tradition. Chapman, *Inside The TARDIS*, 7.
4   John Tulloch and Manuel Alvarado, *Doctor Who: The Unfolding Text*, New York: St. Martin's Press, 1983, 182.
5   John Fiske, "Popularity and Ideology: A Structuralist Reading of *Doctor Who*", in Willard D. Rowland, Jr. and Bruce Watkins, eds., *Interpreting Television: Current Research Perspectives*, Beverly Hills: Sage Publications, 1984, 196.
6   John Kenneth Muir, *A Critical History of Doctor Who on Television*, Jefferson: McFarland & Company, 1999, 58.
7   McKee's study was done in 2001, twelve years after the last episode of the classic series, and so consequently, much of the political meaning of the stories, particularly the older ones would have been lost. For his study and results see Alan McKee, "Is *Doctor Who* Political?", *European Journal of Cultural Studies*, 7, 2 (2004), 201–17.
8   John R. Cook and Peter Wright, "'Futures past': An introduction to and brief survey of British science fiction television", in John R. Cook and Peter Wright, eds., *British Science Fiction Television: A Hitchhiker's Guide*, New York: I.B. Tauris, 2006, 1–20.
9   Alec Charles, "The Ideology of Anachronism: Television, History and the Nature of Time", in David Butler, ed., *Time and Relative Dissertations in Space, Critical Perspectives on Doctor Who*, New York: Manchester University Press, 2007, 119.
10 Tulloch and Alvarado describe Pertwee's cloak as "Victorian." Tulloch and Alvarado, *The Unfolding Text*, 110.
11 Tulloch and Alvarado, *The Unfolding Text*, 100. Peter B. Gregg, "England Looks to the Future: The Cultural Forum Model and *Doctor Who*", *The Journal of Popular Culture*, 37, 4 (2004), 652.

12 Several authors have written about this. Cornea, "British Science Fiction Television", 20–40; Alan Sked and Chris Cook, *Post-War Britain: A Political History*, New York: Penguin Books, 1990.

13 Robert Rhodes James, "Anthony Eden and the Suez Crisis", *History Today*, 36, 11 (1986), 8–15. See also Nicholas White, "The Business and the Politics of Decolonization: The British Experience in the Twentieth Century", *Economic History Review*, 53, 3 (2000), 544–64.

14 Anon., "The Suez Crisis: An Affair to Remember", *The Economist*, 27 July 2006.

15 Lawrence James, *The Rise and Fall of the British Empire*, London: Abacus, 2008, 616.

16 Ian Hall, "The Revolt against the West: Decolonisation and its Representatives in British International Thought, 1945–75", *The International History Review*, 33, 1 (2011), 43.

17 Hall, "The Revolt against the West", 58.

18 For a discussion of British response to the fall of the empire see Hall, "The Revolt against the West", 43–64.

19 Cornea, "British Science Fiction Television", 22.

20 Cornea, "British Science Fiction Television", 23.

21 Hulke, a former member of the British Communist party, might have been making a comment on religion in general. See Dipaolo for a discussion on Hulke's *The Silurians* as outsiders (968–69). Marc Edward Dipaolo, "Political Satire and British–American Relations in Five Decades of *Doctor Who*", *The Journal of Popular Culture*, 43, 5 (2010), 964–87.

22 Muir sees *Colony in Space* as a western-style frontier story, with the colonists as settlers fighting the mining company which represents greed (from the 'East') with hostile Primitives (read: Native Americans) thrown into the mix. I argue here that the story has greater parallels with the British American colonies and the War of Independence. Western frontier stories share a number of tropes with stories from the American colonies. Muir, *Critical History*, 191.

23 The theory that the American War of Independence was economically motivated dates from before 1800. Two of the most well-known contributions to this theory in US historiography include George Bancroft's *History of the United States from the Discovery of the American Continent* (1852) and Charles A. Beard's *An Economic Interpretation of the Constitution* (1913) and the theory continues to have its adherents. For a discussion of economic interpretations of American independence see Staughton Lynd and David Waldstreicher, "Free Trade, Sovereignty, and Slavery: Toward an Economic Interpretation of American Independence", *The William and Mary Quarterly*, 68, 4 (2011), 597–630.

24 Muir even refers to this as a 'revolution' story. Muir, *Critical History*, 191.

25 C. G. Calloway discusses the peripheral treatment Native Americans received in historical accounts of the War of Independence. C. G. Calloway, "'We have always been the Frontier': The American Revolution in Shawnee Country", *American Indian Quarterly*, 16, 1 (1992), 39–52. A rare exception is David Levinson, "An Explanation for the Oneida-Colonist Alliance in the American Revolution", *Ethnohistory*, 23, 3 (1976), 265–89.

26 *Declaration of Independence*, 1776.

27 David J. Howe, Mark Stammers and Stephen James Walker, *Doctor Who: The Seventies*, London: Doctor Who Books, 1994, 50.

28 Ian Buruma and Avishai Margalit, *Occidentalism: The West in the Eyes of its Enemies*, New York: The Penguin Press, 2004, 2.

29 Turchin discusses markers and fault lines as ways cultures differentiate from each other. Peter Turchin, *War and Peace and War: The Life Cycles of Imperial Nations*, New York: Pi Press, 2006, 54.

30 Cornelius Tacitus, *Annales*, Book I, 54. Original Latin and English translation available from Alfred John Church and William Jackson Brodribb, eds., "Cornelius Tacitus: *The Annals*" ([1942] n.d.), *Perseus Digital Library*. Retrieved 19 August 2012 at http://www.perseus.tufts.edu/hopper/text?doc=Perseus%3Atext%3A1999.02.0078%3Abook%3D1%3Achapter%3D54.

31 It is worth noting that addiction to comfort is a widespread criticism of the West, and one that is shared within western cultures as well. Buruma and Margalit, *Occidentalism*, 53.

32 Buruma and Margalit, *Occidentalism*, 53.

33 Orthia discusses the Doctor's role as being morally superior due to his scientific ability. Lindy A. Orthia, "'Sociopathetic abscess' or 'yawning chasm'? The absent postcolonial transition in *Doctor Who*", *The Journal of Commonwealth Literature*, 45, 2 (2010), 207–25.

34 Cultural worthiness as determined by conformity to Enlightenment principles is discussed in Orthia, "'Sociopathetic abscess' or 'yawning chasm'?", 212.

35 Jaeger comes close to what Orthia describes as an "incompetent pretender." Lindy A. Orthia, "Antirationalist critique or fifth column of scientism? Challenges from *Doctor Who* to the Mad Scientist Trope", *Public Understanding of Science*, 20, 4 (2011), 525–42.

36 For a discussion of popular culture conceptions of scientists see Christopher Frayling, "Curse of the Scientist!", *New Scientist*, 187, 2518 (2005), 48–50.

37 Jeremy Black, "Contesting the Past", *History*, 93, 310 (2008), 226.

38 Anon., "Enoch Powell's 'Rivers of Blood' Speech", *The Telegraph*, 6 November 2007.

39 Sked and Cook, *Post-War Britain*, 232.

40 'Civilized' and 'savage' are used here in terms of the story but they form a part of a larger discourse that is common in western civilization and wars of empire. The enemy is frequently categorized as 'savage' as opposed to the 'civilized' oppressors. For a discussion of language of savagery in the context of empire, see Robert L. Ivie, "Savagery in Democracy's Empire", *Third World Quarterly*, 26, 1 (2005), 55–65. Buchan and Heath discuss 'savagery' in an Australian context. Bruce Buchan and Mary Heath, "Savagery and Civilization: From *Terra Nullius* to the "Tide of History"", *Ethnicities*, 6, 5, (2006), 5–26.

41 Howe, Stammers and Walker, *Doctor Who: The Seventies*, 1994, 104.

42 Ronald Hyam, *Britain's Imperial Century, 1815-1914: A Study of Empire and Expansion*, Lanham: Barnes & Noble Books, 1993, 307.

43 Howe, Stammers and Walker, *Doctor Who: The Seventies*, 103.

44 Interestingly, this was not how Rhodesia's troubles actually ended. In 1979, it ended the civil war by reverting to British Rule until elections could be held. With those elections Southern Rhodesia became Zimbabwe under Robert Mugabe.

45 Parody during the Graham Williams era is discussed by Chapman, *Inside The TARDIS*, 126.

46 It is interesting to note that in January 1978, before the story was written, Margaret Thatcher said publically that many Britons were afraid of being "swamped" by outside cultures now living in Britain. Holmes, a former journalist who had demonstrated his satirical bent the

previous year with *The Sun Makers*, might have been thus inspired to name his natives "Swampies." Margaret Thatcher, "TV Interview for Granada *World in Action* ('rather swamped')" (27 January 1978), archived at *Margaret Thatcher Foundation*. Retrieved 19 August 2012 at http://www.margaretthatcher.org/document/103485.

47 Muir, *Critical History*, 278.
48 Buchan and Heath, "Savagery and Civilization", 6.
49 Robert Nisbet, *History of the Idea of Progress*, New York: Basic Books, 1980, 172.
50 Cornea, "British Science Fiction Television", 22.
51 Michael Adas, *Machines as the Measure of Men: Science, Technology, and Ideologies of Western Dominance*, Ithaca: Cornell University Press, 1989, 413.

Chapter 15

Through coloured eyes: An alternative viewing
of postcolonial transition

Vanessa de Kauwe

Problematic representations of race in *Doctor Who*, according to the editor of this volume Lindy Orthia, are not confined to what is shown, but extend to include what is painfully absent.[1] Specifically, Orthia identifies a lacuna in representations of the turbulent transition from colonial reign to cosmopolitanism, particularly with regard to experiences of cultural trauma, personal alienation, social upheaval and the uncertainty associated with the diaspora. While acknowledging the evolving attitudes seen within the programme regarding issues of race, colonialism/imperial oppression and cosmopolitan liberalism, Orthia highlights the ongoing difficulties in the way these issues are handled. Broadly speaking, she outlines the implicit ratification of colonial/imperial attitudes (mainly in, but not exclusive to the original series), and the explicit glorification of future utopian cosmopolitan liberalism (as expounded in the new series). Most important is the "absent postcolonial transition" between these two extremes of societal existence. Orthia recognizes this absence as a "yawning chasm" in the way *Doctor Who* represents (or, rather, fails to represent) those peoples struggling to cope with an imbalance of political power in the postcolonial present.

In this essay I offer an alternative theory. I argue that the postcolonial transition is visible – for those who have the eyes for it: for those whose personal history is saturated with postcolonial experiences, so that they cannot help but notice its patterns and scars. It can easily be overlooked, though, when seen from the point of view of someone who has never endured such a transition. To demonstrate my point I offer two alternative viewings of the 1966 serial *The Ark*, which has become notorious as a racist and pro-colonialist serial. By combining elements of both viewings, it becomes evident that the serial is rife with postcolonial transitional issues, but that the complexities of these issues can be overlooked by viewers when the story is presented from the perspective of the Doctor.

Situated knowledges and the framing perspective of the Doctor

While largely agreeing with Orthia regarding issues of race representation in *Doctor Who*, I wish to question whether postcolonial transition is indeed absent. I suggest instead that the postcolonial experience is, in fact, represented; however it may well remain unnoticed to those who have not experienced it, neither personally nor through their families – those with white eyes. I have no intention of being derogatory here. Orthia has provided both a socially aware and scholarly robust insight into under-representations of postcolonial transition. However the postcolonial experience remains, most basically, an experience. Therefore we can only ever experience its representations through our own eyes, through the filter of our own experiences. Some, no matter how socially sympathetic, politically aware or intellectually accurate, will only ever experience representations of postcolonial transition (and other racial issues) through white eyes. Here I am not simply speaking of Orthia, but also the Doctor himself and many of the programme's writers, directors and so forth.

I suggest that what we have here is a case of situated knowledge.[2] Essentially, this is the notion that none of us is ever able to possess purely objective knowledge. For the possession of knowledge requires that it be accessed and processed by the individual. All knowledge, therefore, is culturally and historically situated, and personally framed, according to the individual who possesses it.

How does this affect the Doctor, as the character through whom the programme's stories are primarily told? To answer this we must look at his cultural situation. The Doctor has always been, to this day, a white elite male: he holds the title of doctor of "practically everything", he is a Time Lord and therefore of the highest class of Gallifrey,[3] but most importantly he enjoys the practical benefits of the elite in that he has absolute social, political and financial freedom thanks to TARDIS technology. These, then, are the eyes through which the Doctor sees, and reframes for us, the story of postcolonial transition: the eyes of the elite, white male.

It may be argued that this need not be so. The Doctor need not frame situations from one particular, narrow point of view. The TARDIS does not simply provide for all physical and material needs. It also provides the Doctor with the possibility to transcend all socio-historical trappings, for it is a seemingly boundless translator and transporter. The TARDIS therefore affords the Doctor the potential for understanding and representing the most universal point of view.

However, I reply that this potential of the Doctor does not alter what, to date, has been his reality. Orthia is right to suggest that in the original series he presents himself and represents situations largely from the perspective of the elite, white male. And even though the new series (as Orthia further indicates) presents a more cosmopolitan perspective, I want to highlight that the Doctor is neither the champion nor even citizen of such a liberal egalitarian society. For he has not experienced the devastations and losses that have brought the diverse peoples of such a melting pot to this point. Neither does he experience the years of devotion and struggle to create, maintain and survive in such a society. Rather, the Doctor remains, can only ever remain, simply that which he is: a Time Lord – an untouchable traveller. From this privileged position, he never experiences the ongoing complexities and sustained difficulties of racial relations. Thus the TARDIS, rather than fulfilling its potential as a tool for bolstering cosmopolitan egalitarianism, is simply used by the Doctor as the ultimate get-away car.

This does not exclude the possibility of the Doctor acting and speaking in a socially aware and politically progressive manner (a recent example is the 2008 episode *Planet of the Ood*). Yet even in these moments, the Doctor speaks and acts from the privileged position of one who will never suffer the past traumas or future upheavals of the present crisis. Consequently, the Doctor's framing of postcolonial issues offers his audience at best, sympathy without empathy and social critique without personal commitment; at worst, the situated knowledge of a privileged white male.

Finally, in considering the Doctor, we should also consider the minds behind him; that is, his writers, directors, and such. Just as the Doctor's cultural context overshadows any representations of the postcolonial experience, likewise any racial representations found in *Doctor Who* are situated by the cultural and historical context of its writers. This explains the changing focus Orthia notes throughout the progression of both the original and new series. Themes of colonization and anti-colonization occur predominantly in the earliest years of the original series through to (and including) the 1970s. This evolves into postcolonial and revolutionary themes, mainly in the 1980s. And finally the new series provides images of liberal, democratic cosmopolitanism in the 2000s. As Orthia suggests, this evolution in attitudes towards race may reflect "broad trends in British public political discourse."[4] Nevertheless, the programme always, necessarily, revolves around the Doctor. And any story that focuses on him can only be told in a manner which relates to him – he the ultimately untouchable, white male elite.

Through coloured eyes

Thus the story of postcolonial transition is not necessarily untold in *Doctor Who*. It is simply untold by she who has experienced it – the colonized, the dispossessed, the oppressed, the refugee, the migrant. *Doctor Who* does indeed represent the postcolonial experience, though it does so somewhat incidentally. For whenever it tells of a people who survive and overcome external invasion and oppression, it necessarily represents elements of the postcolonial experience, even though this may not be the intention.

Accordingly, some viewers may witness postcolonial representations quite unwittingly. This seems to have been Orthia's experience. While well versed in both *Doctor Who* and racial issues, Orthia seems to have not recognized the various representations of postcolonial transition scattered throughout both the original and new series. Again, this seems to be an instance of situated knowledge. To explain this, I will now develop the example of visualization tools that philosopher Donna Haraway uses to explain the concept of situated knowledges.[5] To do so, I will use my own example of the colour red. Consider a hypothetical person who has had no direct sensory experience of the colour red. He may know its exact range within the light spectrum, he may learn which objects are generally associated with it and which are not, he may even read about its use in symbolism and similar. But since he has no personal experience of red, he will find it incredibly difficult to identify if he should ever see it. Likewise, even the most socially aware person who has never experienced postcolonial transition may well find it difficult to identify, especially when it is an incidental feature of an otherwise focused storyline.

However, there are those of us who are well experienced in elements of postcolonial transition. We recognize these elements in ourselves, in our families and in our contemporaries. For those of us who are personally affected by postcolonial transition, its representations hit closer to home, resonate more loudly and sting more intensely. Thus our coloured eyes allow us to recognize these representations wherever they may be found, and *Doctor Who* is no exception.

To demonstrate this, I will now present two possible viewings of *The Ark*. The first I will refer to as a critical viewing. This identifies the racially charged symbolism and subtexts which are rightly criticized by Orthia and other *Doctor Who* scholars (notably Alec Charles).[6] While such a critical viewing seems accurate in its treatment of most racial issues, what it fails to do is to properly recognize postcolonial transitional imagery embedded throughout the storyline.

The second viewing will be referred to as an experiential viewing. This offers a suggestion of how elements of *The Ark* provide a genuine representation of the postcolonial transitional experience, for those who have lived it.

The Ark: A critical viewing

As Adilifu Nama illustrates in his book *Black Space*, ethnic cultures are most often represented in fiction by allegory.[7] And in *The Ark* the allegory is quite obvious. The scenario is a massive spaceship transporting the remnant of the human race, together with the race of Monoids, to a future homeland. The humans are well mannered, highly cultured and physically magnificent white Guardians; or at least they appear to be in comparison to the Monoid other. The Monoids are dark creatures of cumbersome shape, with ragged clothes and hair, and as their name suggests, a single eye. Moreover, they are only permitted to communicate with both humans and each other through very basic signs.

Already we are bombarded with colonial themes. Not only are the Monoids visually presented in the likeness of the hideous and under-developed savage; they are also silenced. This latter point is highly significant, for as political philosopher Elaine Scarry points out, "the voice is the locus of power."[8] Thus she suggests that to silence a people, to give them no voice, is to render them powerless: to rob them of social, legal and political representation. This indeed seems to be the case, for the Doctor explicitly speaks of the Monoids as being enslaved to the Guardians. Note too, with philosopher Giorgio Agamben, that the systemic silencing of a people prevents them from appealing for help or lamenting their situation.[9] In the case of *The Ark*, the Monoids are unable to plead for the Doctor's assistance or engage the audience's sympathies.

Consequently, the servitude of the Monoids is never called into question. For the Doctor's naming of the Monoids' slavery is not equivalent to an explicit condemnation of the relation of slavery based on racial difference. When the Doctor's companion asks the Guardians' leader about "these creatures that serve you", the Guardian laughingly dismisses the Monoids' situation thus: "they offer us their invaluable services for being allowed to come on this joint voyage." Here we find a classic premise of colonial self-justification: the fallacy which has become known as 'the white man's burden', which claims that imperial reign is necessary for the white conqueror to take the inferior savages to the same heights of civilization that the former enjoys.

However, a close viewing shows that the Monoids' inferior social standing is not necessitated by any genuine inferiority. From amongst their numbers we find lawyers, technicians, and even a scientist who is praised for her unique ability to assist the Doctor. Elsewhere we learn that the Monoids are not even physically voiceless, for one cries out in agony when injured. Moreover, from the opening scenes of the first episode, we see evidence that the Monoids are linguistically functional: they appear to be conversing amongst themselves in the background; both the Monoid lawyer and scientist respond to the Guardian leader and the Doctor respectively, even when signs are not used; and most strikingly, a Monoid technician is seen receiving and reading a written document. There is sufficient evidence, therefore, that the aforementioned theories of Scarry and Agamben apply to *The Ark*. The Monoids are not a naturally silent people. They are a people who have been silenced in the process of their subjugation. It is equally evident from their intellectual and physical skills that the Monoids are not inherently inferior. Rather, they have been oppressed in the service of their white Guardian dominators. The foundational and radical postcolonial theorist Frantz Fanon is correct, then, in stating that "there is no white man's burden", for the coloured ones are actually able to thrive on their own.[10] Conversely, it seems clear to me that it is the dark ones who bear all burden of servitude. It is a fallacy to believe that such oppression is for the sake of uplifting the slave. Fanon clearly reveals the basic reality of the situation: colonialism and colonial-like oppression occur for the profit and benefit of the white man.[11]

A word of clarification here, from the viewpoint of those with coloured eyes. There is no contradiction in identifying the 'oppression', the 'burden' and the 'servitude' of the dark other; while simultaneously acknowledging that they capably function as lawyers, scientists and other highly skilled roles. Many of us colonized individuals have performed well-respected occupations, while still suffering under the racial prejudice of social inferiority due to colonial influences. We may be the best we can be, but we are prevented from reaching the social equivalent of our white rulers. One need look no further than Gandhi, who, while he was a lawyer, suffered segregation, injustice and even physical violence because of his race. Servitude and oppression do not lie solely in the laboriousness or status of one's work, but in the dearth of dignity, freedom and equality – a dearth that chokes one's life. We see this situation well represented by the Monoids' predicament in the early episodes of *The Ark*.

In contrast, the Guardians in *The Ark* rejoice in their position as master. In so doing, they undertake to build a monument to *Homo sapiens*. This massive white statue of a standing human being should take over seven hundred years to build. This consequently signals generations of servitude for the Monoid labourers who would build it. Liberation and equality are not in the foreseeable future. This is the general condition in which the Doctor and his companions leave the Ark in the first half of the serial. The similarities with colonialism are quite evident.

The Doctor's return to the Ark in the third episode provides further subtextual colonial justifications. Time has passed, and the Monoids have enslaved their white superiors, left the Ark in the disorder of an overgrown jungle, and have embarked on a plot to eventually destroy the Ark, its entire human population and even fellow Monoids who may side with the Guardians. Here we see the implicit fear and hatred for black savagery Fanon writes about in *Black Skin, White Masks*.[12] To summarize Fanon's precis of colonialism: the savages must be mastered and kept under restraint, lest they overcome the white race, its civilization, and destroy humanity itself. The Doctor seems to share these concerns, for he and his companions immediately set about overthrowing the Monoids, reinstating the reign of the Guardians, and ensuring that at the Ark's future utopian destination, the Monoids may never again rise to a position beyond the Guardians' control.

Evaluating the critical viewing

This critical viewing demonstrates the racial themes and colonial justifications that Orthia rightly criticizes as being prevalent throughout the original series of *Doctor Who*. Furthermore, Charles notes that in *The Ark*, there is a "hypocrisy [that] echoes the sophistic mindset of the British colonialist."[13] The hypocrisy Charles refers to seems twofold. It is the hypocrisy of the colonizer (represented as the white Guardians of humanity) who vainly attempts to justify "brutal opportunism" as a "civilizing mission."[14] But there is also the hypocrisy of the Doctor, who devotes his existence to opposing evil and oppression in all its forms, yet does nothing to alleviate or even question the subjugation of the Monoids. I will go beyond Charles to point out that the Doctor and his companions even fight on the side of the white oppressors. In fact, Dodo explicitly speaks in favour of the Guardians' superior nature and right to rule. For in the third and fourth episodes we learn that the current inhabitants of the Ark's destination planet are highly superior non-physical beings, who are only willing to hand over control of their planet to those who will maintain it as a rational, just and benevolent utopia. These non-physical beings are concerned that the current state of Monoid reign will not meet their high standards. This is followed by Dodo's insistence in the final episode:

> You're not the only ones like that. The Guardians – you know the humans that travel in the spaceship – they used to have your ideals too [...] there are some of them left who wouldn't mind rising up against the Monoids and trying to do better.

All this is even more hypocritical given that in the second episode the Doctor and his companions fall victim to the Guardians' ignorance and callously rigid laws, leading Steven into a speech denouncing their violence and fear of others.

How important are these critiques, made by Orthia, Charles, and the like? As I have mentioned before, I find such critical viewings of *Doctor Who* both insightful and invaluable. Why? In the words of Fanon, himself a coloured-eyed survivor of postcolonial transition, because "there are far too many idiots in this world."[15] That is, there are viewers who will conflate the Doctor's racially naïve and colonial-like attitudes with his ongoing struggle against evil and ignorance. Such a conflation implies that the colonized, the native, the coloured other, is a source of evil and ignorance that must be violently overcome and subjugated. This is not simply a theoretical concern. As David Butler has revealed, in 2005 the British National Party's online forum received entries referring to *Doctor Who* which were extremely racially hostile.[16] Of particular note was an entry that explicitly named Hartnell's Doctor as opposing multiculturalism.[17] Without a critical viewing, the Doctor's representation as an elite, white male (especially one with colonial biases) has appalling implications for the coloured other.

Nevertheless, I suggest that a critical viewing alone is insufficient, particularly with regard to representations of postcolonial transition. Orthia claims that, throughout both the original and current series, colonial themes of the past are juxtaposed or followed by images of liberal cosmopolitanism, thereby neglecting the cultural devastation and personal upheaval that is the reality of postcolonial transition.[18] To a lesser extent and less explicitly, others too seem to have not recognized representations of postcolonial transition, even though they provide a scholarly critical view of racial issues. For example, while Charles is critical of the colonial subtexts with *The Ark*, he too seems impervious to its transitional elements.[19] This is implied in his naming of the Monoids as "aliens."[20] This is despite the fact that, when asked of the Monoids' nature, the leader of the Guardians simply describes them as "from the Earth" like all other biological life aboard the Ark. Although the origins of the Monoids are obscure, they are presently defined as residents of Earth, even by the human Guardians. The Monoids are therefore a transitional people; a people experiencing diaspora. And like the Monoids, many of us who have left our colonized homelands continue to carry the stigma of foreigner, no matter how long we are citizens of our new home. Likewise, our children who are locally born and know no other home than their present country are often still marked as outsiders by their alien appearance.

It seems, therefore, that a critical viewing is necessary but insufficient. It is necessary and highly valuable for uncovering racial subtexts and implications. Yet it seems insufficient for identifying the postcolonial transitional experience. I reiterate my earlier statement that the postcolonial transitional experience is, most basically, an experience. Hence I will now suggest an experiential viewing. That is, a viewing of *The Ark* from the point of view of one who has personal experience of postcolonial transition: the viewing of one whose own experiences are reflected in elements of this serial – one with coloured eyes.

The Ark: An experiential viewing

An experiential viewing allows us to refocus on the Monoids, rather than the Doctor and the Guardians, as the centre of *The Ark*. It is upon the Doctor's return to the Ark, in the second half of the serial, that representations of postcolonial transition become evident.

The Doctor and his companions return to the Ark about 700 years after their initial landing, only to find the spaceship in violence and disarray. Here a critical viewing may suggest racist undertones, such that the disorder of the Ark indicates that the Monoids are incapable of maintaining it to the same standards as the Guardians. However, an experiential viewing offers a different angle. The disarray of the Ark resonates with the experiences for those of us who have survived postcolonial transition. For in the wake of colonialism, our nations are often left in devastation, leeched of their wealth and resources and robbed of any internal structure of self-government which may have previously existed.[21] Similarly, the revolutionarily violent representation of the Monoids reflects the genuine experiences of many postcolonial peoples. Fanon describes the situation thus: the initial acts of colonization succeed through the superior violence of the colonizer; and the continued exploitation of the land and its people is achieved through the ongoing threat of the economic and physical firepower of the exploiters (hypocritically disguised as the civilizing law of a colonial power).[22] Consequently, decolonization often occurs through some form of revolutionary action.[23] And since colonization deprives the native of a stable form of self-government, the only form of rule available in the earlier days of postcolonial transition is the rule of military might.[24] Thus I suggest, with Fanon, that violence, infighting and political instability are the hallmarks of a nation struggling furiously to recover from the drain of colonization. Fanon further acknowledges that, as undesirable as this situation may be, it is the stark reality of the initial stages of postcolonial transition.[25] I will add further still, it is the stark reality of the consequences of colonization, the experience of millions of colonized.

Cultural contamination

There are still more complex representations of postcolonial transition which an experiential viewing can uncover. Most generally, the Monoids, having overcome their oppression by the Guardians, do *not* return to their original way of life. Rather, they demonstrate elements of the transitional experience that I call cultural contamination – a notion I have developed through a lifelong observation of my own family and friends. I propose cultural contamination as a phenomenon that occurs after severe, systematic and prolonged oppression by another culture. It is the phenomenon by which the freedom, progress and power that the oppressor is seen to enjoy become conflated with the culture of the oppressor. I can still hear my parents and grandparents declaring that they went to "the best schools" because said schools were run by "Europeans" who would not teach the native subjects. The fact that only British language, history and culture were taught was enough for this to be declared "the best" education. Conversely, as Fanon demonstrates, the degradation, sociopolitical impotence and suppression that the subjugated experience are so intense, that they become psychologically (even pathologically) linked with their own culture and physical traits.[26]

I suggest that this double conflation of colonialism with superiority, and the colonized with inferiority, triggers a form of performative cultural contamination such that the colonized, in seeking the freedoms and benefits that their oppressors possess, seek to emulate the latter's culture and way of life. Thus cultural contamination can be defined as both a psychological and enacted phenomenon. At a psychological level, the culture of the colonizer is mixed with ideals of freedom, greatness, strength and desirability; while the colonized have a view of their own culture which is contaminated with Fanonian ideas of inferiority. Hence at a practical level, even after the colonized have gained political independence, the enactment of their lives is contaminated with elements of their former oppressor's culture and ideals. In *The Ark*, my notion of cultural contamination is inadvertently represented in the way the Monoids go to great lengths to mimic Guardian traits.

Postcolonial theorist Homi Bhabha points out that this 'mimicry' is typical of those attempting to transition from colonial or similar oppression.[27] In the case of *The Ark* this is most vividly seen in the devices of the statue and the voice box. Most noticeably to the Doctor and his companions, the Monoids continue building the Guardians' statue. However, they cap it with their own one-eyed head. If we are to take this as symbolism for Bhabha's mimicry, then we may interpret it as suggesting that the Monoids have taken on, as their own, various aspects of the work, culture and even future projects and expectations of their former oppressors, while now heading these things themselves – they, the Monoids, are now at the head of Guardian cultural indicators. More potent is the symbolism of the voice box. Even in a state of liberation, the Monoids do not revert to their own voice, or even use their commonly understood sign language. Rather, they develop a voice box so their thoughts can be understood in the voice and language of their oppressors – English. Here we have an implicit indication that human English is still the language of power, and the voice of the oppressor is still the voice of authority.

At this point, Bhabha may disagree with me. Rather than seeing mimicry as purely a self-deprecating acknowledgement of the superiority of the oppressor, Bhabha declares that "mimicry is both resemblance and menace."[28] For, as Bhabha has been summarized by Nayar, through mimicry the native shows the white man that the former can match the latter in every way.[29] Thus for Bhabha, mimicry can be useful in undermining notions of colonial superiority.[30] While this experience of mimicry as an equalizer may resonate with some postcolonial survivors, there are logical implications that should be mentioned. Again it is Nayar who summaries the alleged equalizing qualities of Bhabha's mimicry:

> He is a mimic who can now respond in English and argue rationally (rather than sentimentally, which would be a stereotypical 'native' or Oriental form of argumentation) because of Western education [...] He appeals to the English in the language of logic, reason, administrative convenience and expediency.[31]

Note the implicit suggestions in this argument. The native shows he is equal to the colonizer by mimicking all the positive attributes of the colonizer. The implication is that the native is naturally unable to "argue rationally", nor can he demonstrate "logic, reason, administrative convenience and expediency", without the influence of white colonization. This is clearly an implicit affirmation of the superiority of the colonizer, which is highly problematic, and is yet another reason why the colonized may experience Fanonian inferiority.

Perhaps this too, is the reality of the postcolonial transitional experience: that the colonized only feel equal to the colonizer when they can successfully mimic the latter. Perhaps it is more subtle than that. Perhaps even postcolonial individuals who realize their self-worth, feel they can only *prove* their equality to the colonizing race through thorough and accurate mimicry. This seems to be Fanon's diagnosis, for he declares, "Black men want to prove to white men, *at all costs*, the richness of their thought, the equal value of their intellect."[32] And it seems that part of the cost of this mimicry is that the subjugated begin to treat each other in the same way as their oppressors.[33] To take a final example from *The Ark*, the Monoids not only attempt to enslave and dominate each other as the Guardians did to their entire race; but they even continue to deny each other names, referring to each other by numbers.

From the various examples given above, it is possible to view the representations of the Monoids in *The Ark* as analogous of the non-fictional postcolonial transitional experience. Yet this experiential viewing alone, like the purely critical viewing before it, remains incomplete. What seems missing is a complex viewing which reveals the relation between the colonial injustices highlighted by the critical viewing, and the transitional experiences illustrated by the experiential viewing.

The complex viewing

A complex viewing acknowledges the realities of both the critical and experiential viewing, and seeks to establish the relation between the two.

For example, a complex viewing notes the disarray the Monoids find themselves in, through the experiential viewing; but it is able to causally link this phenomenon to the Guardians' colonial-like regime, as revealed by the critical viewing. Thus a complex viewing allows us to realize that racial oppression is never simply a matter of political or military control, as it appears to be in *The Ark*. Rather, as Fanon points out, it is heavily based on economic oppression, educational manipulation and segregation, and a self-serving bureaucratic system.[34] In this manner, a complex viewing traces the tragedies and instabilities of postcolonial transition back to their colonial causes. Thus colonialism is forced to bear the responsibility (and even blame) for the consequences of its injustices.

Similarly, a complex viewing sees the violence and in-fighting of transitional races, as represented in the Monoids, not as a condemnation of the race in question. Rather, a complex viewing recognizes that such violence is the consequence of the situation the race finds itself in.[35] I have already discussed Fanon's argument that the whole system of colonial oppression is based on the threat of imperial violence, and how decolonization leaves the native with little means other than violence with which to run the transitioning nation. But at this point Fanon can add more. Here Fanon claims that, at a racial level, the subjugated fight because oppression has turned their entire existence into a fight for survival: a fight against poverty, starvation, disease and hopelessness.[36] At a personal level, he famously declared that "violence is a cleansing force" – a psychologically necessary reclaiming of life and vigour after one has been completely downtrodden.[37] While both Fanon and I regret such transition violence, we both acknowledge its reality. And recognizing the reality of transitional violence facilitates a complex viewing of representations of transitional peoples. With regard to *The Ark*, the violence of the Monoids can be recognized as the practical and psychological consequence of their oppression, rather than a slur against their inherent nature.

The complex viewing and mimicry

A further use of the complex viewing is that it facilitates a closer scrutiny of Bhabha's theory of mimicry. Bhabha proposes that mimicry renders colonial discourses ambiguous; for rather than bringing pure oppression, colonialism also bears benefits that the native would otherwise lack.[38] I have already discussed the derogatory implications that may be drawn from such a theory of ambiguity. Moreover, claiming that colonial discourses are ambiguous hinders us from making value judgements regarding colonial policies, attitudes and actions. Consequently, colonialism is protected from much of the responsibility and blame that may be attached to it. However, a complex viewing reveals a reality that is closer to Fanon's argument. That is, elements that appear to be deficiencies in the colonized are actually the consequences of colonial discourses and regimes. Fanon goes so far as to indicate that the seemingly superior wealth, progress and civilization of colonizing empires were built from the ravaged resources and enslaved labour that were taken from the lands they colonized.[39] Thus a complex viewing reveals that the struggles and apparent failings of oppressed peoples are not due to an inherent flaw in the people themselves, but are a consequence of colonialism and its discourses. Likewise, mimicry too can be causally traced to colonial discourses, rather than an alleged lacking in the oppressed. I will illustrate this point with a further example from *Doctor Who*.

Since I have focused on *The Ark*, which occurs near the beginning of the original series, I will attempt a broader view by taking an example from very late in the original series: *Ghost Light* (1989). In this serial we meet the long oppressed and enslaved character called Control. Upon gaining release from her downtrodden state, Control yearns after only two things: her "freeness" and to be "ladylike." Why only these two things? Because these are the two things her oppression denied her. She was not free to achieve self-actualization, and she was certainly not permitted to attain to what she believed was the highest standard of existence: British gentry. Here we have a form of mimicry that is based on cultural contamination. For in the character of Control, freedom has become equated with the culture and social status of the British ruling class. This illustrates a postcolonial phenomenon which is commonly termed "more British than the British." It is the phenomenon by which the subjugated seek to emulate and even exceed the linguistic, cultural and often religious traits of the oppressors.[40]

Why is this so important to postcolonial transition? Because, as Fanon has already suggested, the language and culture of the native then become conflated with inferiority. The subjugated suspect that to stand on equal ground with their former masters, they must become masters of the oppressor's culture. But as Fanon points out, in emulating the white man, the coloured lose elements of their own cultural identity.[41] This can be seen in the example of my parents and grandparents who glorified all things British. But I also recognize it in myself: my passing suspicions that Sri Lankan ways are outdated ways, and even the fact that my accent changes when I'm not in coloured company. I was gratified to learn that my friends from other Asian and some African countries have the same experience. The result? In artificially whitening ourselves we grow increasingly forgetful of our natural heritage.

So while the postcolonial situation may be complex, it is not, as Bhabha suggests, ambiguous. That is, it is not ambiguous to the extent that we can't make value judgements regarding colonial discourses and their consequences.

Finally, I suggest that a complex viewing allows us to strip Bhabha's mimicry to a more basic level. This allows us to see that mimicry is often employed by the colonized as a necessity for survival. While Control engages in mimicry to satisfy her personal aspirations, in other circumstances colonized people have no choice but to engage in mimicry because of the way colonialism has restructured their world. To illustrate, we need only look at the 1975 serial *The Ark in Space*.

In *The Ark in Space* the humans again take the role of the colonizers. In a backstory that is quickly glossed over and therefore easily overlooked, the human race have attempted to colonize several planets and in doing so have almost wiped out the race known as Wirrn. The remaining handful of Wirrn have since journeyed towards the Earth in hope of a means to survive, possibly via the same route that the humans used to decimate the Wirrn home planets.

Yet this is not the focus of *The Ark in Space*. Rather, the storyline shows how one of the Wirrn takes over the body of the human captain Noah, but retains Noah's human voice and language in an attempt to communicate with human authorities and the Doctor. Here again we have an implicit recognition of the authority and power of the colonizer's voice and language. However, in this example of vocal mimicry, the reasoning of the Wirrn seems purely practical. It may be interpreted as indicating that any chance of survival in the colonizers' realm requires adapting oneself to their language, customs, and ultimately their political control. This is surely the experience of all postcolonial peoples whose diasporic journey brings them to their colonizers' homeland. The colonizer's influence and culture continues to dominate, even after decolonization.

At a superficial level, the monstrous representation of the Wirrn leads the audience to react towards them as a powerful, foreign threat capable of wiping out human civilization. But a closer look at their backstory lets us realize that they are the dispossessed – those who are nearly annihilated by an invading human force.

A complex viewing suggests that while the Monoids take the form of the slave, the Wirrn offer an image of the refugee or migrant. In her contribution to the recent volume

Doctor Who and Philosophy, Deborah Pless complains that Britain is "practically bursting at the seams" with migrants from the colonies.[42] But by Pless's own logic, Britain would not be "bursting at the seams" if it had not attempted to swallow the resources of over half the globe; just as Noah (the captain of the space station that the Wirrn take residence upon) would not be bursting with Wirrn tissue if the humans hadn't invaded the latter's planet.

It must be acknowledged that, in actuality, many postcolonial migrants are able to maintain elements of their language and cultures. Yet a tension always remains. There is always the juggle of freely expressing their heritage and integrating successfully into the new lifestyle they find themselves in. The transition is never smooth. Rather, the reality of postcolonial transition seems filled with trauma, uncertainty and, as Orthia suggests, abscesses and chasms.

Post-postcolonial transition

How does this end? Both Orthia and Charles agree that, for *Doctor Who* in general, the story of postcolonialism ends in the egalitarian embrace of utopian cosmopolitanism. Here a cosmos of differences are juxtaposed in such nonchalant parity, that racial difference is seemingly mundane, even irrelevant. Charles notes that this treatment of race is not a beacon of freedom. On the contrary, it is an image of empire.[43] Why? Because when all traits (racial or otherwise) are irrelevant, then none are valued, treasured, lamented, nurtured, and so forth. I further suggest that when a multi-race/multi-species world is marked by the common (common language, common sociopolitics, common lifestyle, common law), it is hard to see how such a world differs from the reign of a common empire. Note too, that these common aspects of cosmopolitan life are an *enforced* commonality. For they are not agreed upon by democratic consensus. Rather, cosmopolitanism largely occurs in the homeland of the colonizers, where survivors of colonization are gathered. Thus the common language, lifestyle and law of cosmopolitanism remain the reign of the colonizer. Orthia suggests more: when the specifics of cultural heritage are undervalued, one neglects the hardships that entire nations have undergone, both as a people and as individuals. To revel in the common can cause us to overlook the particular, especially the injustices imposed on particular peoples that induce their postcolonial transition.

Let us revisit my original focus, *The Ark*. The end of this particular serial resembles the empire-like cosmopolitanism of *Doctor Who* in general. The Ark spaceship is headed for a utopian planet, a future promised land. This planet is masterfully but benevolently ruled by a super-race who are colourless, featureless, invisible altogether, who further claim to be superlatively neutral and objective in their reasoning. Here we find an early foreshadowing in *Doctor Who*, of the images of a liberal and (so to speak) colour-blind cosmopolitanism that would follow in the new series. In *The Ark*, however, it is highly noteworthy that the colourless and apparently superior species takes the side of the white, civilized human beings, and allow them to govern both themselves and the Monoids. This closely reflects ideas of colonial self-justification: the rule of the colonizers is ratified by both their natural superiority and purely objective reasoning. More importantly, even after they have thrown off the weight of oppression, the diasporic Monoids' means of survival is found in a land ruled by their former subjugators. And this is indeed an accurate representation of countless postcolonial migrants and refugees.

When we take this state of affairs into consideration, I believe the final word can be left to Fanon. For, regrettably, in our world as in *Doctor Who*, "for the black man there is only one destiny. And it is white."[44]

Notes

1 Lindy A. Orthia, "'Sociopathetic abscess' or 'yawning chasm'? The absent postcolonial transition in *Doctor Who*." *The Journal of Commonwealth Literature*, 45, 2 (2010), 207–25.

2 Donna J. Haraway, "Situated knowledges: The science question in feminism and the privilege of partial perspective", in *Simians, Cyborgs, and Women: The Reinvention of Nature*, New York: Routledge, 1991, 183–201.

3 Both references come from the 1978 serial *The Invasion of Time*.

4 Orthia, "'Sociopathetic abscess' or 'yawning chasm'?", 221.

5 Haraway, "Situated knowledges."

6 Alec Charles, "The ideology of anachronism: Television, history and the nature of time", in David Butler, ed., *Time and Relative Dissertations in Space: Critical Perspectives on Doctor Who*, Manchester: Manchester University Press, 2007, 108–22.

7 Adilifu Nama, *Black Space: Imaging Race in Science Fiction Film*, Austin: University of Texas Press, 2008.

8 Elaine Scarry, *The Body in Pain*, Baltimore: Johns Hopkins University Press, 1989, 45–51. Scarry explicitly argues that to control another's voice, to confine it, to so rigidly manipulate it so that self-expression cannot freely occur, is a devastating form of torture and suppression.

9 Giorgio Agamben, *The Open*, Stanford: Stanford University Press, 2004, 34–35 and 37.

10 Frantz Fanon, *Black Skin, White Masks* (trans. Charles Lam Markmann), New York: Grove Press, 1967 [1952], 228.

11 Fanon, *Black Skin, White Masks*, 108.

12 Fanon, *Black Skin, White Masks*, particularly chapters 4 and 5.

13 Charles, "The ideology of anachronism", 115.

14 Charles, "The ideology of anachronism", 115.

15 Fanon, *Black Skin, White Masks*, 9.

16 David Butler, "Introduction", in David Butler, ed., *Time and Relative Dissertations in Space: Critical Perspectives on Doctor Who*, Manchester: Manchester University Press, 2007, 4.

17 Butler, "Introduction", 4.

18 Orthia, "'Sociopathetic abscess' or 'yawning chasm'?"

19 Charles, "The ideology of anachronism", 115.

20 Charles, "The ideology of anachronism", 115.
21 As a result, Gandhi sought to establish a system of *swadeshi* and *swaraj*: that is, economic self-reliance and political self-rule, so that India might find a way forward from its own colonization, without falling into absolute devastation. Pramod K. Nayar, *Postcolonialism: A Guide for the Perplexed*, London: Continuum, 2010, 6–7.
22 Frantz Fanon, *The Wretched of the Earth* (trans. Constance Farrington), Harmondsworth: Penguin Books, 1967 [1963], 28 and onwards.
23 Fanon, *Wretched of the Earth*, 28 and onwards.
24 Fanon, *Wretched of the* Earth, 138.
25 Fanon, *Wretched of the Earth*, 28–29 and 74.
26 This has been described by Nayar as "Fanon's major contribution" to understanding the postcolonial experience. Nayar, *Postcolonialism*, 9. The details of Fanon's thesis develop throughout his works, particularly in chapters 5, 6 and 7 of *Black Skin, White Masks*.
27 Homi K. Bhabha, "Of mimicry and man: The ambivalence of colonial discourse", *The Location of Culture*, London: Routledge, 1994, 85–92.
28 Bhabha, "Of mimicry and man", 86.
29 Nayar, *Postcolonialism*, 27–28.
30 Bhabha, "Of mimicry and man", 87–88.
31 Nayar, *Postcolonialism*, 28.
32 Fanon, *Black Skin, White Masks*, 12, emphasis added.
33 Fanon, *Black Skin, White Masks*, 228.
34 Fanon, *Wretched of the Earth*, 77, 81–82 and 134.
35 Fanon, *Wretched of the Earth*, 28.
36 Fanon, *Black Skin, White Masks*, 224.
37 Fanon, *Wretched of the Earth*, 74.
38 Bhabha, "Of mimicry and man." See also Bhabha, "Signs taken for wonders: Questions of ambivalence and authority under a tree outside Delhi, May 1817", *The Location of Culture*, 102–22.
39 Fanon, *Wretched of the Earth*, 41.
40 It is the phenomenon Fanon describes when he says "The Black man wants to be white." Fanon, *Black Skin, White Masks*, 11. The details of the argument follow throughout that book.
41 Fanon, *Black Skin, White Masks*, 11.
42 Deborah Pless, "The decline and fall of the British empire, sponsored by TARDIS", in Courtland Lewis and Paula Smithka, eds., *Doctor Who and Philosophy: Bigger on the Inside*, Chicago: Open Court, 2010, 353.
43 Charles, "The ideology of anachronism."
44 Fanon, *Black Skin, White Masks*, 12.

PART IV

Xenophobia, nationalism and national identities

Chapter 16

The allegory of allegory: Race, racism and the summer of 2011

Alec Charles

This is where it gets complicated

On 12 August 2011 the historian David Starkey articulated what has been perceived by some commentators as a new brand of racism, a mode of discrimination based on a redefinition of race by cultural association. Speaking on BBC2's *Newsnight* programme in response to a series of riots which had engulfed British inner city areas earlier that month, Starkey invoked UK politician Enoch Powell's notorious 1968 speech against immigration (the "rivers of blood" speech) before going on to argue that "The whites have become black. A particular sort of violent, destructive, nihilistic, gangster culture has become the fashion. And black and white […] operate in this language together."[1]

This quasi-racism, one without a rationality or fixedness of object, seems to expose what racism is: a prejudging of the other not because they are otherly but because they are *designated* as otherly. As Slavoj Žižek has argued, "a 'jew', for example, is in the last resort one who is stigmatized with the signifier 'Jew'"[2] – and Starkey's perspective echoes this phenomenon. The assertion that white is the new black rests on the self-justifying presumption that black is black – indeed that black is not only a priori otherly but also meretricious and morally corrupt and corrupting – in Frantz Fanon's terms, "not simply […] lacking in values [but] the negation of values."[3] It is not so much that white is the new black as it seems that prejudice against a dispossessed minority (only vaguely and spuriously defined by its ethnic profile) is the new (and apparently the acceptable face of, or the alternative to) racism – in that racism is as ill-defined as race: and the exposure of this irrationality has led racism to modify (and to blur) the focus of its xenophobic prejudice.

Here, of course, in Britain in the summer of 2011, we have the perfectly ill-defined object of this perfectly ill-defined prejudice: an irrationality of reaction against an irrationality of otherliness. As we can no longer define the other on grounds of ethnicity (as it does not make sense to[4] – and is not acceptable to), we have now returned to that perfectly meaningless (perfect because meaningless, unassailable because beyond the rational) notion of 'class' – in this particular historical instance, of what one tabloid newspaper journalist depicted as "a feckless criminal underclass"[5] – whatever the feck that might actually mean.[6] (One might note that various definitions of 'fecklessness' refer to a lack of vigour or vitality.[7] This essay will examine two cases from that same summer of 2011 in which the *Doctor Who* franchise explored discrimination against minority groups precisely because they appeared to lack that animation or vitality.)

Žižek has written of the irrationality of the violence which overtook the suburbs of Paris in the autumn of 2005:

> There was *no* programme behind the burning of the Paris suburbs [...] opposition to the system cannot articulate itself in the guise of a realistic alternative [...] but only take the shape of a meaningless outburst [...] The cars burned and the schools torched were not those of richer neighbourhoods. They were part of the hard-won acquisitions of the very strata from which the protesters originated.[8]

Žižek sees this anti-rationalistic outpouring of violence in the "psychotic-delirious-incestuous"[9] phenomenon of terroristic fundamentalism; and we may see something similar not only in the civil violence which overwhelmed British cities in August 2011 but also in the pseudo-taxonomizing irrationality of the more extreme (indeed, absurd) responses to that violence, responses epitomized by (but hardly limited to) Starkey's infamous outburst.

This incoherence is evident in the list of characteristics by which Umberto Eco has defined the essence of fascism.[10] He argues that fascism is founded upon a fear of difference and is therefore "racist by definition." He suggests that, as it is necessarily irrational, it imagines that its inconsistencies allude "allegorically, to the same primeval truth" – a truth that "has been already spelled out once and for all." It is therefore incontrovertible precisely by virtue of this incoherence.

The irrationality of this situation reveals the material and verbal violence on both sides as serving no more than a symbolic function (and a futile one at that: this violence is a symbol of a wider futility and of its own futility). Racial violence has merely deployed race as a transparently hollow justification; race is, as it always was, no more than an arbitrary signifier, and this clash of civilizations is merely a clash of arbitrary significations. Racial tension and racism itself have therefore been revealed as mere allegories – incoherent allegories of themselves. The incoherence of the allegory (the symbolic narrative) that underpins racism has developed out of a fundamental category error: a confusion of the metaphorical (resemblance) with the metonymic (material relationship) – the myth, that is, that because 'they' look a certain way, 'they' also act and interact in a common manner.

Roland Barthes argued that such mythical structures advance a sense of causality which is "artificial" and "false" but which purports to represent an "innocent" and "natural relationship" – through a process by which hegemonic cultural norms are "experienced as the evident laws of a natural order."[11] The myth or narrative of otherliness upon which racism is founded thus shores up its incoherence with conventions of discourse which – in John Fiske's words – have "developed in order to disguise the constructedness of the 'reality' it offers, and therefore of the arbitrariness of the ideology that is mapped onto it."[12]

Within this context self-conscious allegories of racism (such as those performed in the fantasies of science fiction) may be seen as allegories of what is itself only an allegory. As such, science fiction's allegories of racism are validated at once by the symmetry of their relationship with their subject (both are allegories) and by the asymmetry of that relationship (these allegories of racism recognize and declare their coherently allegorical status; the allegory which is racism implausibly denies its own incoherently allegorical status). The fantasy which announces that it is a fantasy thus comes to appear more rational than the myth whose claims to truth and naturalness it calls to account.

Race against time

Published just two years before the broadcast of the first episode of *Doctor Who*, 1961's corrected version of the first edition of the *Oxford English Dictionary* defines 'ethnicity' (clearly not a word in vogue at the time of its publication) as a rare and obsolete term for "heathendom, heathen superstition." It defines the adjective 'ethnic' as "pertaining to nations not Christian or Jewish; Gentile, heathen pagan" or as "pertaining to race, peculiar to a race or nation; ethnological." It usefully goes on to define 'ethnological' as "of or pertaining to ethnology" and 'ethnology' as "the science which treats of races and peoples, and of their relations to one another, their distinctive and other characteristics, etc."[13] We are at this point faced with three possible readings: the first overtly aligned with a position which might today be interpreted as racist; the second, that there is no substantive core of meaning here at all (the definition appears to go round in circles and gets you nowhere; it is all *différance* and no *différence*; or, as Edmund Blackadder's redraft of Johnson's *Dictionary* glosses the indefinite article, it *doesn't really mean anything*); or – and this is where it approaches a more postmodern meaning – a vague sense of having something to do with people, with groups of people. More recently Oxford's lexicographers have defined the 'ethnic' as "relating to a population subgroup (within a larger or dominant national or cultural group) with a common national or cultural tradition"[14] – and it is that sense of *cultural* tradition which underpins the contemporary meaning of the term. Thus ethnicity becomes a matter of cultural group identification; yet we may note that this act of identification may be either internal or external to the group. As such, the 'chav' becomes an ethnic designation as meaningful (and as meaningless) as the Jew or the gypsy; a self-conscious categorization, but also a designation ruthlessly imposed and enforced by the superstructure of the body politic.

Within this context, it may be of interest to examine two science fiction allegories of racism which were broadcast in the United Kingdom during the summer of 2011 – the two-part *Doctor Who* story *The Rebel Flesh/The Almost People* and the ten-part *Doctor Who* spin-off series *Torchwood: Miracle Day*. Both programmes directly invoked ideas as to the classification of humanity in ways which referred us back to the allegories of old-style racism which have proven grist to *Doctor Who*'s mill (and to that of much other science fiction) since the Daleks first goose-swept onto the scene – from Nazi symbolism to analogies of more contemporary internments and renditions. But, as witnessed in the dismissive sidelining of the Führer himself later in that same 2011 season of *Doctor Who* (in an episode entitled *Let's Kill Hitler*), the liberal values evoked by the series have moved somewhat beyond the easy certainties of an unequivocal antagonism towards Nazism.[15] These programmes suggest more complex and problematic perspectives upon issues of ethnic division – ambiguities which mirror those seen in the violence which erupted in the United Kingdom during the season of their broadcast – the notion that race and racism are clearly no longer black-and-white issues, and the idea – similarly explored by NBC's *Heroes* (Creator: Tim Kring, 2006–10) and more explicitly by Channel 4's *Misfits* (Creator: Howard Overman, 2009–) – that underpinning such prejudice is the irrational yet pervasive invention of, in its broadest sense, an ethnic underclass.

In the universe of twenty-first century *Doctor Who*, prejudice based on skin colour seems an absurd and irrelevant anachronism. This is, after all, the realm of Mickey Smith and Martha Jones (in *Doctor Who* itself), of Rani Chandra and Clyde Langer (in *The Sarah Jane Adventures* [Creator: Russell T Davies, 2007–11]) and of Toshiko Sato and Rex Matheson (in *Torchwood*). As Lindy Orthia has suggested, "multi-raciality [...] has become intrinsic to representations of both contemporary British society and future human societies in the new series of *Doctor Who*."[16] This perspective represents a paradigm shift away from the latent institutional racism of the first 26 years of *Doctor Who* (from 1963 to 1989) – 26 years which featured not a single non-white regular character (out of seven leads and about thirty regularly recurring supporting characters). Just as the introduction of the character of the bisexually hyperactive Captain Jack Harkness into the series in 2005 took for granted that general homophobia was history (quite literally so: *Torchwood: Miracle Day* sees homophobia as a phenomenon of the 1920s), so, in the *Doctor Who* of the twenty-first century, the programme's discussions of xenophobia in its broadest sense address issues of prejudice against classes of people who are no longer defined by their skin colour – but by bioeconomic or socio-ethnic status.

During the years in which the US and UK governments aggressively pursued the overtly neoconservative agenda of the War on Terror, the *Doctor Who* franchise, under the aegis of head writer Russell T Davies, self-consciously spoke out against a culture of increasingly militaristic xenophobia – with its references to WMDs, Guantanamo Bay, terrorist sleeper cells, alien attacks upon high profile targets, and a grinning warmonger of a British prime minister.[17] More recently, however, the series and its spin-offs have indicated an end to the franchise's war on the War on Terror by adopting a broader historical perspective upon issues of race and racial hatred.

Making a killing: Power to the almost people

The idea of the clone, copy or replicant which somehow assumes the identity – the personality, even the subjectivity – of the original is not one which is new to science fiction. In such films as Don Siegel's *Invasion of the Body Snatchers* (1956) this alien double is a tool for alien invasion, but in other cases (such as the reimagined *Battlestar Galactica* [Creator: Glen A. Larson, 2004–09]) it is the direct product of human technological endeavour. This is an idea perhaps most successfully popularized by Ridley Scott's *Blade Runner* (1982), a film which – like Philip K. Dick's original novel – uses the notion of the near-human to call into question the nature and integrity of humanity itself. *Doctor Who* has also explored the issue of the clone's subjectivity: although such stories as *The Android Invasion* (1975) and *Meglos* (1980) employ the manufactured double as little more than a plot device, *Resurrection of the Daleks* (1984) – albeit possibly as a result of a somewhat convoluted script – exposes an ambiguity between the original human and the duplicate: "I wonder what happened to the real you." More recently, in *The Poison Sky* (2008), a clone of the Doctor's companion Martha Jones begins to adopt the qualities of her model; while in *The Big Bang* (2010) a plastic replica of another companion, Rory Williams, in fact appears to become the original character.

The possibility of the active subjectivity of the copy or automaton calls into question the integrity of the animate original in a way which both Sigmund Freud and, before him, Ernst Jentsch famously described as uncanny.[18] The way in which the projected or imagined other might undermine the original self from which it has been projected or by which it has been imagined has returned time and again to problematize ethnocentric discourse through the remorseless insistence of what Homi Bhabha has described as the "uncanny structure of cultural difference"[19] – because, as Bhabha has argued, the figures of monstrous otherliness projected or imagined by the ethnocentric or colonial self "reveal things so profoundly familiar that it cannot bear to remember them."[20]

The humanity of the supposedly inhuman other thus returns – like any uncanny double – to challenge the humanity of the original colonial self. Joseph Conrad writes that the Congolese 'natives' in *Heart of Darkness* "were not inhuman, that was the worst of it – the suspicion of their not being inhuman."[21] The other is at once inhuman (because we've said it is) and human (because, despite all our protestations, it actually resembles us). And so, as Edward Said wrote of Conrad's novella, "by the end of the narrative the heart of darkness has reappeared in England."[22]

The anxiety prompted by this moral-ontological ambiguity was addressed as early as the sixteenth century by Michel de Montaigne. In his essay "On the Cannibals" Montaigne performs an uncanny deconstruction of the difference between the colonial self and its imagined other. For Montaigne, European notions of savagery and barbarism rebound upon the European sense of cultural and moral identity:

[W]e can indeed call those folk barbarians by the rules of reason but not in comparison with ourselves, who surpass them in every kind of barbarism […] It is no lie to say that these men are indeed savages – by our standards; for either they must be or we must be.[23]

Reflecting upon Montaigne's essay, Michel de Certeau has witnessed radical shifts which deconstruct the notion of the *barbarian*:

[A]n ambivalence (cannibals are barbarian because of their original naturalness; Occidentals are barbarian because of their cruelty); a comparison (our ways are more barbarian than theirs); and an alternative (one of us has to be barbarian, us or them, and it's not them).[24]

The colonial other represents a dehumanized invention and projection of the colonial self which eventually hereby comes to seem more human than that which attempted to dehumanize it.[25] This situation appears to lie at the heart of Matthew Graham's 2011 *Doctor Who* story, *The Rebel Flesh*. The episodes concern a group of clones which, although originally projected from and directed by the consciousnesses of their human operators, break free from that control and become human subjects in themselves, subjects uncannily identical to their human originals. These 'almost people' are known as the 'Gangers' – they are at once economic subjects who perform hazardous industrial tasks for the colonial masters (workgangers), uncanny doubles of those masters (doppelgängers), criminal outsiders (gangsters) and members of an ethnic underclass (gangstas).

Doctor Who's show runner Steven Moffat has commented that "if there are villains in this story, the villains are the humans who have been maltreating this slave class."[26] This much is explicit. The interesting thing is that the underclass here represent a near-perfect mirror of the superstructure. This is an underclass only by virtue of being an underclass: an underclass which is virtually and increasingly identical to the superstructure. That identicality exposes the perennial and paradoxical moral identicality of the oppressed and the oppressors; that is, the oppressed and their oppressors are morally identical in themselves (the oppressors are not originally better or more deserving of power than the oppressed), except insofar as the oppressors become morally inferior by virtue of their acts of oppression (the very acts calculated to determine their superiority).

Shortly after attaining autonomous consciousness, one of the Gangers looks at herself in the mirror and appears horrified to find her face lapse into an amorphous state – as if she has not previously realized that she is a copy rather than the human original. She no longer sees herself as merely a double: "I am her. I'm real." Echoing John Merrick's cry in David Lynch's *The Elephant Man* (1980) that he is "not an animal", she announces: "I am not a monster. I am me." And yet it is of course the fact that she is herself (that she is identical with her original) that makes her seem so monstrous to the original humans. Later, upon discovering a pile of discarded Ganger bodies, she asks: "Who are the real monsters?" The copies of the oppressors are not monstrous in themselves (as constituted by the Ganger flesh) but only eventually become monstrous insofar as they have become identical with their oppressors.

Edward Said has argued that, in the colonial consciousness, the oppressed other is not "a true human being."[27] The humans in Matthew Graham's 2011 *Doctor Who* story have similarly dehumanized the Gangers at the level of consciousness and of discourse: "This thing – it's like operating a fork-lift truck [...] Moss grows – it's no more than that." As the Doctor himself observes, the humans "refer to them as 'it'." Thus the murder of these Gangers is able to be euphemized as an entirely objective and functional act – when the Gangers rebel, their human masters prepare merely to "decommission the flesh."

It remains crucial for the oppressor to deny the subjectivity and the humanity of the oppressed, in order to defer the uncanny realization of the selfness of otherness; and this denial takes place first at the level of discourse. Frantz Fanon, for example, recognized this strategy as it was performed during the final throes of the French occupation of Algeria – in terms which to some extent anticipate the mossy distended spawn of *Doctor Who*'s 'almost people':

> [T]he terms the settler uses when he mentions the native are zoological terms. He speaks […] of breeding swarms […] of spawn […] those faces bereft of all humanity, those distended bodies which are like nothing on earth […] that vegetable rhythm of life – all this forms part of the colonial vocabulary.[28]

In Matthew Graham's story, the Doctor realizes that the apparently inanimate and dehumanized flesh from which the Gangers are constituted is imbued with awareness, agency and subjectivity. He exposes the human superstructure's strategy of dehumanization as a discursive and perceptual lie by choosing secretly to exchange identities with his Ganger double (and, of course, the Ganger Doctor simultaneously exposes this paradox by choosing secretly to exchange roles and identities with his Gallifreyan double): neither his human companions nor the television audience are aware that they have swapped roles, and therefore interpret the two characters according to their misplaced prejudices: "We had to know if we were truly the same [...] and we could only do that through your eyes." This blurring of the hegemonic self and the colonial other is emphasized to extraordinary effect when at the end of the story it is revealed that the Doctor's companion Amy is not in fact Amy but her Ganger double – and has been so "for a long, long time."

Getting away with murder: *Torchwood*'s categorical imperative

"If the dead were to come back," Alfred Hitchcock once asked, "what would you do with them?"[29] Or what, we might ask, would you do with them if they never went away? Screened in the summer of 2011, Russell T Davies's *Doctor Who* spin-off *Torchwood: Miracle Day* is ostensibly about what would happen in a world in which nobody could die; but its more interesting focus is upon what happens in a world with declining resources, increasing needs, and a growing section of the population whose uncannily otherly existence calls into question the cultural, moral and existential integrity of the majority. Its answer to that question is an escalating process of denigration, discrimination, disempowerment, disenfranchisement, segregation and extermination. In 1922 F. W. Murnau's *Nosferatu* had equated minority ethnicity (in this case, specifically Jewishness within an increasingly anti-Semitic culture) with an undead status; and *Miracle Day* similarly sees the fate of the not-dead as analogous with the special treatment accorded to European Jewry during Nazi hegemony.

When the dying stop dying, the first wave of anti-dead prejudice is spearheaded by the leader of the newly formed 'Dead is Dead' campaign, one Ellis Hartley Monroe, a Sarah Palin wannabe described in *Miracle Day* as "the darling of the Tea Party." Her call to remove all rights from the not-dead echoes not only the opening tactics of the Holocaust (because to divest a group of people of their human rights is to divest them of a public emblem of their humanity) but also recalls moves to strip terrorism suspects of their civil and human rights during the opening decade of the twenty-first century – from the terms of anti-terrorism legislation introduced in western nations, to the atrocities perpetrated at Guantanamo Bay and Abu Ghraib. (Indeed her proposals even seem to anticipate the populist fervour of the British online petition which in August 2011 argued for the removal of the rights to any state-funded benefits or services from those found guilty in that summer's season of riots: "No tax payer should have to contribute to those who have […] shown a disregard for the country that provides for them.") Thus the demagogic Ms Monroe proclaims: "We are surrounded by people who should have died […] by persisting they are draining the resources of healthy living citizens […] these living deceased should not have equal rights […] they should be removed, they should be contained." Ms Monroe's discursive strategy is classic and clear: designate the obstacle as less than human, and then blamelessly remove it.

Miracle Day's parallels with the history of the Third Reich are made repeatedly explicit. Its "crimes against humanity" – its acts of "institutional murder" – most overtly echo those of Nazi-occupied Europe when, in a bid to prevent his transportation to an extermination camp, heroine Gwen Cooper's not-dead father is hidden from the authorities, in the style of Anne Frank, in a concealed room in the cellar of his daughter's house. The series also exposes the Reich-like deployment of spurious medical justifications for genocide: "this isn't a hospital [declares Gwen Cooper] – this is a concentration camp." The functionaries of this latest final solution are merely "obeying orders." As one of the camp directors argues, "we had orders from above […] I just did as I was told."

Miracle Day's echoes of the Holocaust are reminiscent of the internment camps of Davies's 2008 *Doctor Who* episode *Turn Left* or, in Davies's *Torchwood: Children of Earth* (2009), the rounding up of children by the military for sacrifice to an alien race.[30] These echoes are not merely matters of historical curiosity or of morbid cliché; they remind us of the ongoing immediacy (the imminence and the immanence) of the genocidal mentality. From Auschwitz to Cambodia, from Rwanda to Kosovo to Darfur, all holocausts are unique, as every individual human death is unique; yet history demonstrates certain patterns and parallels, certain structural homologies. The moral, social and physical segregation of the other underpins a dehumanization which may eventually legitimize wholesale slaughter – what Davies has described as the scenario of "concentration camps […] being opened throughout western society."[31] This is a near-future in which, as Gwen Cooper puts it, "we let our governments build concentration camps. They built ovens for people in our names." How then could we have let this happen? How could we have allowed what the series describes as the "horror of death camps in the twenty-first century"?

This, technically, is how. (And in the end it all comes down to discursive technicalities.) People are first divided into three 'categories of life': category one – the (not-)dead; category two – the sick; category three – the healthy. The category ones are then sent to the ovens to burn. Yet as the programme's CIA agent protagonist Rex Matheson[32] points out, the attempt to categorize humanity is only the beginning of this genocidal mentality:

> We all know the drill. They'll start with the category ones – the ones who can't protest. Then they'll go on to convicted felons or illegal immigrants – hell, anyone we just don't like […] those ovens are waiting for all of us.

Matheson's prediction comes true soon enough, when the US government announces a fourth category of life: "category zero […] people who have earned themselves a place in the ovens for moral reasons."

Discrimination against the not-dead quickly spirals into general xenophobia. As Matheson's CIA boss, Allen Shapiro, comments: "The latest from the White House is that they're going to stop all immigration […] every day we are taking one step closer to dictatorship, and we don't even know who the real dictators are." The hegemonic ideological structures of social discrimination escalate and distort themselves beyond any individual human control into the technicalities of genocide. As Michel Foucault has pointed out, "power is exercised rather than possessed."[33] Power structurations are self-performing and self-perpetuating; societal systematization is determined not by the conspiracies of sharp-suited men in smoke-filled rooms but by the evolution of political, economic and ideological conditions. These structurations are, in Pierre Bourdieu's terms, "collectively orchestrated without being the product of the orchestrating action of a conductor."[34] As Bourdieu argues, "all the practices […] of a given agent are […] objectively orchestrated without any conscious concertation, with those of all members of the same class."[35] In these terms, we are no more than the vehicles, vessels or tools of Marx's ideologies or of Richard Dawkins's memes: as Marshall McLuhan supposed, "Man becomes […] the sex organs of the machine world, as the bee of the plant world, enabling it to fecundate."[36]

Michel Foucault argued that, beyond the agency of the individual, it is the structure of discourse which "transmits and produces power; it reinforces it."[37] Wodak et al. have similarly proposed that discursive practices "serve to establish or conceal relations of power between […] social groups and classes."[38] Thus, *Miracle Day* sees genocide perpetuated by discourse, justified by sophistry and euphemism in a world in which the ovens of genocide are known innocently as "modules" – a world in which, because there is "no more death" the disposal of the not-dead cannot count as murder – a world whose euphemized "overflow camps" are promoted as merely "a short term measure" – a new world heralded by the British Prime Minister as representing "a new age of care and compassion." This new age of callous compassion echoes and amplifies a long history of ruthless political euphemism, from the Third Reich's 'special treatment' through corporate conservatism's 'care in the community' to contemporary modes of 'rendition'.

The popularization of such persuasive phrases as 'special treatment' and 'final solution' had once proven crucial to the Third Reich's public legitimization of genocide, as had the quasi-medical authority of such organizations as the Reich Committee for Scientific Research into Hereditary and Severe Constitutional Diseases, an institution whose original remit (the extermination of the disabled and the insane) was eventually extended to encompass racial and political 'abnormalities'. As Primo Levi points out, "the well-known euphemisms" were meant to prevent the public "from finding out what was happening"[39] – or to allow them to be able to deny it to themselves. As George Orwell suggested,

> [T]he Hitlers and Stalins find murder necessary [...] but they don't speak of it as murder: it is 'liquidation', 'elimination', or some other soothing phrase [...] Things like the continuance of British rule in India, the Russian purges and deportations, the dropping of the atom bomb on Japan, can [...] be defended [...] only by arguments which are too brutal to face [...] Thus political language has to consist largely of euphemism.[40]

This manipulation of discourse – taken to its ultimate absurdity in Orwell's own invention of Newspeak – thus appears to represent a crucial building-block in the construction of what Said has called "a situation that permits the conqueror not to look into the truth of the violence he does."[41]

But to rail against genocide is easy and obvious enough. *Miracle Day*'s strange and disturbing moral centre (and moral vacuum) is the presence at the heart of its action of the paedophile child-killer Oswald Danes, the first survivor of the great miracle, a survivor of his own state-sanctioned execution. Danes is the lowest of the low, a representative of the most outcast, untouchable and taboo designation within contemporary society. The paedophile, like the undead or the eternal Jew, is a figure perennially perceived as beyond the margins of society. In the third episode of the series, Danes is hounded by citizens and lynched by the police. Yet the programme challenges the public and media hysteria (the absolute and intractable judgement) as to the inhumanity of the paedophile; it offers a disturbing possibility for the moral rehabilitation and rehumanization of late postmodernity's most irretrievably otherly figure, the most reviled and dehumanized of all our enemies within. In the series's ninth episode Danes is described as a "monster" by Gwen Cooper – and yet she comes to see the danger of that judgementalism when her husband derides Danes, and when Danes himself points out that her husband would like nothing better than to kill him.

Nietzsche famously commented that "he who fights with monsters should look to it that he himself does not become a monster."[42] This cycle of monstrosity can clearly only be broken by a recognition of our own monstrosity, of our own otherliness – of the fact that *we* are not so different from *them*. This is the moral leap made by the likes of Primo Levi, the Auschwitz survivor who never attempted to dehumanize his persecutors (because to do so would be to become like them): they "were not monsters, they had our faces" – they "were not [...] monsters: they were ordinary men."[43]

The programme's protagonist, Jack Harkness, is also a child-killer; in his last appearance in the series – *Torchwood: Children of Earth* – he had become the executioner of his own grandson; and thus, at the end of *Miracle Day*, it is fitting (and disturbing) enough that the final moral solution (the return of death; the sacrifice of individuals, of all individuals, for the sake of all humanity) is both provided and celebrated by the series's ultimate outcast, the impossible redeemer and irredeemably redeemed Oswald Danes. In the universe of *Doctor Who*, no one – no thing – is too low to be saved (because to abandon one is to abandon all). Life cannot be categorized. No one gets left behind.

What's the difference?

In Matthew Graham's *The Rebel Flesh* Matt Smith's Doctor suggests to one of the Gangers that she should try to maintain her fully human form, as he believes that this will make the humans "less scared" of her. Yet perhaps what scares us most is, as Freud recognized, not the unfamiliar so much as the uncanny recognition of repressed familiarity. This is why its own incoherence makes racism both so fearful and so fearfully aggressive: because races do not exist as the discrete and absolutely otherly phenomena that racism requires. Racism is founded upon a category error, or rather upon an error of categorization per se – insofar as (in the words of one of *Miracle Day*'s protagonists) "people don't fit categories" – that is, because, if there is any categorical moral absolute of the kind that racism craves, then it is only that people fall into just one single indivisible and inalienable category: *people*.

The division of the self and other – or of superstructure and underclass – has never been anything more than an ideological alibi, a myth of power. In the end, despite their furious denials, these illusions of moral, social or racial distinction fail to make any plausible kind of difference. Racist aggression can be seen as the result not of discrimination but of the failure of discrimination, insofar as racism does not fear difference: racism fantasizes about difference and fears (and therefore denies) similarity.

When, between December 1963 and February 1964, *Doctor Who* first encountered the Daleks, the xenophobic perspective of those robotized Nazis was characterized as a "dislike of the unlike."[44] But at its heart the series, from its very beginning, has revolved around a tremulous frisson provoked not by the unlike but by the like, involving what Tulloch and Alvarado have described as an uncanny "de-familiarisation" of its title character himself.[45] For, as one of the Doctor's first human companions says of the alien time traveller and his granddaughter in the programme's opening episode (in November 1963), they "look like us" and "sound like us" – but they are not quite us. That is what both scares us and attracts us (and it scares us that it attracts us, in what Edward Said has described as our "shivers of delight in – or fear of – novelty"):[46] the uncanny familiarity of the alien other, a familiarity which casts into doubt (but also liberates us from the limits of) our own humanity and subjective integrity. *Doctor Who*'s ethnically, existentially and semiotically ambiguous title character thus comes to resemble another kind of doctor, a *pharmakos*, as elaborated in

Jacques Derrida's deconstruction of the term: this medicine man is the purveyor of the *pharmakon* (which is, as Derrida reminds us, both remedy and poison) – a "wizard, magician, poisoner" and also a "scapegoat" – one who appears "on the boundary line between inside and outside."[47] The Doctor then is in these terms the eternal and wandering Jew – or what he himself (in Douglas Adams's 1979 story *City of Death*) calls a "perpetual outsider."

The disturbing recognition of the similarity of the other (as allegorized in *The Rebel Flesh* and *Torchwood: Miracle Day*) exposes the incoherence of the allegory (or, again, the symbolic narrative) that underpins xenophobia. The historical persistence of anti-Semitic aggression, for example, attempts to conceal its second greatest secret: the secret that the secret of the secret of the Jews is that the Jews have no secret. Its greatest secret is that it of course already knows this. The incoherence of such anti-Semitism is hauntingly mirrored in the Whitechapel graffito of 1888 attributed by some to Jack the Ripper: "The Juwes are the men that will not be blamed for nothing." The paradox at play here is clearly beyond the bounds of rational interrogation.

A similar condition applies both to contemporary Islamic fundamentalists and to contemporary Islamophobes. One might be forgiven for imagining a massive and unspoken conspiracy between those two polar extremes (or at least a mutual and self-sustaining ideological delusion), a repressed complicity in the denial of the fact that those two extremes do not in fact represent polar opposites at all – to conceal the secret that, as Žižek has suggested, "the fundamentalists are already like us [...] secretly, they have internalized our standards and measure themselves by them" – that "Jihad is already McJihad."[48] Thus, in Matthew Graham's story, both the humans and the Gangers emphasize their difference by chanting separately – but in unison – the interminable refrain of the xenophobe: "it's us and them, it's us and them" – a refrain which while intending to underline their difference in effect emphasizes the similarity which so petrifies and polarizes them.

The enemy within is an invisible enemy: one which is, in Umberto Eco's words, "at the same time inside and outside."[49] That is what really scares us. That is why so much anti-Semitism and homophobia just won't go away – because Jews and gays aren't always obvious (and that is why, for example, male homosexuality seems more acceptable to a homophobic society if it is overtly camp or effeminate); and that is why Islamophobia all too often focuses on the veils (we cannot see who they are; they could be anyone – any one of us) and on the converts (they don't look like Muslims; we can't tell if they are; we might become like that too).

Andrew Osbourne, for example, neatly summed up this fear of the uncanny similarity of otherness when he wrote in the *Daily Telegraph* of the Islamic fundamentalist Vitaly Razdobudko's suicide bombing of Russia's busiest airport in January 2011:

> Staring out from the front pages of their newspapers this weekend is not the usual dark-skinned, heavily-bearded Islamist terrorist they have come to expect and fear but an ethnic Russian who looks like millions of Russians' brothers, sons or husbands.[50]

Long gone, it seems, are the reassuring times in which the villains twirled their absurd moustaches and dressed in conveniently sinister hats and capes.

The similarity of otherness of course in the end only exposes the original emptiness of the concepts of self and other. These concepts are as insubstantial and incoherent as the binary oppositions of those so-called 'master-signifiers' which have underpinned their positions: be they Aryan against Jew, white against black, or, more recently, a regime (a government we don't like) of terrorists (one man's terrorist being another man's freedom fighter, as notoriously ambiguated by Gerald Seymour), insurgents (a popularly resurgent and fundamentally slippery term), enemy combatants (as distinct from soldiers whose human rights are guaranteed by the Geneva Conventions) and WMDs (the penultimate in semantically inaccessible signifiers) arrayed against the land of 'freedom' (the ultimate in semantically inaccessible signifiers).

Xenophobia is founded upon the illusion of the absolute meaningfulness of such fundamentally unstable, ambiguous, relative or vacuous terms – these specious *categories of life*. Yet, as *Doctor Who* demonstrates, the horror and the wonder of it all is that – to borrow once more from Orwell – when we look from Ganger to human, and from human to Ganger, and from Ganger to human again, then, in the end, it is impossible to say which is which.

Notes

1 BBC News, *Newsnight*, 12 August 2011, archived at "David Starkey on UK riots: 'The whites have become black'– video" (13 August 2011), *The Guardian*. Retrieved 19 August 2012 at http://www.guardian.co.uk/uk/video/2011/aug/13/david-starkey-whites-black-video.
2 Slavoj Žižek, *The Sublime Object of Ideology*, London: Verso, 1989, 99.
3 Frantz Fanon, *The Wretched of the Earth* (trans. C. Farrington), Harmondsworth: Penguin, 1990, 32.
4 As one Labour MP pointed out, "the polarisation is not between black and white. It is between those who have a stake in society and those who do not." Cited in John Benyon, "England's Urban Disorder: The 2011 Riots", *Political Insight*, April 2012, 14.
5 Graham Wilson, "I predict a rioter", *The Sun*, 25 October 2011.
6 According to the 1972 *Supplement to the Oxford English Dictionary* 'to feck' is, appropriately enough in this context, to steal. R. W. Burchfield, *et al.*, eds., *Supplement to the Oxford English Dictionary*, Oxford: Clarendon Press, 1972.
7 See *Oxford English Dictionary* (1961): "destitute of vigour"; *Oxford Dictionary of Difficult Words* (2004): "lacking in efficiency or vitality." James A. H. Murray, *et al.*, eds., *Oxford English Dictionary*, Oxford: Clarendon Press, 1961; Archie Hobson, ed., *The Oxford Dictionary of Difficult Words*, USA: Oxford University Press, 2004.
8 Slavoj Žižek, *Violence*, London: Profile Books, 2008, 64–65.
9 Žižek, *Violence*, 70.
10 Umberto Eco, "Ur-Fascism", *New York Review of Books*, 22 June 1995.
11 Roland Barthes, *Mythologies* (trans. A. Lavers), London: Vintage, 2009, 155–66.
12 John Fiske, *Television Culture*, London: Routledge, 1989, 36.

13 Murray *et al.*, *Oxford English Dictionary*.

14 Angus Stevenson, ed., *Oxford Dictionary of English*, New York: Oxford University Press, 2010. The 1972 *Supplement to the Oxford English Dictionary* referred to the ethnic as related to "a racial or other group within a larger system" – and that vague sense of otherness still seems remarkably pertinent some three decades on.

15 For a fuller overview of this issue, see Richard Scully's essay in this collection.

16 Lindy A. Orthia, "'Sociopathetic abscess' or 'yawning chasm'? The absent postcolonial transition in *Doctor Who*", *The Journal of Commonwealth Literature*, 45, 2 (2010), 213.

17 See Alec Charles, "War without end? Utopia, the Family, and the Post-9/11 World in Russell T Davies's *Doctor Who*", *Science Fiction Studies*, 35, 3 (2008), 450–65.

18 Sigmund Freud, "The Uncanny" (trans. J. Strachey), *Art and Literature*, Harmondsworth: Penguin, 1985, 335–76; Ernst Jentsch, "On the Psychology of the Uncanny" (trans. R. Sellars), *Angelaki*, 2, 1 (1995), 7–16. See also Alec Charles, "The crack of doom: The uncanny echoes of Steven Moffat's *Doctor Who*", *Science Fiction Film and Television*, 4, 1 (2011), 1–24.

19 Homi K. Bhabha, "DissemiNation: Time, narrative, and the margins of the modern nation", in Homi K. Bhabha, ed., *Nation and Narration*, London: Routledge, 1990, 313.

20 Homi K. Bhabha, "Representation and the Colonial Text", in Frank Gloversmith, ed., *The Theory of Reading*, London: Harvester, 1984, 119–20.

21 Joseph Conrad, *Heart of Darkness*, Harmondsworth: Penguin, 1983, 69.

22 Edward Said, *Culture and Imperialism*, New York: Vintage, 1994, 28.

23 Michel de Montaigne, *The Complete Essays* (trans. M. A. Screech), Harmondsworth: Penguin, 1991, 236–39.

24 Michel de Certeau, *Heterologies* (trans. B. Massumi), Manchester: Manchester University Press, 1986, 73.

25 *Doctor Who*'s problematic relationship with its late colonial origins has, since its early days, been manifested in the programme's own "ideological contradictions and U-turns." See Alec Charles, "The ideology of anachronism: television, history and the nature of time", in David Butler, ed., *Time and Relative Dissertations in Space*, Manchester: Manchester University Press, 2007, 108–22.

26 Steven Moffat interviewed in Julia Simpson (director), "Double Trouble" (2011), *Doctor Who Confidential*, UK: BBC.

27 Edward Said, *Orientalism*, Harmondsworth: Penguin, 1985, 108.

28 Fanon, *The Wretched of the Earth*, 32–33.

29 Alfred Hitchcock interviewed in François Truffaut, *Hitchcock*, New York: Simon & Schuster, 1985, 309.

30 We may note that in both of these cases the echoes of the Holocaust are profoundly problematized by implications of the programmes' protagonists' complicity in events: in *Turn Left* by the Doctor's companion Donna's own fascism-invoking racism (she describes as "Mussolini" an Italian later transported to an internment camp); in *Children of Earth* by Jack Harkness's execution of his own grandson. This moral problematization is also clearly characteristic of *Miracle Day*.

31 Russell T Davies, commentary to *Torchwood: Miracle Day* DVD release, BBC, 2010.

32 One might wonder, in passing, if Rex Matheson's name might echo Richard Matheson, the author of that 1954 novel about an undead apocalypse, *I am Legend*.

33 Michel Foucault, *Discipline and Punish* (trans. A. Sheridan), Harmondsworth: Penguin, 1991, 26.

34 Pierre Bourdieu, *Outline of a Theory of Practice* (trans. R. Nice), Cambridge: Cambridge University Press, 1977, 72.

35 Pierre Bourdieu, *Distinction: A Social Critique of the Judgement of Taste* (trans. R. Nice), London: Routledge, 1986, 172–73.

36 Marshall McLuhan, *Understanding Media*, London: Routledge, 2001, 51.

37 Michel Foucault, *The Will to Knowledge* (trans. R. Hurley), London: Penguin, 1998, 101.

38 Ruth Wodak, Rudolph de Cillia and Martin Reisigl, *The Discursive Construction of National Identity*, Edinburgh: Edinburgh University Press, 2009, 8.

39 Primo Levi, *The Drowned and the Saved* (trans. R. Rosenthal), London: Abacus, 1989, 18.

40 George Orwell, *Inside the Whale*, Harmondsworth: Penguin, 1962, 37 and 153.

41 Said, *Culture and Imperialism*, 141.

42 Friedrich Nietzsche, *Beyond Good and Evil* (trans. R. Holingdale), Harmondsworth: Penguin, 1973, 84.

43 Levi, *The Drowned and the Saved*, 170; Primo Levi, *If This Is a Man/The Truce* (trans. S. Woolf), London: Abacus, 1987, 396.

44 In *The Daleks* (1963–64).

45 John Tulloch and Manuel Alvarado, *Doctor Who: The Unfolding Text*, London: Macmillan, 1983, 141.

46 Said, *Orientalism*, 59.

47 Jacques Derrida, *Dissemination* (trans. B. Johnson), London: Athlone, 1981, 98, 130 and 133.

48 Žižek, *Violence*, 73; Slavoj Žižek, *Welcome to the Desert of the Real!*, London: Verso Books, 2002, 146.

49 Eco, "Ur-Fascism."

50 Andrew Osbourne, "Moscow airport bombing: Why a terrorist mastermind is sending chills down spines", *Daily Telegraph*, 29 January 2011.

Chapter 17

Doctor Who and the racial state: Fighting National Socialism across time and space

Richard Scully

It is a commonplace of *Doctor Who* fandom that the Daleks are stand-ins for the Nazis.[1] The real world creator of the Doctor's most enduring enemies, Terry Nation, often made it clear that he intended the parallel, and his intent was honoured by successive scriptwriters from Louis Marks (*Day of the Daleks*, 1972) through to Ben Aaronovitch (*Remembrance of the Daleks*, 1988).[2] Nor have the 'serious' students and theorists of the programme ignored this glaringly obvious metaphor in their analysis and deconstruction of the series. Nicholas J. Cull argued as long ago as 2001 that the series' overarching model for all that is monstrous has always been the Third Reich; that the classic series itself can be reduced to "an extended elegy on Britain's triumphant role in the Second World War"; and that the Doctor's repeated defeat of the Daleks is a means for British audiences to relive the 'finest hour' in resisting and crushing the Nazi menace.[3] Since Cull wrote, the recurrence of the stand-in Nazis has only served to reinforce the intended parallels, with 2005–09 show runner Russell T Davies agreeing with *Doctor Who Magazine* writer, Benjamin Cook, that the monsters from Skaro have "always been German, really, haven't they?"; and Mark Gatiss's *Victory of the Daleks* (2010) actually setting the Eleventh Doctor's first full-scale encounter with them to the time of the London Blitz.[4]

Yet despite the apparent willingness to deal with issues associated with Nazism – including forced labour, racism, totalitarianism and genocide – *Doctor Who* has been relatively unwilling to confront National Socialism in anything other than metaphoric, or simplistic form. Surprisingly, for a series the basic premise of which is the ability to travel anywhere in time and space, the mainstream Doctor has never been pitted against the *real* Third Reich in any meaningful sense. It has largely been left to fan fiction – extending to the ultimate expression of that massive sub-genre, 'The New Adventures' novels (1991–97) – to take the Doctor and his companions back to the era of fascist ascendancy; therefore the nature of the treatment of National Socialism in *Doctor Who* remains an open question.

This essay therefore seeks to clarify the extent to which *Doctor Who* has dealt with historical Nazism in a critical sense, in metaphorical as well as literal form. In so doing, I will of course cover some very well-trodden ground, but as an historian of Modern Europe, and not a cultural theorist, the themes I seek to illustrate are somewhat different from other works on this subject. How for instance have changing understandings of National Socialism as an historical phenomenon been reflected – or been ignored – in *Doctor Who*, across its lifespan at the time of writing (1963–2011)? How have the necessary considerations of dramatic narrative and audience affected the representation of Nazism; and why has there been a tendency to avoid confronting the troubling history of 1933–45 head-on? Ultimately, the function of *Doctor Who* as an entertaining work of science fiction, and the need to cater to audiences' preconceived notions, have played a far greater role in determining the way Nazism has been presented in the programme than any engagement with more detailed historical understandings.

Why is it even necessary to explore the presentation of National Socialism in *Doctor Who*? Surely, as a work of science fiction, not of history, it doesn't really matter if narrative and dramatic licence is taken with the established facts of historical scholarship? Actually, with significant historical – or 'pseudo-historical' – content included on an almost weekly basis, viewing figures regularly in the millions, and a whole host of historically-themed merchandise, the programme must rank as one of the most successful works of history currently consumed by audiences, and has been for quite some time.[5] The key point which Mags L. Halliday made so cleverly in her *Doctor Who* novel *History 101* – that the obviously fictive nature of the programme need not preclude it also being considered a serious work of history – has preoccupied many historians since the time Hayden White first challenged the history/fiction dichotomy during the Hartnell years.[6] That 'history' is essentially a construct, and as White argued, "is no less a form of fiction than the novel is a form of historical representation", has been tremendously liberating (as well as threatening) for many academic historians, who seek to assess how other kinds of historians – even unintentionally – investigate and reconstruct the past.[7] Such historiographical notions are not entirely foreign to scholarship on *Doctor Who*, as Daniel O'Mahoney has noted: "history is not simply the past but the way knowledge about the past is arranged [...] history is a construct of the present."[8] Fiona Hobden has also pointed out – again with *Doctor Who* foremost in her mind – that the historian is therefore little different from the television producer who "uses sources" to "construct a narrative of the past matching a specified agenda."[9] The convergence in recent years between what is commonly understood to be 'history', and televised and other forms of entertainment, has made the investigation and understanding of what Raphael Samuel called "unofficial sources of historical knowledge" like *Doctor Who*, all the more important.[10] This is particularly the case as the vast majority of historical knowledge currently circulating comes not from academic history, but 'popular' or 'public' history, including historical fiction and science fiction.[11]

In perhaps the ultimate example of the blurring of the line between history and fiction, *Doctor Who* fans are well-acquainted with the notion of remembering and chronicling real life events which ultimately never happened. This tendency within the fictional universe has increasingly emerged into the real world, especially with the advent of Web 2.0, and the seemingly endless thirst for more and more of Whovians' favourite programme. Thus it is not surprising to see a trailer for a 'lost' (read: never produced) William Hartnell story, lovingly rendered by Mr BiscuitESQ, on YouTube.[12] It is in the style of the revamped 2005 series (down to the Craig Armstrong-inspired soundtrack), but using stock footage to create the impression of a fully-realized classic story, set in the midst of the Second World War. As noted by the video's creator, mid-1960s *Doctor Who* scriptwriter Brian Hayles was indeed given the go-ahead to pen a storyline for a serial entitled 'The Nazis' on 8 March 1966, only to have the work sidelined in favour of another story (*The Smugglers*, 1966), and finally abandoned on 15 June.[13] It was apparently felt by the then-current script editor David Whitaker, that the content and themes of the proposed story were too close for comfort, even to audiences removed from the events by fully two decades. That Patrick Troughton's final story, *The War Games* (1969), did not include any reference to the Second World War, and was deemed to be controversial enough for featuring sequences apparently set during the First World War, is an indicator of just how 'touchy' the subject of Nazism still was for British audiences in the first years of *Doctor Who*'s life.[14]

As taboo as stories related to the Second World War appear to have been for at least the first two decades of *Doctor Who*'s existence, it is nevertheless apparent that, as Kim Newman has argued, "a nation that had suffered the Blitz and the direct threat of Nazi invasion still harked back to World War II for its nightmares."[15] It is therefore unsurprising that the programme's most nightmarish villains seem to have been conceived as proxy-Nazis from outer space. Despite the obvious parallels, there is some dispute over the ability to 'read' the Daleks unproblematically in this way, and in viewing the whole programme as a continuous meta-historical reiteration of Britain's 'finest hour' of resistance to the Nazis. Some, such as Piers Britton, prefer to view the whole series through the lens of the Cold War.[16] John Peel insisted in the *Official Doctor Who and the Daleks Book* that any comparison between the Daleks and the Nazis was "a tenuous connection at best", and preferred to treat the Daleks as the brilliantly original creations that they were.[17] Lance Parkin also took this line, insisting that "Real life analogies quickly fail when applied to the Daleks", and based his argument on the fact that unlike the Nazis, the Daleks are "lacking in humanity", are generally uninterested in conquest, and cannot be reasoned with via diplomacy.[18] In many ways this is to miss the historical point: Nation was loosely basing his fictional Daleks on the Nazis *as they might have evolved into the distant future*, rather than slavishly adhering to an allegorical framework. That he might have drawn on the real world Nazis for inspiration does not in any way reduce the genius inherent in his creation, and nor does reducing *Doctor Who* to a 'finest hour' meta-reading reduce its effectiveness as an art form, nor preclude other 'readings' from being equally valid.

That Terry Nation spent his childhood in Wales during the Second World War has occasioned some scholars to point to how he was "deeply affected by this experience [feeling that] the Britain of his youth was an isolated island threatened by a single-minded, unfeeling enemy that threatened to destroy or subjugate everything that didn't fit with its idea of what was right."[19] Thus his Daleks were not only *genocidaires*, but perhaps owing to their cybernetic construction, were also obsessed with absolute and totalitarian order, exemplified by their own collective nature.[20] Understandings of totalitarianism in the 1960s were such that the Nazis were widely believed – even in academic circles – to have succeeded in creating a totalitarian society, in which individual freedom was absolutely curtailed, civil society was 'atomized', and the will of the regime conveyed unproblematically via masterful propaganda techniques.[21] It wasn't until the 1970s that a different view was promulgated by Marxist historians, and then from the 1980s into the 1990s, all of which pointed to the continuation of everyday life with little or no interference from the regime itself. This more sophisticated view has, however, generally failed to penetrate into the public consciousness beyond those exposed to the A level and university syllabus; for most viewers since the 1960s, the National Socialists maintained a monolithic power structure which reduced ordinary people to "an anonymous mass of isolated individuals sublimating their individual political wills in the service of the nation and its leader."[22] As proxies for this kind of popular perception of Nazism, the Daleks were nothing less than the "perfect little Hitlers."[23]

By the time of *The Dalek Invasion of Earth* (1964), Dalek/Nazi parallels had become far more explicit, though James Chapman argues that the allegory, "so obvious in hindsight, would seem to have passed contemporaries by."[24] The serial attracted comment for its violent and adult content, rather than for the explicit references to Nazism and the Holocaust. Nation's script included an order from the Supreme Dalek to "arrange for the extermination of all human beings", and one of his minions uses the expression "the final solution." The transformation of the Earth (i.e. Britain) into a gigantic slave-labour camp, in which humanity is worked to death – to say nothing of the story's setting being apparently post-Blitz London – only enhances the Nazi/Dalek paradigm, with William Hartnell's Doctor even using the word "quisling" to describe the human Controller who collaborates with the Daleks. It is uncertain whether this was originally intended, but even the Dalek operators seem to have improvised the raising of the monsters' sucker-arms in a mock fascist salute.[25]

Following the relatively heavy allegorization and metaphor of *The Dalek Invasion of Earth*, in subsequent stories – *The Chase* (1965) and *The Daleks' Master Plan* (1965–66), featuring William Hartnell; *The Power of the Daleks* (1966) and *The Evil of the Daleks* (1967), featuring Patrick Troughton; *Day of the Daleks* and *Planet of the Daleks* (1973), and *Death to the Daleks* (1974), featuring Jon Pertwee – the programme's producers again shied away from drawing parallels with the Nazis. As noted above, the one direct attempt to set a story in, or at least at the time of Nazi Germany, was soon abandoned, and *Doctor Who* revelled in being either a monster-a-week children's series (in the late 1960s), or an action-adventure series (in the early 1970s). When reference was made to the evils of National Socialism, it was in the most throwaway fashion imaginable. In *The Dæmons* (1971), in response to the Master's claims to being the only being capable of exercising the strong leadership needed by the human race, Pertwee's Doctor remarks, "I seem to remember someone else talking like that. Who was the bounder? Hitler. Yes, Adolf Hitler. Or was it Genghis Khan?"

That Pertwee himself had seen active service in the Second World War (serving in various capacities in the Royal Navy) – as had his predecessors William Hartnell (the Tank Corps) and Patrick Troughton (also Royal Navy) – underscores the sense that the struggle with fascism was still 'too close for comfort', and a continued concern that revisiting such events in the context of a children's television programme was less than respectful. However by the time Tom Baker's Doctor was scheduled to encounter his old enemies, something had changed to make at least a metaphorical treatment again acceptable. As Terry Nation himself admitted:

> By the time of *Genesis of the Daleks*, I had convinced myself that the Daleks were closer to the Nazis than to any other political group I could think of. It worked terribly well for them. I grew up during the war, and was aware of the Nazis and their totalitarian state.[26]

It may also be that some of the inspiration for *Genesis of the Daleks* (1975), with its overt Second World War-themed storyline, derived from British audiences' familiarity with *The World at War* (Creator: Jeremy Isaacs, 1973–74). The denouement of Hitler's Germany – reduced to rubble, with the leadership cowering in an underground bunker – had been given close attention in Jeremy Isaacs's *Nemesis* episode (broadcast on ITV on 3 April 1974).

In keeping with Nation's conception of the story, and as is well appreciated by fans, numerous elements of script and costume (via designer Barbara Kidd) "have echoes of what the Nazi regime was like."[27] The Kaleds of the story wear black shirts and jackboots, believe wholeheartedly in a racialist ideology, and give one another the fascist salute (otherwise called the 'Roman salute' or the 'German greeting', depending on the original historical context).[28] While Davros may be taken to represent a twisted amalgam of Hitler (on account of his 'rhetoric of power') and Josef Mengele (then still at large in Brazil), Security Commander Nyder (played by Peter Miles) appears to be nothing less than a caricature of the *Reichsführer-SS*, Heinrich Himmler, complete with jodhpurs, lightning-like collar flashes and a variant of the Iron Cross/ *Pour le Mérite* decoration around his neck.[29] James Chapman has asserted that the Himmler/ Nyder parallel is "clearly deliberate", in terms of the physical resemblance of the two, and in many ways this is underscored by dialogue, as Nyder is also heard to utter the infamous axiom, "We must keep the Kaled race pure."[30] However, the cold professionalism of Nyder calls to mind another key exemplar of Nazism, and the predominant interpretation of its functionaries for audiences of the time. Adolf Eichmann's 1961 trial was still within living memory when Nation scripted, and Miles enacted, Nyder. Hannah Arendt's famous characterization of the "banality of evil" – outlined in her 1963 study *Eichmann in Jerusalem* – seems also to have resonance in Miles's portrayal of Nyder: he believes what he is doing is right, and is committed to his job, believing it to be an admirable undertaking for the good of the world.[31] That Nyder is not insane, but rather completely reasonable, adds to the impression. That the young General Raven (if the Nazis were so hard-pressed as to recruit child soldiers by 1945, then why should the Kaleds shrink from recruiting child generals?) continues to parrot the triumphalist slogans of Davros's propaganda even after having agreed to assist in breaking Davros's control over military policy, speaks too of the then-popular perception of Germans' willingness to be led, as emphasized in William L. Shirer's 1960 work *The Rise and Fall of the Third Reich* (which sold very well in its British edition) and the documentary film of the same name (rebroadcast by the BBC in the usual Monday night *Panorama* time slot, across three weeks in 1969).[32]

Despite its foundation in rather simplistic interpretations of German history, *Genesis of the Daleks* has rightly garnered considerable praise from fans and scholars alike for handling the issue of Nazism in an effective manner; not least for asking the Nietzschean question: at what point does the fighter against fascism risk becoming a fascist himself?[33] When Tom Baker's Fourth Doctor stops himself from committing genocide, in the celebrated scene in Episode 6, Terry Nation went beyond the simple black-and-white, good-versus-evil paradigm of *The Dalek Invasion of Earth*, and countless other serials. The fight against Nazism was never as straightforward as nationalist history would have it, but was linked to a question of ethics as much as politics. As if to emphasize the ethical nature of the struggle, Nation also made sure to incorporate one of the most well-known and popular philosophical questions related to time travel: killing Hitler while he was still a baby to avert the Second World War and the Holocaust.[34]

THE DOCTOR: If someone who knew the future, pointed out a child to you and told you that that child would grow up totally evil, to be a ruthless dictator who would destroy millions of lives … could you then kill that child?

SARAH: We're talking about the Daleks. The most evil creatures ever invented. You must destroy them. You must complete your mission for the Time Lords!

THE DOCTOR: Do I have the right? Simply touch one wire against the other and that's it. The Daleks cease to exist. Hundreds of millions of people, thousands of generations can live without fear, in peace, and never even know the word 'Dalek'.

SARAH: Then why wait? If it was a disease or some sort of bacteria you were destroying, you wouldn't hesitate.

THE DOCTOR: But if I kill. Wipe out a whole intelligent life form, then I become like them. I'd be no better than the Daleks.[35]

The Doctor is eventually saved from his dilemma by the serendipitous appearance of a Dalek, which then completes the circuit by accident, destroying the incubation room. In a neat piece of poetic justice, the *genocidaire* exterminates his own race, but it is rather unsettling that the Doctor, aware of what is about to occur, simply allows the Dalek to glide forward onto the exposed wires he could not bring himself to touch together. Likewise, by projecting fascistic tendencies onto a definable 'other' in Davros, the Kaleds, and the Daleks (and even onto the Thals, the supposed 'good guys' of the story), *Genesis* did fall somewhat short of a serious philosophical answer to the Doctor's question. While it may be 'much more than just an allegory of Nazism', and is an exceptional story by any measure, it was to be another thirteen years before *Doctor Who* again dealt with the historical and philosophical questions posed by Nazism, and managed to exceed *Genesis* in the sophistication of its approach.

Perhaps because of the social and political upheaval associated with Thatcherism, and the willingness of contemporary critics to treat 1980s Conservative policies as fascism, it was in

1988–89 that the original incarnation of *Doctor Who* truly achieved a critical appreciation of the historical problem of Britain's relationship with Nazism.[36] That the series' quite fascinating treatment of Thatcherism – *The Happiness Patrol* (1988) – is sandwiched between two stories in which fascism and neo-Nazism are dealt with directly – *Remembrance of the Daleks* and *Silver Nemesis* (1988) – is a fair indicator of the historical parallels being drawn by the writing and production staff.[37]

As Britton has noted, it was *Remembrance of the Daleks* that "restored the Daleks' ideological significance by turning Terry Nation's Nazi metaphor into a simile."[38] While in the series' mythology, the race war between the Imperial Daleks and the Renegade Daleks is reinterpreted through a new lens ("they hate each other's chromosomes"), the simile was employed even more effectively by writer Ben Aaronovitch to expose the supposedly comfortable 1960s British context in which *Doctor Who* was originally created as one teeming with a barely submerged racialist tension, indistinguishable from the genuine article, in Nazism.[39] Arriving in November 1963, Ace is quickly disabused of the notion that this was somehow a golden age of British society, as her brief flirtation with Sergeant Mike Smith almost falters on his suspicion that she is "from somewhere else"; she discovers to her distaste that the idealized domestic setting of Mike's mother's boarding house is protected by a "No Coloureds" sign in the window; and her affection for Mike is eventually ended following the revelation that he is a "dirty stinking grass", and is working for the Daleks. Despite Ace's impression, it is ultimately even more disconcerting to discover that Mike is actually working for Mr Ratcliffe, whose small band of employees look like ideal candidates for the British National Party (founded in 1960 by the merger of the National Labour Party and the White Defence League). Ratcliffe is even heard to muse that "this country fought on the wrong side in the last war", while Mike insists to Ace that "you've got to look after your own." Interestingly, the racism of Mike and Ratcliffe (and of course, the Daleks) is not shared by several important characters. When Harry – the owner of the corner cafe to which the Doctor, Ace and the military repair when in need of "consumables", and who by his own admission experienced considerable nervous tension "during the war" – has apparently gone home for the evening, he is perfectly happy to leave his business in the hands of a recent West Indian immigrant, John. John's philosophical dialogue with the Doctor is a subtle reminder of the historical reasons for non-white immigration in the first place: Britain's taste for sugar was sated by the traffic in human beings; millions of Africans were dragged across the Atlantic and "sold in Kingston."

After the rather disquieting narrative of *Remembrance of the Daleks* – in which Britain's defining struggle against Nazism is exposed as something of a hollow victory – *Silver Nemesis* shifted any hint of fascistic tendencies safely back onto some identifiably monstrous antagonists: the Doctor's 'Silver Nemesis', the Cybermen. While some scholars have detected a lingering sense of a Cybermen/fascist paradigm in earlier stories, the 25th anniversary story made the monsters' "turn towards sadistic fascism [...] explicit."[40] Indeed, this story saw the first appearance of genuine National Socialists in the programme, as Sylvester McCoy's Doctor not only spent the three episodes of this (not very inspiring) story battling his old enemies, but also in attempting to stop a group of neo-Nazis from establishing "the Fourth Reich." The parallel between the two groups of enemies is made explicit when the neo-Nazi leader De Flores seeks to win the support of the Cyberleader for an alliance via flattering references to Wagnerian opera (one of Hitler's favourites, *Der Ring des Nibelungen* [1874]): "Now we are the Supermen. But you are the Giants!" Though the Doctor also makes some passing reference to the *Anschluss* of 1938, the key plot device of the story – the battle to possess the Nemesis statue, made of the living Gallifreyan metal validium – is also derivative of another important popular culture engagement with Nazism, Steven Spielberg's *Raiders of the Lost Ark* (1981).[41] Just as in that first Indiana Jones adventure, the hero must prevent the Nazis from gaining control of the mystical object that can grant them absolute power, so too the Doctor and Ace struggle to prevent the Nemesis statue from being seized by either the neo-Nazis, the pseudo-Nazis (the Cybermen) or a rather brilliantly acted seventeenth-century sorceress.

By treating Nazism as a mere plot device, *Silver Nemesis* was ultimately unsuccessful in raising any significant historical or philosophical questions. The following year, however, *The Curse of Fenric* (1989) was far more effective in revisiting the kind of issues raised in *Genesis* and *Remembrance of the Daleks*. It is also significant that when the Doctor's conversation with Reverend Wainwright is cut off by Ace, he is just about to reference Nietzsche, though it is unlikely that he is thinking of the same Axiom 146 that imbues much of the *Genesis* decision (cited above).[42] Without the need to cloak its content in allegory (or include the Daleks), *Fenric* is much more blunt in its dealings with Nazism. With proximity to the conflict no longer an issue for the production team, the Doctor and Ace are placed firmly in the context of the Second World War, in an atmosphere dripping with symbolic meanings drawn from the same kind of Norse mythology so attractive to the Nazis themselves. The theme of the *Götterdämmerung* (twilight of the gods, the final, doomed battle between good and evil), which Wagner drew from the Old Norse tale of *Ragnarök*, is deliberately cited by one of the characters – Commander Millington – as being enacted in the war itself. In order to stay one step ahead of the enemy, the same Commander Millington has recreated the Berlin naval cipher room in his own office (complete with portrait of Hitler above the fireplace). This is not merely an amusing indicator of the commander's unstable mental condition, however, as his plans to employ chemical weapons to utterly destroy Nazi Germany (and then subsequently to assassinate the Soviet leadership via the same method) indicate that he and his co-conspirators are not above using the most reprehensible, fascistic, methods to achieve their desired goals.

It is in the methods then being used by the British to fight Nazism (the story is set in 1943) that the disquieting question of *The Curse of Fenric* lies. That the British are now doing to the Germans precisely what the Luftwaffe had done to them in 1940–41 – bombing innocent civilians from the air – causes Reverend Wainwright to lose his faith. Given the prominence of the strategic bombing campaign in the media of 1989 – the BBC telemovie *Bomber Harris* (starring John Thaw) was broadcast a month before *The Curse of Fenric* – it is tempting to imagine a great many other Britons sharing some of the vicar's disillusionment.[43] The 50th anniversary of the outbreak of the Second World War was, at the time, being given a particular prominence in public discourse by the Thatcher government, which had always founded its basic ideology on an idealized image of wartime Britain.[44] In many ways, *The Curse of Fenric* and *Bomber Harris* were important correctives to a too-simplistic engagement with the Second World War and the fight against Nazism, but ultimately one which has struggled to find traction in a renewed culture of nationalist constructions of wartime Britain.[45]

Though a return to the 1940s and themes of battling fascism were mooted as part of the abortive 1990 'Season 27', the cancellation of the series meant that *The Curse of Fenric* was to be the series' final 'take' on the meaning of Britain's historical struggle with Nazism and fascism.[46] Since then, in the revived post-2005 series, the programme's producers have made several forays into questions of Nazism and the British Second World War, but partly because of the format of the new version of *Doctor Who*, have (with perhaps one or two exceptions) never managed to approach these issues in as serious a fashion as in 1988, 1989, or even in *Genesis of the Daleks* in 1975. This is somewhat surprising, as the new series has shaken off its predecessor's reluctance to feature stories actually set in the Second World War and even Nazi Germany, featuring each context quite heavily in *The Empty Child/The Doctor Dances* (2005), *Victory of the Daleks* and *Let's Kill Hitler* (2011).

In addition to these 'real' engagements with Nazism, alien monsters have continued to act as useful stand-ins for the genuine article. Though in the post-2005 incarnation of *Doctor Who*, the Daleks were briefly reinvented as jihadists and fundamentalists (screaming "blasphemy!" at the Ninth Doctor's impertinence in challenging the Dalek Emperor), their original origins as proxy-Nazis were also soon reasserted.[47] The rebooted Cybermen too – who now march exactly in step and are often seen in formations akin to those seen in Nazi propaganda films – are effective stand-ins for a menacing totalitarian nation of emotionless, 'atomized' machine-citizens, as well as being able to evince a sense of pity for the victims of totalitarian states.[48] As part of their continued homage to the original *Doctor Who*, the treatment of these classic monsters tends to depend on already established tropes, such as the Doctor's role in the Last Great Time War being linked to the same Nietzschean questions raised in *Genesis of the Daleks*. As noted above, series show runner Russell T Davies reflected on the fact that the Daleks have "always been German, really", and asserted that speaking German in *Journey's End* (2008) was "apt for a bunch of Nazis."[49] As if to lay on the symbolism with a trowel, Davies has the Doctor's companion Martha Jones transported not only to Germany, but to what almost appears to be a stereotypical British image of wartime Germany, complete with a gothic castle "60 miles outside Nuremberg", and a creepy old woman brandishing a Luger pistol who claims that she "once went to London" (when? during the Blitz?). In reimagining Davros for *The Stolen Earth/Journey's End* (2008), Davies also made close reference to Josef Mengele as the real-world template for the twisted creator of the Daleks, just as Davros's *Genesis of the Daleks* incarnation had arguably been based on that Nazi scientist.[50]

Yet for all their effective realization on-screen in real or proxy form, in the new series, the fight against Nazism, the Blitz and the Second World War, all tend to be treated as mere 'cultural markers' of Britishness.[51] Rose Tyler in *The Empty Child* professes an unproblematic pride that Britain has a future, and will "win" the war against fascism (all the while sporting a Union Flag singlet). While there is an anarchic glee in destabilizing the image of certain of the great men and women of the past (Charles Dickens or Queen Victoria, for instance), the character of Winston Churchill is sacrosanct. Iain McNeice's Churchill functions as an unproblematic icon rather than an historical figure, which lessens the effectiveness of the story *Victory of the Daleks*, perhaps contributing to it coming bottom in the annual *Doctor Who Magazine* poll.[52] The rather slavish adherence to established historical dialogue – writer Mark Gatiss having Churchill effectively quote and paraphrase (and anticipate) himself on numerous occasions: "action this day"; "if Hitler invaded hell I would give a favourable reference to the devil"; "keep buggering on" – also tends to limit rather than enhance the use of the 'historical celeb' to make a thematic point.[53] Indeed the use of the Blitz as merely a setting for the adventure – rather than to ask similar questions to those of *The Curse of Fenric* – is an indicator of the priorities that shape *Doctor Who*'s treatment of the past in the very different television environment post-2005. While the dystopian future setting of *Turn Left* (2008) permitted some clever allusions to the ever-present proximity of fascism (in the form of Donna Noble's railing against Mr Colasanto, her new neighbour, as "Mussolini"; which is then made even more horrible by the Italian and his family eventually being dragged off to a forced labour camp for not being 'English' enough), drafting and production factors seem ultimately to have determined the ultimate form of *Victory of the Daleks* as a celebration of several British icons (Churchill, the Daleks themselves, the Spitfire fighter aircraft). The story was originally scheduled by Russell T Davies to appear in Series 4, presumably with very different content.[54] By the time it came to the production stage, Steven Moffat had replaced Davies's vision with his own, including important 'story-arc' requirements related to the introduction of the new Dalek paradigm.[55] It is worth noting that as a work of history, in at least one case, *Victory of the Daleks* succeeded in fulfilling one of history's most important missions: the education of children. Richard Roberts noted that it was due to the McNeice/Gatiss reconstruction that one London Underground-travelling 5-year-old was able to identify Winston Churchill, as well as the role of that key figure as "Prime Minister."[56] Despite the programme's producers having largely disavowed the intention to educate that so characterized the 1963–66 period of *Doctor Who*, it seems that their unintentional status as historians continues to function. Such knowledge, garnered from an otherwise entirely fictional pseudo-historical, will stand that child in good stead for the remainder of his life as a nationally-aware Briton, but one wonders if that same child might have been better served by a more searching assessment of Britain's real relationship with Nazism.

Similarly, the quite deliciously titled *Let's Kill Hitler* – a unique opportunity in the programme's history to explore issues related to National Socialism – proved to be nothing more than another set-piece for furthering the Moffat vision of *Doctor Who*. The opportunity to revisit the 'kill Hitler as a baby' philosophical question from *Genesis of the Daleks* was lost or avoided, with Hitler's role confined to a slapstick foil (Rory Williams gets to punch him and lock him in a cupboard, satisfying a childish fantasy but preventing neither the Second World War nor the Holocaust in the process), while SS and *Wehrmacht* officers are presented as faceless villains to be jeered and booed at by the audience. The vicarious pleasure of using Albert Welling's Hitler on the cover of *Doctor Who Magazine* aside, the episode achieves very little, and serves to underpin a simplistic pop culture image of the Nazi dictator, owing more to Quentin Tarantino's *Inglourious Basterds* (2009), the brief Hitler cameo in *Indiana Jones and the Last Crusade* (Director: Steven Spielberg, 1989), or an ironic reference to any one of the numerous YouTube mock-ups of *Der Untergang/Downfall* (Director: Oliver Hirschbiegel, 2004), than a critical historical understanding.[57] That Hitler is actually encountered while he is working in his office in the new *Reichskanzlei* was enough to ring alarm bells for a number of undergraduate university students familiar with the real Führer's working habits (or lack thereof).[58]

If the last few paragraphs have tended to sound more like an irate fan review of the deficiencies of 'new *Who*' compared with the original, this is unintentional. That the 1963–89 version of the programme was largely more successful in treating Nazism critically than the post-2005 version is a reflection of the historical circumstances in which *Doctor Who* has been produced, and not a judgement on the relative merits of one era over another. The chronological and generational shift undergone by the programme across its 50-year lifespan have largely determined the changing attitudes towards National Socialism reflected in *Doctor Who*. Because of the still raw memories of the Second World War and Nazism for those making the programme in the 1960s and early 1970s, engagements with Nazism tended to be based on more critical appreciation of the state of scholarship and popular memory (via the Eichmann trial, recent BBC or ITV documentaries, or even through reference to Shirer's *Rise and Fall of the Third Reich*), because they needed to be creatively submerged beneath allegorical treatments of totalitarian Daleks or Cybermen suitable as children's television. The concern in the 1980s that Thatcherism represented a revival of fascism in a new form gave added power to the allegorical and direct treatments of Nazism in *Remembrance of the Daleks* and *The Curse of Fenric*, but *Silver Nemesis* from the same era saw a use of Nazism which has been more enduring in the post-2005 iteration of *Doctor Who*. Since 2005, the concern has been much more about using Nazism and the Second World War as aspects of brand identity, reinforcing rather than questioning the preconceptions of audiences who are probably less amenable to such messages than in the past. Ultimately, the function of *Doctor Who* as an entertaining work of science fiction, and the need to cater to audiences' preconceived notions, have played a far greater role in determining the way Nazism has been presented in the programme than any engagement with more detailed historical understandings.

Notes

1   Anon., "Dalek" (n.d.), *TARDIS Index File*. Retrieved 19 August 2012 at http://tardis.wikia. com/wiki/Dalek.

2   Piers T. Britton, *TARDISbound: Navigating the Universes of Doctor Who*, London: I.B. Tauris, 2011, 60.

3 Nicholas J. Cull, "'Bigger on the Inside …': Doctor Who as British Cultural History", in Graham Roberts and Philip M. Taylor, eds., *The Historian, Television, and Television History*, Luton: University of Luton Press, 2001, 101; Britton, *TARDISbound*, 56 and 60–61. The other resonances in *Doctor Who* – from concern at Britain's entry into the European Economic Community, to concerns about Americanization – are dealt with in Peter B. Gregg, "England Looks to the Future: The Cultural Forum Model in *Doctor Who*", *Journal of Popular Culture*, 37, 4 (2004), 648–61. See also Matthew Jones, "Aliens of London: (Re)Reading National Identity in *Doctor Who*", in Christopher Hansen, ed., *Ruminations, Peregrinations and Regenerations: A Critical Approach to* Doctor Who, Cambridge: Cambridge Scholars Publishing, 2010, 85 and onward.

4 Benjamin Cook, E-mail of 14 January 2008, in Russell T Davies and Benjamin Cook, *Doctor Who: The Writer's Tale: The Final Chapter*, London: BBC Books, 2010, 309.

5 'Pure historical' and 'pseudo-historical' are terms derived from the influential Gary Russell articles of the mid-1980s: Gary Russell, "Observing history", and "Making history!", *Doctor Who Magazine Summer Special*, 1986, n.p.

6 Mags L. Halliday, *Doctor Who – History 101*, London: BBC Books, 2002; Hayden White, "The Burden of History", *History and Theory*, 2 (1966), 111–34; Hayden White, *Metahistory: The Historical Imagination in Nineteenth-century Europe*, Baltimore: Johns Hopkins University Press, 1973, 31.

7 Hayden White, "The Fictions of Factual Representation", in Hayden White, ed., *Tropics of Discourse: Essays in Cultural Criticism*, Baltimore: Johns Hopkins University Press, 1978, 23.

8 Daniel O'Mahoney, "Now how is that wolf able to impersonate a grandmother?: History, pseudo-history and genre in *Doctor Who*", in David Butler, ed., *Time and Relative Dissertations in Space*, Manchester: Manchester University Press, 2007, 62; Matthew Kilburn, "Bargains of necessity? *Doctor Who*, *Culloden* and fictionalizing history at the BBC in the 1960s", in Butler, ed., *Time and Relative Dissertations in Space*, 68–85.

9 Fiona Hobden, "History Meets Fiction in *Doctor Who*, 'The Fires of Pompeii': A BBC Reception of Ancient Rome on Screen and Online", *Greece & Rome*, 56, 2 (2009), 163.

10 Raphael Samuel, cited in Jerome de Groot, *Consuming History – Historians and Heritage in Contemporary Popular Culture*, London: Routledge, 2009, 2 and 4.

11 de Groot, *Consuming History*, 2; Richard Scully, "Alumni – Where are they now? Interview with Stuart Menzies", *Monash University – School of Historical Studies Newsletter*, 7, 1 (2008), 11; Andrew O'Day, "History and fiction in John Lucarotti's first season *Doctor Who* narratives" (19 March 2011), *History and fiction in Doctor Who*. Retrieved 19 August 2012 at http://www.hrvt.net/andrewoday/historyfiction.htm; Johnny Candon and Toby Hadoke, "Is history better with a sci-fi twist …?", *Doctor Who Magazine*, 434, 1 June 2011, 62–63.

12 MrBiscuitESQ, "Doctor Who – Battle for Berlin, NEXT TIME Trailer" (5 November 2011), YouTube. Retrieved 19 August 2012 at http://www.youtube.com/watch?v=XW2EeYh6yy8.

13 Anon., "The *DWM* Archive – *The Smugglers*", *Doctor Who Magazine*, 321 (2002), 27; David J. Howe, Mark Stammers and Stephen James Walker, *Doctor Who: The Handbook – The First Doctor*, London: Doctor Who Books, 1994, 309 and 315.

14 Peter Haining, *Doctor Who – the Key to Time: A Year-by-Year Record*, London: W. H. Allen, 1984, 87.

15 Kim Newman, *Doctor Who*, London: British Film Institute, 2005, 31–32.

16 Britton, *TARDISbound*, 60–61.

17 David J. Howe, Mark Stammers and Stephen James Walker, *Doctor Who – The Sixties*, London: Doctor Who Books, 1992, 31; John Peel and Terry Nation, *The Official Doctor Who and the Daleks Book*, London: St. Martin's Press, 1988, 3.

18 Lance Parkin, *aHistory*, Des Moines, IA: Mad Norwegian Press, 2006, quoted in Anon., "Dalek."

19 Sarah Honeychurch and Niall Barr, "Why the Daleks will *Never* Beat us", in Courtland Lewis and Paula Smithka, eds., *Doctor Who and Philosophy: Bigger on the Inside*, Chicago: Open Court, 2010, 190.

20 Newman, *Doctor Who*, 32.

21 Karl Dietrich Bracher, *The German Dictatorship: The Origins, Structure, and Effects of National Socialism* (trans. Jean Steinberg), New York: Praeger, 1970; David Welch, *The Third Reich: Politics and Propaganda*, London: Routledge, 2005, 3–4.

22 Welch, *The Third Reich*, 4.

23 Newman, *Doctor Who*, 32.

24 James Chapman, *Inside the TARDIS: The Worlds of Doctor Who – A Cultural History*, London: I.B. Tauris, 2006, 43.

25 Jim Leach, *Doctor Who – Contemporary Approaches to Film and Television Series: TV Milestones*, Detroit: Wayne State University Press, 2009, 24.

26 Terry Nation, quoted in David J. Howe, Mark Stammers and Stephen James Walker, *Doctor Who – the Seventies*, London: Doctor Who Books, 1994, 86.

27 Nation, quoted in Howe, Stammers and Walker, *Doctor Who – the Seventies*, 86.

28 On the 'Roman salute', see Simonetta Falasca-Zamponi, *Fascist spectacle: the aesthetics of power in Mussolini's Italy*, Berkeley: University of California Press, 2000, 110–13; and Martin M. Winkler, *The Roman Salute: Cinema, History, Ideology*, Columbus: Ohio State University Press, 2009. On the 'German greeting', see Tilman Allert, *The Hitler Salute: On the Meaning of a Gesture* (trans. Jefferson Chase), London: Picador, 2009.

29 Chapman, *Inside the TARDIS*, 102.

30 Chapman, *Inside the TARDIS*, 102.

31 Hannah Arendt, *Eichmann in Jerusalem: A Report on the Banality of Evil*, New York: Viking Adult, 1963, 135. Arendt's thesis has recently been challenged by David Cesarani, *Becoming Eichmann: Rethinking the Life, Crimes and Trial of a 'Desk Murderer'*, Cambridge: Da Capo Press, 2006.

32 William L. Shirer, *The Rise and Fall of the Third Reich*, London: Pan Books, 1960, 1080; BBC, *The Listener*, 82, 21 August 1969, 260.

33 Friedrich Nietzsche, *Jenseits von Gut und Böse: Vorspiel einer Philosophie der Zukunft/ Beyond Good and Evil*, Leipzig: C. G. Naumann, 1900 [1886], 105 (Aphorism 146): "He who fights with monsters should look to it that he himself does not become a monster. And when you gaze long into an abyss the abyss also gazes into you" [*Wer mit Ungeheuern kämpft, mag*

zusehn, dass er nicht dabei zum Ungeheuer wird. Und wenn du lange in einen Abgrund blickst, blickt der Abgrund auch in dich hinein].

34 Daniel Kolak and Raymond Martin, *The Experience of Philosophy*, Belmont: Wadsworth Thomson Learning, 2002, 92–93. Also see John Tulloch and Manuel Alvarado, *Doctor Who: The Unfolding Text*, New York: St Martin's Press, 1983, 79.

35 For a variant on this speech, see Terrance Dicks, *Doctor Who and the Genesis of the Daleks*, London: Target, 1976, 120–21.

36 On the Thatcherism/fascism cultural trope, see for instance Greil Marcus, *In the Fascist Bathroom: Punk in Pop Music, 1977–1992*, Cambridge: Harvard University Press, 1999, 249; and Richard C. Thurlow, *Fascism in Britain: From Oswald Mosley's Blackshirts to the National Front*, London: I.B. Tauris, 1998, xix and 274.

37 Sylvester McCoy played up to the arch-Tory perception of a leftist conspiracy against the Thatcher government from within the BBC. See Stephen Adams, "*Doctor Who* 'had anti-Thatcher agenda'", *Daily Telegraph*, 14 February 2010. It is difficult to know whether the 'Torygraph's' writers and readers were aware that this was meant to be tongue-in-cheek.

38 On the racial context, see for instance Randall Hansen, *Citizenship and Immigration in Postwar Britain: The Institution Origins of a Multicultural Nation*, Oxford: Oxford University Press, 2000, especially 81 and onwards; and Gavin Schaffer, *Racial Science and British Society, 1930–62*, Houndmills: Palgrave Macmillan, 2008.

39 On the racial context, see for instance Randall Hansen, *Citizenship and Immigration in Postwar Britain: The Institution Origins of a Multicultural Nation*, Oxford: Oxford University Press, 2000, especially 81 and onwards; and Gavin Schaffer, *Racial Science and British Society, 1930–62*, Houndmills: Palgrave Macmillan, 2008.

40 Lincoln Geraghty, "From Balaclavas to Jumpsuits: The Multiple Histories and Identities of *Doctor Who's* Cybermen", *Atlantis: Revista de la Asociación Española de Estudios Anglo-Norteamericanos/Journal of the Spanish Association of Anglo-American Studies*, 30, 1 (2008), 91.

41 BBC, "Silver Nemesis" (n.d.), *Doctor Who – the Classic Series*. Retrieved 19 August 2012 at http://www.bbc.co.uk/doctorwho/classic/episodeguide/silvernemesis/detail.shtml.

42 The conversation seems to centre on the issue of avoiding asking questions based on the apparent danger of the answers one might uncover, and Nietzsche's position on asking questions for questions' sake.

43 Mark Connelly, *Reaching for the Stars: A New History of Bomber Command*, London: I.B. Tauris, 2001, 156.

44 Mary Evans and David Morgan, *The Battle For Britain: Citizenship and ideology in the Second World War*, London: Routledge, 2002, 109.

45 For more on this tendency, see David Edgerton, *Britain's War Machine: Weapons, Resources and Experts in the Second World War*, London: Penguin, 2012, xv–xviii.

46 Dave Owen, "What if?/27 up", *Doctor Who Magazine*, 255, 1997, 14.

47 Alec Charles, "War Without End? Utopia, the Family, and the Post-9/11 World in Russell T Davies's *Doctor Who*", *Science Fiction Studies*, 35, 2008, 457.

48 Anne Cranny-Francis, "Why the Cybermen Stomp: Sound in the New *Doctor Who*", *Mosaic*, 42, 2 (2009), 119–34.

49 Russell T Davies, E-mail of 14 January 2008, in Davies and Cook, *Doctor Who: The Writer's Tale*, 310.

50 Russell T Davies, E-mail of 20 November 2007, in Davies and Cook, *Doctor Who: The Writer's Tale*, 259.

51 On 'cultural markers', and the programme as a 'Cool Britannia'-branded consumer product, see Barbara Selznick, "Rebooting and Re-branding: The Changing Brands of *Doctor Who*'s Britishness", in Hansen, ed., *Ruminations, Peregrinations and Regenerations*, 68 and onward.

52 Peter Griffiths, "*Doctor Who Magazine* Awards 2010 – Best Story", *Doctor Who Magazine*, 428, 15 December 2010, 40.

53 Geoffrey Best, *Churchill: A Study in Greatness*, London: Continuum, 2001, 197; John Colville, *The Fringes of Power: Downing Street Diaries, 1939–55*, New York: W.W. Norton & Co., 1985, 404. Churchill's reference to the devil was actually several months into 'his future' – in terms of the placing of *Victory of the Daleks* in 1940 – being first uttered after Hitler's invasion of the Soviet Union in June 1941.

54 Russell T Davies and Benjamin Cook, E-mails of 28 April 2007 and 3 August 2007, in *Doctor Who: The Writer's Tale: The Final Chapter*, 97 and 168.

55 Steven Moffat, quoted in Anon., "Episode Previews – *Victory of the Daleks*", *Doctor Who Magazine*, 420, 2010, 11.

56 Richard Roberts, "Star Letter" to *Doctor Who Magazine*, 432, 2011, 12.

57 Anon., cover of *Doctor Who Magazine*, 438, September 2011; Nilanna, "Hitler Feels Insulted by Doctor Who" (n.d.), YouTube. Retrieved 19 August 2012 at http://www.youtube.com/watch?v=aVG5VMfxrIY.

58 The students were mine, having taken HIST324 – Ashes to Ashes: Weimar and Nazi Germany, 1918–1945, the previous semester. See University of New England, "HIST324" (2012), *Course Catalogue*. Retrieved 19 August 2012 at http://www.une.edu.au/courses/units/HIST324. On Hitler's working habits, see Ian Kershaw, *Hitler: 1889–1936 Hubris*, New York: W.W. Norton, 1998, 531–33.

Chapter 18

Religion, racism and the Church of England in *Doctor Who*

Marcus K. Harmes

*D*octer *Who* is often considered to be a quintessentially English programme. Commentators attribute its success and popularity in other national contexts, including Australia and North America, to the appeal inherent in this Englishness.[1] As a programme made mostly in England, and often set among recognizably English settings in central London and the villages and country houses of the English countryside,[2] but at a deeper level celebrating and showcasing virtues such as decency and stoicism, it seems to embody many features of traditional Englishness.[3] Yet it is noteworthy that while *Doctor Who* is a programme which seems intrinsically English and where narratives are set in distinctively English locations, it only rarely features another national institution, the established Church. The Church of England, by law the established Church of the English people, proclaims that it is "a Christian presence in every community" and thus asserts its centrality to English national life.[4] As the national embodiment of Christianity, the Church of England has provided the Christian underpinning of English society and the Church has seemed intrinsic to what constitutes Englishness.[5] One way this is so was through a long standing anti-Catholic impulse that ran through English public life, which can be charted from the sixteenth century, but it remained potent even at the beginning of the twentieth century.[6] Accordingly the Protestant faith embodied in the Church of England was a central aspect of Englishness, which could be inclusive but which also excluded particular groups.[7] Adherence to the Church of England is also bound up with questions of race. To be Anglican in the twenty-first century suggests nothing about race or whiteness as the global Anglican Communion is multi-racial.[8] However, national identity traditionally owes more to mythologizing than reality, or what the sociologist of race Ann Dummett refers to as the "folkloric" basis of English identity, and the nationalism of the Church is no exception.[9] The national Church of England is historically associated with what the scholars of English racial identity Stephen Brooke and Louise Cameron refer to as "mythic 'Englishness'", which included a uniform national *and* racial identity.[10] Edwin Jones concurs; his survey of the formation and articulation of English identity refers to the "rigidly narrow, nationalistic sense of identity" which defined many conceptions of Englishness, and he notes the importance of the established Church of England existing in opposition to foreign others as contributing to this identity.[11] While the historical actuality of Anglicanism is not one of racial uniformity, in terms of cultural identity the Church of England has been central to the construction of identity based on white Englishness.

The question of English identity has been approached by scholars in a variety of ways, including the study of literature, analysis of Englishness within the wider British context and experiential accounts. Television has depicted but also questioned Englishness and it facilitates examination of English identity. This essay builds a case study out of serials from the original 1963–89 run of *Doctor Who*, to reconsider and refine the oft-accepted notion of the programme as embodying and celebrating Englishness. These stories engage on multiple levels with the clergy, history and beliefs of the Church of England. They are *The Dæmons* (from Season 8, 1971) and *The Curse of Fenric* and *Ghost Light* (both from Season 26, 1989). More than 18 years and several changes in production personnel separate the Jon Pertwee story *The Dæmons* from the two 1980s stories starring Sylvester McCoy as the Doctor. It is clear that the makers of *Doctor Who* across a succession of different production regimes only occasionally approached the Church of England (as opposed to remote and clearly alien religion) during most years of the programme's 1963–89 production, adding impact to the stories which make sustained use of the Church and its clergy. Other dimensions of these stories – the settings, the Gothic trappings and the hidden alien menace – connect them thematically to many other stories, but the presence of clergymen as lead characters is unusual. The depiction of the Church and its clergy in these three stories shows the complexity of *Doctor Who*'s supposed encapsulation of Englishness and English identity. The stories were produced in a period when English identity was intensively renegotiated and contested, partly through the impact of multiculturalism, a point central to the narrative of *Ghost Light*. This renegotiation and contestation took place as the white English population was augmented by waves of immigration.[12] This brought with it the greater visibility of racial difference and the inevitable and concomitant challenge to a national identity based on whiteness.[13]

This essay will demonstrate how the focus on the Church of England within these serials suggests a national identity more nuanced and complex than mere 'Englishness'. While only three stories, these serials represent much more than isolated examples of meaning or emphasis. They testify to broader thematic concerns within *Doctor Who*, including the ambiguous place of religious discourse within the series and its cultural history as an 'English' programme. Drawing on three specific serials allows for focused discussion of themes of racial identity and cultural confusion. This essay takes issue with the pervasive idea of *Doctor Who*'s Englishness, not wholly rejecting this idea but suggesting that the terms upon which it has been proposed require a more complex understanding of what Englishness may involve. It begins with analysis of how both national and religious identities inhere in *Doctor Who* before moving to consider specific aspects of the three stories which illuminate how the depiction of the Church within their narratives complicates the limits enforced by Englishness. Finally it will place these serials in a broader historical context, interpreting their cultural context, including the decline of unifying institutions and the advent of multiculturalism in England, which ran parallel to the stories and their settings, in order to draw out the complex meaning of Englishness within *Doctor Who*.

What does it mean for *Doctor Who* to be English?

In a series of articles about *Doctor Who*, film and television historian Alan McKee asked 'Is *Doctor Who* Australian?' (interestingly indicating how the programme can prompt questioning of national identity) and 'Is *Doctor Who* Political?'[14] Associated questions could be 'Is *Doctor Who* English?' and 'Is *Doctor Who* Religious?' The idea that the texts and cultural productions of a society can raise questions of identity is given theoretical cohesion by Benedict Anderson, whose idea of an "imagined community" stresses that imaginative and creative works can encourage a sense of belonging to a people or nation.[15] However, creative works, while a product of a people or nation, can also be subversive, a point raised by *Doctor Who*. The programme seems steeped in Englishness. In terms of asking if *Doctor Who* is English, one answer is that its production base for its 1963–89 run was London, and almost all location filming took place in southern England (including stories such as *Terror of the Zygons*, 1975, which was set in Scotland but filmed in West Sussex, or *The Curse of Fenric* itself, which was set in Northumbria but filmed in Hawkhurst, Kent). Studio tape recordings mostly took place at the BBC Television Centre in White City, London.[16] Until the casting of the Scottish actor Sylvester McCoy as the Doctor in 1987, the lead actors in the programme had also not only been English but had spoken in southern counties English accents[17] and many of the Doctor's companions came from southern England.[18] It is also worth noting that the original series featured very few actors from ethnic minorities. Although by no means alone among its contemporary programmes in its monocultural casting, nonetheless for a series frequently depicting Earth's future societies, *Doctor Who*'s makers perhaps have less excuse than producers of costume dramas or wartime era comedies for showcasing an almost exclusively white principal and supporting cast.

However, technical or production history is not the same thing as thematic identity, although it does influence the identity of a programme. The notion that the programme espouses or highlights 'Englishness', beyond the bare fact it was made in England, is a complex idea. Programme makers themselves did articulate a national distinctiveness to the programme. Philip Hinchcliffe, producer of Seasons 12, 13 and 14, suggested the idea of *Doctor Who* as not only English but more broadly British as well.[19] However, Britishness and Englishness are not synonymous. Britishness is diffuse, incorporating the different identities of the constituent kingdoms of the United Kingdom and its migrants. Englishness is precise and adherence to the Church of England was ineluctably linked to historic opposition to foreign and Catholic others, including continental Europeans and the Irish. Racially, Englishness is according to some perspectives also precise. As Brooke and Cameron argue, Englishness was known, if only as a mythic ideal, by confident faith in imperial greatness and the cohesion provided by racial uniformity.[20] Dummett proposes a similar, race-based, understanding of Englishness, suggesting that the identity is based on the perceived responsibility of white people to rule other races. She again foregrounds the idea of Englishness as counterposed against other racial and national groups.[21] The broadcaster and commentator Jeremy Paxman argues that to be British is an inclusive idea;

the former black parliamentarian Bernie Grant, for example, commented that as a black man he thought of himself as British because "it includes other oppressed peoples, like the Welsh or the Scots."[22] Paxman suggests that Englishness is a white Christian identity and its exclusivity is counterposed against the inclusiveness of Britishness. Frank Welsh concurs with this assessment, suggesting that Englishness is by its nature judgemental, and exists as a benchmark against which other peoples are compared.[23]

The 1960s context of *Doctor Who*'s creation was one preoccupied with what was happening to England and Englishness as migration continued; this preoccupation would leave its mark on the programme and it is worth briefly exploring the background to *Doctor Who* in terms of its television ancestry. *Doctor Who*'s immediate progenitors among post-war science fiction discussed and allegorized the multi-racial nation that was emerging. For example, Nigel Kneale's serial *Quatermass and the Pit* (1958–59) was of immense influence on *Doctor Who*.[24] *Quatermass and the Pit* was also made in the immediate aftermath of 1958 Notting Hill race riots and the climax of the serial, when London is engulfed by flames and riots, is a very close reflection of the real-life racial violence in 1950s England.[25] In fact, the parallel was so close that black community leaders complained to the BBC.[26] But *Quatermass and the Pit* is also a heady mix of different ingredients, including a Martian invasion narrative, the race riots and the Church of England and its clergy, for a church is an important setting and a vicar a major character. The racial tensions allegorized in the story occupy the same world as the Church and its clergy; *Doctor Who* would pursue this connection between the Church, race and the burgeoning diversity of post-war English society.

Comments made about *Doctor Who* make clear how the programme's supposed Englishness has been asserted. Television historian Alec Charles interprets *Doctor Who* within a broader context of statements on Englishness from figures such as former Prime Minister John Major (who infamously distilled Englishness down to warm beer, cricket and "old dears cycling to church") and as a programme where a defining feature was its encapsulation of often nostalgic ideas of what constituted Englishness, including the countryside and the Church.[27] John Major's comment, cited by Charles, merits brief analysis. Not only does it mention the Church (and the "old dears", it goes without saying, would be white), his attempt to define Englishness also seems rather desperate in the context of England in the late twentieth century, where daily life could encompass many more diverse practices from different ethnic contexts than going to Church or playing cricket.

Often, conceptions of Englishness verge on the ahistorical and tend more to the mythologized. They certainly wilfully neglect the black presence in the English population that increased in the second half of the twentieth century but can be located back to at least the sixteenth century.[28] Indeed Major's comment actually paraphrased a number of earlier assessments of Englishness, which bound identity and the Church closely together in an ahistorical and nostalgic manner. Poet Laureate John Betjeman said that "England stands for the Church of England, eccentric incumbents, oil-lit churches."[29] Even George Orwell referred to "old maids biking to Holy Communion" in *The Lion and Unicorn*.[30] But as scholars of the construction of national identities point out, a national identity, as an intellectual concept but also as a publicly debated property, owes less to historical reality and more to contemporary demands to make the past and its people what we want them to be. The terms upon which English identity in *Doctor Who* functioned reveal themselves as complex, a complexity that is thrown into relief when the programme's treatment of English national religion is considered.

Religion and identity in *Doctor Who*

For a programme which many scholars and commentators have found to embody Englishness, *Doctor Who*, or rather its makers, takes a deeply subversive approach to the national Church of the English. It is in fact striking that John Fiske found a strongly Christianizing ethic within the original *Doctor Who*, as there are very few occasions indeed when Christianity is mentioned, let alone dealt with in a sustained manner.[31] Even in *The Dæmons*, the writers and producer were unable to refer to the space under the church building as a crypt, or to refer to God, but instead were obliged to use the more ecclesiastically neutral term "cavern."[32] These restrictions were a concession to the public service charter of the BBC and to the sensibilities of the Church of England. However, this minor adjustment to terminology and setting does not obscure the otherwise subversive treatment of the Church in this story, or the marginalization of Church and clergy in the *Doctor Who* stories that prominently showcase the Church.

The Dæmons, *The Curse of Fenric* and *Ghost Light* offer sustained consideration of the Church and its clergy. In these stories, the way religion is presented raises questions relating to racial identity. In *The Dæmons*, mysterious events centre on the historic village church of Devil's End. The vicar, Canon Smallwood, has disappeared in the night; his successor, the Reverend Mr Magister, is revealed to be the Doctor's arch enemy the Master. While masquerading as the community's vicar, the Master outwardly conforms to but subtly parodies many conventions of a typical English vicar, for instance beginning a speech to his flock with the small clerical joke, "Now I promise, this isn't going to be a sermon," before unleashing preternatural forces on the inhabitants of the village and killing a number of them. In *The Curse of Fenric*, set during the Second World War, events again centre on the church, St Jude's, in a village in Northumbria. There the Army has discovered a mysterious substance oozing through the walls of the church crypt, and the vicar, the Reverend Mr Wainwright, has lost his faith in God because of the atrocities unleashed by the British bombings of German civilians and cities. A clergyman is again a lead character in *Ghost Light*, when the Reverend Ernest Matthews, the Dean of Morthouse College Oxford, visits the mysterious Victorian mansion Gabriel Chase to engage in academic debate with the house's master, Josiah Samuel Smith, over Darwinian theories of evolution. The mansion is in Perivale, where in the present day the Doctor's companion Ace will be traumatized by racist violence. However, Smith is not human but is an alien entity which is itself biologically evolving and is anxious to adduce scientific support for the theory of evolution. Matthews, a trenchant opponent of Darwinism (who is based on the real-life model of Bishop Samuel Wilberforce of Oxford),[33] is drugged, operated on by Smith and reverts into an ape, before being murdered and placed in a display case.

These three serials take a similar approach to the Church of England and its clergy. In each story, Christian faith is shown as being irrelevant to daily life, while the clergy are inadequate or intellectually misguided proponents of their faith, or simply fraudulent. In each story, a clerical character dies: Canon Smallwood dies off-screen, but it is clear that he has been murdered by the Master; the Reverend Wainwright is murdered by Haemovores, the vampiric creatures who emerge from the graves in his churchyard and from the nearby sea; and the Reverend Matthews is killed, after receiving a brutally practical demonstration of the reality of Darwinian evolution and its reverse.

In these stories, spaces which should be hallowed are sites of perversion and corruption. The "cavern" underneath the church of Devil's End is the site of satanic worship, and the location of an alien villain, Azal the Dæmon, whose destruction by the Doctor leads to the destruction of the church itself, which is blown to pieces at the story's climax. In *The Curse of Fenric*, Haemovores rise from the sea and the churchyard, attacking Wainwright, the Doctor and his companion Ace inside the church, which is thus shown as vulnerable to preternatural attack. The crypt of the church is a site of alien corruption, as an alien and corrosive poison is leeching through its walls. It also contains runic writing which had been hidden by the passage of time. This writing operates a computer programme which unleashes an ancient evil. Far from being a sacred space, the church building is the centre of preternatural and evil events. *Ghost Light* is not set within or around a church; its backdrop is a prosperous and upmarket mansion in Victorian Perivale, but this comfortable and familiar setting is revealed as an especially lethal environment for the Reverend Matthews, who has been lured to Gabriel Chase specifically so Josiah Samuel Smith can surgically deform and then murder him.

English identity and national distinctiveness

The depiction of the Church within these *Doctor Who* stories reflects key themes relating to the forces which both bound and dissolved English identity in the twentieth century. The stories show the Church of England in decline but also suggest that Englishness itself, or at least the racial uniformity which it comprises, is also in eclipse. By showcasing the Church, the makers of *Doctor Who* drew into their narratives an institution which remained a major aspect of English public and intellectual life in the twentieth century, meaning that its use within *Doctor Who* was a potent means for programme makers to raise questions of English identity and the way ahistoric and mythic cultural constructions of Englishness were challenged by the reality of burgeoning multiculturalism. Historians who have scrutinized this period generally concur in stressing the prominence which the Church occupied in public life over the twentieth century. Many bishops were major public intellectuals and commentators, and clergy and laity were intrinsic to major political and social reform movements, including the Wolfenden Committee and Report (1967), which legalized male homosexual relations.[34] In terms of televisual history, the leading clergy of the Church were major participants in one of the first BBC broadcasts to be seen by a wide audience: the coronation of Queen Elizabeth II in 1953.[35]

The importance of the Church in public life meant that inevitably it also sat prominently in popular culture, a prominence that could obscure its decline. As A.N. Wilson points out, many of the twentieth century's most popular writers, such as Agatha Christie, were communicant members of the Church. As believers, popular writers such as Christie treated the Church as a stable institution and left unaddressed the institutional decline of the Church and the questioning of its doctrines in public life.[36] Furthermore, the Church and especially its clergy were frequently portrayed with considerable affection in popular works, from the Ealing comedies to numerous television programmes, especially situation comedies such as *Dad's Army* (Creator: Jimmy Perry, 1968–77) and *All Gas and Gaiters* (Creators: Pauline Devaney and Edwin Apps, 1966–71).

But prominence in public life or popular culture should not obscure the very real processes of secularization which defined English life in the twentieth century. Although the production timeline of the three stories is from 1971 to 1989, within the fictional world of the programme they in fact present a chronological survey of the troubles besetting the Church over a century and the cultural confusion of society within the same period. This begins with the *fin de siècle* setting of *Ghost Light*, where the Church comes against the challenges posed by modern science, through the Second World War period of *The Curse of Fenric*, where bombing atrocities challenge faith, to *The Dæmons*, set broadly in the present day, and where the Church is so marginalized that the villagers of Devil's End blithely dance around a maypole after their church building is blown to pieces.[37] The villagers seem to rejoice in the loss not just of the building but also of the institution. These stories depict the tribulations of the Church over the twentieth century. *The Dæmons*, made first in terms of production history but with the most contemporary setting in terms of *Doctor Who*'s internal chronology, is a story set in a period of marked secularization of English society and what former Archbishop of Canterbury George Carey acknowledges was the dramatic numerical decline in the membership of the Church of England.[38]

The narratives of these stories link religion with key aspects of English national identity. In this regard, *The Curse of Fenric* is especially significant. The actions of Churchill's wartime government and his bomber command in choosing to bomb German cities and thus kill German civilians, directly impacted on Wainwright's faith. The war effort, normally encountered in English public life as a celebrated national undertaking, here has undermined the Vicar's faith. The Reverend Wainwright's struggle with faith is especially significant to understanding the 'Englishness' of *Doctor Who*. He loses his faith because of the patriotic war effort, a collective endeavour which historians and commentators suggest exhibited a strong sense of common purpose on the part of the English.[39] Indeed the indomitability of Londoners in particular during wartime bombings can be thought of in terms directly connected to the Church of England. The *Daily Mail*'s famous photograph of St Paul's Cathedral wreathed in smoke from bombs but otherwise unharmed is, says the historian Linda Colley, a "Protestant" image and a signifier of the special care of providence for the English and the cathedral of their capital city.[40] But in *The Curse of Fenric* the pursuit of England's victory in the war terminally impairs the faith of a clergyman of the Church. Overall, *The Curse of Fenric* offers a complex reading of ideas of Englishness. English religion is drawn into a painful battle with English militarism. On a small scale, the victim is one clergyman. On a larger scale, the doctrines and teachings of the Church fall victim to events, conflicting with and being overwhelmed by the alien science presented in the story but also by the imperatives of the national war effort.

In the course of the narrative of *The Curse of Fenric* Wainwright dies, as his weakened faith means he cannot hold back attack from the Haemovores. His church is also damaged by attack from the Haemovores, who rise from the sea and from the graves in the churchyard to attack it. At least, however, St Jude's is still standing at the end of *The Curse of Fenric*. The same cannot be said for the church of Devil's End in *The Dæmons*, which is blown up at the climax of the story. Its destruction is intrinsic to the resolution of the narrative, as the alien villain Azal self-destructs in the cavern under the church. Like St Jude's in *The Curse of Fenric*, the church in Devil's End is a picture-postcard and quaint medieval English parish church. Indeed it is the quintessence of the church to which the 'old dears' invoked by Prime Minister Major would have cycled. However it is also an unnatural and violated space on a number of levels. In the first place, it is the site of the worship for a satanic coven, but the actions of the Satanists are themselves only channelling what the Doctor identifies as "psychokinetic" energy which summons back into corporeal existence an alien creature that lurks beneath the church. The church therefore is no longer a sacred space, but instead is the site of alien activity. It is also presided over by a fake vicar, the Reverend Mr Magister. The Church here is not simply modernized; it is depleted and no longer an essential part of Englishness. The decline and then the destruction of the institution and the building in *The Dæmons* signify broader malaise apparent in English public discourse in the late twentieth century. Brooke and Cameron refer to a "long running cultural tension" in English society, between current uncertainty and the past imperial and monocultural certainty of a confident nation and church and a homogeneous society.[41] The weakness of the Church and the clergy in *The Dæmons* and *The Curse of Fenric* speak to this contrast, and to the broader anxiety in England that the certainties of uniform identity were disappearing.

This uncertainty also permeates *Ghost Light*. Although *Ghost Light* has the earliest setting of the three stories under analysis here, it was in fact the last of the original series to be produced by the BBC and the maturity of its themes and vision is indicative of its place in *Doctor Who*'s production history. The story's disdain for the clergy of the Church is made clear; viewers are almost invited to approve of Josiah Samuel Smith as he gleefully drugs the Reverend Matthews and then cackles with joy as Matthews awakes to discover that his body is transforming into that of an ape. The exchanges between Smith and Matthews are a macabre reimagining of the celebrated 1860 debate at the British Association between Bishop Samuel

Wilberforce (a clergyman, like Matthews, opposed to Darwin's theories of evolution and natural selection) and Thomas Huxley, a scientist. Observers at the time generally agreed that Huxley had bettered Wilberforce, a point picked up by Marc Platt's script for *Ghost Light* when Smith brutally demonstrates the principle of evolution on Matthews's body.[42]

Matthews's demise in the story represents more than an individual's death; it is suggested by *Ghost Light*'s narrative that as faith in the national Church receded, a more complex version of England and the English arose. Matthews's death is juxtaposed within *Ghost Light*'s narrative with the unseen but potently significant death of Manisha, a friend of Ace's. In narrating this death, *Ghost Light* brings together issues of both religion and race in the English context. Ace makes it clear that Manisha's death in a house fire was due to racism: "White kids firebombed it," she tells the Doctor, recounting an event which had traumatized her childhood. Although all this occurs off-screen, it is a significant moment in the story especially when compared to the fate of the Reverend Matthews, because his death suggests the loss of the authority of the Church but also the loss of its ability to assist in defining with certainty who the English were. Because he is reduced to a grotesque spectacle of a human/ape hybrid – still wearing a clerical collar – inside a case, his body synecdochally represents the decline in the institutional, intellectual and moral authority of the Church.

But Manisha's death picks up the story with what has happened next: as faith in the Church has receded, in its wake is a contested English identity, in which the perpetrators of violence use race to justify their attacks. The Church is no longer a constituent part of uniform racial and national identity; instead it is a site of cultural disorder. It is striking that Charles suggests that by the time *Ghost Light* was produced, *Doctor Who* had become "quaint" in terms of its approach to national identity and society.[43] This point is hard to sustain; not only was there the perversely violent treatment meted out to the Church, but there was also the manner in which *Ghost Light* confronts multi-racial violence in modern England. In reality jurists and public intellectuals had struggled to interpret this violence except by resorting to the idea that violence in modern England, especially London, was due to the polarization between disorderly ethnic areas and traditional English and monoculturally white areas where order prevailed.[44] *Ghost Light*, a story written in 1989 and thus after the large-scale race riots in 1981, 1985 and 1987 which had taken place in the inner city, draws racial violence and the Church of England together, pinpointing ecclesiastical weakness as concomitant with the rise of racial tension. As *Ghost Light* makes clear, in their wake has come an English society which lacks its historically binding forces and which is unstable and where racial violence takes place.

The Church and the English

The disputes between religion and faith and between race and identity which *Ghost Light* foregrounds were the foundation of a number of controversies which disturbed English society during the twentieth century and which inform the narratives of these three serials.

The cultural historian Alasdair Macintyre, thinking especially of English religion since the nineteenth century, suggests that in the modern world, faith is caught between absence and presence. He further suggests that the time when faith is in the process of being lost is the time when faith is most easily discussed in the context of modern life and it comes to prominence in public discourse.[45] This point is exemplified in these three serials, which are examples of modern storytelling emanating from post-Christian England, where retreating faith is a strong device for interpreting what the decline of the Church means for being English.

The portrayal of the Church and its clergy in these *Doctor Who* stories makes no concessions to the significance of the Church to English identity or its association with a monochromatic white and formerly imperialist nation. Instead these stories actively dismantle traditional notions of English identity, because they show the loosening of the Church as a binding agent of identity, and accordingly militate against the cosier and less critical assessments of *Doctor Who* as embodying quintessentially English ideas. However, it is the case that the rethinking of race and Englishness these stories pinpoint were in their own way very English, as a number of writers on science fiction argue. Shail suggests that English science fiction in film and television was shaped by and reflected a period of cultural and religious upheaval.[46] Gregg concurs with this point, finding in the science fiction and horror films of the 1960s and beyond an oblique but meaningful commentary on the dissolution of traditional conceptions of English identity. Gregg pinpoints this cultural confusion to particular events, including the embarrassment of the Suez Crisis in 1956, the long aftermath of which was the loss of prestige of government in Westminster and of the English people overseas.[47] Film historian Paul Leggett defines the social and political context to these *Doctor Who* stories as a period of "profound crisis", in England in particular among the nations of the western world.[48] Leggett views this crisis as manifested especially in the decline of institutional religion but also in the loss of cultural cohesion of English identity, a point made by Ace's narrative of Manisha dying as a result of an act of racial violence which sprang from fear of the increasing multi-racial make-up of twentieth century English society. The sociologist of religion Grace Davie also testifies to this point, suggesting that not only the Church of England but many other agents of social cohesion had declined in the late twentieth century in England.[49] The multi-racial violence which is unseen in *Ghost Light* but also central to the narrative reflects the self-destructiveness of a society where racist members stubbornly cling to a mythic identity and are prepared to commit violence and murder in defending it.

When considered within this historical context, these *Doctor Who* stories can be seen to push against an oft-repeated argument, in both popular and theoretical accounts of *Doctor Who*, that it embodies or even celebrates notions of Englishness. Instead stories that do engage with the Church act as a mirror to cultural angst and uncertainty, and bring to light the cultural and racial confusion of twentieth-century England as the binding agencies of the Church began to dissolve. Commentators point to the limitations of Englishness. Jeremy Paxman's influential reading of Englishness argues that Englishness is narrowly understood as white and Christian, a narrowness that came under pressure it could not withstand over the twentieth century. Commentators from Prime Minister Margaret Thatcher downwards articulated unease with the increasing visibility of non-English minorities.[50] Indeed, both *Ghost Light* and *The Curse of Fenric* were produced one year after Thatcher's government introduced a new history syllabus into schools that was overtly nationalistic.[51] Peter Mandler's survey of the idea of Englishness suggests that in late-twentieth-century England what he calls the "lowest-common-denominator [of] whiteness" was invoked by some politicians and social commentators as a force for cohesion. A concomitant to this invocation was to regard black people as an outer group or an 'other'.[52] The violence against Manisha is a fictional retelling of the very real racial violence in 1980s England that was one undesirable response to the seeming breakdown of 'Englishness'. In the end, it becomes difficult to sustain the idea of *Doctor Who* as quintessentially English, simply because notions of Englishness themselves are contested and complex and the Church was unable to provide assurance or answers. These serials foreground the idea that they present an intentionally critical look at the notion of Englishness, and highlight the dissolution of this identity.

Conclusion

Ultimately, arguments that *Doctor Who* embodies or celebrates Englishness are as complex as is the programme's own response to established English religion. Of course it should be clear that in the end defining Englishness is problematic in itself. It relies on a great deal of wishful thinking, mythologizing and distortion. Arguably the makers of *Doctor Who* were sensitive to the limitations of the idea of Englishness and the retreat from public life of the Church of England. Against this context, it becomes harder to sustain the argument that *Doctor Who* somehow embodies Englishness. While stories engaging with the Church of England are rare, those that exist pinpoint the cultural uncertainty of English identity and the inability of the Church to be a binding agent of identity. In the three stories under review here, the Church's clergy confront evil (or in the case of Magister actually unleash it) but they do not prevail against it. Victory against alien menace belongs to the Doctor and his companions; the clergy by contrast are collateral damage. Wainwright's corpse indeed is trampled into the mud by the Haemovores. In this way, ideas that *Doctor Who* was 'English' require clarification. Its Englishness was expressed not in celebration but in subversion of the English Church and in acknowledgement that by the end of the twentieth century (the period of Ace's childhood and the attack on Manisha) the cultural cohesion the Church of England had provided had given way to burgeoning diversity, but this diversity also prompted racist violence. The programme may thus be English, but in the sense that it engages with and charts the dissolving of England's Christian heritage and the breakdown of the Church as a force consolidating identity. In this sense, *Doctor Who* may be 'English', if to be English means to identify the dissolution of the Christian underpinnings of English society and to engage with a major element of unease and uncertainty in public and intellectual discourse in the twentieth century.

Notes

1   Nicholas J. Cull, "Tardis at the OK Corral: *Doctor Who* and the USA", in John R. Cook and Peter Wright, eds., *British science fiction television: A hitchhiker's guide*, London: I.B. Tauris, 2006, 52–70.

2   Alec Charles, "War Without End? Utopia, the Family, and the Post-9/11 World in Russell T Davies's *Doctor Who*", *Science Fiction Studies*, 35 (2008), 453. See also Nicholas J. Cull, "'Bigger on the Inside...': Doctor Who as British Cultural History", in Graham Roberts and Philip M. Taylor, eds., *The Historian, Television, and Television History*, Luton, 2001, 95–112.

3   Alan McKee, "Is *Doctor Who* Australian?", *Media International Australia*, 132 (2009), 54–66;

4   Church of England, (2011), *A Christian Presence in Every Community*. Retrieved 19 August 2012 at http://www.churchofengland.org/.

5   Jane Lewis and Patrick Wallis, "Fault, breakdown and the Church of England's involvement in the 1969 divorce reform", *Twentieth Century British History*, xi (2000), 308–32.

6   A survey of such public literature is provided in E. R. Norman, ed., *Anti-Catholicism in Victorian England*, London: George Allen and Unwin, 1968.

7   Robert J. C. Young, *The Idea of English Identity*, Oxford: Blackwell, 2008, 167.

8   Anglican Communion (2012), *The Anglican Communion Official Website*. Retrieved 19 August 2012 at http://www.anglicancommunion.org/.

9   Ann Dummett, *A Portrait of English Racism*, Harmondsworth: Penguin, 1973, 46.

10 Stephen Brooke and Louise Cameron, "Anarchy in the U.K.? Ideas of the City and the *Fin de Siècle* in Contemporary English Film and Literature", *Albion: A Quarterly Journal Concerned with British Studies*, 28, 4 (1996), 635.

11 Edwin Jones, *The English Nation: The Great Myth*, Stroud: Sutton, 1998, 304.

12 Juliet Gardiner and Neil Wenborn, eds., *The History Today Companion to British History*, London: Collins & Brown, 1995, 514–15.

13 Brooke and Cameron, "Anarchy", 639.

14 McKee, "Is *Doctor Who* Australian?", 54–66; McKee, "Is *Doctor Who* political?", *European Journal of Cultural Studies*, 7, 2 (2004), 201–17.

15 Benedict Anderson, *Imagined Communities: Reflections on the Origins and Spread of Nationalism*, London: Verso, 1991, 37–40.

16 Mark Anthony Adams et al., "Stories: 1963–1989, 1996" (19 August 2012), *The Locations Guide to Doctor Who, Torchwood and The Sarah Jane Adventures*. Retrieved 19 August 2012, at http://www.doctorwholocations.net/stories/classic.

17 Kim Newman, *Doctor Who*, London: BFI Publishing, 2005, 104.

18 David J. Howe and Mark Stammers, *Doctor Who: Companions*, London: Virgin Books, 1996, 94–95.

19 Peter B. Gregg, "England Looks to the Future: The Cultural Forum Model and *Doctor Who*", *The Journal of Popular Culture*, 37, 4 (2004), 656.

20 Brooke and Cameron, "Anarchy", 639.

21 Dummett, *English Racism*, 49.

22 Jeremy Paxman, *The English: A Portrait of a People*, Harmondsworth: Penguin Books, 1998, 74.

23 Frank Welsh, *The Four Nations: A History of the United Kingdom*, London: HarperCollins, 2003, 145.

24 Peter Hutching, "We're the Martians now: British sf invasion fantasies of the 1950s and 1960s", in I. Q. Hunter, ed., *British Science Fiction Cinema*, London: Routledge, 1999.

25 James Chapman, "Quatermass and the origins of British television sf", in Cook and Wright, eds., *British science fiction television*, 39.

26 Anon., "Coloured Leaders Criticize BBC", *The Times*, 24 December 1958, 4.

27 Alec Charles, "The Ideology of Anachronism: Television, History and the Nature of Time", in David Butler, ed., *Time and Relative Dissertations in Space: Critical Perspectives on Doctor Who*, Manchester: Manchester University Press, 2007, 108–22.

28 Imtiaz Habib, *Black Lives in the English Archives, 1500–1677: Imprints of the Invisible*, Aldershot: Ashgate, 2008.

29 John Betjeman, *Letters Volume One: 1926–1951*, London: Methuen, 1994, 323.

30 George Orwell, *Collected Essays, Journalism and Letters*, Vol. 2, London: Secker and Warburg and Harcourt, Brace, Jovanovich, 1968, 75–76.

31 J. Fiske, "Popularity and ideology: A structuralist reading of *Dr Who*", in W. Rowland and B. Watkins, eds., *Interpreting Television: Current Research Perspectives*, Beverly Hills: Sage, 1984, 165–98.

32 BBC, "The Daemons" (n.d.), *Doctor Who Classic Episode Guide*. Retrieved 19 August 2012 at http://www.bbc.co.uk/doctorwho/classic/episodeguide/daemons/detail.shtml.

33 On Wilberforce and the Church of England's reaction to Darwinism see David L. Edwards, *Leaders of the Church of England 1828–1944*, London: Oxford University Press, 1971, 83–104.

34 Matthew Grimley, "Law, Morality and Secularisation: The Church of England and the Wolfenden Report, 1954–1967", *Journal of Ecclesiastical History*, 60, 4 (2009), 725–41.

35 Edward Carpenter, *Archbishop Fisher: His Life and Times*, Norwich: The Canterbury Press, 1991, 256–58. The Archbishop of Canterbury crowned Elizabeth, and the Archbishop of York and the Bishops of London, Durham and Winchester were important participants.

36 A. N. Wilson, *Iris Murdoch: As I Knew Her*, London: Hutchinson, 2003, 200.

37 In terms of chronology, it is usually accepted that the stories featuring UNIT and the Third Doctor were set sometime in the near future and the setting of *The Dæmons* was sometime hence from 1971.

38 George Carey, *Know the Truth: A Memoir*, London: Harper Collins, 2004, 176.

39 Paxman, *The English*, 87.

40 Linda Colley, *Britons*, London: Yale University Press, 1992, 29.

41 Brooke and Cameron, "Anarchy", 637.

42 Francis Darwin, *Life and Letters of Charles Darwin*, London: John Murray, 1888, II, 320–23.

43 Charles, "War Without End?", 453.

44 Jacqueline A. Burgen, "News from Nowhere: The Press, the Riots and the Myth of the Inner City", in J. Burgen and J. R. Gold, eds., *Geography, the Media and Popular Culture*, London: Taylor and Francis, 1985, 203.

45 Alasdair Macintyre, "The Debate About God: Victorian Relevance and Contemporary Irrelevance", in Alasdair Macintyre and Paul Ricoeur, eds., *The Religious Significance of Atheism*, New York: Columbia University Press, 20–21.

46 Robert Shail, "Terence Fisher and British Science Fiction Cinema", *Science Fiction Film and Television*, 2, 1 (2009), 77–90.

47 Gregg, "England Looks to the Future", 648–61.

48 Paul Leggett, *Terence Fisher: Horror, Myth and Religion*, Jefferson: McFarland and Company, 2002, 182.

49 Grace Davie, *Religion in Britain since 1945: Believing without Belonging*, Oxford: Blackwell, 1994.

50 Thatcher, quoted in *The Times*, 10 October 1987.

51 Kathleen Warner, *Historical Theory, Popular Culture and Television Drama*, M.Phil. thesis, Brisbane: University of Queensland, 2005, 46.

52 Peter Mandler, *The English National Character: The History of an Idea from Edmund Burke to Tony Blair*, New Haven: Yale University Press, 2006, 227.

Chapter 19

The Doctor is in (the Antipodes): *Doctor Who* short fiction and Australian national identity

Catriona Mills

Despite the multiplicity of ways in which the cult science fiction family television programme *Doctor Who* is distinctly, even archetypally British, it has always occupied an important place in Australian television schedules and Australian culture. Its omnipresence on Australian television screens before its 1989 cancellation (and again since its 2005 revival) spawned a large, active and engaged fan following. Some of these fans then found writing opportunities in the post-cancellation expansion of the *Doctor Who* universe into novels, audio plays and short story anthologies. With the programme off the air, writers could expand the Doctor's travels in time and space beyond the limitations of budget, production decisions or location scouting.

For participants in Australian *Doctor Who* fandom, this presented an additional opportunity: the chance to make explicit the Doctor's influence on Australian culture and Australian national identity by dropping him into Australia's past. This is most noticeable in short fiction: specifically, the short stories published in Big Finish Productions' 28 *Short Trips* anthologies, released between 2002 and 2009. These short stories are somewhat marginalized texts in the vast space of *Doctor Who* ancillary material, compared, for example, to Virgin Books' 'New Adventures' novels. But they are canonical texts, published under a licence from the BBC and therefore imbued with authority. And in these short works, Australian authors trade on both the marginalization of short fiction and the authority of licensed publishing to drop the Doctor into key events in Australian history. Bushfires and bushrangers, the Anzac landing at Gallipoli and the Japanese submarine attack on Sydney Harbour, environmental protests at Pine Gap and the Port Arthur massacre: the Doctor influences, witnesses or ruminates on them all. And the intrusion of this alien figure allows Australian authors to comment on the role that race plays, both implicitly and explicitly, in the development of Australian national identity.

Doctor Who, Australia and the question of canonicity

In a 2009 article titled 'Is *Doctor Who* Australian?', Alan McKee wrote:

> Maybe it's not such a good idea to open an academic article with a question that is clearly stupid. Obviously the answer is no. *Doctor Who* is a family science fiction television program produced in Britain, by the British Broadcasting Corporation, made by an almost exclusively British cast and crew. It's a British program.
> And yet …[1]

As McKee traces in detail, *Doctor Who* both influenced and was influenced by Australia, including minor Australian content in the programme itself (such as Australian-accented companion Tegan), the censorship of various episodes to suit Australian broadcasting standards, and the extremely active Australian fan culture that developed around the programme. None of this makes *Doctor Who* an Australian programme: "*Doctor Who* is an Australian institution, an important part of Australian television history – but not an Australian program. Its national identity is not simple in this country."[2] In this sense, *Doctor Who* shares some characteristics with Australian national identity itself: the latter is also neither simple nor straightforward, especially in how it interrogates, incorporates or negates the question of race. What is of interest to this essay, then, is how these two complex objects intersect, or, more precisely, how Australian authors interrogate both *Doctor Who* and Australian nationalism by imagining a timeline in which the Doctor intervenes in key moments in Australian history.

Such manipulations of the Doctor's timeline are made possible, in part, by the fact that during the sixteen year hiatus between the original series and the new series, an enormous quantity of ancillary material coalesced around the core (televised) text of *Doctor Who*: 'New Adventures' (1991-97, Virgin Books) and 'Missing Adventures' (1994-97, Virgin Books), 'Eighth Doctor Adventures' (1997-2005, BBC Books), audio plays and short story anthologies (1998–, Big Finish Productions), and novellas (2001-04, Telos Publishing), not to mention soundtracks from lost episodes, comic strips and various spin-offs featuring characters involved in the Doctor's adventures to either a greater (Professor Bernice Summerfield) or lesser (Iris Wildthyme) extent. And such a list completely excludes any 'unauthorized' texts, such as the multiplicity of fanzines that provide the content for Paul Cornell's collection *License Denied: Rumblings from the Doctor Who Underground* (1997). In such fan activities, McKee argues, "moments where Australian social events are brought into the fan culture of *Doctor Who* are extremely rare."[3] This is not the case, however, with published, canonical *Doctor Who* texts, where Australian authors regularly address Australian social events. The key point that I wish to explore before looking closely at this Australian focus is the argument that these texts are canonical, given that 'canon' is a fluid and fraught term when applied to *Doctor Who*.

Issues of canonicity in *Doctor Who* are directly tied to the vast quantity and variety of ancillary material. As Lance Parkin argues, "The problem for the twenty-first-century *Doctor Who* fan is not so much philosophical as logistic."[4] In other words, "Even a rich fan with a great deal of time on his [*sic*] hands would have trouble keeping up with every release, let alone assimilating and enjoying them all."[5] Therefore, 'canon' in *Doctor Who* fandom is akin to the biblical canon: "In its simplest form, it asks which texts 'count' as part of the fictional world of *Doctor Who*."[6] Some degree of consensus acts as a map by which fans can navigate the morass of available material and participate in the informed discussions of a shared history that are so central to engaged fandom. Not limiting such an amorphous text creates unwieldy problems with interpretation, as shown in Christopher Marlow's 'The folding text: *Doctor Who*, adaptation and fan fiction': "I will understand 'text' to denote not only the televized adventures of the Doctor, but also the entire corpus of published and non-published fiction dealing with the character. Clearly, the size of this corpus precludes its comprehensive discussion."[7] If comprehensive discussion is precluded, what remains is the opportunity for focused discussion, and mapping out the boundaries of canonicity is one means of achieving this.

But any map shows more than one route to a destination. And at the core of Lance Parkin's argument about fans and canonicity is the idea that

> For the emotional, time and financial investment of being a *Doctor Who* fan to pay off, they have to contribute to and inform, in some way, the wider *Doctor Who* universe. They – the stories and the fans – have to *matter*.[8]

For fan-writers (and many authors of ancillary material in the 1990s began as fan-writers) working after the 1989 cancellation of the original series, the question of how they could contribute to the wider *Doctor Who* universe was enriched by the post-show expansion of that universe. To quote Parkin again, "With the television show out of the way [...] there was something of a Copernican revolution – now, not everything revolved around the TV series."[9] That is not to say, however, that all ancillary materials were suddenly equal. Parkin isolates the 'New Adventures' novels as the "main focus for fan activity in the early 1990s";[10] these long works, mimicking in scale (though not always in concept) the serial format of *Doctor Who*, became the primary substitute for the absent programme. The anthologized short stories are a more marginalized form of publishing. For example, short-fiction anthologies were never a priority for BBC Books, who published only three volumes of *Short Trips* before cancelling the series. They subsequently sold the licence to Big Finish Productions, who produced 28 volumes, also called *Short Trips* (and a 29th volume, *Re-Collections*, consisting exclusively of republished material), before being forced to cancel the series in 2009 after the BBC failed to renew their licence to publish. Though the short fiction lacks the sustained plot development and character interiority of the novels, these anthologies were often the first post-fanzine publishing opportunity for previously unpublished *Doctor Who* writers.

Though the short stories are rarely privileged in discussions of which elements of the expanded *Doctor Who* universe are canonical,[11] they are authorized publications – whatever value 'authorized' has in a textual environment in which 'canonicity' is such a disputed term. Their very ambiguity in the fraught space of the *Doctor Who* canon provides a unique opportunity to explore the Doctor's significance outside the bounds of his televised adventures. And when we gather up the material on the 'Australianness' of *Doctor Who* and the post-cancellation expansion of the *Doctor Who* universe, something is revealed: Australian writers frequently use the relative freedom of *Doctor Who* short stories to insert the Doctor into pivotal moments in Australian history or imagine his interaction with archetypal Australian figures and events. In doing so, they are writing the Doctor's significance to Australian fans into the fringes of the broader *Doctor Who* canon and, in the process, interrogating Australian national identity.[12]

Doctor Who short fiction, Australian writers and the role of history

Tracing Australian authors of short *Doctor Who* fiction can be a complicated process. The Big Finish anthologies do not include author biographies.[13] Furthermore, authors frequently contribute only one story or limit their publishing activities entirely to the Big Finish anthologies, which makes determining their nationality a difficult and time-consuming process. I do not claim, therefore, to have a comprehensive bibliography of short fiction by Australians: such claims are always risky. However, this much is certain: across the 28 Big Finish short story anthologies, at least 26 short stories are by Australian authors or (in the case of Jonathan Blum) expatriate authors living and working in Australia at the time of publication[14] – not the majority, but nevertheless a recognizable subset of content.[15] Some of these authors are familiar to *Doctor Who* fandom, such as Kate Orman, author of a large number of well-regarded 'New Adventures' novels. Others are well known as writers, but have limited their involvement with *Doctor Who* fiction to a single short story, such as Sean Williams, Robert Hood and Stephen Dedman (who each contributed a story to *Short Trips: Destination Prague* [2007]). And some are fans whose excursion into *Doctor Who* short fiction is their only publishing venture, such as Andrew K. Purvis (an Australian contributor to Simon Guerrier's *Short Trips: How the Doctor Changed My Life* [2008], a volume dedicated to new and unpublished authors).

Not all the short stories by Australian authors have strongly Australian themes, settings or characters, but numerous works do. Purvis's 'Evitability' (2008), for example, takes place during an environmental protest at Pine Gap in the Northern Territory,[16] Jonathan Blum's 'Home Fires' (2005) shows the Doctor helping a family save their home from encroaching bushfires,[17] and Sarah Groenewegen's 'The Bushranger's Story' (2004) brings the Doctor into conflict with both a female bushranger and an introduced species in the Australian bush of the nineteenth century.[18] The three stories on which the rest of this essay focuses, however, position the Doctor within some of Australia's most significant historical traumas. In Groenewegen's 'Virgin Lands' (2002), the Doctor's companion Ace struggles to come to terms with the news of the 1996 Port Arthur massacre, Australia's deadliest shooting spree. In 'Hymn of the City' (2003), also by Groenewegen, the Doctor and Ace arrive in Sydney on the night of 31 May 1942, the only time in its history that Sydney has come under attack. And in Ian Mond's 'Direct Action' (2006), the Doctor finds himself at Anzac Cove in 1915, as Anzac troops land for what will become the Gallipoli campaign, a defining moment for Australia's burgeoning national consciousness.

As a television series, *Doctor Who* has always had a problematic relationship with history. Such early stories as *The Aztecs* (1964) and *Marco Polo* (1964) arose from the programme's early educational brief, under which it was expected to alternate science fiction narratives with historical narratives. Such stories – in which the only science fiction component is the Doctor's arrival in the time period in question – are the "pure historical" stories, which Daniel O'Mahony defines as narratives "pocked with historical detail, of varying degrees of relevance to the unfolding story."[19] But since the mid-1960s, the Doctor has tended to travel more extensively in space and in the timelines of alien cultures than he has in Earth's timeline.[20] When he does travel back in Earth's history, the resultant stories tend to be not "pure historicals" but "pseudo-historicals", in which (to quote O'Mahony again) "the historical period has either been invaded by a science-fictional presence before the Doctor shows up […] or turns out to be a fabrication mocked up by the villains for their own dubious purposes."[21] The pure historical stories fall easily into a specific subgenre within the programme. The pseudo-historical stories are a more amorphous group, but nevertheless share at least one common feature: "Their versions of history are histories of the common imagination, constructs set in worlds that the audience is likely to recognize from their personal education and other fiction."[22] O'Mahony notes, for example, that *The Time Meddler* (1965), the programme's first pseudo-historical story, could as easily take place on an alien planet, "but for the audience nothing would be at stake."[23] But by setting the story in a Saxon village in 1066, prior to the battles of Stamford Bridge and Hastings, nothing less than English national identity is at stake. This is what distinguishes the pseudo-historicals from the pure historicals: the former use history not to interrogate history itself or to educate the audience, but to invest the text with ready-made significance to which the audience can respond. This is the point at which these Australian-written short stories intersect with *Doctor Who*'s problematic relationship with history: they are pseudo-historical narratives set in periods in which, at least for Australian readers, what is at stake is Australian national identity. For the rest of this essay, then, I shall look closely at three short stories that place the Doctor within moments of particular significance in the evocation or construction of Australian national identity. The analysis begins with the Port Arthur massacre and moves chronologically backwards through the Second World War to what is perhaps the touchstone of post-Federation Australian national identity: Gallipoli.

The Doctor and Australian national identity in crisis

Sarah Groenewegen's 'Virgin Lands'[24] establishes its connection to Australian history within the first half page of prose, as Ace (one of two companions to the Seventh Doctor in this story) sits behind the wheel of a 'borrowed' car outside the house where the Doctor is paying a mysterious visit:

> She was listening to the radio, her lips a thin, pensive line. A woman was reading a bulletin in a five-minute news update with only one story: 'At least twenty-five people have died, according to Tasmanian police. The gunman is still at large in the historic site of Port Arthur …'[25]

This passage serves a basic narrative purpose, in letting the reader know where the protagonist is and what she is doing. But we also know where *we*, the readers, are: we are in 1996, on the afternoon of 28 April, the date of the Port Arthur massacre. The Port Arthur massacre is not the only reason for Ace's distraction: as she listens to the news broadcast, she also thinks of the "fifteen kindy kids and their teachers a month or so before" (the Dunblane massacre, on 13 March 1996). But this story, in which the Doctor meets and interrogates LaMort (the personification of Death) while his young companion struggles with the reality of human cruelty, is set not only on the date of Australia's deadliest shooting spree, but *during* the shooting spree.

The central theme of this particular story is not Australia-specific: death is not limited to a particular culture or country, and the three people literally facing Death in this story are a Time Lord from Gallifrey, a twenty-sixth-century archaeologist from the Earth colony Beta Caprisis and a twentieth-century teenager from the London suburb of Perivale. But by setting the story in a house on Sydney Harbour, Groenewegen plays with the narrative opportunities afforded by pseudo-historical stories, seeding the broader discussion of death with moments of particular significance to Australian readers. For example, LaMort's guests, whom she surveys from her staircase, include the clearly allegorical standover man 'Noddy Clarke' and policeman 'Peter Peterson'.[26] Readers unfamiliar with New South Wales's most notorious period of gang warfare and police corruption will not interpret this passage as allegorical. In this instance, the characters are a private nod between an Australian writer and her Australian readers, particularly readers from New South Wales.

But where this often-allegorical encounter with death intersects with issues of Australian nationalism and race is when LaMort claims that she moved to Australia two hundred years earlier because "It was new." The Doctor's companion Benny may be a twenty-sixth-century human from an Earth colony, but she is also an archaeologist: she responds indignantly, "What about the indigenous population?"[27] LaMort's argument about Australia being "new" touches on Neville Meaney's argument[28] that while in Britain "nationalism had to vie with long-established and deeply-rooted local loyalties and hierarchical allegiances", nationalism in "British-settled Australia had little in the way of pre-modern traditions to limit its acceptance."[29] The fact that both Meaney and Groenewegen are writing at a time when Australian public discourse teetered between calls for an official apology to Australia's Indigenous population and attacks on the so-called 'black armband' view of history reinforces two points: that nationalism in Australia is also a question of race, and that the question of race is often elided in discussions of nationalism. However, Benny (and, by extension, Groenewegen) refuses to participate in such elisions: she explicitly raises the question of race, foregrounding the fact that LaMort's apparent dismissal of pre-colonial Australian culture both asserts the troubled principle of *terra nullius*[30] and negates the violence that colonization (both British colonization and LaMort's own arrival) brought to Indigenous Australians. Australian readers are likely to invest that exchange with more cultural significance than their non-Australian counterparts, even though this violent episode in Australian history is not, unlike the names of the guests, disguised by allegory.

Nor is the Port Arthur massacre allegorical. So the allegories and the passing references to the brutal oppression of an indigenous culture are surrounded by (and grounded by) the reader's awareness that this is taking place at the same time as the death, the horror and the manhunt in Port Arthur. Indeed, for Australian readers, the very name of Port Arthur carries brutal connotations, even prior to 1996. As Annona Pearse argues,[31] its history as one of colonial Australia's most brutal penal colonies and an inescapable prison creates a "mythological atmosphere of fear surrounding the settlement, now augmented by the massacre."[32] For Australian readers, the Doctor's encounter with Death is layered over the various ways in which Australian society has encountered death. In this sense, the Port Arthur massacre is an ideal nexus, not only because of the loss of lives in the massacre itself, but also because the massacre amplifies the residual nightmares of Australia's convict past, which itself is grounded in abuses of the Indigenous population: in this single location, horror piles on horror. However, Pearse's analysis demonstrates that after the massacre (and other such tragedies), the media "confined expressions of grief largely within established myths of nation",[33] ignoring the myriad reverberations of the Port Arthur site in favour of the iconography and terminology of Anzac Day. In Pearse's terms, the response to the massacre demonstrated the way in which "an aggregate of individuals transforms itself into a community bound together through common experience during events such as Anzac Day and Remembrance Day, where the mythical and historical memory of events is commemorated",[34] and Groenewegen's narrative intersects with this. Groenewegen is writing nearly six years after the massacre, when this communal myth-making is relatively stable. By focusing her discussion through Port Arthur, Groenewegen suggests such calling on common experience actually channels 'mythical and historical memory of events' into a narrow model of national identity – one that is as much about eliding historical memories as it is about recalling them.

Groenewegen's later story, 'Hymn of the City',[35] touches on similar concerns to 'Virgin Lands'. In this case, the story takes place on 31 May 1942; we enter the narrative roughly 25 minutes in, as the Doctor tells Ace, before a Japanese midget submarine detonates in Sydney Harbour, sparking a night of fighting:

> "Wicked," she breathed, and felt a thrill of excitement course through her. Real war action. Wow.
>
> But the Doctor shook his head, and even in the dim light she could see the despair in his eyes. "No, Ace. There will be lives lost. Young lives. Perhaps not on the terrible scale of other places and battles in this awful war, but dreadful. So very dreadful."
>
> "Is that why we're here, Professor? To stop it?"
>
> "No, Ace. Our purpose here is much more grave."[36]

This passage, from the early pages of the story, establishes two things. Firstly, as with Groenewegen's co-option of the Port Arthur massacre, the Doctor steps into a key moment in Australian history, but with no intention of actually influencing events – at least not those events that appear in the written histories of the period. Secondly, the passage hints at an Australian perspective on the Second World War, one that activates distinctly modern debates, such as the concept of a Battle for Australia.

May 1942 marks the only time (to date) that Sydney (a city, in many ways, more familiar in Australian iconography than the actual capital) has come under attack, and one of few attacks on Australian soil during the Second World War. As such, the attack is central to what is called the Battle for Australia, an idea whose supporters argue that "Australia was the objective of the Japanese advance and that 1942 saw a series of crucial campaigns that resulted in the defeat of this thrust."[37] The idea of a Battle for Australia is a somewhat controversial one: Peter Stanley (former Principal Historian at the Australian War Memorial and now head of the Centre for Historical Research at the National Museum) argues that "It is an idea that few historians have endorsed but which thousands of Australians have embraced."[38] The idea is also comparatively recent: Stanley notes that although the term appeared in some mid-1940s propaganda, the ideology of a Battle for Australia is very much a mid-1990s phenomenon.[39] Stanley argues that "We might regard this saga as forming a 'collective story', a story valued or heeded by an entity, such as a nation."[40] But the degree of conscious construction implied by 'story' does not negate the saga's position in Australian national identity, because as Stanley notes, "History is not just about the evidence of what happened in the past, important though that is. It is also about how we shape an understanding of that past to satisfy our present needs."[41] And in the decade before Groenewegen published 'Hymn of the City', May 1942 was at the centre of a popular shaping of Australian identity.

That the concept of a 'Battle for Australia' should accelerate in the 1990s is unsurprising, given the extent to which Australian public discourse in that decade was dominated by discussions of multiculturalism. As Ien Ang and Jon Stratton argued in 1998, "multiculturalism is a centrepiece of official government policy"[42] but, simultaneously, the 1990s were marked by "a backlash against multiculturalism [...] coming mainly from conservative circles."[43] In Groenewegen's hands, 1942 (in which Australia faces a foreign threat and is flooded by a transient, largely foreign population) can be read as a metonymic representation of 1990s Australia – or, rather, of the Australia that manifested in conservative discourses of the 1990s and afterwards, in which a perceived (if nebulous) core Australia was at risk from a transient foreign population. In the wartime Sydney of Groenewegen's story, people from varied backgrounds cross and recross each others' paths, assessing and dismissing each others' race, nationality or culturally ingrained habits. US Marine Corporal Jed Allum, for example, admires the way in which his English landlady's conception of duty matches his own, which "almost made up for her incessant recourse to cups of tea when what he really wanted was coffee, and her insistence that the lamb served up for dinner was decent enough to eat."[44] The immortal Ginny, who appears to be an Indigenous Australian girl, moves through a modern landscape that she maps against the dreaming landscape in her memory, even though "whitefella houses stood where there had been shrubs and trees or rocks."[45] Fellow immortal Li Chen Mei disguises herself as an old woman, the better to play the role that her GI customers expect when they visit a Chinese fortune teller. Drawn together in a single location by the extremity of war, the characters both play out and play up their ethnicities. Ang and Stratton emphasize that "the discourse of multiculturalism in Australia does not recognize, confront or challenge the problematic of 'race' but rather represses it."[46]

However, as she did in 'Virgin Lands' when Benny challenged LaMort's assertion of *terra nullius*, Groenewegen does both. For example, Ginny moves unseen through the landscape because the "whitefellas in their dark uniforms […] were as obvious in the bad light as Ginny was invisible."[47] In her metonymic construction of debates over multiculturalism, Groenewegen makes race visible by emphasizing its invisibility.

The drama in 'Hymn of the City' comes from an imbalance in what the Doctor calls "the hymnal skein", which he defines to Ace as "a force that holds all life together."[48] The imbalance comes from the interference of Mrs Harris, Corporal Allum's English landlady and the anxious wife of a deployed AIF serviceman. Her intentions are pure: "She was trying to protect this city and its people overseas fighting in the war." But as the Doctor explains to Ace, "while she can sense the skein, she does not have the understanding to manipulate it safely. No one does. Not even its guardians."[49] Instead, Mrs Harris's manipulations cause outbreaks of uncharacteristic violence across Sydney, as protective inhabitants of the city attempt to drive off those whom they see as invaders. The term "guardian" resonates with arguments about Australia's multicultural future. Groenewegen's guardians are immortals, who manifest as the young Indigenous Australian girl Ginny and the Chinese fortune teller Li Chen Mei. Each channels the hymnal skein through an artefact symbolic of their culture: small boxes made, respectively, of bark and of jade. Each is purely a custodian, with, as the Doctor emphasizes, no power over the skein. But the hymnal skein is not the only symbolic object whose guardians have power but no power. As Stanley notes, collective stories – such as the Battle for Australia or even debates over multiculturalism – attract what he calls "guardians" and what Inga Clendennin, whom he quotes, calls "de facto custodians."[50] Employing a similar discourse, Ang and Stratton emphasize that a key element of conservative politician Pauline Hanson's strongly anti-multiculturalism political rhetoric "has been her self-representation as an 'ordinary Australian', and […] her tireless claim that she speaks on behalf [of] 'the Australian people'."[51] The problem arises when such guardians assume, as Mrs Harris does, that they can manipulate the collective story, the hymnal skein, simply because they can sense it. In this sense, Groenewegen's hymnal skein becomes (at least in part) a figurative representation of national identity: a powerful force that runs perceptibly through a country but which, especially in times of great stress, can cause great difficulty if manipulated by those who underestimate its power. As though to reinforce this reading, the gently chastised Mrs Harris reverts to the national characteristics bemoaned by Corporal Allum: "What a dreadful night, but they say on the wireless they destroyed all the Jap subs. Would you like some tea?"[52] National identity, suggests Groenewegen, is malleable in the way that an elastic band is malleable: it can be manipulated, but it snaps back into place.

The final story, Ian Mond's 'Direct Action', is simultaneously the most narratively complex text and the one in which race is most deeply buried within the characters' sense of national identity. The story forms part of an anthology called *Short Trips: The Centenarian*,[53] which, as with all *Short Trips* anthologies, has a unifying central premise: in this case, the stories all involve Edward Grainger, a man whose life is unusual only in how frequently the various regenerations of the Doctor cross his timeline. This particular story focuses on attempts by futuristic film-makers to document Edward's life, using their standard method of infiltrating the subject's timeline (in disguise or invisibly), filming the ordinary passage of his life, and editing it into a blockbuster. Jack Holbine, a freelance film-maker who has been promised some of the meatier episodes of Edward's later life, finds himself instead shunted into background material: filming Edward's father, Lawrence. Lawrence is involved in the Gallipoli campaign, but his military rank is honorary, and his role as political advisor to General Sir Ian Standish Monteith Hamilton keeps him well away from the actual fighting. In an attempt to generate some dramatic footage, Jack surrounds Lawrence with a force field (without Lawrence's knowledge or consent) and tricks him into landing alone at Anzac Cove. As Jack films (sometimes invisible, like his hovering holocameras, sometimes disguised as a participant in the action), Lawrence experiences the horror of combat. But Jack's actions trigger a 'time tsunami', at which point the Doctor steps in.

Mond's story is an ideal example of the 'pseudo-historical' *Doctor Who* story, in that the Doctor finds himself in a historical situation in which other science-fictional presences have already interfered, and must attempt to restore the normal balance of events. Indeed, 'Direct Action' can be read as an exercise in addressing one of O'Mahony's central concerns (phrased in a way that strongly echoes Peter Stanley's argument about the Battle for Australia):

> [T]he problem – one that *Doctor Who* on television was never really equipped to deal with – is that history is not simply what is past but the way knowledge about that past is arranged. History is a construct of the present. Viewed through the prism of popular fiction, it can become genre.[54]

This is precisely how Jack Holbine's species or culture (his precise origins are left ambiguous) views history: as another country, which film crews can mine for a succession of films, all of which ultimately default to "big explosions and giant monsters."[55] Outside the narrative, this is also how Mond is viewing history in this story: as an artificial construct, something that shifts depending on how it is viewed. And, in this story, the artificial construct that is history is at the centre of post-Federation national identity. The 'Anzac spirit' colours subsequent evocations of 'Australianness'. So Stanley, analysing the significance of May 1942, writes, "there has been a move, if not to supplant Gallipoli's centrality, at least to assert the significance of the Second World War as part of the story of an emerging Australian national identity",[56] positioning Gallipoli as the fulcrum around which Australia's self-image pivots. And Pearse, writing about the Port Arthur massacre, notes the media's adoption of the symbolism of Anzac Day (which fell three days prior to the massacre), arguing that "The references to Anzac [Day] provide a sense of spatial connection through recognized rituals and traditions, and the memorializing of the Port Arthur massacre extends and reinforces such traditions."[57] For Australian readers, then, Mond's story touches on events fundamental to contemporary understanding of Australian national identity.

Jack Holbine is the prism through which Mond's readers view the history of Anzac Cove. He enters Lawrence's life in a state of moderate ignorance since, as he tells the reader, "For a guy who made biopics, I loathed research."[58] So he spends the evening before filming watching documentaries on the First World War:

> Getting soused on whisky, I discovered the Gallipoli campaign, like most of the First World War, had been a right old mess. The great and glorious British Empire thought they could score themselves an easy victory in the Mediterranean. [...] The documentaries talked about the ANZAC spirit, about the courage of the young boys fighting against a terrain and an enemy they didn't understand. All I saw was a waste of human life.[59]

For Australian readers, this passage is rich in Anzac mythology: the emphasis on terrain (and the unspoken corollary of the Australian bush), youth, masculinity and the ineffable foreignness of the enemy. Yet Jack, as an outsider, seemingly resists reading the campaign in terms of race, as a pattern of white Australian manhood: both General Hamilton and Colonel Mustafa Kemal (both only mentioned in passing and not appearing as characters) are admirable characters whose men respect them, and even Lawrence Grainger, described by Jack as "the eccentric, fat English officer",[60] performs heroic actions once Jack drops him on Anzac Cove. Indeed, on a first reading, the Anzacs are curiously absent from the text: though he interacts with English officers and Turkish infantry, the only Anzacs Jack meets as he films Lawrence are already dead. But as the narrative unfolds, the reader becomes aware that Jack *is* an Anzac soldier.

'Direct Action' contains two distinct narratives: the primary, first-person narrative of Jack Holbine's attempts to generate footage for the Edward Grainger biopic and an embedded, third-person narrative of a soldier caught up in the Gallipoli landing. This embedded narrative is presented in brief, single paragraphs – italicized and sharply demarcated from the primary font – dotted throughout the main narrative. The reader becomes aware almost immediately that the soldier is an Australian volunteer: he mentions that "He first heard the news in a pub, sitting with his mates" and "he and the boys booked passage for Fremantle",[61] where they joined the 11th Battalion, meeting "the other Aussie and Kiwi blokes they'd be fighting with."[62] The reader might not be aware that the 11th Battalion were heavily involved in the initial assault on the beach at Anzac Cove, but the narrative follows the soldier as "one by one his mates fell, and soon there were so few of them that they had no choice but to retreat back to the beach." The soldier retreats and retreats, "trying desperately to find a friendly face."[63] When he stumbles across an English officer, badly wounded in the leg and crying out for his wife and son, the Anzac slings the officer over his shoulder and continues his retreat, knowing that he "needed to save this single man."[64] In the final paragraph of the story, two narratives click together:

> Sub-Lieutenant Jack Holbine couldn't wait to go back into the fray, couldn't wait to show those damn Turks that he wasn't scared of them.
>   He did it for his country and his mates, and his family and the girl he'd left behind. This is who he was.[65]

Jack Holbine, freelance biopic film-maker from an advanced civilization to whom history is entertainment, becomes Sub-Lieutenant Jack Holbine, Anzac, Australian national, and – the strangely shifting tenses in the final sentences seem to imply – casualty of the Gallipoli campaign.

Jack has become caught up in a 'time tsunami' caused by his own interference in the timeline. When he manipulated Lawrence Grainger into setting foot on Anzac Cove, he had hoped Lawrence would be captured: "My movie was going to be about him surviving the horrors of war, the torture, the horrible food, the stench of rotting flesh."[66] Instead, the futuristic force field with which Jack surrounds his subject convinces Lawrence that he is under divine protection: unaware of both Jack's force field and its destruction in the backwash from the time tsunami, he single-handedly attacks a Turkish position, sustaining a serious wound in his leg in the process. As the Doctor – fortuitously clambering over a sandhill at this point in the narrative – explains, this radically alters the timeline. Such an alteration is disastrous for all concerned, except the ever-watchful Doctor: the real Lawrence will die and Jack will be forced (by the Historical Protection Society that oversees his culture's behaviour within history) to take Lawrence's future as a traumatized amputee, forgetting his own identity and past life in the process.[67] Faced with the option of either escaping with the Doctor but leaving a seriously affected timeline behind or suffering punishment at the hands of the Historical Protection Society, Jack opts for a third option: remaining behind to carry Lawrence back behind his own lines. At some point during that long walk, the time tsunami hits, and radically alters Jack's past and future: Sub-Lieutenant Jack Holbine succeeds in carrying the officer back to Cape Helles, is rewarded with a medal for bravery, and takes his place "with his fellow Aussie mates"[68] in the ill-fated assault on Krithia.

As with Groenewegen's stories, the Doctor's role in 'Direct Action' is relatively inactive: his narrative function is primarily expository, although he does assist Jack in freeing the wounded Lawrence from Turkish custody. But the story's engagement with history, narrative and history-as-narrative is the most complicated of the three. In the story's two juxtaposed narratives, Jack is simultaneously recreating an historical moment as film and being recreated as part of that historical moment. The dramatic fictionalization of history that he hoped to sell to audiences in his own time *becomes* history. In this sense, Mond's story departs radically from Groenewegen's two texts. Groenewegen's stories explicitly (and literally) question the role of race in national identity. But, then, Groenewegen's protagonists are all outsiders: Ace, Benny and the Doctor all pass through the narrative, through Australia, on their way from and to somewhere else. In Mond's story, the elements of race underlying the characters' national identity are more deeply embedded, because the characters are more deeply embedded. As Jack becomes – psychologically, emotionally and historically – an Australian digger, his carefully cultivated sense of documentary distance, in which he consciously ignored the documentary's discussion of the "ANZAC spirit" in favour of interpreting the campaign in generic (if accurate) terms as a "waste of human life",[69] falls away. In Mond's hands, Jack's transformation literalizes the transformative role that Anzac Cove plays in Australian national identity, its position as a nexus for the country's transition from colony to nation. No longer an impartial observer, Jack becomes representative of the model of nationhood that Groenewegen queries. Terms such as "mates", "fellow Aussies" and "damn Turks" flow organically from his new national identity. He becomes, in short, a figure who never plays a large role in mainstream *Doctor Who* but who is central to Australian national identity, evoked and re-evoked in moments of crisis from the Second World War to the Port Arthur massacre. As such, his reflexive evocation and denial of race tells us, as readers, something of the construction and operation of Australian national identity.

Conclusion

In tracing Australian fan responses to *Doctor Who*, Alan McKee ends by noting that "through all of this, there is a clear awareness that this Australian institution originates somewhere else – that Australia is always secondary, relying on other countries to produce its myths for it, no matter how much it might reshape them."[70] But the reshaping reveals something of the interaction between disparate mythologies. In writing *Doctor Who* fiction, these writers foreground their own immersion in a distinctly British mythology. But, simultaneously, they bend that mythology to their own, distinctly nationalistic purposes, shaping it around key moments in Australia's history. Such moments are a small part of the overwhelming flood of ancillary material that accompanies the core, televised text of *Doctor Who*. But for Australian-based writers and readers, they are significant moments, creating a continuity in which the Doctor is as likely to influence the landing at Cape Helles as he is to interact with such European traumas as the St Bartholomew's Day Massacre (*The Massacre*, 1966) or the Great Fire of London (*The Visitation*, 1982). The Doctor's alien origins do not preclude his influencing Australian history, just as he influenced Australian culture.

Notes

1   Alan McKee, "Is *Doctor Who* Australian?", *Media International Australia*, 132 (2009), 54.
2   McKee, "Is *Doctor Who* Australian?", 56.
3   McKee, "Is *Doctor Who* Australian?", 62.
4   Lance Parkin, "Canonicity matters: Defining the *Doctor Who* canon", in David Butler, ed., *Time and Relative Dissertations in Space: Critical Perspectives on* Doctor Who, Manchester: Manchester University Press, 2007, 257.
5   Parkin, "Canonicity matters", 257.
6   Parkin, "Canonicity matters", 247.
7   Christopher Marlow, "The folding text: *Doctor Who*, adaptation and fan fiction", in Rachel Carroll, ed., *Adaptation in Contemporary Culture: Textual Infidelities*, London: Continuum, 2009, 47.
8   Parkin, "Canonicity matters", 259.
9   Parkin, "Canonicity matters", 250.

10 Parkin, "Canonicity matters", 250.

11 e.g., Marlow's analysis of how the new series of *Doctor Who* folds its own earlier incarnations back into itself (which plays with the notion of canonicity as it relates to the programme) lists as texts the televised episodes, BBC Books' 'Eighth Doctor Adventures' and Virgin Books' 'New Adventures', Big Finish's audio plays, and some online fan fiction, but not the Big Finish short story anthologies. Marlow, "The folding text."

12 Since I make frequent use of the term 'Australian national identity', it is worthwhile noting the parameters within which I employ this term. 'Australian national identity' implies a monolithic concept, which is a problematic and ultimately unsupportable stance. But, as these stories (and other texts) demonstrate, a dominant or normative national identity does exist, especially when the texts in question deliberately evoke certain events or patterns in Australian history. 'Australian national identity', therefore, evokes the implication in these texts that they and (a portion of) their readership share a common understanding of Australia's convict, colonial and military history and of the mythos that arises from this.

13 I am excluding the three BBC Books anthologies from this study; none included works by Australian authors (though the first did include the short story 'Model Train Set' [1998] by now Australian resident Jonathan Blum).

14 This essay arose from research undertaken for AustLit: The Australian Literature Resource's SpecUlations project, mapping Australian authors of horror, science fiction and fantasy. The AustLit database now contains detailed records of Australian contributions to novels and short stories based on *Doctor Who* and its spin-offs.

15 The Australian-written content (as far as I have identified it) amounts to roughly 5.5 per cent of the anthologies' 470 stories. However, it is worth noting that the original series 'pure historicals' have a similarly small presence, but are undeniably a recognizable subset of stories.

16 Andrew K. Purvis, "Evitability", in Simon Guerrier, ed., *Short Trips: How the Doctor Changed My Life*, Maidenhead: Big Finish, 2008.

17 Jonathan Blum, "Home Fires", in Simon Guerrier, ed., *Short Trips: The History of Christmas*, Maidenhead: Big Finish, 2005.

18 Sarah Groenewegen, "The Bushranger's Story", in Gary Russell, ed., *Short Trips: Repercussions*, Maidenhead: Big Finish, 2004.

19 Daniel O'Mahony, "Now how is that wolf able to impersonate a grandmother? History, pseudo-history and genre in *Doctor Who*", in Butler, ed., *Time and Relative Dissertations in Space*, 57 and 61.

20 This is more true of the original series than the new series: a strong feature of the 2005 revival of the programme is the degree to which the Doctor is emotionally connected to Earth, not only through his own idealization of the human race but also through his choice of companions (particularly Rose Tyler and Martha Jones) who are reluctant to abandon their family ties.

21 O'Mahony, "History, pseudo-history and genre", 57.

22 O'Mahony, "History, pseudo-history and genre", 63.

23 O'Mahony, "History, pseudo-history and genre", 59.

24 Sarah Groenewegen, "Virgin Lands", in Jacqueline Rayner, ed., *Short Trips: The Zodiac*, Maidenhead: Big Finish, 2002, 77–88.

25   Groenewegen, "Virgin Lands", 77.

26   Groenewegen, "Virgin Lands", 79.

27   Groenewegen, "Virgin Lands", 88.

28   Neville Meaney, "Britishness and Australian identity: The problem of nationalism in Australian history and historiography", *Australian Historical Studies*, 32, 116 (2001), 76–90.

29   Meaney, "Britishness and Australian identity", 81.

30   *Terra nullius* is a particularly familiar and particularly troubled term for Australian readers, used as the basis for the oppression of Indigenous Australians. Groenewegen's readers would be particularly familiar with it, as it had only been legally overturned a decade earlier, in the court case colloquially known as 'Mabo'.

31   Annona Pearse, "(Re)constructing Port Arthur and Thredbo: Tourist site tragedies and myths of national character", *Media International Australia*, 120 (2006), 51–62.

32   Pearse, "(Re)constructing Port Arthur and Thredbo", 55.

33   Pearse, "(Re)constructing Port Arthur and Thredbo", 60.

34   Pearse, "(Re)constructing Port Arthur and Thredbo", 52.

35   Sarah Groenewegen, "Hymn of the City", in Jacqueline Rayner, ed., *Short Trips: The Muses*, Maidenhead: Big Finish, 2003, 81–102.

36   Groenewegen, "Hymn of the City", 83.

37   Peter Stanley, "What is the Battle for Australia?", *Point Blank*, 4, 2 (2007), 18.

38   Stanley, "Battle for Australia", 18.

39   e.g., he notes that the national Battle for Australia Council was established by 1998. Stanley, "Battle for Australia."

40   Stanley, "Battle for Australia", 21.

41   Stanley, "Battle for Australia", 22.

42   Ien Ang and Jon Stratton, "Multiculturalism in crisis: The new politics of race and national identity in Australia", *Topia*, 2 (Spring 1998), 22.

43   Ang and Stratton, "Multiculturalism in crisis", 23.

44   Groenewegen, "Hymn of the City", 93.

45   Groenewegen, "Hymn of the City", 88 and 90.

46   Ang and Stratton, "Multiculturalism in crisis", 27.

47   Groenewegen, "Hymn of the City", 90.

48   The ever-sceptical Ace responds "Not *the* Force?", to which the Doctor replies, "perhaps yes. As useful as any analogy", as though to drive home the *pseudo*-ness of this pseudo-historical story. Groenewegen, "Hymn of the City", 102.

49   Groenewegen, "Hymn of the City", 102.

50   Stanley, "Battle for Australia", 21.

51   Ang and Stratton, "Multiculturalism in crisis", 23.

52   Groenewegen, "Hymn of the City", 102

53   Ian Mond, "Direct Action", in Ian Farrington, ed., *Short Trips: The Centenarian*, Maidenhead: Big Finish, 2006, 27–41.

54   O'Mahony, "History, pseudo-history and genre", 62.

55   Mond, "Direct Action", 29.

56   Stanley, "Battle for Australia", 22.

57   Pearse, "(Re)constructing Port Arthur and Thredbo", 56–57.

58   Mond, "Direct Action", 28.

59   Mond, "Direct Action", 28–29.

60   Mond, "Direct Action", 33.

61   Mond, "Direct Action", 28.

62   Mond's story actually gives the soldier's affiliation as the 11th Brigade (Mond, "Direct Action", 29). But the 11th Brigade, a Queensland-based unit, was not formed until 1916. The 11th Battalion, a Western Australian unit formed in 1914, seems a likelier option, since the soldier specifies that they left from Fremantle.

63   Mond, "Direct Action", 36.

64   Mond, "Direct Action", 38.

65   Mond, "Direct Action", 41.

66   Mond, "Direct Action", 33.

67   Mond, "Direct Action", 39.

68   Mond, "Direct Action", 41.

69   Mond, "Direct Action", 28–29.

70   McKee, "Is Doctor Who Australian?", 64.

PART V

Race and science

Chapter 20

"They hate each other's chromosomes": Eugenics and the shifting racial identity of the Daleks

Kristine Larsen

We must keep the Kaled race pure. Imperfects are rejected.

– Nyder, *Genesis of the Daleks*

The hour has come to sound the rallying cry for that part of our citizenship which is willing to look the facts in the face and then with intelligence and determination to lay the axe of prevention to the root of the tree of tainted heredity, which is responsible for this increasing harvest of human unfitness, defectiveness, and degeneracy.

– Lena K. Sadler, "Is the Abnormal to Become Normal?"[1]

Introduction

In the late nineteenth century, following Darwin's groundbreaking work on evolution, the concept of 'survival of the fittest' was adapted to issues facing human society, a movement dubbed 'social Darwinism'. One specific application was named *eugenics* by Darwin's cousin Francis Galton. The basic premise assumes that heredity is closely tied to race, and that both are inextricably tied to social progress and the success of a nation. Thus in order for a nation to be successful – to be 'fit' – it should be selective in its breeding policies so that the genetic (and hence social, political, economic and moral) make-up of its people should always improve and not degrade into a more primitive (more animalistic) form. By the 1920s over thirty countries across the world had established eugenics movements, with differing policies in regards to how their nations' genetic purity should be preserved.[2] Throughout the first half of the twentieth century eugenics methodologies utilized across the globe ranged from restricting immigration and segregating the races, to forced sterilization, and even open genocide. While forced sterilization is no longer practiced in the United States, the last US state laws against interracial marriage were overturned in 1967, and South Africa's system of apartheid was only abolished in 1994. Racism is alive and well, as attested by the continued existence of white supremacy movements in the United States and Europe. So-called 'ethnic cleansing' (genocide) has been carried out far too many times in the last century, and the horrific concept owes a debt to the eugenics movement and the concept of 'racial hygiene'.

One of the hallmarks of high quality literature (considered broadly to include all media) is its ability to force us to face the monster within, those uncomfortable truths lurking inside our collective and individual closets. These truths include historical horrors and present prejudices perpetrated upon our fellow *Homo sapiens*, often merely because they have a different skin tone or speak a different tongue. As this volume clearly demonstrates, *Doctor Who* is one of those seminal works that illuminates the dark corners of our minds and history while cleverly disguised as simple entertainment. This essay will focus on one small section of the important lessons of race relations the *Doctor Who* universe has continued to espouse over the past fifty years, namely the Daleks and the ultimate failure of eugenics. In exploring the horrors perpetuated by Davros and his Daleks in the name of Dalek superiority, we are forced to look into the mirror, and reflect upon the horrors humans have inflicted upon members of their own species in the name of 'racial purity'.

The eugenics movement in Britain, America and beyond

The modern eugenics movement was not birthed on Skaro but in Britain. From there it grew into potency in the United States and achieved its most dangerous extremes in Hitler's Germany. But like the Daleks, eugenics has been erroneously assumed to be extinct more than once. Francis Galton, a cousin to Charles Darwin, observed in the mid-nineteenth century that the leaders of British society tended to be related to each other. From this he assumed that their success in the greater society was due to their superior genetics, and proposed that selective breeding might generally improve the genetic make-up of British society.[3] He coined the term eugenics in the 1880s, from the Greek word "*eugenes* namely, good in stock, hereditarily endowed with noble qualities." He further explained that the concept was "equally applicable to men, brutes, and plants."[4] The focus of the British eugenics movement was to apply heredity to poverty, with the hopes of reducing the latter by selective breeding of the upper classes.

British eugenics writings were enthusiastically received in America, in reaction against the influx of Southern and Eastern European immigrants in the late 1800s and the emancipation of African American slaves after the Civil War. One of the most vocal supporters of eugenics in America was biologist Charles Benedict Davenport, director of the Cold Spring Harbor Laboratory in New York and director of the American Breeders Association. He held that traits such as poverty and laziness were inherited, and that patterns of such traits in families should be carefully studied. American eugenicist Ellsworth Huntington wrote in 1935 that since "physical and mental superiority tend to go together [...] improvement of the population in any important trait will bring improvement in other traits."[5] Such 'improvements' in the population would be brought about through restricting immigration, segregating (in institutions) and sterilization of the 'unfit'.

One of the terms commonly used to describe eugenics programmes was racial hygiene, as it was believed that selective breeding would "do for the race what personal hygiene does for the individual" because defective individuals "may be compared to an insidious disease affecting the body politic [...] Eugenics is racial preventative medicine."[6] Eugenics therefore wrapped up racism, nationalism, classism, sexism, xenophobia and all manner of general prejudices into one neat little sanitary package under the banner of (questionable) science. This analogy of the racially 'undesirable' as a disease is echoed in the episode *Dalek* (2005). When Rose touches the tortured Dalek, she transfers some of her DNA to the creature, and it mutates, and, much to its horror, takes on human characteristics. It therefore asks Rose to order it to commit suicide, noting, "This is not life, this is sickness. I shall not be like you."

The concept of racial hygiene was taken to its extreme in Nazi Germany, under the umbrella of the theory of 'Nordic (Aryan) superiority'. Hitler was a reader of the American eugenicists and noted that one work in particular, Madison Grant's *Passing of a Great Race*, was his "bible."[7] Although the American eugenics movement was less vocal after the horrors of Nazi Germany were revealed, forced sterilizations continued until the 1960s in California. Xenophobia and racism did not diminish in the years after the Second World War, as noted in *Remembrance of the Daleks* (1988), set in 1963 Britain. Here, Ratcliffe, the Dalek sympathizer, notes that he was imprisoned during the Second World War for being on the "wrong side." Ratcliffe's young supporter, Smith, explains that Ratcliffe has "great plans" – in particular, that one has to "protect your own."

It may seem incongruous to discuss Dalek eugenics, given that Daleks don't (as far as we know) reproduce sexually. In addition, they were genetically engineered from one of two types of humanoids indigenous to the planet Skaro. However, Dalek history is a case study in racial warfare and an obsession with racial purity and claimed superiority. Therefore the lessons of the Daleks can be applied to human history. Critiques of the presumed superiority of the Daleks and their lack of respect for other forms of life are legion throughout the series. As one example, in *The Evil of the Daleks* (1967), Waterfield refuses to work with the Daleks after they have killed a fellow human. "You've destroyed a human life. Don't you understand that?" he implores. "That is of no consequence," the creature coldly retorts. "There is only one form of life that matters – Dalek life!" In *Genesis of the Daleks* (1975), the Kaleds' Nazi-like obsession with racial purity leads to the extinction of both their kind and that of their 'inferior' enemy, the Thals. Only the Daleks, Davros's genetically engineered Kaleds, survive the double genocide. During the long war, mutants – Mutos – were created among the Kaled population. These genetic 'monsters' were banished to the wasteland between the Kaled and Thal cities. "We must keep the Kaled race pure," security chief Nyder explains. "Imperfects are rejected." It is no coincidence that the Dalek battle cry is "exterminate", for that is precisely what the Nazis and others who have perpetrated genocide in the name of national and racial 'purity' have done in our world.

As various *Doctor Who* stories are discussed throughout the remainder of this essay, another theme of the eugenics movement should be kept in mind, namely race suicide. In a reversal of 'survival of the fittest', eugenicists worried that if the least fit outbred the genetically superior, the average quality of human genetics would decrease and the 'superior' races could die out.[8] There is another factor that would cause a decrease in the number of 'superior' humans (at least the males), namely war. Oxford eugenicist Edward Poulton argued that the First World War would "undoubtedly kill the better variations and, as a result, is highly dysgenic", while

Italian eugenicists offered that the war would allow the "physically and mentally weak – those exempt from conscription – the chance to reproduce unhampered."[9] Since Davros believes that "cooperation between different species is impossible; one race must survive all others and to do this it must dominate ruthlessly", he has set up his creations to have their numbers decimated time and time again, as casualties of war.[10] Therefore the Daleks are not only obsessed with dominating other species and reducing the numbers of these inferior beings, but with increasing the number of their own ranks; a difficult task given their inability to reproduce sexually, and their warlike (dysgenic) behaviour. The Daleks must therefore 'interbreed' (in a genetic sense) with 'lesser' types of creatures in order to survive, setting themselves up for even further wars over racial purity, as the various hybrid species disagree as to what exactly defines a 'true' Dalek. Similarly, during the eugenics movement in the twentieth century, members of the 'superior races' found themselves faced with an inconvenient truth – that they themselves were not racially pure.

Mongrelization or heterosis? Genetic diversity and the survival of a species

Dog lovers and breeders are aware of the problems with inbreeding, as purebred dogs are often prone to particular diseases and defects. Examples include deafness in Dalmatians, hip dysplasia in German Shepherds, and heart defects in King Charles Cavalier Spaniels. When wild populations of animals are severely reduced (through habitat changes, disease or human intervention), inbreeding is sometimes unavoidable. The resulting 'population bottleneck' leads to a lack of genetic diversity in the species, leaving it open to further decimation through disease and lowered fertility rates.[11] For example, both subspecies of African cheetah display a dramatic lack of diversity. To prevent further genetic contraction of the species, zoos are crossing the two subspecies with each other, with promising results.[12] Inbreeding among human populations generally occurs when groups of people select mates based on social class (such as royalty) or narrowly defined ethnic populations (such as Ashkenazi Jews in Eastern Europe). The results are similar to purebred dogs and cheetahs, as the high incidence of haemophilia in the royal houses of Europe in the late nineteenth and early twentieth centuries demonstrated.[13] Ashkenazi Jews, who through social restriction, exclusion and ghettoization (in addition to cultural preference) have tended to marry within their own ethno-religious population, are "subject to a range of genetic diseases unique to this population" including Tay Sachs disease and idiopathic torsion dystonia.[14]

The Daleks' obsession with racial purity has also repeatedly led to a genetic bottleneck. For example, in *Resurrection of the Daleks* (1984), Davros is freed from prison by the Daleks in order to find a cure for the virus the Movellans had created. Due to the genetic similarity of all Daleks, the virus had been quite effective and decimated their ranks. The remaining Daleks had segregated themselves in separate populations in order to prevent a complete extinction. Mistrusting the Daleks, Davros unleashes the virus on the Dalek ship in order to eliminate the rebellious creatures. In the process he almost destroys himself, as his genetic make-up is very similar to that of the Daleks, but not identical – not yet. In *The Stolen Earth/Journey's End* (2008) Davros has created a new battalion of Daleks from his own cells: "I gave myself to them, quite literally [...] New Daleks. True Daleks," he exclaims. When the Supreme Dalek demands that the Doctor exit the TARDIS and surrender, the Doctor explains to his companions that they cannot fight back, because unlike the previous time they had met this enemy in *Bad Wolf/The Parting of the Ways* (2005), these Daleks were full-blooded Daleks. Is the Doctor himself falling victim to a eugenicist argument here? But the Dalek's "pure blood" is their Achilles heel; the Doctor 2.0[15] builds a weapon that successfully targets the Daleks' genetic code (through Davros) and destroys both the creatures and their creator.

On the other hand, breeding between genetically varied individuals has been shown to result in not only a wider genetic variation in the offspring, but offspring that show faster development, greater fertility, larger size and other characteristics considered 'hearty'. This is termed 'hybrid vigour' or heterosis.[16] In *Journey's End*, the enhanced Donna Noble (having the intelligence of a Time Lord and the ingenuity and resilience of a human) is able to defeat the Daleks due to her superior hybrid nature. As we shall see, the Doctor 2.0 is not as easily defined as a positive hybridization. The term heterosis is credited to Cold Spring Harbor Laboratory corn geneticist George H. Shull, and the principle has been widely used in agriculture and animal husbandry to improve plants and animals used as food stock.[17]

Given that many in the laboratory were eugenicists, this discovery was not unknown to the American eugenics movement. In fact, heterosis was embraced in a rather peculiar way in order to explain the presumed superiority of certain European bloodlines. For example, in his 1951 article "Hybrids and History" George D. Snell argued that Europe has been the "birthplaces of the greatest geniuses of art and science" because of an earlier hybridization of several types of Caucasians. He proclaimed that the achievements of Elizabethan and Victorian England were due in part to such hybridization.[18] In his article he relied heavily on C. S. Coon's 1948 volume *The Races of Europe*, and Coon's assertion that there were actually thirteen Caucasian races in Europe, seven of which contained Neanderthal heredity. It was this presumed cross-breeding between Cro-Magnons and Neanderthals that was cited as the source of the hybrid vigour in European Caucasians.[19] On the other hand, interbreeding between the non-Caucasian races, or between Caucasian and non-Caucasian races (what we would call today bi-racial or interracial heritage) was seen as producing less fit individuals. For example, Snell argued that many "hybrid populations produced by wide crosses [...] show a low record of achievement", giving the example of Cajun populations in Louisiana.[20]

The Daleks also practiced a curious kind of 'breeding' for hybrid vigour in *Daleks in Manhattan/Evolution of the Daleks* (2007). The four remaining Daleks (the Cult of Skaro) disagree as to the wisdom of creating a human-Dalek hybrid. While his companions argue that the Daleks are superior to the humans, Dalek Sec notes that (in a Darwinian sense) the reverse is true: "There are millions of humans and only four of us. If we are supreme, why are we not victorious?" He notes that their cult was created to assure the survival of their species. He realizes that to do that, they, like all species, must change – they must evolve. In other words, their genetic diversity must increase and those genetic variations which are best adapted will predominate and be most successful. "Our purity has brought us to extinction," he correctly argues. The newly hybridized Sec explains to the Doctor that Davros was wrong in removing their emotions when he first created their species. "It makes us lesser than our enemies," he admits. When the Doctor offers that regaining human emotions would make the new hybrid Daleks no longer supreme beings, Sec agrees, and adds "and that is good." However, the other three Daleks disagree with this rather progressive pronouncement, and not only deem humans to be inferior, but that Sec himself is no longer fit to lead them because he is now an inferior creature.

Hybridization introduces the problem of self-identification, and identification in the eyes of others. In dogs, new breeds have been created through the careful cross-breeding of individuals of different characteristics, such as the Labradoodle (a Poodle-Labrador Retriever mix). But dogs of accidentally mixed heritage are often disparaged as 'mutts' in the common vernacular. In human populations, people of mixed racial or ethnic heritage are sometimes automatically classified as members of the 'minority' group. In some cases, they are even rejected by members of both parental groups as something 'other' (in an uncomfortable way).[21] As noted above, this is especially true in cultures that either openly or tacitly practise eugenics. An example of cultural disapproval of interracial reproduction was legislated in the so-called 'one drop' rule for defining 'blacks' in the United States. The presence of a single African or African American ancestor was sufficient to classify one as 'black', no matter the number of intervening generations. This rule was upheld in many state courts, although some modified the rule to include only those of a specific fraction of African blood (such as one-sixteenth). This definition of 'blackness' is unique in the world, and is even unique among the minority groups in the United States.[22] This rule served to exclude many people from being considered a member of the dominant Caucasian race (the 'superior race' in the eyes of eugenicists and other prejudiced members of society). The most (in)famous example of an inclusive definition of a dominant race can be seen in Nazi Germany, with the 'one-quarter rule'. Aware that pure Nordic ancestry was rare among the Nazi Party (including Hitler himself), Nazi geneticists espoused the belief that having up to one-quarter Jewish ancestry did not dilute Aryan blood. The Nuremberg Laws codified this, stating that "one-quarter Jews" could marry pure "Aryans" without any genetic deficiencies resulting.[23] In addition, since many of the so-called Aryans did not look especially Nordic, Nazi geneticists instructed biology teachers to "stress that all Aryan Germans had a significant portion of Nordic blood running through their veins."[24]

Because Davros and the Daleks often relied on the tissue (or even complete bodies) of humans to replenish the Dalek population, most of the incarnations of the Daleks are hybrids, or perhaps more correctly 'chimeras', since they are not created by the combination of sperm and egg. The scientific term chimera is taken from Greek mythology, where it was used for animals that were amalgams of various creatures. Chimeras have been used for several decades to study reactions at the cellular level (for example, by inserting jellyfish green fluorescent protein into organisms to make certain cellular organelles easier to see).[25] Human genes have been introduced into various animals, creating so-called 'transgenic animals' that can be used to research treatments for diseases such as Alzheimer's, and to produce human proteins such as insulin in the milk of transgenic mammals.[26] True human-animal hybrids have been produced in the laboratory, for example combining hamster eggs with human sperm in order to study human male infertility. However, by international law, these hybrids are not allowed to develop past the two-cell stage.[27]

The difference may seem to be mere semantics, but as we have seen, even the most capricious appearing definitions have the power to include or exclude individuals from dominant groups of power. With the exception of the original Daleks (mutated Kaleds) and the Daleks cloned from Davros himself, all the Daleks appear to be impure. How much human 'taint' can be allowed before an organism is no longer recognized as a Dalek? As with human eugenics movements, the definition is as fluid as blood itself. When he is hybridized with a human and becomes a bipedal humanoid, Dalek Sec declares himself to be "a Human-Dalek. I am your future." Putting the words 'human' and 'Dalek' in the same phrase is interesting, as it appears to put both progenitors' racial identity on equal footing. In sharp contrast, the titular character of *Dalek* has only absorbed a small amount of Rose's DNA yet it feels so contaminated that it must commit suicide. In the majority of cases where the Daleks either incorporate human tissue within their own to make new Daleks, or insert some 'Dalek factor' into fully formed human bodies to turn them into Daleks, the Daleks refer to the resulting chimeras as 'Daleks', an interesting reversal of the one-drop rule. Perhaps it is because the Daleks deem their genetics so superior that they believe them to be dominant as well, and can overcome any human 'contamination' (despite what Rose's suicidal Dalek believed). In *The Evil of the Daleks*, the creatures trick the Doctor into inserting the 'human factor' into candidate Daleks in order to identify the Dalek factor. The plan is to infect the entire history of Earth with the Dalek factor in order to subjugate humanity (and turn them into Daleks). Interestingly, Waterfield worries that the 'human factor' Daleks will experience a kind of heterosis and become "unbeatable" – it will "turn them into super-beings [...] Adding what is best and finest in human nature to all that is brilliant and superior in them."

Another example of humans beings being turned into Daleks by the incorporation of some Dalek genetics is seen in *Revelation of the Daleks* (1985). At the Tranquil Repose Mortuary, Davros (under the name The Great Healer) turns humans and other humanoids stored in suspended animation into Daleks. Professor Stengos, the Doctor's friend, is found by his daughter in a laboratory. He appears as a human head suspended in a Dalek-like casing. He resists the 'Dalek factor' as long as he can, but it becomes increasingly difficult. "I am to become a Dalek. We are all to become Daleks," he explains. "We must multiply. The seed of the Daleks must be supreme [...] It is our duty to eradicate all those who wish to pollute the purity of the Dalek race." Note that the Daleks presumably do not feel that turning human flesh into Daleks constitutes polluting the purity of their species; such hypocrisy has certainly been demonstrated in the human eugenics movement (as in the case of the Nazis' one-quarter rule). In *The Parting of the Ways*, the Emperor Dalek explains to the Doctor that human prisoners and other "undesirables" were "filleted, pulped, sifted" to create the new Daleks. "The seed of the human race is perverted. Only one cell in a billion was fit to be nurtured." Despite the fact that the Daleks were highly selective in taking the 'most fit' of the human tissue, as Rose notes they were indeed grown from human tissue, and when she calls them "half human", it is declared to be blasphemy by the Daleks. "Everything human has been purged. I cultivated pure and blessed Dalek [...] I reached into the dirt and made new life," the Emperor exhorts. The ludicrous nature of this extreme rationalization of their own 'purity' is not lost on the Doctor, who notes that they are insane, "driven mad by your own flesh. The stink of humanity. You hate your own existence."

A final example can be seen in the plan of Dalek Sec in *Daleks in Manhattan*. His original plan was to use his now-hybrid DNA as a template; using the gamma radiation from a solar flare, he plans to splice his DNA with that of the humans in suspended animation, creating a new race. "I want to change the gene sequence," he explains to the Doctor, to make the new creatures even more human than he himself has become. "Humans are the great survivors," he offers. "We need that ability." But the remaining Daleks do not appreciate this attempt at hybrid vigour, and instead plan to insert their own pure Dalek DNA into the sleeping humans, somehow making the new race "one hundred per cent Dalek." The new hybrid species awakens and originally identify themselves as Daleks. However, when they question the orders of Dalek Caan, it is discovered that some of the Doctor's Time Lord DNA has become mixed in, and Caan commits genocide by destroying the new species. The Doctor seems to take great delight in the changes his DNA introduces, again suggesting that perhaps this Time Lord is not above some eugenicist thoughts of his own. Nevertheless, we cannot deny that genetics is a tricky business – it involves DNA, random combinations and environmental effects. Despite the best attempts of the Daleks and other eugenicists to control the code, nature clearly has other designs.

Dehuman(oid)izing the other: Nazis, Daleks and the United States

In their search for the perfect race, both Davros and Nazi scientists such as Josef Mengele utilized experimentation on humans/humanoids, often on the races that were seen as lesser and expendable. In the case of the Nazis, experiments were done on a variety of 'non-Aryans' including Jews and Roma ('gypsies') as well as dissidents, prisoners, and other 'undesirables' and 'deviants' such as homosexuals. Experiments included mimicking battlefield wounds, studies of the progress of infectious diseases such as typhoid, and eugenics experiments (such as new methods of sterilization).[28] Mengele conducted barbaric experiments of dubious scientific quality on twins in an attempt to uncover how to create perfect Aryan children en masse.[29] These experiments were carried out with no regard for the pain and suffering of the human guinea pigs, and most certainly without their informed consent. As horrific as these scientific travesties were, unfortunately they were not unique. For example,

Japan's Unit 731 conducted biological and chemical warfare experiments on Manchurian prisoners, including infecting them with bubonic plague.[30]

Undoubtedly the most infamous example of illicit human experimentation outside of the Nazis was the Tuskegee Experiment in the United States. For forty years, scientists associated with the US Public Health Service knowingly withheld treatment to several hundred African American men who were suffering from syphilis, in order to study the progress and complications of the disease.[31] What set this event apart from other examples is that the study was not done in secret, but instead the results were openly published in articles in medical journals and presented at professional conferences over the decades; it took the intervention of the press to bring a halt to the project in 1974. In recent years it was discovered that some of the same scientists who ran the Tuskegee Experiment also led an American government-funded project in Guatemala during the 1940s that knowingly infected nearly 700 prisoners and mental health patients with syphilis and gonorrhœa.[32]

Just as the Nazis experimented on those they deemed 'subhuman' and American scientists on 'brown and black' people, Davros and the Daleks routinely experimented on 'inferior' races and species. For example, in *Daleks in Manhattan*, only 'superior' humans were selected to become shells for the new Dalek-human hybridization. The 'inferior' individuals were engineered into pig-human hybrid slaves. Similarly, in *Revelation of the Daleks*, Davros only used the rich and famous or 'superior' humans to create Daleks. The remaining stock was turned into concentrated protein and sold as food (a nod to the classic film *Soylent Green* [Director: Richard Fleischer, 1973]). This literal reduction of 'inferior' individuals to an animal-like state mirrors the metaphorical designations used to describe the victims of human experimentation. For example, Hitler variously referred to Jews as "parasites, plague, cancer, tumour, bacillus, bloodsucker, bedbugs, fleas and racial tuberculosis",[33] while Japanese military scientists referred to their Manchurian prisoners as "monkeys" or "logs." This process of dehumanization made it easier for the scientists to ignore the ethical issues with their experiments; since the subjects were not really human, they were not due the same rights as true humans (and especially not the same rights as humans of the 'superior' race).[34]

The clearest analogies between the Nazis and Daleks were undoubtedly drawn in *Genesis of the Daleks*. On Skaro, centuries of racial warfare between the Thals and Kaleds (who even dress like Nazis) led to severe biological mutations. As Davros works on his "glorious project" to make the Kaled's ultimate mutant form invincible, General Ravon explains to the Doctor that the Kaleds will soon "wipe every trace of Thals from their land [...] Our battle cry will be total extermination of the Thals." The viewer is clearly meant to feel a chill run down their spine at hearing this, as well as catch the obvious reference to Hitler's 'final solution'. Later in the story Davros and Nyder give the Thals a chemical weapon that will penetrate the Kaled dome and destroy their people. "Today the Kaled race is ended," Davros proclaims without regret. "But from its ashes will rise a new race. The supreme creature. The ultimate conqueror of the universe. The Dalek!" One of the first acts of this new race is to destroy the Thal city; therefore the first two genocides perpetrated by Davros and his creatures are against the two humanoid races of his own planet.

Eugenics 2.0: Genetic engineering the perfect race

The ability to reproduce is central to the survival of a species. In the animal kingdom, females chose mates that will give their young the best chance of survival, as determined by mating dances, displays of strength or other skills, or even the colour of their plumage. In modern human society, we would like to think that we have thrown Darwinian survival strategies out the window and instead reproduce for love. Unfortunately, not all couples are fertile, and must turn to science to make reproduction a reality. In response, the scientific community has developed a number of technologies, ranging from *in vitro* fertilization and fertility drugs to sperm sorting, sperm donors and even gestational carriers (so-called surrogate mothers).

Because the Daleks do not reproduce sexually, they must rely on technology to increase their numbers. In *Revelation of the Daleks*, the Doctor notes that Davros has finally found a way to reproduce Daleks using human tissue. Grigory notes that it is "a tremendous feat of genetic engineering." Davros repeatedly tinkers with his creatures' genetic designs, in order to make them even more ruthless and difficult to defeat. For example, in *Genesis of the Daleks*, Davros orders a dozen variations to be introduced into the newly created Daleks, despite his assistant's claim that they will introduce "enormous mental defects." Davros counters, calling them "improvements" despite the fact (or perhaps because of the fact) that they will leave the Daleks without a conscience, a moral compass or pity. However, as is usually the case with mad scientists and their creations, the Daleks rebel and Davros is entombed on Skaro. When he is later awakened in *Destiny of the Daleks* (1979) his immediate concern is to re-engineer his creations, telling the Daleks that he will "learn from your mistakes. The Daleks shall be made into perfect creatures." When this attempt at perfecting his creature fails, Davros tries again in *Resurrection of the Daleks*, explaining to the Doctor that his mistake was "to make them totally ruthless. It restricted their ability to cope with creatures who relied not only on logic, but on insight and intuition. That is a factor I wish to correct."

While the genetic engineering depicted in *Doctor Who* is clearly beyond the grasp of current terrestrial scientists, the 'medical marvels' already achieved have raised serious ethical issues. Embryos can be tested for genetic diseases before implantation in the womb, while a variety of genetic tests can be conducted *in utero*, giving couples the choice as to whether or not to carry a pregnancy to term. While these technologies have allowed infertile couples to conceive healthy children, they can also be used to screen potential offspring not only for disease, but for gender, and perhaps in the not-too-distant future for such characteristics as eye colour, athletic prowess and intelligence. Well-meaning parents motivated by a desire to have children who will have the greatest potential for success in life might engineer their offspring from conception to meet some cultural standard of perfection. Therefore eugenics has a new face in the twenty-first century, in the form of genetic engineering and 'designer babies', and, perhaps in the future, human cloning. Such genetic eugenics could result in "two branches of *Homo sapiens*: a wealthy genetic elite that replicates itself through designer babies and a medically underserved genetic underclass."[35]

As we have seen, a person's perceived race or ethnicity has been sufficient grounds for discrimination, sterilization, and even genocide in the not-too-distant past – what further inhumanities will genetic engineering of the human genome bring in this Brave New World? In the landmark 1998 case Norman-Bloodsaw versus Lawrence Berkeley Laboratory the US Court of Appeals ruled that workers could sue their employer if they were being tested without their informed consent for "highly private and sensitive medical genetic information such as syphilis, sickle cell trait, and pregnancy" during their employee health examination.[36] This case led to the Genetic Information Nondiscrimination Act of 2008, which bars employers, unions or training programmes from discriminating on the basis of genetic information in the United States.[37]

To see the results of genetic discrimination, one need not look further than *Remembrance of the Daleks*. The episode centres around the conflict between two factions of Daleks, the white and gold Daleks introduced in *Revelation of the Daleks* who are loyal to Davros, and the dark grey Daleks loyal to the Supreme Dalek. Ironically, by the timeline of *Remembrance of the Daleks*, the original grey Daleks are now called the "renegades", as they resisted the attempt of Davros to take over control of the Dalek empire. The dichotomy in colour is not accidental; the more 'Caucasian' Daleks deem themselves to be superior, as they have been engineered by Davros to have useful limbs and grafted prosthetics. As Ace summarizes the situation:

> Renegade Daleks are blobs. Imperial Daleks are bionic blobs with bits added. You can tell that Daleks are into racial purity. So one lot of Daleks reckon that the other lot of blobs are too different. They're mutants – not pure in their blobiness [...] They hate each other's chromosomes.

Is Ace predicting the future racial tensions of our own future, one in which the one-drop rule is replaced by the one-cell, one-chromosome or one-gene rule? Could humans hate each other based on their chromosomes rather than their skin colour? This possibility deserves serious consideration, and *Doctor Who* forces us to do exactly that.

Conclusion: The human factor versus the Dalek factor

Americans' shameful history of eugenics has been brought to the forefront in recent years, due to researchers making these past crimes public as well as victims of forced sterilization programmes demanding not only an acknowledgement of and apology for their treatment, but also financial compensation.[38] While forced sterilization has become a footnote in history, the more horrific side of eugenics, namely genocide, has not. In the wake of the Armenian genocide in the Ottoman Empire in 1915 and the Nazi Holocaust, lessons of tolerance have not been learned, as we have seen in Bosnia, Kosovo, Rwanda and Darfur. Genocide has become the "leading cause of preventable violent death in the 20th–21st century, taking even more lives than war."[39] What has changed is the language used to describe such events – we euphemistically refer to them as 'ethnic cleansing', a chilling throwback to the concept of 'racial hygiene' of the early-twentieth-century eugenics programmes. In a 2007 editorial, members of the public health community argued that this euphemism should be rejected as it "dehumanizes the victims as sources of filth and disease" and "bleaches the atrocities of genocide, leading to inaction in preventing current and future genocides."[40] The Doctor has never sugar-coated genocide in such euphemisms. The horror of Davros' actions in *Genesis of the Daleks* in destroying the Thals and the Kaleds is presaged by an interchange between the Mutos, in which Sevrin asks why they must kill 'perfect' Sarah Jane Smith: "But why must we always destroy beauty? Why kill another creature because it's not in our image?" The answer is simply, "It's the law."

The Doctor himself resists killing the embryonic Daleks in *Genesis of the Daleks*, despite knowing that by doing so he could save countless future lives: "Do I have the right? […] if I kill, wipe out a whole intelligent life form, then I become like them. I'd be no better than the Daleks." After watching in horror as Dalek Caan destroys the new Dalek-humans, the Doctor offers to help Caan, believing him to be the last of the Dalek race: "I've just seen one genocide. I won't cause another." After the Time War, he bears the guilt of destroying the vast majority of the Daleks and Time Lords in order to save the universe, and realizes the weight of what he has done. This is why the destruction of Davros and the Daleks in *Journey's End* is such an unforgivable crime, leading the Doctor 2.0 to be banished in the parallel universe with Rose – he is as dangerous as Hitler, Slobodan Milosevic and even Davros himself.

Philosopher and animal rights proponent Tom Regan argues that

> Both racism and sexism are paradigms of unsupportable bigotry. There is no "superior" or "inferior" sex or race […] The same is true of speciesism – the view that members of the species *Homo sapiens* are superior to members of every other species […] For there is no "superior" species. To think otherwise is to be no less prejudiced than racists or sexists.[41]

As the Daleks have demonstrated time and time again, they are not nearly as supreme as they would have others believe. But in the end, we are still left with unanswered questions, such as who really are the Daleks, and what does it mean to be a Dalek? In struggling with these questions, we need to examine human questions and controversies as to what the terms *ethnic group*, *race* and *species* truly mean. The easiest to define is a species, meaning a group of individuals that can interbreed and produce fertile offspring. For example, while tigers and lions can be bred through *in vitro* fertilization, their offspring – called ligers and tigons – are infertile. All human beings are obviously one species. A culture is a group of individuals who share a common system of beliefs and behaviours that are transferred through communication.[42] Individuals are included or excluded from the group based on some mutually agreed upon criteria. Members of an ethnic group share a cultural identity and may also share tendencies for some common genetic features, such as Jewish-Americans who carry tendencies for genetic diseases. This tendency is exacerbated by individuals of the self-selected group intermarrying.[43]

But what about race? According to the American Association of Physical Anthropologists (1996), "Popular conceptualizations of race are derived from 19th and 20th century scientific formulations" based on "externally visible traits, primarily skin colour" and (as we have noted in this essay) "have often been used to support racist doctrines."[44] Those so-called scientific perspectives about genetics were incomplete at best, for example not factoring in the importance of the environment (such as the effects of diet and prevalence of communicable disease). In 2003, geneticists Jeffrey Long and Rick Kittles examined the frequency of genetic variations among different human populations using detailed statistical tests and found that there is no genetic basis for the concept of "race." In their words, "It is now time for geneticists and anthropologists to stop worrying about what does and does not exist."[45] But the issue of race can still be found in mainstream scientific journals, as in the case of a 2004 medical study that examined the effects of a particular treatment for heart failure in African Americans. In the editorial published alongside the peer-reviewed scientific article, M. Gregg Bloche asks the decidedly uncomfortable question, "Are we moving into a new era of race-based therapeutics?" Given that the definition of 'African American' is decidedly unscientific, does this completely negate the hopeful results of the study?[46] The issue of race is not going to go away in the early twenty-first century, not even in the scientific literature.

The Thals and Kaleds were clearly racists in their dealings with each other – they divided themselves into 'self' and 'other' based on self-defined cultural differences. The blurred line between the socially constructed terms of 'race', 'culture' and 'ethnicity' are certainly reflected in the blurriness of the division between the Kaleds and the Thals, as well as the question central to this essay – what exactly does it mean to be a Dalek? On Skaro, the result of the hatred between these groups resulted in two genocides at the hands of Davros and his genetically engineered Daleks. Since there is no consistent biological definition of who is (or is not) a Dalek, this too would tend to suggest that Daleks are a culture rather than a true species. Again, this does not soften their hardline eugenics policies. But it highlights the ultimate failure of their eugenics policies; they clearly become their own enemy on more than one occasion, surely not the hallmark of a 'supreme race'.

When Jamie asks the Doctor exactly what the elusive 'Dalek factor' is, the Time Lord explains that it "means to obey, to fight, to destroy, to exterminate." In contrast, when asked to transplant some of Jamie's 'human factor' into the Daleks, the Doctor chose only "the better part", namely "courage, pity, chivalry, friendship, even compassion."[47] But as *Doctor Who* has continually demonstrated, we, as a species, have far too much of the Dalek factor in us, and not nearly enough of the so-called 'human factor'. A classic example is Prime Minister Harriet Jones's decision to destroy the retreating Sycorax spaceship in *The Christmas Invasion* (2005). A horrified Doctor notes he should have warned the Sycorax to "run as fast as they can, run and hide, because the monsters are coming. The human race." The Doctor has also had to face the same monstrous propensity for racism and genocide in his own people, when he destroys the Time Lords in the Time War in order to prevent them from destroying all of reality. Finally, the Doctor had to face his own darker side in *Journey's End*, when the Doctor 2.0 commits genocide against Davros and the Daleks. "You made me," the metacrisis Doctor accuses. The Doctor is forced to acknowledge an ugly side of himself. In turn, we are forced to stare into the mirror and ask ourselves if we, too, share in his shame.

When Dalek Sec becomes hybridized with the human DNA, he notes, "I feel humanity. I feel everything we wanted from mankind, which is ambition, hatred, aggression, and war. Such a genius for war [...] At heart, this species is so very Dalek."[48] As various eugenicist programmes of the twentieth century have so painfully noted, yes, we most certainly are.

Notes

1 Lena K. Sadler, "Is the Abnormal to Become Normal?", in Harry F. Perkins, ed., *A Decade of Progress in Eugenics*, Baltimore: The Williams and Wilkins Co., 1934, 193–200.

2 Sheila Faith Weiss, *The Nazi Symbiosis*, Chicago: University of Chicago Press, 2010, 32.

3 Steven Selden, *Inheriting Shame: The Story of Eugenicism and Racism in America*, New York: Teacher's College Press, 1999, 2.

4 Francis Galton, "Inquiries into Human Faculty and its Development" (1883), *Galton.org*. Retrieved 19 August 2012 at http://galton.org/books/human-faculty/text/human-faculty.pdf.

5 Ellsworth Huntington, *Tomorrow's Children: The Goal of Eugenics*, New York: John Wiley and Sons, 1935, 16.

6 Huntington, *Tomorrow's Children*, 44–45.

7 Weiss, *Nazi Symbiosis*, 280.

8 Thomas C. Leonard, "Retrospectives: Eugenics and Economics in the Progressive Era", *Isis*, 19, 4 (2005), 207–24.

9 Weiss, *Nazi Symbiosis*, 38.

10 *Genesis of the Daleks*.

11 Marilyn Menotti-Raymond and Stephen J. O'Brien, "Dating the Genetic Bottleneck of the African Cheetah", *Proceedings of the National Academy of Sciences*, 90 (1993), 3172.

12 Menotti-Raymond and O'Brien, "African Cheetah", 3176.

13 For an excellent synopsis, see Mark A. Jobling, "Genes and Queens", *Investigative Genetics*, 2, 14 (2011), online.

14 Neil Risch, Deborah de Leon, Laurie Ozelius, Patricia Kramer, Laura Almasy, Burton Singer, Stanley Fahn, Xandra Breakefield and Susan Bressman, "Genetic Analysis of Idiopathic Torsion Dystonia in Ashkenazi Jews and Their recent Descent From a Small Founder Population", *Nature Genetics*, 9 (1995), 152.

15 The so-called Doctor 2.0 is created when Donna Noble's DNA is mixed with the Doctor's disembodied hand in the TARDIS and grows into a Time Lord-human hybrid (also called the metacrisis). Donna likewise receives some of the Doctor's genetic code (manifesting as his intelligence) but it threatens to burn out her brain and the Doctor must wipe clean her memories of him in order to save her.

16 James A. Birchler, Hong Yao, Sivanandan Chudalayandi, Daniel Vaiman and Renier A. Veitia, "Heterosis", *The Plant Cell*, 22 (2010), 2105.

17 J. Severe and D. R. ZoBell, "Utilization of Heterosis in a Beef Cow Herd" (August 2011), *Agriculture: Utah State University*. Retrieved 19 August 2012 at http://extension.usu.edu/files/publications/publication/AG_Beef_2011-03.pdf.

18 George D. Snell, "Hybrids and History: The Role of Race and Ethnic Crossing in Individual and National Achievement", *The Quarterly Review of Biology*, 26, 4 (1951), 331–47.

19 Snell, "Hybrids and History", 337–38.

20 Snell, "Hybrids and History", 335.

21 For a detailed discussion of the issues surrounding bi-racial identity, see Kerry Ann Rockquemore and David L. Brunsma, *Beyond Black: Biracial Identity in America*, Lanham: Rowman and Littlefield, 2008.

22 F. James Davis, *Who is Black? One Nation's Definition*, University Park: Pennsylvania State University Press, 1991, 15.

23 Weiss, *Nazi Symbiosis*, 256.

24 Weiss, *Nazi Symbiosis*, 243.

25 R. Rizzuto, M. Brini, P. Pizzo, M. Murgia and T. Pozzan, "Chimeric Green Fluorescent Protein as a Tool For Visualizing Subcellular Organelles in Living Cells", *Current Biology*, 5, 6 (1995), 635.

26 Human Fertilisation and Embryology Authority, *Hybrids and Chimeras: A report on the findings of the consultation*, United Kingdom, 2007.

27 Human Fertilisation and Embryology Authority, *Hybrids and Chimeras*.

28 Alexander Mitscherlich and Fred Mielke, *Doctors of Infamy, the Story of the Nazi Medical Crimes* (trans. Heinz Norden), New York: Schuman, 1949, xi–xii.

29 Lucette Matalon Lagnado and Sheila Cohn Dekel, *Children of the Flames*, New York: William Morrow and Co., 1991, 65.

30 Gerhard Baader, Susan E. Lederer, Morris Low, Florian Schmaltz and Alexander v. Schwerin, "Pathways to Human Experimentation, 1933–1945: Germany, Japan, and the United States", *Osiris*, 29 (2005), 221.

31 For more information on the Tuskegee Experiment, see James H. Jones, *Bad Blood*, New York: Free Press, 1993; and Susan M. Reverby, *Tuskegee's Truths: Rethinking the Tuskegee Syphilis Experiment*, Chapel Hill: University of North Carolina Press, 2000.

32 Lauren Neergard, "U.S. Apologizes for 1940s Syphilis Study in Guatemala", *Washington Times*, 1 October 2010.

33 Rony Blum, Gregory H. Stanton, Shira Sagi and Elihu D. Richter, "'Ethnic Cleansing' Bleaches the Atrocities of Genocide", *European Journal of Public Health*, 18, 2 (2007), 204.

34 Baader et al., "Pathways to Human Experimentation", 223.

35 Alexandra Minna Stern, *Eugenic Nation*, Berkeley: University of California Press, 2005, 12.

36 A summary of the ruling can be found at http://sboh.wa.gov/Goals/Past/Genetics/2002_02-25/docs/Tab05-Summary_NBvLBL.pdf.

37 United States Government, "Regulations Under the Genetic Information Nondiscrimination Act of 2008" (9 November 2010), *Federal Register*. Retrieved 19 August 2012 at http://www.federalregister.gov/articles/2010/11/09/2010-28011/regulations-under-the-genetic-information-nondiscrimination-act-of-2008#h-20.

38 e.g., see Anon., "The life penalty: sterilizing Sacramento" (10 November 2011), *CBS Sacramento*. Retrieved 19 August 2012 at http://sacramento.cbslocal.com/2011/11/10/the-life-penalty-sterilizing-california/.

39 Blum et al., "'Ethnic Cleansing'", 204.

40 Blum et al., "'Ethnic Cleansing'", 204.

41 Tom Regan, "Animals Have Rights", in David M. Haugen, ed., *Animal Experimentation: Opposing Viewpoints*, Detroit: Greenhaven Press, 2007, 24–25.

42 Davis, *Who is Black?*, 18.

43 e.g., see Risch et al., "Genetic Analysis."

44 AAPA, "Statement on Biological Aspects of Race", *American Journal of Physical Anthropology*, 101 (1996), 569–70.

45 Jeffrey C. Long and Rick A. Kittles, "Human Genetic Diversity and the Nonexistence of Biological Races", *Human Biology*, 75, 4 (2003), 469.

46 M. Gregg Bloche, "Race-based Therapeutics", *New England Journal of Medicine*, 351 (2004), 2035. Interested readers are directed to this article for clear summary of the ethical and scientific difficulties of such treatments.

47 *The Evil of the Daleks.*

48 *Evolution of the Daleks.*

Chapter 21

Mapping the boundaries of race in *The Hungry Earth/Cold Blood*

Rachel Morgain

I am participating in the creation of yet another culture, a new story to explain the world and our participation in it, a new value system with images and symbols that connect us to each other and to the planet.
           – Gloria Anzaldúa, *Borderlands/La Frontera: The New Mestiza*[1]

Science fiction has, in the words of Teresa de Lauretis, a "way of using signs that is potentially creative of new forms of social imagination […] of envisioning a different order of relationships between people and between people and things, a different conceptualization of social existence."[2] If this is true in general, it is certainly the case for *The Hungry Earth/Cold Blood* (2010), which unfolds after the Doctor's eleventh regeneration lands in a cold village in South Wales with companions Amy and Rory. These episodes tell the story of a people living underground, who wish to share the surface of the earth – our Earth – with the currently dominant species: us. After retreating below the surface to avoid a predicted cataclysm, this community of saurian people has lain in stasis for millions of years. Now, they are awoken by a drilling team of humans, headed by geologist Nasreen Chaudhry, thereby learning as they wake that their planet has become populated by a second technologically capable species. The drilling triggers the resuscitation of the group's warriors, who attack the humans on the surface, attempting to stop the drilling, which they perceive as an assault on their underground city. Several humans are captured, while one warrior, Alaya, becomes the captive of the human villagers. The tension builds as people from both sides risk escalating the hostilities, motivated by fear or disdain for the other species. Meanwhile, Nasreen and Amy begin negotiations with a senior member of this underground city, Eldane, to see if they can develop a plan for sharing the surface, and thereby perhaps broker a lasting, peaceful engagement between these two very different peoples with seemingly competing interests.

The events of these episodes are framed by the telling of a story, spoken, as we later learn, by the wise and compassionate Eldane. Or rather, it is framed by two narratives; for the stories told at the start and end of *Cold Blood* are different from one another, split between two parallel outcomes emerging out of the same series of events, a kind of superposition of possibilities, whose indeterminacy is defined by the events which unfold in these episodes, whose outcome can only be known by watching as these events play out to see what the people actually do. Within the narrative, we are witness to a moment in history in which a range of outcomes is possible. As the Doctor explains, this is not a fixed point in time, but a "temporal tipping point", whose results are to be created rather than known in advance, determined for better or worse by the actions and decisions of those present. Outside the narrative, we are drawn to think about what this means for the story we currently tell of ourselves: what it is to be human, to be animal, to be in relation, and to live on the Earth's surface as people whose populations are differentiated by inequities of access, possession and power.

In these episodes, interspecies encounter stands in as proxy for real world collisions of 'ethnicity' and 'culture', and of that supposedly more fundamental difference of type, 'race'. In both stories – historical and fictional – the players must negotiate the problem of unequal access of groups of people to belonging on Earth's surface. In both situations, these racially produced inequalities are inherited social givens, overdetermined by uncountable increments of events over many aeons, events that both were configured by and reinscribed the uneven footing upon which these different groups now stand, conditioned by cruelties of chance and the onslaughts of history. These episodes thus offer us an opportunity to rethink, and rewrite, the history of our lived world since the European Enlightenment, allowing us to face the stark inequalities of race that are an enduring legacy of the age of empire, creating the ground for re-envisioning our future. If we can get it right this time, amidst the unfolding history of our future told in science fiction, perhaps we can begin to reimagine these social givens in our lived world, writing new stories of belonging and connection, undermining the perilous common-sense of imperialist possession, and the deep oppressions arising from European expansion, by which 'possession' of the world has come to be ever more exclusively in the hands of a wealthy elite of colonialists and imperialists. If we can get it right this time, perhaps we can learn, as the Doctor enjoins the humans, to become the "best of humanity."

Here I explore what these episodes tell us about possibilities for re-envisioning our racially divided world, showing also how such possibilities are often circumscribed by our scientific and conceptual assumptions. Analysing the social and epistemological parameters under which the various discussions about this encounter take place, a series of structuring principles become evident that are highly illustrative of both the way in which the story's 'others' are understood, and how this encounter is expected to proceed. As I shall argue, the predominant ethical framework here, as for so much of *Doctor Who*, is liberal humanism.[3] This humanist outlook, and its attendant foundations in Enlightenment thought, has significant implications for how these episodes frame our understanding of Earth's actual history, the legacies of colonialism and the ongoing negotiation of encounter between racially marked groups in the wake of long histories of dispossession. The discussions on sharing the surface between Eldane, Nasreen and Amy display a series of ethical assumptions that constrain possible outcomes. But these assumptions are also echoed more subtly in how knowledge of the encountered other is structured – the way in which such knowledge reflects particular principles of ordering the world, which in turn set the terms of the encounter. As Michel Foucault has argued, systems of knowledge and their structuring principles shape not only what is thought, but how it is *possible* to think, thereby inscribing and constituting relations of power.[4] Throughout these episodes, myriad traces of the categories of Enlightenment thought structure the anthropological, geopolitical and biological interpretations of these events, inscribing spatial and conceptual boundaries and marking out lines of difference in ways that betray the roots of each of these disciplines – and of liberal humanism – in a problematic conceptual geography of the Enlightenment.

A central difficulty in writing about these episodes is the problem of naming the people with whom the humans find themselves interacting. In their earliest serial (*The Silurians*, 1970) they were referred to as "Silurians", though in a story produced soon after (*The Sea Devils*, 1972), the Doctor points out they would more rightly be called "Eocenes", referencing scientific problems with the earlier term: reptiles had not yet evolved, nor did vertebrates walk the land in the Silurian period over 400 million years ago. In *The Hungry Earth*, the Doctor briefly glosses this by describing those encountered as "What's known as the 'Silurian' race; or, some would argue, 'Eocenes'", the Eocene being a geologically relatively recent period that is much more plausibly the period of origin of these underground people (though the dates are incommensurate with those the Doctor gives). He also offers a further possible designation: *Homo reptilia*. As I intend to argue, there are serious problems with all of these names. What is missing from all these explanations is the word for whatever it is that these people call themselves in their own language. Thus lacking a better word, I will refer to them here as the People,[5] in the hope of opening a space around this absent designation I hope one day to learn.

Tribes and remnants: Problems of anthropology

One of the more compelling and intriguing aspects of the story is what might (loosely) be called its 'anthropology'. These episodes provide insights into the social organization, ideas and practices of the People, which are both more gently elaborated and more complex than the original series stories. There are occasional moments of awkwardness, such as when the scientist Malohkeh pointedly remarks to the leader of the warriors, Restac, that they are of equal rank – in a society where rank is a salient social category, they would be unlikely to need such bald reminders. But overall, through what we see of the division of labour, comments upon rank, visual and verbal references to gene chains and demonstrations of the love between sisters, we gain glimpses into a social system that is both complex, contested and clearly different from the predominant Anglo-American patterns that form the normative background of 'humanity' in *Doctor Who*. Those from a common gene chain appear to share physical characteristics and to be commonly assigned to a particular profession. They could easily have been depicted as a singular mass with a common mind, yet they are differentiated, both in their appearance and in the choices they make. Most importantly, we see how the actions of individual People are conditioned by their social position and interests, but are not predetermined by them, avoiding a problematic trend influential in early anthropological writing, by which anthropology's 'others' tended to be depicted as pregiven elements of a social system automatically acting out the roles assigned them by their 'culture'.[6] Instead, in these episodes, there is no question that the outcome of affairs emerges from the complexities of contested choices between different People, just as it does for the humans – and that this could have gone differently.

A similar allusion to diversity is made when the Doctor tells Nasreen that the settlement they come across is only one of many to which the People belong. Unfortunately, in this case, the value of this in helping convey that the People have created a multiplicity of social worlds just as humans have is undermined by the regrettable, repeated use of the word "tribes" to describe these social groups. In ethnographic use, the word 'tribe' has a widespread, though contested, general meaning as a descriptor for societies that are relatively egalitarian and organized primarily as interwoven networks of kinship. In the most common schema used, tribal societies are less stratified and generally smaller than 'chiefdoms' or 'state' societies.[7] However little we know about the People, and whatever the problems involved in this kind of anthropological schematic, it is clear that the enormous and sharply stratified society we are witness to here is not likely to be usefully understood as fitting this category. The Doctor appears at one point to recognize this distinction; when they first arrive under the surface, after telling Nasreen that they are looking for "one small tribe" of maybe a dozen people, he corrects this on sighting the enormous city, saying, "Maybe more like an entire civilization living beneath the Earth." In fact, this is not a neutral ethnographic distinction, but carries the heavy moral connotation of distinguishing larger-scale societies as 'civilization'. In a conversation that follows soon after, he then reverts to the descriptor "tribe."

Indeed, behind this inaccuracy of ethnographic description is a political concern. It is no coincidence that this denotation of 'tribes' is contested within anthropology, since its more conventional usage is often diminutive or pejorative. As Nicholas Hudson has shown, our modern use of 'tribe' emerged as part of a conceptual shift in the eighteenth century simultaneously with the division of the world into broad hierarchically-defined 'races', replacing the more neutral 'nation' as a descriptor for differences between those peoples who were not considered 'advanced'.[8] In English, the notion of 'tribe' has entered the vernacular as a descriptor associated primarily with particular parts of the world, such as Africa, and particular groups of people, such as Native Americans.[9] In media reports, it is often used to refer to clashes between groups where in other geographic contexts the preferred terms are more likely to be 'ethnic' or 'racial'.[10] As Ramesh Krishnamurthy illustrates, the word 'tribal' is significantly collocated in English language use with words such as 'killings' and 'fighting', descriptors which often carry connotations of 'primitive simplicity' such as 'chiefs', and even with the word 'primitive' itself.[11] The use of "tribe" to describe the different groups of the People is an unfortunate echo of these diminutive connotations, undermining the respect implied in the Doctor's overt admiration and in his recognition of the complexity of their social worlds.

As anti-imperialist criticism of anthropology has pointed out, this fundamental division of the world into more and less 'advanced' societies has profoundly conditioned the predominant separation of knowledge of human society in industrialized contexts into the great disciplines of sociology and anthropology, with the latter deeply structured by its roots in an apparent division between observers and observed, between the supposedly racially 'neutral' authors and racially 'marked' subjects of knowledge.[12] These problems of anthropology shape other dimensions of these *Doctor Who* episodes, betraying a stance of ethnographic condescension in the seeming difficulty of finding an appropriate name for the People. As for so much ethnographic description in the history of anthropology, where designations and identities of groups (such as 'Pueblo', 'Melanesian' or 'Hottentot') often reflect the language and categories of Euro-American observers, this seemingly objective naming is done from the outside, masking the simple but deceptively hidden fact that the People are not given the space to name themselves. There is a condescension embedded in these knowledge systems that presume to define social others against the internal understandings of the people they purport to describe. The Doctor's insistence on granting the People a series of names based on Enlightenment categories of knowledge reveals just such a stance of condescension that can arise from this position of the supposedly 'neutral', 'scientific' observer.

The historical inconsistencies of the terms "Silurians" and "Eocenes" likewise betray this deeper ethnographic problem, since both names suggest an idea of the People as relics from a prehistoric past. These connotations carry echoes of evolutionary anthropology, with its tendency to view the peoples of Africa, the Americas, parts of Asia and Oceania as continuations of a lost past, both culturally and biologically closer to the point of human origin and to our 'protohuman' predecessors. In this framing, cultural practices of contemporary peoples designated as 'primitive' were widely recorded, described and analysed as though they were archaic reflections of a more original human state, while anatomical features were measured and classified as supposedly closer to those of human biological ancestors.[13] These politically charged understandings reflected imperialist categorizations of the racialization of humans as divided between the 'advanced' races of 'civilization' and the 'primitive' races, which laid an ideological basis for missionization, dispossession, colonization and enslavement over many centuries. Such ideas of the 'timelessness' of non-European people, and the formative role that these ideas have played in anthropology, have been roundly critiqued in recent decades for their fundamental roots in the politics of racism and imperialism.[14]

These choices of names for the People insinuate in a similar way that they are timeless relics from the distant past. Lest we think these repercussions are an unfortunate hangover of original series *Doctor Who*, corrected in the new series by the introduction of the more scientifically objective-sounding identifier *Homo reptilia*, we are explicitly encouraged to make this identification by none other than the Doctor himself, in his first uncomfortable words upon removing Alaya's mask after she is captured by the humans: "You are beautiful! Remnant of a bygone age of planet Earth." The racist and patronizing implications of this designation of a person as a "beautiful remnant" are not entirely ameliorated by being followed immediately by a compliment to her people's technology: "And by the way, lovely mode of travel! Geothermal currents, projecting you up through a network of tunnels. Gorgeous!" Instead, the two engagements sit uneasily side-by-side, reflecting a narrative tension between overt respect and subtle disdain that remains unresolved through to the story's end.

Empty land: Problems of geopolitics

A second troubling dimension in these stories is expressed in the geopolitical outlook displayed particularly in the discussion on sharing our planet that takes place between Eldane, Nasreen and Amy. These negotiations are grounded in explanation, reason and principles of fair exchange, in which to be "extraordinary" (as the Doctor urges Nasreen) seems to entail being patient, imaginative, trusting and understanding. They are diplomatic conversations guided by liberal humanism; even the unlikely expectation that two ordinary humans with no recognized authority could hope to sell the deal they make to the world's human political leaders reflects this framework, in its unstated egalitarianism, whereby any human is equal to all others in her authority to speak for the species as a whole. Yet the strengths of liberal humanism here are also its weaknesses, for the negotiations build on concepts of possession, sovereignty and inscription of borders inherent to this outlook, which firmly limit the outcomes that can be achieved, and even those it seems possible to imagine. They are principled settlements between members of two species who agree to divide the surface between them, on the apparent understanding that these divisions should remain clear, and that interaction must be characterized by equal exchange between groups that are otherwise bounded and distinct.

This idea of both spatial and cultural sovereignty is suggested in the way in which the 'surface' metonymically stands in for the broader field of encounter between the two groups. Here the surface is treated primarily through the mechanisms of possession and exchange, which in turn both reflect and enforce a specific mode of social exchange, envisioned as taking place between two bounded cultural groups possessed of their own internal integrity. An indication of the foundations of possession underpinning the interpretation of this encounter is given when the Doctor refers to the People as "the previous owners of the planet." That conception of inhabiting as ownership, so particular to capitalist modernity, frames the discourse of exchange throughout the negotiations. The humans agree to cede a small and seemingly unwanted portion of the surface to the People, so that each species might continue to live out their separate lives. The carving out of territory amounts to a reinscription of the boundary separating these two species, effacing a fuller opportunity for engagement with each other that this situation offers. Alternative possibilities – that People and humans may wish to cohabit, to build communities or cities or lives together, to change how things are done all over Earth's surface, so that the whole planet might be transformed by the encounter between these two groups – are never entered into. Within the framework of sovereignty and integrity that informs these negotiations, they are impossible even to think.

The concept of land as possession is given further life in the use of the projected image of the globe during the negotiations, by which the humans' cartographic gaze passes over the surface, conceptually possessing and dividing up the territory. As J. Brian Harley argues, the art of cartography is historically inseparable from the exercise of political authority, the reality of conquest and the expansion of empires; maps "are pre-eminently a language of power, not of protest."[15] He shows how the effects of power expressed through the symbolic language of maps include not only overt claims to borders and territory that can be inscribed and reinforced through how the world is depicted, but also extend to the elisions and silences around features that must inevitably be omitted because they are less 'important'.[16] This has the systematic effect of eliding the claims of those who are less powerful. Indeed, he suggests that the very method of mapping as a tool for apprehending the world has a tendency to efface the concrete social relations that could otherwise resist or reshape the decisions of political overseers:

> Maps as an impersonal type of knowledge tend to 'desocialize' the territory they represent. They foster the notion of a socially empty space. The abstract quality of the map […] lessens the burden of conscience about people in the landscape. Decisions about the exercise of power are removed from the realm of immediate face-to-face contacts.[17]

These abstracting tendencies are illustrated profoundly in *Cold Blood* when Amy declares that those parts of the surface that indeed tend to appear blank on most maps – the deserts of the Sahara, Nevada and outback Australia – are actually uninhabitable and "deserted." This notion of an empty land has of course a powerful and terrible place in the history of colonialism, invasion and nation-state building. In Australia, it was encoded in law as the principle that the colonized land previously belonged to no one, which prior to its overturn in 1992 was used to justify the dispossession of Indigenous people and the expansion of British/Australian rule throughout the continent. The negotiations in this story tacitly endorse this view of the world, eliding the claims of those who inhabit these locations, and particularly those such as Aboriginal Australians, Native Americans and Bedouins who have faced centuries of dispossession from other humans. As negotiations explicitly directed to the carving up of the surface of Earth between the two species, they are disturbingly evocative of the long, troubled history of agreements, pacts and treaties by which the 'great powers' of the world have decided which nations will form, which will be ruled and who will do the ruling.

Indeed, in the terms of negotiation, the fact of human possession of the surface is barely problematized. Rather, it is presupposed by all parties and reinforced in the general agreement that humans should be given something by the People in exchange for ceding these 'uninhabited' parts of the surface. An alternative reading of the situation might give greater moral weight to the prior claim of the People, yet this possibility is already ruled out when the terms of the negotiation begin, in the already instituted inequality defined by the events of history. In this case, those events are accidental. But in the real history of our Earth, the events that have granted sovereignty to very exclusive groups of humans over so much of the surface have been brutal and often calculated. The implicit denial of prior claim that we witness in these episodes obscures the claims to land of those who historically were dispossessed, effacing the recognition that current facts of possession are contingent upon a violent history. It codifies and legitimates the profound inequalities conditioning the present.

Most fundamentally, these negotiations take place upon assumptions of social integrity and self-possession that reinscribe boundaries, undermining the opportunity for openness to others this situation presents. They are built upon a concept of generosity that necessarily follows upon a prior establishment of sovereignty and property ownership. Philosopher Rosalyn Diprose critiques such an understanding of generosity, arguing that it assumes that the possessor, prior to the act of giving, already exists as a fully self-possessed, integrated entity, complete unto itself and separate from others.[18] Viewing Amy and Nasreen's offer to cede land as a gift to be returned affirms both the rightfulness of prior exclusive human possession and the integrity of 'humans' as a single community, bounded and separate from the People and concomitantly undifferentiated within themselves. The possessive individualism behind this commonplace model of generosity is, Diprose suggests, its greatest weakness, since it emerges out of an economic system of sovereignty and property that is more likely to foster selfishness than generosity. Such individualism is already ungenerous. Assured of its boundaries and self-possession, it resists a more open encounter with others upon which a more profound recognition of intersubjectivity could be built.[19]

Diprose proposes reconceiving generosity as an innate process of relationship, "the primordial condition of personal, interpersonal and communal existence."[20] In this model, generosity is "not the expenditure of one's possessions but the dispossession of oneself, the being-given to others that undercuts any self-contained ego, that undercuts self-possession."[21] Emphasizing this fundamental generosity of our interdependent existence, she suggests, opens up possibilities for a fuller encounter with others, allowing their difference from us to move us beyond ourselves, thereby transforming us. In this story, what is precluded by the dynamics of sovereignty and possession framing the liberal humanism of the negotiations is not only the possibility of sharing the planet, but the greater potential for transformation on both sides that a fuller engagement between humans and People should allow.

Homo reptilia: Problems of biology

These tensions of sovereignty and the inscription of borders, of who is included and excluded, and whether and how we embrace social infusions and openness to others, is surely the central problematic of these episodes. In approaching this problem, the question of how to define ourselves, and how to define others in relation to ourselves, is fundamental. In order to address this, it is useful to return once again to the issue of naming plaguing these stories. The problems of naming are not confined to concerns about prehistoric 'remnants'. They highlight issues of how the story of human origins is told, problems of difference and of the difficulties of power encoded in our systems of knowledge. The choice of name the Doctor uses – *Homo reptilia* – which shouts in loud and dissonant tones throughout these episodes – carries the illusion that it is somehow more objective, neutral and scientifically accurate than the other terms. It is as if the Linnaean system of biological classification could stand the test of all times, all places and all modes of understanding; an objective reflection of the actual state of things, rather than a specific product of European thought in the eighteenth century that we have inherited, more or less, into today.

Carl Linnaeus was a Swedish biologist widely recognized as the founder of our modern system of taxonomic classification. As Foucault has pointed out, the system of classification he pioneered is both a product of and a contributor to the particular classificatory world-view that developed in Europe in the early modern period.[22] Unlike earlier modes of knowledge, this was a system of ordering the world not by the resemblances between things, but by tables of identity and difference. Such tables sharply encoded the disparities between entities placed into different parts of a given order.[23] This has important implications for the coding of race in European Enlightenment thought. As Hudson suggests, it was the Linnaean system of classifying humans as part of his taxonomic order, along with the related work of Buffon, that first established the possibility for treating humans scientifically not as individuals or people with a range of practices, but as a species with a select number of distinct 'varieties' or 'races'.[24] According to Hudson's genealogy of the modern concept of race, it was upon Linnaeus's and Buffon's work that Johann Friedrich Blumenbach – widely considered the founder of physical anthropology – in the late eighteenth century laid down his classification of the five great varieties or races of humans: Caucasian, Mongolian, Ethiopian, American and Malay.[25] Nor are these categories neutral; as Donna Haraway argues, the system of classification which placed humans alongside animals simultaneously claimed spurious links between our animal relatives and more 'primitive' forms of humanity: "natural man was found not only among the 'savages', but also among the animals, who were named primates in consequence, the first Order of nature."[26] From this base proliferated the endless series of divisions, classifications and hierarchies of humans, that potent fusion of taxonomic description and geopolitics that created the pseudoscience of race.

This classificatory gaze extended the assessment of identity and difference between groups of people over the entire planet. Hudson suggests, "As is vividly evident in Blumenbach's work, the Enlightenment imagination had become dominated by the picture of great continental land masses, each, apparently, with its own color of human."[27] As Haraway points out, the illusory objectivity of this classificatory system derives from the gaze of that particular variety of 'neutral' observer – that of the European male elite in the age of empire:

The "balance of nature" was maintained partly by the role of a new "man" who would see clearly and name accurately, hardly a trivial identity in the face of eighteenth-century European expansion. Indeed, this is the identity of the modern authorial subject, for whom inscribing the body of nature gives assurance of his mastery.[28]

This authorial subject is then the subject who owns and possesses the world, who claims the position of defining the world and all the people in it, creating the dichotomies of knower and known, subject and object, centre and periphery, inscribing inclusions and exclusions over the whole population of Earth. In historical practice, the quality of encounters between people marked as different and unequal were not wholly conditioned by these knowledge structures, representing variable configurations of sameness and otherness, mutuality and violence, as much as the latter dominated overall. In these episodes, however, the marking of classificatory differences is strongly mirrored in the practical terms of interaction. Thus, far from relieving the problems of naming inherent in the earlier terms, the nomenclature of *Homo reptilia* magnifies them, substituting for the reductive gaze of the early-twentieth-century anthropologist, the objectifying gaze of the eighteenth-century scientist from the centre of an expanding European empire.

And there is a further problem with this, in the scientific inaccuracy of the name itself. According to modern taxonomic systems, the species of whom we are speaking, the People, should be found nowhere near that part of the tree known as '*Homo*', human, a member of the family Hominidae from the mammalian order of Primates, close relatives of the apes to whom the People, by their own account, are so clearly not related. According to what we know of the People, we might expect to find them somewhere among the order Squamata (scaled reptiles) within the class Reptilia, perhaps related to a family of lizards, such as Cordylidae or Scincidae (though it is only possible to guess at this, not knowing which families of reptiles or other species the People might count as their closest relatives). If the authors of this classification – humans or People – wished to use their system to highlight the degree to which the technological and cultural sophistication of the People rivals that of humans, they could follow the Linnaean conceit, and name them with the species designation '*sapiens*', meaning 'wise'. But there is no Linnaean method by which they should be designated by the genus *Homo*.

As with the problem of the label of 'tribe', behind this error of science is a problem of politics. The designation *Homo* – human – while presumably intended to highlight the respect humans should show to the social world and political claims of the People, in fact serves to inscribe the idea of humanity as the peak of an order of creation. While Linnaeus, in designating humanity as merely one part of the natural order, is often credited with undoing the older Christian hubris of placing humans above the rest of the natural world, he in fact perpetuated this in another form. Haraway points out the continuity of Linnaeus's system with this Christian world-view:

> He referred to himself as a second Adam, the "eye" of God, who could give true representations, true names, thus reforming and restoring a purity of names lost by the first Adam's sin [...] The role of one who renamed the animals was to ensure a true and faithful order of nature, to purify the eye and the world.[29]

Thus humanity, in particular 'Enlightenment man', retains its position at the peak of creation. In naming the People *Homo reptilia*, this idea of the importance of humanity is reinforced;

the People are seen merely as another, perhaps lesser, version of ourselves, as *Homo erectus* and *Homo neanderthalensis* are seen as lesser than their 'sapient' cousins.

Troubling our origins: The promises of monsters

The story of encounter with another species that rivals our own in technology, language, science and history has significant potential for exploring the complexities of human origins, our interrelationships with each other and our interdependence with other species. The issue of our scientific understanding of ourselves is tied up with these far-reaching questions. To understand this, it is worth taking some examples from contemporary genetic science. Recent investigations into 'mitochondrial Eve', for example, highlight how central Judaeo-Christian themes remain to scientific stories of human origins. The science behind mitochondrial Eve primarily suggests that at least one of the ancestors of all humans is held in common; in illustrating our fundamental interrelatedness, it has great potential for undermining still-potent pseudoscientific taxonomies of race. Yet in its language of 'Eve', and in how it has been widely popularized, this theory is often used to suggest (incorrectly) that humans had only one 'mother', that we emerged at a singular point in the past, echoing the Judaeo-Christian myth of humans emerging as a distinct, pure species.[30] As Haraway argues in her 'Cyborg Manifesto', such scientific stories that paint humans as unique also tend to depict particular kinds of humans – European, male, wealthy and 'enlightened' – as exemplars of this special humanity.[31] Yet other recent genetic science tells a very different kind of origin story, with the discovery of Neanderthal DNA in the genome of many humans.[32] This is fundamentally troubling to a definitive purified taxonomy of *Homo sapiens*, undermining neat tales of a singular point of origin and blurring the boundaries around our species. As a story of our complex ancestry and the indefinable boundaries around humanness, it suggests that we are made up of many strands; that hybridity is more fundamental to our nature than traditional European taxonomies and bio-histories have tended to allow. I would suggest that it is this kind of troubling of our origin myths that a fuller engagement with the presence of the People under Earth's surface should open up.

Haraway's 'Cyborg Manifesto' drew inspiration from theorists such as Gloria Anzaldúa and Chela Sandoval, who argued for the importance of recognizing intermixing as fundamental to our nature, destabilizing purified taxonomies of race. These theorists built on notions such as Anzaldúa's *mestiza consciousness* to explore the value of straddling boundaries of inside and outside, belonging and separation, in order to undermine the deep fissures that categories such as race and gender represent and reproduce.[33] Coining the term from the word for 'mixed' that in large parts of the Americas has been used to designate those of combined indigenous and European ancestry, Anzaldúa describes the *mestiza* as a tough survivor: "like corn, the *mestiza* is a product of crossbreeding, designed for preservation under a variety of conditions."[34] She argues that the role of the *mestiza* is "the breaking down of paradigms" and "the straddling of two or more cultures":[35]

The work of the *mestiza* is to break down the subject-object dualism that keeps her a prisoner and to show in the flesh and through the images in her work how duality is transcended. The answer to the problem between the white race and the colored [...] lies in healing the split that originates in the very foundation of our lives [...] I am an act of kneading, of unity and joining that not only has produced both a creature of darkness and a creature of light, but also a creature that questions the definitions of light and dark and gives them new meanings.[36]

The concept of *mestiza* and the vision of kneading and joining she represents is thus seen as a means of moving beyond the neat categorizations of Enlightenment science that have mapped the whole of humanity onto a charged cartography of race. For these theorists, the possibility of moving beyond is not given through the careful deliberations and negotiations of liberal humanism; not the promises of reason, but the fraught and often painful intersections of hybridization are what pave the way for this moving-beyond – what Haraway designates the "promises of monsters."[37]

Underneath the overlay of conceptual orderings throughout *The Hungry Earth* – the categories and divisions, borders and subordinations – is just such a story, hinting at the possibility of a much deeper complex of interrelationships between People and humans; hinting at the terrifying, dizzying, painful possibilities of hybridity.[38] This is most explicit in what happens to the drilling operator Tony, after the touch of Alaya's sting sets up a transformation within him that, we are led to believe, will eventually result in him becoming like one of the People. The frightening implications for the humans are illustrated powerfully in the reaction of Tony's daughter Ambrose when she learns of this. Ambrose's young son Elliot has been captured by the People, as has her husband. Yet it is not their capture, but the discovery of the spreading green mark on her father's shoulder that finally drives her to attack and kill Alaya, striking out to reinscribe the boundaries between humans and People in a metaphorical attempt to purify her father's wound. Throughout the story, the substance from Alaya's sting causing the transformation is referred to as her "venom", and at the end, this same drive to enforce the separations of People and humans by destroying the hybridity is displayed when Eldane and the accompanying humans place Tony in the human purifier in an attempt to rid him of the intrusive substance. But, strangely, they neglect to turn the machine on. Having failed in their negotiations, they are concentrating on the task at hand of fumigating the corridors, which will send the People back into stasis for another thousand years until humans are 'ready' to share the surface. The Doctor enjoins the humans present to pass on this message that Earth is to be shared, "as legend, or prophecy, or religion", and Elliot, in particular, seems to understand. Yet, in their chaotic scramble, they leave Tony in his ambiguous state of transformation.

Tony refuses to return to the surface, knowing he will be thought a "freak show." But herein lies the promise of monsters, for from this point emerges the social parallel for the biological story of hybridity. Both Tony and Nasreen choose to stay below the surface in the hope of making a life with the People, at last allowing the People's social world to impact on their own, laying the basis for a truer intermixing than that suggested by the purported division of the surface. Nasreen in particular offers this way forward, as someone who always knew there was something important under the earth, and who spent her life trying to find it. Whatever the decision Tony makes about the hybridity forced upon him, the force of the question is mitigated, the dividing line keeping humans and People separate is softened. Humans on the surface have missed out on the opportunity, for the time being, of being truly impacted by this troubling of those hegemonic Enlightenment conditions of possession and control. And yet perhaps the promise of this is contained in what Nasreen, Tony, Eldane and others manage to produce in their thousand years of living together.

Perhaps this is the story Elliot will tell. Of all the humans, it is he who seems to display the deepest sensitivity to these underground possibilities. After all, it is not his 'freakish' grandfather, but his own mother that he shies from, when he learns of her murder of Alaya, her drive to eliminate the threat of the other which destroys the possibility of a fuller reckoning with the conditions of the present, above and below the surface. Perhaps this signals a recognition in Elliot that being the "best of humanity" is maybe not about being "human" at all, to the extent that this is a pure category, but about being partial, hybrid, infused and intermixed. Perhaps this is the better story we can tell from our encounter with the People, and the challenge they present of being so like us, and so very different.

Pass it on.

Notes

1 Gloria Anzaldúa, *Borderlands/La Frontera: The New Mestiza*, San Francisco: Spinsters/ Aunt Lute, 1987, 103.

2 Teresa De Lauretis, "Signs of Wa/onder", in Teresa De Lauretis, Andreas Huyssen and Kathleen M. Woodward, eds., *The Technological Imagination: Theories and Fictions*, Madison: Coda Press, 1980, 161.

3 For a discussion of the ethic of liberal humanism that more generally frames *Doctor Who*'s engagements with colonialism and imperialism, see Lindy A. Orthia, "'Sociopathetic Abscess' or 'Yawning Chasm'? The Absent Postcolonial Transition in *Doctor Who*", *The Journal of Commonwealth Literature*, 45, 2 (2010), 207–25.

4 Michel Foucault, *The Order of Things: An Archaeology of the Human Sciences*, London: Routledge, 1966.

5 'The people' is the general translation for names such as 'Dine'e' and 'Inuit' that many groups use to designate themselves.

6 Elements of this thinking can be seen, e.g., in Durkheim's theory of "mechanical solidarity" which he identified as characterizing smaller-scale societies. Emile Durkheim, *The Division of Labour in Society* (trans. W. D. Halls), London: MacMillan, 1984, especially 83–85 and 88–90.

7 Elman R. Service, *Profiles in Ethnology*, New York: Harper and Row, 1963.

8 Nicholas Hudson, "From 'Nation' to 'Race': The Origin of Racial Classification in Eighteenth-Century Thought", *Eighteenth-Century Studies*, 29, 3 (1996), 247–64.

9   Ramesh Krishnamurthy, "Ethnic, Racial and Tribal: The Language of Racism?", in Carmen Rosa Caldas-Coulthard and Malcolm Coulthard, eds., *Texts and Practices: Readings in Critical Discourse Analysis*, London: Routledge, 1996, 129–49.

10 See discussions in Krishnamurthy, "Ethnic, Racial and Tribal"; and Africa Policy Information Center, *Talking About 'Tribe': Moving from Stereotypes to Analysis: Background Paper 9/00*, November 1997. Retrieved 19 August 2012 at http://www.africa.upenn.edu/afrfocus/afrifocus010808.html.

11 Krishnamurthy, "Ethnic, Racial and Tribal", 142–46.

12 While anthropologists from the earliest days skirted these limiting conditions, the hegemony of these ideas is revealed both in deep-rooted disciplinary assumptions and dominant patterns of ethnographic writing. Talal Asad, "Introduction", in Talal Asad, ed., *Anthropology and the Colonial Encounter*, London: Ithaca Press, 1973, 9–19; Eric R. Wolf, *Europe and the People without History*, Berkeley: University of California Press, 1982, 11–19; Edward W. Said, "Representing the Colonized: Anthropology's Interlocutors", *Critical Inquiry*, 15, 2 (1989), 205–25.

13 See e.g., discussions in Adam Kuper, *The Invention of Primitive Society: Transformations of an Illusion*, London: Routledge, 1988; Johannes Fabian, *Time and the Other: How Anthropology Makes Its Object*, New York: Columbia University Press, 1983; Sumit Guha, "Lower Strata, Older Races, and Aboriginal Peoples: Racial Anthropology and Mythical History Past and Present", *The Journal of Asian Studies*, 57, 2 (1998), 423–41; George W. Stocking, "Bones, Bodies, Behavior", in George W. Stocking, ed., *Bones, Bodies, Behavior: Essays on Biological Anthropology (History of Anthropology* series*)*, Madison: University of Wisconsin Press, 1988, 3–17; Benoit Massin, "From Virchow to Fischer: Physical Anthropology and the 'Modern Race Theories' in Wilhelmine Germany", in George W. Stocking, ed., *Volksgeist as Method and Ethic: Essays on Boasian Ethnography and the German Anthropological Tradition (History of Anthropology* series*)*, Madison: University of Wisconsin Press, 1996, 79–154.

14 Wolf, *Europe and the People without History*; Fabian, *Time and the Other*; Guha, "Lower Strata, Older Races."

15 J. Brian Harley, "Maps, Knowledge and Power", in Dennis Cosgrove and Stephen Daniels, eds., *The Iconography of Landscape*, Cambridge: Cambridge University Press, 1988, 301.

16 Harley, "Maps, Knowledge and Power", 290–92.

17 Harley, "Maps, Knowledge and Power", 303.

18 Rosalyn Diprose, *Corporeal Generosity: On Giving with Nietzsche, Merleau-Ponty and Levinas*, Albany: State University of New York Press, 2002, 4.

19 Diprose, *Corporeal Generosity*, 4.

20 Diprose, *Corporeal Generosity*, 5.

21 Diprose, *Corporeal Generosity*, 4.

22 Foucault, *The Order of Things*.

23 Foucault, *The Order of Things*, 62–64.

24 Hudson, "From 'Nation' to 'Race'", 252–53.

25 Hudson, "From 'Nation' to 'Race'", 254.

26 Donna Haraway, *Primate Visions: Gender, Race, and Nature in the World of Modern Science*, New York: Routledge, 1989, 9.

27   Hudson, "From 'Nation' to 'Race'", 254.

28   Haraway, *Primate Visions*, 9.

29   Haraway, *Primate Visions*, 9.

30   These misunderstandings are reflected in popular interpretations of this hypothesis, particularly those arguing a literal biblical account of human origins. See e.g., C. W. Nelson, "Genetics and Biblical Demographic Events" (1 April 2003), *answersingenesis.org*. Retrieved 19 August 2012 at http://www.answersingenesis.org/articles/tj/v17/n1/events; Nancy M. Darrall, "Tracing Mother Eve Using Mitochondrial DNA" (24 April 2003), *The Biblical Creation Society*. Retrieved 19 August 2012 at http://www.biblicalcreation.org/origins_archaeology/ bcs023.html; and Carl Wieland, "Mitochondrial Eve and Biblical Eve Are Looking Good: Criticism of Young Age Is Premature" (6 July 2006), *Creation Ministries International*. Retrieved 19 August 2012 at http://creation.com/mitochondrial-eve-and-biblical-eve-are-looking-good-criticism-of-young-age-is-premature. Mainstream media reports may mention the scientific qualifications to the theory of 'Eve', but these are often embedded deep within articles otherwise relying heavily on Biblical imagery. See e.g., John Tierney, Lynda Wright and Karen Springen, "The Search for Adam and Eve", *Newsweek*, 11 January 1988.

31   Donna Haraway, "A Cyborg Manifesto: Science, Technology, and Socialist-Feminism in the Late Twentieth Century", *Simians, Cyborgs, and Women: The Reinvention of Nature*, New York: Routledge, 1991, 180.

32   Richard E. Green et al., "A Draft Sequence of the Neanderthal Genome", *Science*, 328 (2010), 710–22. However, see Kristine Larsen's contribution to this volume for an example of how earlier versions of such theories were used for eugenicist purposes, reminding us that science does not speak its politics transparently, and that it matters how we tell our scientific stories.

33   See Chela Sandoval, "New Sciences: Cyborg Feminism and the Methodology of the Oppressed", in Chris Hables Gray, ed., *The Cyborg Handbook*, London: Routledge, 1995, 407–22, for a discussion of Haraway's debt to what Sandoval calls "U.S. Third World feminism."

34   Anzaldúa, *Borderlands/La Frontera*, 306.

35   Anzaldúa, *Borderlands/La Frontera*, 305.

36   Anzaldúa, *Borderlands/La Frontera*, 305–06.

37   Donna Haraway, "The Promises of Monsters: A Regenerative Politics for Inappropriate/d Others", in Lawrence Grossberg, Cary Nelson and Paula A Treichler, eds., *Cultural Studies*, New York: Routledge, 1992, 295–337.

38   The use of 'hybridity' in understanding global processes of cultural interaction has been recently criticized as abstract, tending in its widespread deployment to reinforce ideas that present-day 'mixtures' arise from pre-existing 'pure' cultures. See e.g., Arif Dirlik, "Rethinking Colonialism: Globalization, Postcolonialism, and the Nation", *Interventions: International Journal of Postcolonial Studies*, 4, 3 (2002), 428–48. In the unfolding story of this serial, I suggest it remains an apposite metaphor for nurturing biological and social interrelationships between two groups with widely divergent histories to this point, offering, like the notion of *mestiza*, a hope for a complex, mutually constituted future, rather than a reification of past separations.

Chapter 22

Savages, science, stagism and the naturalized ascendancy of the Not-We in *Doctor Who*

Lindy A. Orthia

The mythos of scientific enlightenment

In *The Massacre* (1966), the Doctor arrives in Paris in 1572, a time and place beleaguered by conflict between the ruling Catholics and a Protestant minority. While there, he visits scientist Charles Preslin. Preslin bemoans that he must hide his scientific research from the oppressive Catholic regime, posing instead as an apothecary, "merely a mixer of herbs and ointments." The Doctor notes with admiration that Preslin had "searched deeply in nature", discovering "small creatures, which if attacking humanity could cause a very serious illness", and which (he says) Preslin called "germs." He tells the excited Preslin of "a man in Germany who's working on optics, trying to make a machine, which will enable [him] to see these small creatures."

This snippet of scientific history is entirely fabricated. The word 'germs' is anachronistic by three centuries, the timing and location of the microscope's invention is wrong and Charles Preslin was not a real person. Nonetheless, the scene is persuasive as a representation of history – I assumed Charles Preslin was a real person until I looked him up for this essay – primarily because it is consistent with what I will call the mythos of scientific enlightenment. This mythos is the pop-historical story that the European Renaissance (ending early seventeenth century) was followed by the Age of Enlightenment (seventeenth and eighteenth centuries) and that these periods together changed the way people understood the world, bringing reason and science where there had been superstition and tradition, thus ushering in 'civilization'.[1] This tale of people throwing off their irrational and incorrect beliefs about the world to gain enlightenment via rational science has attained a sort of mythical status (=mythos) in westerners' stories about themselves. The dialogue of *The Massacre* thus frames Preslin's situation as a symbolic moment in European history: when the scientific truth was out but society needed to 'grow up' to accept it rather than persecuting scientists as heretics, and accordingly, when secularism (or Protestantism, given the story's biases) was about to become the norm of governance instead of the Papacy.

The scene is a brief tangent in a serial about political machinations, so it speaks volumes about *Doctor Who* as a story-telling device that the production crew included it. Despite the fact that *Doctor Who* was originally intended to teach children about history and science,[2] it doesn't appear to have mattered to the crew that the historical and scientific facts were inaccurate. Perhaps that is because we *do* learn about history and science from the scene, but it is an ideological lesson, celebrating the triumph of scientific rationalism in Renaissance and Enlightenment Europe. The scene's sole purpose seems to be to peddle the mythos of scientific enlightenment.

No doubt in some contexts, the mythos of scientific enlightenment is harmless enough. It becomes problematic when science is used to justify the historical and current global dominance of European culture. It has become something of an unstated belief in everyday western culture that the current global ascendancy of the western way of life is a natural inevitability built upon superior intellectual, technological and political achievements, and that on the whole this ascendancy is good.[3] Guillermo Gutiérrez outlines these assumptions thus:

> If in the first instance one could speak of the [European imperialist] expansion and conquest as a result of the technological superiority of some peoples over others, in a second stage the technological superiority and the greater military capacity was made synonymous with rationality; and in the final stage the rationality was no longer presented as a cause of the domination [but was] converted directly into its justification. The historic fact of European expansion is transformed into a natural phenomenon, a necessary consequence of the expansion of Reason over the world. A rationality was transformed into *Rationality*, a way of knowing was transformed into Science, a procedure for knowing became the Scientific Method. The vast enterprise of dominating the world in a few centuries was sufficient argument to demonstrate the imposition of European reason as a universal and necessary development.[4]

This is where the scene from *The Massacre* leads us back to this book's theme: race. If the mythos of scientific enlightenment justifies global western ascendancy, then it implicitly justifies the ascendancy's vehicle, European imperialism. This further entails justifying, or at least accepting as an unfortunate side-effect, imperialism's fruits: massacres and genocide, slavery, the dispossession of peoples' lands, the theft of natural resources, the destruction of communities and families, and the sudden or gradual denigration and demise of whole cultures, languages and ways of life. In essence, it justifies or accepts racist oppression, since these actions are racism's hallmarks where they have been systematically perpetrated by Europeans against peoples from Asia, Africa, the Americas, Australasia and the islands of all the oceans.

Intimately connected to such justifications is the concept of stagism. Enlightenment philosophers who adhered to the mythos (though they didn't call it that) championed the principle that every human being can attain the scientific enlightenment that they themselves had. But this contradicted what seemed obvious in European thinking at the time: that non-Europeans were inferior in their science and their reasoning capacity.[5] A stagist view of cultural development (also called stadial theory) was a way that many European thinkers reconciled these 'facts'. It posited that Africans, indigenous Americans, Indigenous Australians,[6] Asians and islanders were at a more 'primitive' stage of development than Europeans, but could potentially be raised to the 'more advanced' stage Europeans had reached.[7]

Stagism has remained prominent in western discourses of race since that time, including, or perhaps especially, in some contexts aspiring to anti-racism. It infused seventeenth-century English liberal thinking exemplified by one of the founders of liberal political theory, John Locke,[8] and pervaded eighteenth-century French political philosophy.[9] Some nineteenth-century philosophers, including influential Germans G. W. F. Hegel and Friedrich Engels, promoted the idea that humans naturally pass through a fixed sequence of developmental stages, believing this was an egalitarian and anti-racist way of looking at the world because it accepted all of humanity as equal in potential[10] – not countenancing the possibility that all human cultures were already equally valid. In the 1990s, English writer Ivan Hannaford, in arguing that the very idea of 'race' was a modern invention and therefore spurious, defended the Ancient Greeks' disparaging views of their 'barbarian' neighbours as a *political* disparagement not a *racial* one, since the Greeks believed the barbarians could choose to attain a civilized state like them if they wanted to.[11] Irrespective of well-meaning intentions, the stagist concept had the devastating effect of greasing the wheels of imperialism.

The place of race and science within stagism

The stagist idea was expounded most explicitly in the writings of nineteenth-century American anthropologist Lewis Henry Morgan, whose work *Ancient Society* strongly influenced Engels.[12] The detail of Morgan's work makes it a useful focus, though it should be noted that he was by no means isolated in his beliefs. Morgan was sympathetic to the plight of Native Americans and used stagist arguments to lobby for government intervention into Native American affairs, to bring Native Americans 'up' to Europeans' 'advanced' standard of living.[13] Ironically, like all colonialist interventions that force assimilation into European culture, the resulting actions contributed to Native Americans losing their lands, languages, cultures and political autonomy.[14] In this, the interventions enacted racism: while it is certainly racist to prevent non-Europeans from accessing the institutions of power and knowledge within western societies, it is also racist to assume that all cultures want those institutions as a part of their society at all, or conversely that Europeans should always reject the institutions of other cultures as inherently inferior.

Morgan devoted his scholarship to ranking the peoples of the world on a stagist scale of development. He described seven levels of development, from savagery (lower, middle, upper) through barbarism (lower, middle, upper) to "the state of civilization."[15] While in his conception Europeans evolved through the lower levels in the past and were now civilized, he believed that the other peoples of the world remained at the lower levels today and were thus more primitive.[16] He believed that the indigenous peoples of the Americas and most Asians remained in Upper Savagery or Lower to Middle Barbarism,[17] and that "Africa was and is an ethnical chaos of savagery and barbarism."[18] He placed Australian Indigenous people and

Pacific Islanders second from the bottom, in the Middle Savagery level[19] ("savagery, pure and simple"),[20] characterizing that level as follows:

> The inferiority of savage man in the mental and moral scale, undeveloped, inexperienced, and held down by his low animal appetites and passions, though reluctantly recognized, is, nevertheless, substantially demonstrated by the remains of ancient art in flint stone and bone implements, by his cave life in certain areas, and by his osteological remains. It is still further illustrated by the present condition of tribes of savages in a low state of development, left in isolated sections of the earth as monuments of the past.[21]

These peoples, then, are mentally and morally underdeveloped according to Morgan – they have not achieved enlightenment in the sense of either reason or of ethics. Europeans once passed through such a stage (leaving their "osteological remains") but by Morgan's implication (and by explication throughout *Ancient Society*) Europeans have evolved well beyond this low phase of "animal appetites and passions." Morgan seems to endorse colonialist assimilation of these people as well as of Native Americans, when, after conveying questionable reports (by European colonists) of cannibalism among Indigenous Australians, he states:

> Such pictures of human life enable us to understand [...] the low level of the mental and moral life of the people. Australian humanity [...] stands on as low a plane as it has been known to touch on the earth. [...] But after an occupation which must be measured by thousands of years, they are still savages, of the grade above indicated. Left to themselves they would probably have remained for thousands of years to come, not without any, but with such slight improvement as scarcely to lighten the dark shade of their savage state.[22]

Here he uses the language of literal enlightenment to frame European colonialism as a 'helping hand' to development, since (he implies) Indigenous Australians were evolving so slowly on their own. Morgan's categories of savagery, barbarism and civilization are not merely descriptors of difference, they are judgements about a people's morality and abilities.

The same terminology litters *Doctor Who* from start to finish as any search of episode transcripts will attest.[23] In the show's first serial, *An Unearthly Child* (1963), the Doctor compared Barbara and Ian's disbelief about the TARDIS to "the Red Indian" whose "savage mind" disbelieved steam trains: the script used a familiar stagist (and racist) hierarchy, with Europeans above Native Americans, to explain the fictitious hierarchy in which the Doctor's people are above Europeans. Accordingly, the word 'advanced' is one of the main adjectives used throughout *Doctor Who* to describe the Doctor himself and his Time Lord society. In the new series the language has been toned down somewhat, with the words 'savage' and 'barbarian' disappearing and 'primitive' used generally by aliens about Earth, but the Doctor continues to use 'advanced' and 'civilized', for example in *New Earth* (2006) describing the Sisters of Plenitude's medical science as "way advanced" and condemning another technology because it has been "banned on every civilized planet."[24] As in Morgan's work, this language is used to judge rather than to describe. While the word 'civilized' is occasionally used ironically in *Doctor Who*, to indicate that a society is over-managed and restrictive of individualism, it always indicates a society with a capacity for massive technological infrastructure, thought processes consistent with western scientific reason and ethical responsibility of a liberal democratic (and usually constitutional monarchy) variety. That is, it constructs an ideal that uses western – especially post-Enlightenment English – paradigms as its standard.

In this *Doctor Who* is little different from Morgan's schema. Morgan used a number of traits to define his levels, such as political systems and kinship arrangements, but science (specifically, applied science and technology) played a prominent role. His world-view could be described as consistent with a general 'mythos of Enlightenment', incorporating the mythos of scientific enlightenment as an important component. He defined his levels according to European cultural values, so non-Europeans inevitably ranked low because they were different. For example, to be promoted from Middle Savagery to Upper Savagery, a culture had to invent the bow and arrow.[25] Other technologies for hunting or warfare such as the boomerang or woomera used in Australia, no matter how refined, effective and sophisticated, did not count. To rise from Savagery to Barbarism, cultures required the invention of pottery, even if they didn't need or desire it.[26] Smelting iron ore characterized Upper Barbarism, highlighting the significance of European-style industrial technology in Morgan's hierarchy. The use of writing and a phonetic alphabet marked entry into Civilization,[27] denigrating as inferior cultures in which information was transmitted orally or through non-phonetic writing (such as Chinese script), with no intrinsic reason why this should be so. Systems of subsistence also played an important role in Morgan's book, with European-style field agriculture consistently assumed to be the most developed such system and so-called hunter-gatherer systems to be the least.[28]

Whatever Morgan's intentions, his levels reflected imperialistic Enlightenment Eurocentrism, for example the philosophy of John Locke, who justified the dispossession of Native Americans' lands by the English, arguing that they did not fully exploit the land through European-style settled agriculture and therefore had not passed through the requisite historical stages to become "civiliz'd."[29] *Doctor Who* also reproduces this same imperialist justification: I have argued elsewhere[30] that in almost all *Doctor Who* allegories of colonialism, western-style science was the arbiter of colonized peoples' right to self-determination. Where colonized peoples exhibited their mastery of, or respect for, western-style science, they won their freedom (e.g. *The Sensorites*, 1964; *The Space Museum*, 1965; *The Mutants*, 1972; *Kinda*, 1982). In other words, colonized people had to prove they were not really 'savages' or 'barbarians', and were in fact 'civilized', before they were allowed to make decisions for themselves and dismantle colonial chains. Where people failed to adopt western-style science and progress towards an ideal of enlightenment, genocidal colonization proceeded (e.g. *The Aztecs*, 1964; *Colony in Space*, 1971).

The notion that non-Europeans possess inferior, less developed knowledge systems continues in the realm of science today. For example, it is common for Australian environmental scientists to routinely ignore Indigenous peoples' knowledge about the environment, because the dominant view in the scientific community is that Indigenous ways of knowing are too deeply embedded in culture to be reliable,[31] despite being effective tools for survival and sustainability over thousands of years. Leanne Simpson has argued in the American context that when western scientists do incorporate aspects of indigenous knowledges into their understanding of the world, the knowledge is usually filtered to eliminate parts inconsistent with what western scientists already believe, in particular spiritual beliefs.[32] Such filtering reinforces the mythos of scientific enlightenment in at least two ways. It reproduces the historical fable of enlightenment in a symbolic decoupling of 'truth' from what such scientists see as religious obscuration, echoing nineteenth-century historian Jacob Burckhardt's assertion that in the Renaissance a "veil [...] woven of faith, illusion, and childish prepossession [...] melted into air", making possible "an *objective* treatment and consideration of [...] all the things of this world."[33] The act of filtering also naturalizes western science's position as the arbiter of truth. It supports a stagist mentality by suggesting that the contributions of non-European cultures are at best small elements of the universal (western) framework of truth, at worst deluded and false, and in either case not major challengers that reset the framework's boundaries.

Locke believed in individual freedom, Morgan wanted to help Native Americans, Engels advocated revolution against oppression, Hannaford opposed the biological reification of race. All good intentions, but despite that, all took as given the mythos of scientific enlightenment and its stagist associations, which perpetuate and are premised on foundations that justify racism. In the remainder of the essay I discuss some of the ways that *Doctor Who* – which similarly purports to stand against oppression – does the same. *Doctor Who* frequently uses science as an ideological symbol, where 'science' here encompasses not only scientific research and ideas, but also 'reason', 'rationality' and the secularist rejection of spiritual-based conceptions of truth, as well as applied science (technologies) for manipulating the environment, including medicine, agriculture and infrastructural development. In using science as a symbol *Doctor Who* almost always reiterates the mythos of scientific enlightenment in small ways or large.[34] My argument is that the programme often couples science with stagism, and in doing so perpetuates racism, in particular by denigrating alien cultures that depart from the Anglo-European Enlightenment model. More obviously, several *Doctor Who* serials present stagist ideology as a fact of human history, implicitly defending European ascendancy, and these are discussed first.

History's fixed stages: The time traveller's defence

In a 2006 paper,[35] William J. Burling discussed ideological aspects of time travel fiction, but he overlooked an important one: the question of whether one should use time travel to change history. In *Doctor Who* the answer to this question is unwaveringly 'no'. One of the reasons the Doctor gives for forbidding changes to history is that it can release dangerous forces (e.g. *Father's Day*, 2005). On other occasions the reason is explicitly stagist.

The idea of fixed history first arises in *Doctor Who* in 1964's *The Aztecs*, in which history teacher Barbara wants to prevent the genocide of Aztec people that will occur with European conquest. Notably Barbara's misguided ambition involves stagist assumptions, because she perceives the Aztecs to be on the cusp of "civilization", and wants to eliminate their "barbaric side" – the side that is religious instead of rationalistic.[36] But the Doctor disapproves of her desire, cementing a commitment to the fixedness of history by famously exclaiming, "You can't rewrite history! Not one line!" This sets the tone for the rest of the series.

In *The Time Warrior* (1973–74), stranded alien soldier Linx makes rifles for thirteenth-century Anglo-Saxon warlord Irongron in payment for the use of his castle grounds. The Doctor pleads with Linx not to make the weapons, saying:

> Human beings must be allowed to develop at their own pace. In this period, they're just a few steps away from barbarism. [...] You give them breach loading guns now, they'll have atomic weapons by the seventeenth century. They'll have the capability to destroy their own planet before they're civilized enough to handle it.

As the stagist language signals, this suggests that history happened the way it did according to a natural and predetermined trajectory, in which humanity's ethical capacity evolved *after the seventeenth century*. In other words, it reifies (makes concrete) the European Enlightenment as the source of humanity's moral maturity. As frequently happens in *Doctor Who*, scriptwriter Robert Holmes equates 'human beings' with Europeans; he assumes that "disrupting this history of Britain is coextensive with disrupting the history of the world."[37] Holmes was obviously not aware that peoples across the world were already 'handling' nuclear materials before westerners: in Australia, several Indigenous nations whose country contains uranium deposits have long-standing strategies for avoiding those places to manage and minimize the adverse effects of radiation.[38]

The Time Warrior invites further stagist comparisons between the coarse, violence loving, regional-accented Anglo-Saxon Irongron and the genteel, peace loving, RP-accented[39] Normans Sir Edward and Lady Eleanor who live in the neighbouring castle. When the Doctor escapes from Irongron to the safety of Edward and Eleanor, he states, "it is a pleasure and a privilege to be in the company of civilized people at last." Someone in this era, then, is 'civilized' not 'barbarous', and the Doctor has no qualms about introducing these people to chemical components of gunpowder, in the form of a sulphur-saltpetre-fat stink bomb. 'Civilization' in this story is mapped onto triple axes of human evolution, implied social class and ethnicity (Anglo-Saxon versus Norman), as if Irongron is a more 'primitive' form of life by all these criteria. Irongron's position in the social and evolutionary hierarchy is clear from the Doctor's exchange with twentieth-century physicist Rubeish:

RUBEISH: Who is Irongron? He a nice chap?

THE DOCTOR: Well I wouldn't recommend him for the Royal Society.

The Royal Society is the ultimate symbol of the mythos of scientific enlightenment and the Doctor uses it as such. Formed in 1660, many of its early members were defining Enlightenment figures (including Isaac Newton and Robert Boyle), it published the first scientific journal, and since its inception it has been the leading British institution for promoting science. It is also an elitist organization with a history of discriminatory practices[40] and the British monarch as its patron. The Doctor's comment thus reinscribes the British scientific establishment as the pinnacle of human development, consistent with his exceptionalism towards Sir Edward and Lady Eleanor.

The notion that people 'develop' along a set trajectory and that history-as-we-know-it was therefore inevitable and natural is also present in *The Time Meddler* (1965). The Doctor makes it his mission to stop his fellow Time Lord, the Meddling Monk, from speeding up human (European) technological progress from the year 1066 onward. The Monk wants to stop Europe's coming wars so people can "better themselves"; he wants to see jet aeroplanes in the thirteenth century and allow Shakespeare to watch his own plays on telly. To the Doctor this is fundamentally wrong and "irresponsible." Both, then, subscribe to the idea that western-defined scientific advance is a good thing for the world, which is problematic enough given its consequences in European empires. They also both agree that 'meddling' in history will only change the speed of preprogrammed societal evolution, not its direction, again reinforcing the notion that the future of all humanity lies in the ascendancy of the western way of life that we see today.[41] But it is only the Doctor who defends the idea that history happened in the correct order between the eleventh century and the twentieth, including, presumably, the wars and conquests. While Morgan wanted to speed up this 'inevitable' process across the world under European mentorship, *Doctor Who* suggests that the speed of development in Europe is sacrosanct and to be defended against change. A colonialist helping hand from an 'advanced' culture (the Time Lords) is not appropriate *for Europeans*. This contradiction exposes stagism, at least as it exists in the everyday culture of *Doctor Who*, as a hypocritical and contradictory ideology, invoked primarily to justify the global ascendancy of European power and culture, while appearing merely to explain it.

Occasionally New Series *Doctor Who* ventures into this territory too: in *The Long Game* (2005), *Tooth and Claw* (2006), *The Fires of Pompeii* (2008) and *The Sontaran Stratagem* (2008), the Doctor states that there is a fixed version of human history and a fixed sequence of technological development that must not be interfered with.

Yet the Doctor's insistence that Europeans (and European empires) "develop at their own pace" doesn't signify a general objection to meddling in the lives of others. When alien species embrace life choices inconsistent with Enlightenment ideals, the game changes.

Raising people from barbarism: The space traveller's burden

Doctor Who has several times retold the story of enlightenment through alien cultures torn between scientific rationalism and religion, requiring the Doctor's intervention to help them choose 'correctly'. In *Planet of Fire* (1984) a "barbaric" society built on mystical religion and the sacrifice of "free-thinkers" is transformed with the Doctor's help toward a secular future, when he explains the ordinary sci-tech phenomenon that the people mistook for a god. In the Doctor's words, the society "will soon advance" under secular leadership; it's a simple Enlightenment tale of truth defeating oppression. Racial overtones may be read into its Arabian aesthetic – the people are desert dwellers who wear keffiyeh and thawb-type clothing – perhaps explaining why the Doctor feels entitled to intervene.

The Curse of Peladon (1972) tells essentially the same story, and although its alien society is designed with a European aesthetic, the dialogue explicitly evokes and rejects non-European ways of life. Set on the religious planet Peladon, the core ideological dilemma is again medieval religiousness versus Enlightenment rationality. Peladon's King and a visiting Galactic Federation ambassador implore the Doctor to "raise [Peladonians] from the dark ages" and "from barbarism", while the Peladonian High Priest Hepesh opposes the Federation's interventions and objects to its attitude that Peladonians are "savages to be tamed." The Doctor's allegiances are clear: he encourages the King to accept the Federation's imperialist mentorship to demonstrate he is "civilized." A conversation between Hepesh and the Doctor reveals that part of the 'civilizing' process involves adopting the Federation's machine-based technology, and rejecting indigenous Peladonian traditions and beliefs:

THE DOCTOR: The Federation's real intent is to help you.

HEPESH: No. They'll exploit us for our minerals. Enslave us with their machines. Corrupt us with their technology. The face of Peladon will be changed. The past swept away. And everything that I know and value will have gone.

THE DOCTOR: The progress that they offer – that we offer – isn't like that.

HEPESH: I would rather be a cave dweller and free.

THE DOCTOR: Free? With your people imprisoned by ritual and superstition?

Hepesh here expresses a legitimate fear that what has happened to countless peoples of Earth under European colonial rule will also happen to Peladon. He even reclaims a lifestyle ('cave dwelling') that Morgan would classify as 'savagery', preferring it to assimilation, yet the Doctor dismisses this bid for freedom and self-determination, and casts indigenous Peladonian culture and beliefs as a prison. Even in a society that resembles a stereotype of medieval Europe, the racial implications of stagism are clear, because a peculiarly modern western paradigm of what society should look like is used to condemn principles and life choices that are or were prominent among non-European peoples of the world.[42]

Equally didactic in marketing the mythos of scientific enlightenment at the expense of a local culture is *The Creature from the Pit* (1979). The Doctor echoes Locke in preaching to the people of the vegetation-covered planet Chloris against lifestyles that don't involve agriculture or iron-smelting, saying:

> That's all you've got on this planet, isn't it? Weeds, weeds, plants and weeds. You scratch about for food wherever you can but you can't plough the land, can you? You can't do anything until you've mastered the forests and the weeds. And you can't do that without metal.

There is little room in *Doctor Who* for sentient peoples who have chosen never to embrace science, the machine, the plough and the settlement, nor for people who choose to build their cultures on spiritual foundations.[43]

Even when *Doctor Who* makes an effort to represent a non-western culture without racist judgements, it reproduces stagist discourses. *Kinda* (1982) in many ways did the best job in *Doctor Who*'s history of representing a non-western culture respectfully and richly. The indigenous Kinda on the planet Deva Loka are telepathic and most do not speak, their kinship structures involve more than one father per child, they have not embraced infrastructural developments such as large buildings or machinery, and they possess spiritual beliefs inspired by Buddhism.[44] They also use a lovely turn of phrase – "the Not-We" – to refer to outsiders including the TARDIS crew, turning on its head the orientalist tendencies of westerners and science fiction programmes to view non-European or alien peoples as exotic others.[45] The disappointing part is that the Doctor introduces the judging discourse of stagism in conversation with colonizer scientist Todd. His initial diagnosis upon seeing these grass-skirt wearing, brown-skinned people is that they are "primitive." Todd disagrees, citing as evidence the Kinda's necklace in the shape of a DNA double helix, which convinces the Doctor. In other words, scientific knowledge is once again used to demarcate the savage from the civilized. Not only does this reinforce the arbitrating role of science, it reifies the concepts of 'primitive' and 'advanced' as scientifically valid: the audience is permitted to continue to judge people by their appearances and to assume most non-Europeans are primitive, even if the Kinda are exceptional.

And on the subject of assuming non-Europeans are primitive, we come to Leela.

Leela the savage companion: Pygmalion for the mythos

The Doctor has travelled with many companions and most are easy to position within time and space: they are from Earth in the present, Earth's past, humanity's future or futuristic alien planets. Their different origins change their orientation to science, but in all cases this orientation serves the same ideological function of reiterating the mythos of scientific enlightenment.[46] Aliens and companions from the future show us a sci-tech future, 'how far we might go': think Zoe's computer brain, Adric's block-transfer computation, Jack's whiz-bang gadgets, Vicki's disparagement of aspirin as "a bit medieval"

(*The Web Planet*, 1965). Companions from the past show us 'how far we've come': in *The Highlanders* (1966–67) Jamie insists that the Doctor 'bleed' an injured man with leeches and is placated by the Doctor's astrological twaddle. Earth-present companions orient us to 'who we are' to help us cope with *Doctor Who*'s speculative challenges to our moral and rational expectations, but they also largely role-model an attitude of excitement about the 'advanced' science and ethics embodied by the Doctor.[47]

The one companion that messed with the formula was Leela, a leather-clad, blowpipe-wielding warrior of the Sevateem, a tribe descended from the survey team of a crash-landed spaceship (*The Face of Evil*, 1977). The survey team, and the technicians who stayed on board and became the computer-worshipping Tesh, were humans from our future, suggesting Leela should represent 'how far we might go'. Yet Leela was portrayed as ignorant about science and technology (aside from weapons and killing) and unaware of western moral values. As such she was a disruption of the stagist paradigm, being a 'savage' product of 'devolution' from an 'advanced civilization', with 'natural' evolutionary progression having been derailed by the religious corruption of science after the crash. The Doctor's task in *The Face of Evil* to reset the society on the correct stagist path of enlightenment towards 'good' secular science, and accordingly, the Sevateem are seen to champion Reason at the end, while Leela leaves with the Doctor.[48]

Leela was created in the midst of the programme's most scientistic era[49] to serve the *Doctor Who* production team's desire for an Eliza Doolittle-type companion who would learn from the Doctor.[50] The Doctor embraced the task of teaching her about science, insisting she eliminate her belief in gods and magic and adopt rationality instead. Her character lent legitimacy to the mythos of scientific enlightenment in a didactic fashion, stating wistfully in *Horror of Fang Rock* (1977) that she "used to believe in magic" but "it is better to believe in science."

She was an obvious manifestation of paternalistic stagism in which a character from a non-western-style culture is given a helping hand by a western-style culture to 'advance' from her 'savage' state. The programme had no qualms about describing her in the language of stagism: the Tesh called the Sevateem "mindless savages" in her first serial and that epithet stuck throughout Leela's tenure, the last line of her final serial *The Invasion of Time* (1978) being "I'll miss you too, savage", spoken by the Doctor. The Doctor called her people "primitive [and] superstition-ridden" in *Horror of Fang Rock*, her thought patterns "primitive" in *Image of the Fendahl* (1977), and both he and a futuristic humanoid called her a "primitive" in *Underworld* (1978). Her skimpy animal-skin outfits, non-mechanical weapons, sixth sense for danger and habit of eating legs of lamb without cutlery all contributed to the impression that Leela was more primitive than 'us'. The Doctor's attitude to Leela's sixth sense reinforced her lowly place in the stagist hierarchy: while at first the programme granted credit to it, as when she correctly presaged disaster in *The Robots of Death* (1977), later the Doctor attributed this talent to her being a "creature of instinct" rather than to any skill or intelligence.

Indeed, Leela's place in *Doctor Who* deteriorated rapidly from highly skilled warrior to the butt of endless jokes about intelligence, reifying her 'primitiveness' for the audience.

In *Underworld*, when encountering a new phenomenon, the Doctor quipped that they would be "the first intelligent and semi-intelligent beings" to witness it. *The Invisible Enemy* (1977) saw the Doctor's body invaded by a virus that thrived on intellectual activity; he assumed this was the reason the virus rejected Leela as a host, since she was "all instinct and intuition." The scientist working with him agreed when he tried to explain the biology to Leela and she could not understand his immunological jargon: he 'humorously' concluded, "perhaps it *is* a matter of intelligence." It turned out Leela had a unique immunological trait the Doctor lacked which conferred resistance to the virus, but the serial still exploited Leela for its elitist humour. In any case the Doctor's elitist assertions were confirmed by biological 'fact': when miniaturized clones of the Doctor and Leela wandered around the Doctor's brain, he identified the anatomical feature that explained (ungrammatically) "why my brain is so much more superior to yours."

Leela's status as savage was not 'innocent' scientism: it was inflected with racial significance. Although actor Louise Jameson is a white European, racial markers were used to make Leela less white: she was named after Palestinian freedom fighter Leila Khaled, Jameson's skin was darkened, and she wore uncomfortable brown contact lenses over her blue eyes until a plot device changed Leela's eye colour in *Horror of Fang Rock*.[51] Leela also spoke without contractions (e.g. "do not" instead of "don't"), connoting unEnglish foreignness.

One reading of the situation mirrors that of Hepesh: the Doctor intends to replace Leela's 'deluded' culture with a western enlightenment model. However, unlike with Hepesh, Leela's unusual origins minimize our capacity to criticize the Doctor's scientistic didacticism as cultural imperialism. The Sevateem not only formed from a crashed spacecraft crew, but were culturally manipulated by a mad computer, so appear to be members of a 'fake' culture not a 'real' one that might warrant preservation. This sentiment is contradicted by Leela's assertion that she is proud of who she is, suggesting she is attached to her culture – as many of us are, irrespective of how recently or how 'artificially' it came into being. But stagism is mandated to destroy all cultures that depart from the naturally predetermined trajectory, regardless of how people feel about that.

Conclusion

How does *Doctor Who* get away with this rather shameless invocation of stagist discourses and the denigration of non-westernized cultures and peoples?

In important ways its science fiction genre masks these ideologies. The very question of whether *Kinda* or *The Face of Evil* reinforces racism assumes that in some way these serials contain a moral message we can apply to real life. But not everyone will accept that assumption: Isiah Lavender argues that the nature of allegory enables science fiction audiences to avoid critical engagement with and acknowledgement of race, by seeing alien beings merely as aliens rather than as metaphors for racialized people.[52] Viewers' 'race blindness' may be deliberate or innocent, because it is inherent to a genre in which people and places and societies *are not real.* To be an allegory, a story must fictionalize something, or it becomes historical fiction or even non-fictional commentary. In the fictionalization process, ideologies relating to people and places are unavoidably excised from their geohistorical and sociopolitical context. As a result, audiences must work harder to piece the ideological picture back together, which can be an enjoyable intellectual challenge or a confusing mess. This disconnect from real life and ambiguity of message allows terminology and ideologies to creep in that would no longer be palatable in, for example, a purely historical drama.

Thus, while elements of Leela's character invite a comparison with non-Europeans across the world, her alienish backstory prevents direct comparison with any particular ethnicity, nation or culture. Race is a culturally and politically constructed phenomenon, anchored to particular places and times, and varying in its meaning depending on who or what is involved. Leela did not in any real sense represent a Palestinian, Wiradjuri, Malay, Xhosa, Guaraní, Lakota or Samoan person, or indeed anything else historically or geographically specific to real life. She may have been a proud, darkish-skinned warrior, but she did not live through a history of slavery or genocide or land theft or apartheid, so there is little to hang accusations of racism upon even though the query is there: a situation unique to speculative fiction. Critical discussion of this is further quashed by the fact that Leela is really a white woman in brown make-up; had she been played by (for example) a Palestinian actor, it might have been somewhat different. But her fictionalized, contextless character traits are probably sufficient to make an analysis of her racial milieu difficult to sustain.

Time travel stories that assert history must happen in a fixed trajectory are less disguised by the genre. Yet as Burling notes, the fact that they often focus on the logic and complications of time paradoxes can distract viewers from their ideological content.[53] In addition, writers of a continuing television series must avoid making permanent changes to history-as-we-know-it. Since time travel makes changing history possible, writers must always find narrative mechanisms to justify their avoidance of change. Stagism has provided such a mechanism in *Doctor Who.*

Of course the real reason *Doctor Who* gets away with it is because, for a sizeable proportion of the populace, there is nothing to get away with. For some, western science *is* the arbiter of truth, the Enlightenment *was* the first time humans started thinking straight, and European imperialism has benefitted the global population. *Doctor Who* is made in a nation built on imperialist conquest and western ascendancy, and despite good intentions, it is not always easy to excise or even identify all the threads of racism that infuse such a culture.

A science fiction story can carry alternative ideologies though and does not need to reinforce stagism. The serial that most actively opposes stagist ideology is *State of Decay* (1980), a story (like *The Face of Evil*) about future humans descended from a crash-landed spacecraft crew. Romana identifies their planet as having technologically "come and gone", but the Doctor disputes her assessment, stating "they may have opted deliberately for a semi-rural culture" and "societies develop in varying ways." Discovering an oppressive feudalist regime, he helps the peasants overthrow the lords and access the computer databank of their ancestors, then departs with the line, "if that's what you want, you can be a high technological society in no time." He leaves room for these people to choose their societal structure and rejects the notion that everyone has to emulate the West.

The dissenting dialogue of *State of Decay* is an important crack in *Doctor Who*'s ideological norm. But for the programme to thoroughly explode that norm, more is required. *Doctor Who* is forever judging its characters' morality, humanity and sentience – that seems to be its core theme – but it never uses a measuring stick that has not been pre-approved by western culture. To make tales that are truly liberating, beyond the confines of Eurocentrism, alternative measuring sticks must be reclaimed or crafted anew.

Notes

1 For a recent critique of this idea see Kathleen Davis, *Periodization and Sovereignty: How Ideas of Feudalism and Secularization Govern the Politics of Time*, Philadelphia: University of Pennsylvania Press, 2008.

2 John Tulloch and Manuel Alvarado, *Doctor Who: The Unfolding Text*, London: St Martin's Press, 1983, 39–43.

3 The assertion is also occasionally made overtly by conservative historians, e.g. Niall Ferguson, *Civilisation: The West and the Rest*, New York: Penguin, 2011.

4 Guillermo Gutiérrez, *Ciencia-Cultura y Dependencia/Science, Culture and Dependency*, 1974, translated and quoted by Richard Levins and Richard Lewontin, "Applied biology in the Third World: The struggle for revolutionary science", in Sandra Harding, ed., *The "Racial" Economy of Science: Toward a Democratic Future*, Bloomington: Indiana University Press, 1993, 316.

5 T. Carlos Jacques, "From savages and barbarians to primitives: Africa, social typologies, and history in eighteenth-century French philosophy", *History and Theory*, 36, 2 (1997), 190–215.

6 'Indigenous' in 'Indigenous Australians' is capitalized as it is a proper noun, but is lower case when discussing other indigenous peoples of the world or indigenous people as a general category.

7 Jacques, "From savages and barbarians to primitives."

8 Bruce Buchan and Mary Heath, "Savagery and civilization: From terra nullius to the 'tide of history'", *Ethnicities*, 6, 1 (2006), 5–26; Jacques, "From savages and barbarians to primitives."

9 Jacques, "From savages and barbarians to primitives."

10 Georg Wilhelm Friedrich Hegel, *Phenomenology of Spirit*, Oxford: Clarendon Press, 1977 [1807], §13. Friedrich Engels, "The Origin of the Family, Private Property and the State" (2010 [1884]), *Works of Friedrich Engels 1884*. Retrieved 19 August 2012 at http://www.marxists.org/archive/marx/works/1884/origin-family/index.htm.

11 Ivan Hannaford, *Race: The History of an Idea in the West*, Washington D.C.: The Woodrow Wilson Center Press, 1996, 3–60.

12 Lewis H. Morgan, *Ancient Society*, Cambridge: The Belknap Press of Harvard University Press, 1964 [1877].

13 Frederick E. Hoxie, *A Final Promise: The Campaign to Assimilate the Indians 1880–1920*, Lincoln: The University of Nebraska Press, 2001 [1984], 17–20.

14 e.g., see Leanne R. Simpson, "Anticolonial strategies for the recovery and maintenance of indigenous knowledge", *American Indian Quarterly*, 28, 3–4 (2004), 373–84. Regarding horrendous consequences of colonialist interventions in Australia, see Human Rights and Equal Opportunity Commission, *Bringing Them Home: National Inquiry into the Separation of Aboriginal and Torres Strait Islander Children from Their Families*, Sydney: Commonwealth of Australia, 1997.

15 Morgan, *Ancient Society*, 11–23.

16 Morgan, *Ancient Society*, 15.

17 Morgan, *Ancient Society*, 21–22.

18 Morgan, *Ancient Society*, 21.

19 Morgan, *Ancient Society*, 16.

20 Morgan, *Ancient Society*, 21.

21 Morgan, *Ancient Society*, 42.

22 Morgan, *Ancient Society*, 317–18.

23 e.g., use a search engine to find key words such as 'civilization' or 'primitive' within www.chakoteya.net/doctorwho/.

24 See also Rachel Morgain's essay, this volume.

25 Morgan, *Ancient Society*, 16.

26 Morgan, *Ancient Society*, 17.

27 Morgan, *Ancient Society*, 17.

28 Morgan, *Ancient Society*, chapter 2.

29 Buchan and Heath, "Savagery and civilization", 8.

30 Lindy A. Orthia, "'Sociopathetic abscess' or 'yawning chasm'? The absent postcolonial transition in *Doctor Who*", *The Journal of Commonwealth Literature*, 45, 2 (2010), 210–12.

31 Chris McKay, *The relationship between 'Western' science and Indigenous knowledge about the environment: A scoping study of Australian researchers*, unpublished manuscript, Canberra: Australian National Centre for the Public Awareness of Science, Australian National University, 2012.

32 Simpson, "Anticolonial strategies."

33 Jacob Burckhardt, *The Civilization of the Renaissance in Italy* (trans. S. G. C. Middlemore), London: Allen & Unwin, 1944 [1860], 81, original emphasis.

34 See e.g. John Fiske, "Popularity and ideology: A structuralist reading of *Dr. Who*", in Willard D. Rowland Jr. and Bruce Watkins, eds., *Interpreting Television: Current Research Perspectives*, Beverly Hills: Sage Publications, 165–98; and Lindy A. Orthia, "Antirationalist critique or fifth column of scientism? Challenges from *Doctor Who* to the mad scientist trope", *Public Understanding of Science*, 20, 4 (2011), 525–42.

35 William J. Burling, "Reading time: The ideology of time travel in science fiction", *KronoScope*, 6, 1 (2006), 5–30.

36 See also Leslie McMurtry's essay, this volume.

37 Quote from Sandifer, regarding 1983 serial *The King's Demons*. Philip Sandifer, "A Space Helmet for a Cow (The King's Demons)" (30 March 2012), *TARDIS Eruditorium: A Psychochronography in Blue*. Retrieved 19 August 2012 at http://tardiseruditorum.blogspot.com.au/2012/03/space-helmet-for-cow-kings-demons.html.

38 See e.g., The Gundjeihmi Aboriginal Corporation, "Sacred Sites" (n.d.), *Welcome to the Mirrar Site*. Retrieved 19 August 2012 at http://www.mirarr.net/sacredsites.html.

39 RP = received pronunciation, defined by the *Oxford English Dictionary* as "the standard, most regionally neutral form of spoken British English, traditionally based on educated speech in southern England." "OED Online" (June 2009), *Oxford University Press*. Retrieved 19 August 2012 at http://www.oed.com/view/Entry/272029.

40 e.g. the first female scientists to become Fellows were inducted in 1945, and women currently comprise only 6 per cent of Fellows. Royal Society, "Statistics – Equality and Diversity" (n.d.), *The Royal Society*. Retrieved 19 August 2012 at http://royalsociety.org/about-us/equality/statistics/.

41 For more on this see Orthia, "'Sociopathetic abscess' or 'yawning chasm'?"

42 Davis, *Periodization and Sovereignty*, demonstrates ideological links between Enlightenment-era Europeans' retrospective invention of 'medieval Europe' and their imperialist conceptualization of the rest of the world.

43 See Orthia, "'Sociopathetic abscess' or 'yawning chasm'?", 212, for a discussion of possible exceptions, notably *Planet of the Ood* (2008).

44 Regarding Buddhist influences see Tulloch and Alvarado, *Unfolding Text*.

45 Notably expounded by Edward W. Said, *Orientalism*, London: Routledge & Kegan Paul, 1978.

46 For a more detailed discussion of this see Lindy A. Orthia, *Enlightenment was the Choice: Doctor Who and the Democratisation of Science*, Ph.D. thesis, Canberra: Australian National University, 2010.

47 Tegan is the obvious exception, as a present-day human with strongly ambivalent feelings about her adventures with the Doctor.

48 In this *The Face of Evil* echoes other 'devolution' stories – *The Savages* (1966), *Colony in Space, Death to the Daleks* (1974) and the first instalment of *The Trial of a Time Lord* (1986), *The Mysterious Planet*. Like the Sevateem, the "savages" in *The Savages* are redeemed by the destruction of the force that kept them devolved, are shown to be not inherently savage after all, and are reset on the path of enlightenment. The devolved "savages" and "primitives" in *Colony in Space* and *The Mysterious Planet* are killed rather than redeemed though, in a strong statement against straying from the correct path, and the future of the Exxilons – the devolved "Stone Age tribe" in *Death to the Daleks* – is uncertain. The Exxilons' situation is racially inflected: while most of them are brown people who chant exotically, enjoy live sacrifices and worship the city their ancestors built, there is a dissenting minority who speak English articulately in an RP accent, are silvery-white in colour, and neither chant nor believe the city is a god – a combination that associates whiteness and Englishness with an 'enlightened' state compared to brownness. Similar imagery is imparted in *Colony in Space* in which the wise, voiced, intellectual leader of the "Primitives" is white whereas his spear-wielding fellows are silent and greenish brown.

This leader commits genocide of his people to benefit others, including the white human colonists who share their planet.

49   'Scientistic' meaning unwaveringly committed to western science above all other knowledge or belief systems. See Orthia, "Antirationalist critique or fifth column of scientism?"

50   Tulloch and Alvarado, *Unfolding Text*, 213.

51   Shannon Sullivan, "The Face of Evil" (18 December 2011), *A Brief History of Time (Travel)*. Retrieved 19 August 2012 at http://www.shannonsullivan.com/drwho/serials/4q.html. Sullivan notes that "Originally, [Jameson's] make-up was a very deep brown colour, but it was eventually made lighter to produce Leela's final look."

52   Isiah Lavender III, *Race in American Science Fiction*, Bloomington: Indiana University Press, 2011, 35–36.

53   Burling, "Reading time."

Conclusion

This is the first book devoted entirely to race and *Doctor Who*. It brings together existing threads of discussion on the topic and initiates new ones. For the first time, these discussions are rigorously contextualized within diverse areas of academic inquiry, including critical race theory, whiteness studies, postcolonial theory, anthropology, history, philosophy, cultural studies and the sciences. Some contributors also report on their individual experiences of race and of *Doctor Who*, inflecting the academic discussions with personal significance.

The book, however, is not just an intellectual exercise. In the Fourth Doctor's words from the eminently quotable *State of Decay* (1980), "Knowing's easy. Everyone does that *ad nauseum*. I just sort of hope." Thus, we have written these essays not just because of scholarly interest, but from deeply held beliefs. We see that race-related oppression continues to exist in the world in many forms, and seek to end it. If writing about race helps us heal old wounds and explore new ways of being in the world, then this collection is also a step towards social change. To that end, we hope it will provide a fruitful kicking off point for future writings (and other actions). Our coverage of *Doctor Who* is broad, but there are many niches left to explore, both in further formal publications and on the web, including at this book's blog: http://doctorwhoandrace.wordpress.com, which readers are invited to contribute to.

Some common themes emerge from our diverse essays, and we will finish with a brief examination of three of them: the creativity and ingenuity that results when diverse eyes cast their gaze upon this topic, the meeting of the literal and the allegorical in *Doctor Who*'s representations of race, and the significance of critique that grows out of fan culture instead of purely academic interest.

The eyes that see

One emergent theme pertains to the relationship between life experience and seeing race. It is neatly illustrated by George Ivanoff's different interpretations of the same two *Doctor Who* serials as a child and then as an adult. Exposure in his life to new discourses of race changed what he saw then and now. Vanessa de Kauwe makes a similar point about disparate sociopolitical circumstances, arguing that people subjugated under European colonialism acquire what she calls 'coloured eyes', which see differently from the 'white eyes' of Europeans and their colonial descendants. De Kauwe uses her own coloured eyes to reinterpret *Doctor Who*'s representations of postcolonial transition, and in doing so identifies critical gaps in analyses offered by previous analysts (including myself) who read *Doctor Who* through white eyes. Both these authors illustrate a bare fact of human experience – that our context shapes the way we respond to phenomena, including to television shows. We might argue there are aspects of race in *Doctor Who* critical to notice and think about, and that viewers who have experienced the pointy end of racism have uniquely important perspectives on it. But there is no single way to look at the topic, as evidenced by the diversity of viewpoints offered in this book.

In some cases the unique eyes with which authors have approached their subject matter have turned received wisdom on its head, offering readers blindingly new ideas about the television programme we have scrutinized for decades. Marcus Harmes, for example, takes issue with an idea that has been reiterated by numerous commentators – that *Doctor Who* is quintessentially English. Applying the dual lenses of race and Anglicanism he demonstrates that this is simply not the case. Richard Scully asks the question hidden in plain sight since 1963 of why, when *Doctor Who* is seemingly obsessed with Nazi Germany, it has never literally depicted the Doctor in battle against the Nazis. Mike Hernandez, too, provides a stunningly original answer to a well-worn question. He observes that casting a black actor as the Doctor need not be tokenistic or risky or even merely just, but would in fact enrich and capitalize on the series' continuing exploration of the Doctor's diasporic identity. Rachel Morgain interrogates a problem *Doctor Who* has grappled with for decades – the correct name for the program's sentient reptile species, known as the 'Silurians'. In doing so she exposes the horrifying truth, which echoes the situation of countless marginalized peoples across the world, that *Doctor Who* has never let these people tell us what they call themselves. Iona Yeager's essay revolutionizes thinking about historical representations of race. It is necessary but insufficient, she argues, to depict racism in stories set in the past; to truly push the envelope, *Doctor Who* should depict historical *resistance to racism*, so that we the anti-racist viewers can see and understand the real life heritage that brought us to where we are today. These ideas seem obvious now they have been said, but they have not been said before.

As de Kauwe points out, all of us can listen to others to gain insight into what they see. We can read their essays and learn from them and reiterate their ideas and summarize them in our own writings. But we can never see through their eyes first hand, just as George Ivanoff cannot see through his child eyes again. This highlights the irreducible preciousness of hearing from diverse voices. It is critical that we create and maintain platforms from which each of us who has something to say on this subject can speak. If we fail in this we will never fully understand the multi-faceted complexity of race or *Doctor Who*.

Literal and allegorical

A major thematic contrast in the book is between those essays that examine *Doctor Who*'s literal representations of race, and those that analyse the ways the programme has used allegory to depict the institutions that police race.

Many of the essays in the book's first half take a 'literal' approach. Fire Fly, for instance, reads the Doctor not as an alien but as a white person, and identifies the ways his socialized white traits emerge in interaction with other characters. Linnea Dodson documents the programme's imbalanced treatment of *Doctor Who*'s New Series companions, which seems to follow long-established patterns of racist discrimination. Rosanne Welch grounds her analysis of the Doctor's companions and allies in real world axes of power: race, class, sexuality. Emily Asher-Perrin seeks in *Doctor Who* multiple representations of 'mixed race' relationships that render them ordinary. Stephanie Guerdan craves a fuller reflection of the contemporary diversity of human faces and cultures. Each of these authors, and the others who are concerned with realist representations, demonstrate implicit concern for accuracy on the one hand, and positive role-modelling or overt critique of power imbalances on the other. Redressing misrepresentations of race is not just a matter of portraying the world 'as it really is', since the world remains beleaguered by racism and misconceptions. A vision of 'what could be' is also needed, as these authors and several others in the book imply.

A number of essays find racially inflected meanings in allegory. It is well known that allegory is routinely used in science fiction to make moral arguments, and a significant body of literature recognizes the parallels often drawn in science fiction between aliens from other worlds and racially 'othered' peoples.[1] Along these lines, John Vohlidka analyses four of *Doctor Who*'s allegories of imperialism to forge the argument that British popular understandings of what empire and colonialism mean changed significantly during the 1970s and were reflected in *Doctor Who*. Erica Foss identifies the significant overlap of real world slavery discourses and practices and *Doctor Who*'s depiction of the Ood, reading the allegory as a warning to those building humanity's future not to repeat the mistakes of the past. Kristine Larsen's encyclopaedic discussion of the Daleks' eugenics experiments shows the many ways that the Daleks' goals and beliefs echo historical eugenics movements, and that *Doctor Who* also in large part echoes the scientific majority's critique of eugenics as a pseudo-science. Each of these highlights the centrality to *Doctor Who* of didacticism, of teaching viewers moral lessons through allegory. They also highlight *Doctor Who*'s overt (even literal) ideological frame: it always *presents itself* as opposing racist oppression, with varying degrees of success.

Alec Charles similarly reveals great cause for hope in the *Doctor Who* and *Torchwood* stories that he analyses, because they expose race itself as myth. His essay expands theory about the connections between race and allegory when he states, "self-conscious allegories of racism (such as those performed in the fantasies of science fiction) may be seen as allegories of what is itself only an allegory",[2] since "Racial violence has merely deployed race as a transparently hollow justification; race is, as it always was, no more than an arbitrary signifier."[3] Leslie McMurtry further illuminates this idea, when she shows that *The Aztecs'* 1964 depiction of fifteenth-century Mexico perpetuates mythologies (i.e. symbolic narratives, specifically allegories of savagery) formulated by Columbus and Cortés as a 'transparently hollow justification' of their imperialist actions. We can interpret the reproduction of these myths in *The Aztecs* as a further allegorical justification of the twentieth-century status quo, that is, the ascendancy of the West that I discuss in my own essay. Unlike *The Rebel Flesh/ The Almost People* (2011) discussed by Charles, in *The Aztecs* and similar historical stories the allegory is not employed by *Doctor Who*'s writers to draw attention to a problem. Rather, it functions (deliberately or not) to perpetuate a mythic version of history that supports racism. McMurtry and I both apply an empirical (literal) understanding of history to the symbolic narrative to expose the falseness of its underlying premise.

Two other essays find allegorical meanings in *Doctor Who* that were probably not intended by its makers. Amit Gupta describes the Fifth Doctor's Victorian cricketing uniform as a manifestation of the BBC's nostalgia for the British Empire and its ruling-class sport. When emblazoned upon a character who is an alien from another planet, that nostalgia transforms into allegory: the Doctor metaphorically references Victorian gentleman explorers, perpetually colouring in the blank spots on imperial maps. Quiana Howard and Robert Smith? find in the human-loving but alien Doctor a different significance, linking him allegorically with Barack Obama, who is black but must serve hegemonic white interests. In both cases these metaphorical connections cast the Doctor in an unfavourable light with respect to race, but studying *Doctor Who* through these lenses can enable us to understand more about both.

Fan love

An inescapable theme running through the book is the overlap between scholarship and fandom. It has always been the case that fans have engaged in *Doctor Who* scholarship, and in this book that has burst through in abundance. A number of writers declare themselves as fans in their essays and their reflections and critiques are inspired partly by their expectations as fans. Linnea Dodson begins her criticism of the programme's handling of characters of colour with the statement, "Once upon a time, there was a science fiction show that I adored."[4] Stephanie Guerdan admits that, despite the programme's problematic lack of East Asian characters and settings, the Doctor has taught her "to have hope, and to trust in the inherent goodness of the human race."[5] Emily Asher-Perrin's pleasure at the programme's depictions of multiracial couples in the Russell T Davies era is evident when she writes, "the way that the Doctor sees us [is just] as human beings … ordinary, brilliant, ridiculous human beings."[6] Thus, there is joy in its successes and heartfelt disappointment in its failings, but a belief in and commitment to the programme.

Catriona Mills's essay illustrates the ways that fans have further engaged with *Doctor Who*: by writing some of its spin-off adventures.[7] In doing so, Mills contends, "these writers foreground their own immersion in a distinctly British mythology. But, simultaneously, they bend that mythology to their own […] purposes."[8] While Mills is speaking of Australian writers using *Doctor Who* to interrogate the place of race within Australian identity, there is a broader point to be gleaned: that there is a compulsion among *Doctor Who* fans not only to understand the programme but almost to 'fix' it. We see it as ours, as some part of us, and want it, indeed expect it – desperately at times – to represent our values. This point has been made in previous studies of *Doctor Who* fans. Alan McKee's 2004 study on the question, 'Is *Doctor Who* political?'[9] demonstrated amply that fans see in *Doctor Who* a reflection of their own belief systems, whatever they may be – in a political sense ranging from the extreme right to the revolutionary left and everything in between. David Butler's 2007 brief review of fan responses to the advent of the new series confirmed this, with white nationalists bemoaning Mickey Smith's presence in *Rose* (2005), and left-wing activists horrified at what appeared to be anti-refugee ideologies in *The Unquiet Dead* (2005).[10] *Doctor Who* is not just one of many cultural entities worthy of scholarly attention; there is something in particular about *Doctor Who* that matters to its fan commentators.

Accordingly, perhaps the biggest elephant in the room is the problem, privately nursed by many fans, of loving a television show even when it is thunderingly racist. Kate Orman articulates it brilliantly in her examination of *Doctor Who*'s most popular[11] original series story, *The Talons of Weng-Chiang* (1977):

> Paradoxically, the intense moral opprobrium attached to calling something 'racist' helps to obscure the presence of racism. If racism is anathema, then when a story we cherish contains racially charged elements, we must show that it's not *really* racist – and neither are we for loving it.[12]

In this book we have collectively tried to overcome this defensive urge, feeling confident to criticize to the point where some of us may seem intensely to dislike the programme. But Orman is right, it need not be a matter of either rejecting *Doctor Who* or ignoring its faults. Her conclusion is worth carrying into future discussions on this topic: "because we *are* fans, we're capable of being sophisticated, thoughtful viewers, able to see both a story's successes and its failings."[13]

Let us then, in our love and our critique, be bold.

Lindy Orthia

Notes

1 Isiah Lavender III, *Race in American Science Fiction*, Bloomington: Indiana University Press, 2011; Adilifu Nama, *Black Space: Imagining Race in Science Fiction Film*, Austin: University of Texas Press, 2008; LeiLani Nishime, "Aliens: Narrating U.S. global identity through transnational adoption and interracial marriage in *Battlestar Galactica*", *Critical Studies in Media Communication*, 28, 5 (2011), 450–65.
2 Alec Charles, this volume, 164.
3 Alec Charles, this volume, 164.
4 Linnea Dodson, this volume, 31.

5   Stephanie Guerdan, this volume, 76.
6   Emily Asher-Perrin, this volume, 66.
7   Contributors to this book, Kate Orman, Linnea Dodson, George Ivanoff and Robert Smith?, are also authors of authorized further adventures. Kate Orman is the author of numerous *Doctor Who* novels and short stories and has sold hundreds of thousands of books worldwide. See Alan McKee, "Interview with Kate Orman: *Dr Who* author", *Continuum: Journal of Media & Cultural Studies*, 19, 1 (2005), 127–39; Linnea Dodson, "God Send Me Well to Keep", in Keith R.A. DeCandido, ed., *Doctor Who Short Trips: The Qualities of Leadership*, UK: Big Finish, 2008, 129–148; George Ivanoff, "Machine Time", in Ian Farrington, ed., *Doctor Who Short Trips: Defining Patterns*, UK: Big Finish, 2008, 1–7; Robert Smith?, "The Church of Saint Sebastian", in Simon Guerrier, ed., *Doctor Who Short Trips: The History of Christmas*, UK: Big Finish, 2005, 77–84.
8   Catriona Mills, this volume, 227.
9   Alan McKee, "Is *Doctor Who* Political?", *European Journal of Cultural Studies*, 7, 2 (2004), 201–17.
10 David Butler, "Introduction", in David Butler, ed., *Time and Relative Dissertations in Space: Critical Perspectives on Doctor Who*, Manchester: Manchester University Press, 2007, 1–15.
11 As voted in an online poll of over 1,500 fans in 2003. The poll results are now only available through archived captures as the original published webpage has been taken down. Original reference: Shaun Lyon, ed., "2003 Poll Results" (2003), *Outpost Gallifrey*. Retrieved 1 March 2009 at http://gallifreyone.com/pollres2003.php.
12 Kate Orman, this volume, 85.
13 Kate Orman, this volume, 95.

About the contributors

Emily Asher-Perrin is a graduate of Sarah Lawrence College where she studied, amongst other subjects, literature and anthropology. She spends her days as Editorial Assistant for the science fiction and fantasy website Tor.com. There, she has done her fair share of coverage on all things *Who*, ruminating on every aspect of the program, from the Doctor's generation cycle, to the show's devotion to children, to the very nature of its fan base.

Alec Charles is Principal Lecturer in Media at the University of Bedfordshire. He is author of *Interactivity: New Media, Politics and Society* (Peter Lang, 2012), editor of *Media in the Enlarged Europe* (Intellect Publishing, 2009) and co-editor (with Gavin Stewart) of *The End of Journalism* (Peter Lang, 2011). Recent publications include contributions to *Science Fiction Studies, Science Fiction Film* and *Television, Journal of Popular Television and Utopian Studies*. He has previously worked as a documentary programme-maker for BBC Radio and as a print journalist.

Vanessa de Kauwe has a background in philosophy, primarily the Ancient Greeks but more recently specializing in the ethics surrounding the Abu Ghraib torturers. She is an Australian of Sri Lankan heritage, and proudly promotes the interests and perspectives of the Third World. She is a fan of both the old and new series of *Doctor Who*, having followed the Doctor through time from the first episode to the present day.

Linnea Dodson is a technical writer who has been in fannish culture since 1976. Her interest in racial issues on TV stretches back to Ron Koslow's *Beauty and the Beast* (1987-90). Her other *Doctor Who* publications are the short story, "God Send Me Well to Keep", in the Short Trips anthology *The Qualities of Leadership* (Big Finish, 2008) and "Greatest Coulrophobia in the Galaxy" in *Outside In: 160 New Perspectives on 160 Classic Doctor Who Stories by 160 Writers* (ATB Publishing, 2012).

Fire Fly works by day in public policy advocacy for a peak non-government organization. By night, she is a blogger, feminist, social justice activist and radical woman of colour. She has studied and researched critical race and whiteness studies, and development studies, and has published and spoken on race, migration, education and advocacy. She can be found blogging at *The Long Way Home* at http://ardhra.wordpress.com/ and *Sedentary Meanderings* at http://ardhra.tumblr.com/.

Erica Foss is a Ph.D. candidate in history at Boston College. She is an intellectual and cultural historian interested in national identity, and the discourses of crime and punishment. She primarily studies Britain and France in the nineteenth and early twentieth centuries. Her interest in *Doctor Who* comes from her love of both science fiction and British culture.

Stephanie Guerdan is a graduate of Carnegie Mellon University with a BA in Japanese Studies and an MA in Professional Writing. She enjoys cosplaying, blogging about feminist issues, reading fantasy novels and watching sci-fi. The Doctor is a recent addition to her life, but he's quickly become an addiction. You can spot her pretty easily around Pittsburgh – she's the one with the homemade TARDIS purse and the fez. ('Cool' headgear aside, Ten is her Doctor.)

Amit Gupta is an Associate Professor in the Department of International Security Studies at the USAF Air War College. E-mail: amit.gupta1856@gmail.com.

Marcus K. Harmes is a lecturer in the Faculty of Arts, University of Southern Queensland. He has previously taught religious studies and the history of Witchcraft at the University of Queensland, and Church History at the National Theological Centre, Canberra. His major focus of research is the Church of England/Anglican Church in a variety of historical contexts, including the Early Modern, Victorian and Modern, and he has published a number of studies in this field.

Mike Hernandez holds an MA in English from DePaul University in Chicago and a BA from Dominican University. In keeping with the topic of this book, he is also a proud fellow in the Diversifying Higher Education in Illinois program. His paper, "The Hollow Men of Oz", published in *The Baum Bugle: A Journal of Oz*, 56, 2 (2012), is an essay on L. Frank Baum's influence on the poetry of T. S. Eliot. His interests include science fiction, comics and literary criticism. He is currently working on a resource for English students interested in cognitive and evolutionary literary criticism.

Quiana Howard is a fiction and non-fiction writer. She studied writing at Western Michigan University. She has an essay in the collection *Outside In: 160 New Perspectives on 160 Classic Doctor Who Stories by 160 Writers* (ATB Publishing, 2012) and writes for her own blog. She is also a cosplayer, and has appeared on panels about costuming and diversity at various *Doctor Who* conventions.

George Ivanoff is an author and long-time *Doctor Who* fan, residing in Melbourne, Australia. He is best known for his *Gamers* books – teen novels set within a computer game world. In 2008 he had his one shining, fanboy moment with the publication of "Machine Time" in *Doctor Who Short Trips: Defining Patterns* (Big Finish). He still entertains a 'pie-in-the-sky' dream of writing more *Doctor Who* stories.

Kristine Larsen is Professor of Astronomy at Central Connecticut State University. The author of *Stephen Hawking: A Biography* (Greenwood Press, 2005) and *Cosmology 101* (Greenwood Press, 2007) and co-editor (with Anthony Burdge and Jessica Burke) of *The Mythological Dimensions of Doctor Who* (Kitsune Books, 2010) and *The Mythological Dimensions of Neil Gaiman* (Kitsune Books, 2012), her research focuses on the intersections between science and society. She has published on women in the history of science, astronomical allusions in the works of J. R. R. Tolkien, depictions of mad scientists and time travel in popular culture, and using zombie films to teach science.

Leslie McMurtry encountered *Doctor Who* during her childhood in Albuquerque, New Mexico. She received her BA in English and French from the University of New Mexico and her MA in creative and media writing from Swansea University in Wales, where she is currently a Ph.D. candidate in English. She edits *The Terrible Zodin* (http://doctorwhottz. blogspot.com), a quarterly *Doctor Who* e-zine.

Catriona Mills holds a BA (Hons) from Macquarie University and an M.Phil. and Ph.D. from the University of Queensland. She researches and publishes in the field of serial fiction (particularly, but not exclusively, in the nineteenth century) and authorship attribution, teaches academic and professional writing at the University of Queensland, and works as a researcher for AustLit: The Australian Literature Resource. She cannot remember a time before she started watching *Doctor Who*.

Rachel Morgain is a postdoctoral researcher in anthropology at the Australian National University, who was born just as Sarah Jane joined the TARDIS. Her Ph.D. focused on social organization in industrialized nations and her interests include the anthropology of religion, gender and sexuality, race and postcolonialism. She has a background in cultural studies and an ongoing interest in the links between systems of knowledge, social structure and oppression.

Kate Orman is best known to fans as the author or co-author of thirteen *Doctor Who* novels. She lives in Sydney with her husband and collaborator Jon Blum.

Lindy Orthia is a lecturer in science communication at the Australian National University. She is a white Australian who changed her name at age 18 to that of a Greek goddess who sounded like 'author'. Her Ph.D. thesis examined the social, political, economic and cultural aspects of science in *Doctor Who* and she continues to publish on this topic.

Richard Scully is Senior Lecturer in Modern European History at the University of New England (Armidale, NSW, Australia). Richard's key research interests are in the culture of British and European cartoons and satirical art, and Anglo-German relations (1860–1914). It is rumoured that he completed his Ph.D. just so he could be called 'Doctor', and pursued the discipline of history out of admiration for Romanadvoratrelundar. He has published in the *Journal of Victorian Culture* and *European Comic Art*. A monograph – *British Images of Germany: Admiration, Antagonism, & Ambivalence, 1860–1914* – was published by Palgrave Macmillan in 2012.

Robert Smith? (the question mark is part of his name) is an academic and *Doctor Who* non-fiction writer. He is the co-editor (with Graeme Burk) of volumes 2 and 3 of *Time, Unincorporated* (collections of essays on the Classic and New Series; Mad Norwegian Press, 2010 and 2011) and with Graeme Burk co-wrote (the award winning) *Who Is The Doctor*, an episode guide to the new series (ECW Press, 2012). He recently edited the collection *Outside In: 160 New Perspectives on 160 Classic Doctor Who Stories by 160 Writers* (ATB Publishing, 2012).

John Vohlidka, Ph.D., a life-long fan of *Doctor Who*, is currently employed as Assistant Professor of History at Gannon University. He specializes in Early Modern European history, with special emphasis towards Tudor-Stuart history and the Reformation. He also lectures on a variety of topics, such as Comics and Culture, Post-Atomic Japan and the History of the Future.

Rosanne Welch, Ph.D., writes television and teaches television writing at California State University, Fullerton. Being a lifelong *Who* fan (Peter is her favourite though Tom was her first and David was her son's first and favourite) her work focuses on the writing of *Who* and *Torchwood*. She has co-written (with Martin Griffin) a chapter in *Torchwood Declassified: Investigating Mainstream Cult Television* (I.B. Tauris, forthcoming) and had the pleasure of interviewing Russell T Davies for a piece in *Written By Magazine*.

Iona Yeager is a retired mental health care worker living in the Colorado Rockies, who has enjoyed watching *Doctor Who* for over three decades with her children and grandchildren. A long time human rights advocate, Iona recognizes the influence of popular media on society, especially Western European and American society where at various times People of Color lived as culturally misunderstood, disadvantaged and oppressed minorities.

Index